MW00852067

Nuer Religion

NUER RELIGION

NUER RELIGION

BY

E. E. EVANS-PRITCHARD

PROFESSOR OF SOCIAL ANTHROPOLOGY
AND FELLOW OF ALL SOULS COLLEGE
IN THE UNIVERSITY OF OXFORD

OXFORD
AT THE CLARENDON PRESS
1956

Oxford University Press, Amen House, London E.C. 4

GLASGOW NEW YORK TORONTO MELBOURNE WELLINGTON
BOMBAY CALCUTTA MADRAS KARACHI CAPE TOWN IBADAN

Geoffrey Cumberlege, Publisher to the University

————

PRINTED IN GREAT BRITAIN

PREFACE

I HAVE previously written two books on the Nuer, a cattle-herding people dwelling in the swamps and savannah of the southern Anglo-Egyptian Sudan. *The Nuer. A Description of the Modes of Livelihood and Political Institutions of a Nilotic People* was published in 1940 and *Kinship and Marriage among the Nuer* in 1951. The present volume, *Nuer Religion*, completes a study of the Nuer which began in 1930.

Accounts of religion in writings on the Nuer are generally meagre and superficial. The only detailed treatment is in Father J. P. Crazzolara's *Zur Gesellschaft und Religion der Nueer* (1953), much of which appeared earlier in volume viii of Father W. Schmidt's *Der Ursprung der Gottesidee* (1949) Those who read his account will see that it differs in many respects from what I now present, though less with regard to fact than in emphasis and interpretation.

Although Nuer religious ideas and practices were a part of their way of life which greatly interested me, it was that to which I was able to give least attention during my short residence of a year in Nuerland. It was necessary to learn their language and to study their manner of livelihood and their family, kinship, and political activities before giving close attention to the more difficult problems of their religious thought These tasks, all the heavier in the arduous conditions in which they had to be carried out, left me little time to pursue anything which could be called a systematic inquiry into religious matters. What I record I witnessed myself or is information given spontaneously during talks about other and more practical affairs or in comment on some event or experience. Such observations may, however, be more valuable in a study of religious thought than those derived from purposive inquiry. This is especially so when a people lack, as the Nuer do, anything which offers easy scope for such an inquiry, for they have nothing which can properly be called dogma, liturgy, and sacraments (*in sensu stricto*), and they lack a developed religious cult and mythology. This is doubtless one of the reasons why for the most part those who have written about the Nuer have said so little about their religion.

(v)

A study of Nuer religion is a study of what they consider to be the nature of Spirit and of man's relation to it I had previously spent many months among the Azande people of the Nile-Uelle divide. From my earliest days among them I was constantly hearing the word *mangu*, witchcraft, and it was soon clear that if I could gain a full understanding of the meaning of this word I should have the key to Zande philosophy When I started my study of the Nuer I had a similar experience I constantly heard them speaking of *kwoth*, Spirit, and I realized that a full understanding of that word was the key to their—very different—philosophy. The attempt to reach it and. even more, to present my conclusions has occupied me for a long time and has proved to be a formidable task. The difficulties which had to be overcome will be very apparent in the pages which follow, but I mention some of them now

One of the difficulties of presentation has been the different senses the word *kwoth* may have. I have tried to overcome it by speaking of 'God' when the word has a sense near enough to our own conception of God to permit the usage; of 'Spirit' where it refers, either in Nuer or, more frequently, in my exposition, to spiritual nature rather than to any definite, precise, or stated form; and of 'a spirit', 'the spirit', and 'spirits' where it specifically denotes some particular spiritual figure or figures other and lesser than God. The reasons for making these distinctions will become clearer as the book proceeds, and it will then also be perceived why it is impossible to adhere to them rigidly or to use them without any ambiguity.

A further difficulty relates not to Nuer words but to our own. Although the considerable literature on primitive religions which appeared towards the end of the last century and the early years of the present century made us familiar with such terms as animism, fetishism, totemism, mana, tabu, and shamanism, their meanings are still obscure. The very fact that some of these terms are borrowed from native languages is an indication of the failure to build up an adequate and agreed-upon terminology in Comparative Religion, a subject which, moreover, has been since sadly neglected, especially in this country. In these circumstances sometimes even communication is difficult If I speak of 'spear' or 'cow' everybody will have pretty much the same idea of what I speak of, but this is not so when I speak of 'Spirit', 'soul', 'sin', and so forth

This difficulty is not easily overcome, because it is not merely a matter of definitions but involves also personal judgement. It would be useless to deny this and rash to ignore it. It may be said that in describing and interpreting a primitive religion it should make no difference whether the writer is an agnostic or a Christian, Jew, Muslim, Hindu, or whatever he may be, but in fact it makes a great deal of difference, for even in a descriptive study judgement can in no way be avoided. Those who give assent to the religious beliefs of their own people feel and think, and therefore also write, differently about the beliefs of other peoples from those who do not give assent to them. This is not the place to discuss further this difficulty. I merely wish to recognize that it exists and that it introduces into writings about religion complications which are not present when writing about, for example, kinship or husbandry

I am, of course, well aware that Nuer religion is very unlike what we know in general about Negro religions. One cannot even say that it is a typical Nilotic religion. It is certainly very unlike the religion of the Anuak, of the Luo of Kenya, of the Acholi, of the Alur, or of the Shilluk. Indeed, only the religion of the Dinka can be said to have strongly marked affinities with it, and it can be further said that in some respects the religions of these two peoples resemble less other Negro religions than some of the historic religions. They have features which bring to mind the Hebrews of the Old Testament Professor C. G. Seligman clearly sensed this, as his account of the Dinka and Nuer shows, and Miss Ray Huffman, an American Presbyterian missionary who spent many years among the Nuer, remarks that 'the missionary feels as if he were living in Old Testament times, and in a way this is true'.[1] When, therefore, I sometimes draw comparisons between Nuer and Hebrew conceptions, it is no mere whim but is because I myself find it helpful, and I think others may do so too, in trying to understand Nuer ideas to note this likeness to something with which we are ourselves familiar without being too intimately involved in it.

[1] C. G. and B Z Seligman, *Pagan Tribes of the Nilotic Sudan*, 1932, chaps iv–vi; Ray Huffman, *Nuer Customs and Folk-Lore*, 1931, pp. 56–57 This raises questions which lie outside the scope of the present volume They are discussed by C. G Seligman, op cit , 'Prolegomena', and in his earlier 'Some Aspects of the Hamitic Problem in the Anglo-Egyptian Sudan', *Journal of the Royal Anthropological Institute*, 1913, also by P W Schmidt, op cit., pp. 571 seq

PREFACE

I have to emphasize that this is a study of religion So strong has been rationalist influence on anthropology that religious practices are often discussed under the general heading of ritual together with a medley of rites of quite a different kind, all having in common only that the writer regards them as irrational; while religious thought tends to be inserted into a general discussion of values. Here the view is taken that religion is a subject of study *sui generis*, just as are language or law Consequently I do not feel that I am obliged to describe fully such ceremonies as those that take place at initiations, engagements, weddings, &c., which on no definition of religion can be regarded as religious phenomena, but only to indicate what, if anything, in them has religious significance. Likewise, I do not consider that I have to discuss Nuer moral judgements in general, but only in so far as they more immediately concern their religious thought and practice.

The chapters of this book were first written to be delivered as lectures, mostly in university courses at Oxford, though some were written for more formal occasions Chapter I was a Presidential Address to the Royal Anthropological Institute (1951), Chapter XI the Henry Myres Lecture to the same Institute (1954), Chapter IV the Monro Lecture in the University of Edinburgh (1952), Chapter V a lecture to the University of London Anthropological Club (1954), and Chapter X an address delivered at the Fourth International Congress for Anthropology and Ethnology in Vienna (1952). Some repetition is inevitable in this form of presentation but I have eliminated all that was avoidable.

I thank the editors of the following journals for permission to reprint what has appeared in them: *Journal of the Royal Anthropological Institute, Man, Sudan Notes and Records, Africa, African Affairs, American Anthropologist, Annali Lateranensi, Anthropological Quarterly,* and *Sociologus.*

I owe a very great debt to Dr. R. G Lienhardt. He has read the whole of this book at various stages of its growth and has made many suggestions which I have adopted. We have discussed its contents so often that I am scarcely able to say what I owe to him and what I do not. I can only say that I doubt whether I would have written it at all if it had not been for his interest and encouragement. His help has been all the more valuable, and the more generous, in that it was given in the light of as yet unpublished conclusions he had reached by his study of Dinka religion,

a study fuller and deeper than I was able to make of Nuer religion
Dr. Lienhardt also made inquiries on my behalf among the Nuer
themselves.

I am also most grateful to Dr. Mary Smith of the American
Presbyterian Mission at Nasser on the Sobat river. Her parents,
also at one time members of that Mission, are old and much
esteemed friends who helped me unreservedly during my residence among the Nuer; and she was brought up among the Nuer,
to whom, like her parents, she has devoted her life. I sent this
book out to her, chapter by chapter. She confirmed many conclusions, added new information, and made some criticisms.

Dr. P. J. Bohannan and Mr. J. M. Beattie kindly read through
the book in manuscript. I received also some useful comments on
the contents of Chapter V from Professor Dorothy Emmett and
Mr. Brian Farrell. Professor A. N. Tucker has given me advice
on linguistic matters. Mr. F. D. Corfield has again allowed me to
include some of his excellent photographs. Plate XV is from a
negative lent to me by Major-General Sir Charles Gwynn. I am
indebted to the late Mr. Henry Balfour, Mr. T. K Penniman, and
and Mr. Louis Clarke, for the drawings of specimens in my collec-
tions in the Pitt-Rivers Museum at Oxford and the University
Museum of Archaeology and Ethnology at Cambridge. Fig. 3 is
reproduced, with her permission, from Mrs. Grace M. Crowfoot's
Flowering Plants of the Northern and Central Sudan. I thank the
Government of the Anglo-Egyptian Sudan for a grant of money
towards the cost of publication.

It is sad that I must now say a final farewell to a people who
have for so many years occupied my thoughts. I was a *ger*, what
they call a *rul*, an alien sojourner, among them for only a year,
but it was a year's relationship of great intensity, and the quality
of a relationship counts for more than its duration. This final
volume of my trilogy is dedicated to them in memory of an
experience which has greatly influenced my life.

E. E. E.-P.

Oxford
January 1956

CONTENTS

LIST OF ILLUSTRATIONS

PLATES

TEXT-FIGURES

ERRATA

Page 44, seven lines from bottom. *for* '*Ruah*' *read* '*Ruah*'

Page 45, line 3: *for* 'extirpation' *read* 'expiration'

Page 69, two lines from bottom: *for* 'prosrated' *read* 'prostrated'

Page 234, last line: *for* 'patricular' *read* 'particular'

Page 306, seven lines from bottom *for* 'diu' *read* 'diu'

Page 317, line 1 of par 2 *for* 'characterstics' *read* 'characteristics'

CHAPTER I

GOD

I

THE Nuer word we translate 'God' is *kwoth*,[1] Spirit Nuer also speak of him more definitely as *kwoth nhial* or *kwoth a nhial*, Spirit of the sky or Spirit who is in the sky. There are other and lesser spirits which they class as *kuth nhial*, spirits of the sky or of the above, and *kuth piny*, spirits of the earth or of the below. I discuss the conception of God first because the other spiritual conceptions are dependent on it and can only be understood in relation to it.

The Nuer *kwoth*, like the Latin *spiritus*, the Greek *pneuma*, and the English derivatives of both words, suggests both the intangible quality of air and the breathing or blowing out of air. Like the Hebrew *ruah* it is an onomatope and denotes violent breathing out of air in contrast to ordinary breathing.[2] In its verbal form it is used to describe such actions as blowing on the embers of a fire; blowing on food to cool it, blowing into the uterus of a cow, while a tulchan is propped up before it, to make it give milk; snorting; the blowing out of air by the puff fish; and the hooting by steam pressure of a river steamer. The word is also found, and has the same general sense, in some of the other Nilotic languages.

As a noun, however, *kwoth* means only Spirit, and in the particular sense we are now discussing it means *kwoth nhial* or *kwoth a nhial*, Spirit of the heavens or Spirit who is in the heavens, the copula *a* in the second designation being one of the verbs we translate 'to be'. *Nhial* is the sky, and combined with verbs the word may also refer to certain natural processes associated with the sky, as raining and thundering; but it may also have merely the sense of 'on high' or 'above'. We may certainly say that the Nuer do not regard the sky or any celestial phenomenon as God, and this is clearly shown in the distinction made between God and

---

[1] The word has been variously spelt by European writers I shall throughout use *kwoth* (pl. *kuth*), neglecting the genitive and locative forms.

[2] Norman H. Snaith, *The Distinctive Ideas of the Old Testament*, 1944, chap vii

the sky in the expressions 'Spirit of the sky' and 'Spirit who is in the sky'. Moreover, it would even be a mistake to interpiet 'of the sky' and 'in the sky' too literally.

It would equally be a mistake to regard the association of God with the sky as pure metaphor, for though the sky is not God, and though God is everywhere, he is thought of as being particularly in the sky, and Nuer generally think of him in a spatial sense as being on high. Hence anything connected with the firmament has associations with him. Nuer sometimes speak of him as falling in the rain and of being in lightning and thunder Mgr. Mlakic says that the rainbow is called the necklace of God.[1] I have never heard a spontaneous reference to the sun as a divine manifestation, but if one asks Nuer about it they say that it too belongs to God, and the moon and the stars also. They say that if a man sees the sun at night this is a divine manifestation, and one which is most danger-ous for him; but I think that the light they say is occasionally seen is not regarded as an appearance of the physical sun but as some peculiar luminous vision. When Nuer see the new moon they rub ashes on their foreheads and they throw ashes, and perhaps also a grain of millet, towards it, saying some short prayer, as 'grandfather, let us be at peace' or 'ah moon, *nyadeang* (daugh-ter of the air-spirit *deng*) we invoke (God) that thou shouldst appear with goodness. May the people see thee every day. Let us be (*akolapko*).' Mgr. Mlakic says that they mark their foreheads with ashes in the form of a cross and that it is called *ngei kwoth*, God's sign.[2] I must add that the language is here figurative, even playful. They may address the moon, but it is God to whom they speak through it, for the moon is not regarded, as such, as Spirit or as a person.

It would be quite contrary to Nuer thought, as I have remarked, and it would even seem absurd to them, to say that sky, moon, rain, and so forth are in themselves, singly or collectively, God. God is Spirit, which, like wind and air, is invisible and ubiquitous. But though God is not these things he is in them in the sense that he reveals himself through them In this sense, which I discuss further in Chapter V, he is in the sky, falls in the rain, shines in the sun and moon, and blows in the wind These divine manifesta-

[1] *The Messenger*, 1943-4 (I have not seen the original articles but only a typewritten copy of them, so I cannot give page references)
[2] Ibid

tions are to be understood as modes of God and not as his essence, which is Spirit.

God being above, everything above is associated with him This is why the heavenly bodies and the movements and actions connected with them are associated with him. This is why also the spirits of the air are regarded as *gaat kwoth*, children of God, in a way other spirits are not, for they, unlike other spirits, dwell in the air and are also thought of as being in the clouds, which are nearest to the sky This is why also the *colwic* spirits are so closely associated with God, for he touched them with his fire from heaven and took them to himself. Some birds also are spoken about by Nuer as *gaat kwoth*, especially those which fly high and seem, to us as well as to Nuer, to belong to heaven rather than to earth and therefore to be children of light and symbols of the divine. The feeling that they are in a measure detached from the earth is enhanced in the case of migratory birds[1] by their disappearances and reappearances. I have heard the idea expressed that in their absence from Nuerland they have gone to visit God's country. This is probably no more than poetic fancy, but we can say that the disappearance of these birds strengthens the allegory of God's children which arises from their ability to do what man cannot do, fly towards heaven and God Twins also, in a very special sense, are *gaat kwoth*. They belong to the above, and Nuer say that they are birds. The Jikul clan and the Gaanwar clan, whose ancestors fell from heaven, are also *ji kwoth*, God's people, for that reason and are thought to have special powers.

Thus anything associated with the sky has virtue which is lacking in earthly things. Nuer pathetically compare man to heavenly things. He is *ran piny*, an earthly person and, according to the general Nuer view, his ghost is also earth-bound. Between God and man, between heaven and earth, there is a great gulf, and we shall find that an appreciation of the symbolism of the polarity of heaven and earth helps us to understand Nuer religious thought and feeling and also sheds light on certain social features of their religion, for example the greater prestige of prophets than of priests.

[1] I am indebted to Miss Ray Huffman and Dr Mary Smith for the information that, among others, these are the pied crow, the kite, the pelican, the maribou stork, the eagle, the crested crane, the Cape Paradise flycatcher, the wagtail, and the durra-birds.

Before discussing furthei the separation of God from man I will mention some of the chief attributes of God. He is in the sky, but his being in the sky does not mean that he is not at the same time elsewhere, and on earth. Indeed, as will be seen, Nuer religious thought cannot be understood unless God's closeness to man is taken together with his separation from man, for its meaning lies precisely in this paradox.

Nuer say that God is everywhere, that he is 'like wind' and 'like air'. According to Father Crazzolara,[1] he may be spoken of by the epithets *jiom*, wind, and *ghau*, universe, but these words only stand for God in poems or in an allegorical sense and are illustrations of the liking the Nilotic peoples show in their poetry for metonymy and synecdoche. God is not wind, but *cere jiom*, like wind; and he is not *ghau*, the universe, but *cak ghaua*, the creator of the universe. Another poetic epithet by which he may be referred to is *tutgar*. This is an ox-name, taken from an ox of the kind Nuer call *wer*, which has wide spreading horns and is the most majestic of their beasts (Plate I) The name is a combination of two words: *tut*, which has the sense of 'strength' or 'greatness', and *gar*, which has the sense of 'omnipresent', as in another of God's titles, *kwoth me gargar*, the omnipresent God (*gargar* can also be translated 'limitless').[2] But the commonest Nuer way of trying to express their idea of the nature of God is to say that he is like wind or air, a metaphor which seems appropriate to us because it is found throughout the hierological literature of the world and we are particularly familiar with it in the Old Testament Among the Nuer the metaphor is consistent not only with the absence of any fixed abode of God but also of any places where he is thought particularly to dwell, for air and wind are everywhere. Unlike the other spirits God has no prophets or sanctuaries or earthly forms.

God, Spirit in the heavens who is like wind and air, is the creator and mover of all things Since he made the world he is addressed in prayers as *kwoth ghaua*, Spirit of the universe, with the sense of creator of the universe The word *cak*, used as a noun, can mean the creation, that is, all created things, and hence the

[1] Op cit p 72.

[2] Dr. Mary Smith tells me that if a ne'er-do-well is asked how he expects to live he may reply '*kwoth e gargar*', 'God is limitless' (in his power to aid), in the same way as a man may say of the earth or of the universe that it is *gargar*, limitless.

PLATE I

Ox with spreading horns

nature or character proper to a person or thing, it can be used in a
very special sense to refer to an abnormality, *cak kwoth*, a freak;
and, though I think rarely, it is used as a title of God, the creator,
as in the expression *cak nath*, creator of men. As a verb 'to create'
it signifies creation *ex nihilo*, and when speaking of things can
therefore only be used of God. However, the word can be used of
men for imaginative constructions, such as the thinking of a name
to give a child, inventing a tale, or composing a poem, in the same
figurative sense as when we say that an actor creates a part. The
word therefore means not only creation from nothing but also
creation by thought or imagination, so that 'God created the
universe' has the sense of 'God thought of the universe' or 'God
imagined the universe'.

Professor Westermann wrote at the dictation of a Nuer an
account of how God created the world and made all things in it.
It begins '*Me chak koth nath, chwo ran thath*', which he has
translated 'When God created the people, he created man '[1] It will
be observed that he has translated two different words, *cak* (*chak*)
and *tath* (*thath*), by 'create', but they have not quite the same
sense. for whereas *cak* means creation *ex nihilo* and in thought or
imagination, *tath* means to make something out of something
else already materially existing. as when a child moulds clay into
the shape of an ox or a smith beats a spear out of iron. The sentence would therefore be better translated 'When God created
people then he made (or fashioned) man.' The distinction is similar to that between 'created' and 'made' in the first chapter of
Genesis, 'created' there being a translation of the Hebrew *br'*,
which can only be used for divine activity.

The complementary distinction made in Genesis between 'the
heaven and the earth' is made, by implication at least, in a slightly
different way by the Nuer. A parallelism often heard in their
prayers is '*e pinydu, e ghaudu*', 'it is thine earth, it is thy universe'
Piny is the down-below, the earth in the sense of the terrestrial
world as the Nuer know it. *Ghau* has many meanings—world,
sky, earth, atmosphere, time, and weather—which taken together,
as they should be in a context of prayer, mean the universe
Another common, and related, strophe in prayers is '*e ghaudu,
e rwacdu*', 'it is thy universe, it is thy word'. *Rwac* in ordinary

---

[1] Diedrich Westermann, 'The Nuer Language', *Mitteilungen des Seminars fur
Orientalische Sprachen*, 1912, p 115

contexts means speech, talk, or word, but when used in prayers and invocations in the phrase '*e rwacdu*', 'it is thy word', it means the will of God, and when used in reference to creation it has almost the meaning of the creative word 'he created the world, it is his word'.

The Nuer can hardly be said to have a creation myth, though our authorities[1] record some fragmentary accounts of the creation of men, parts of which I have myself heard These state that men were created in the Jagei country of western Nuerland at a certain tamarind tree, at the foot of which offerings, and according to Mr. Jackson sacrifices, were sometimes made till it was destroyed by fire in 1918. Many details in the versions given by Mr. Jackson and Captain Fergusson are clearly foreign, either Dinka or in Mr. Jackson's account Shilluk and in Captain Fergusson's account possibly even Atwot or Mandari, and I regard Father Crazzolara's version as the closest to Nuer tradition In this version the tamarind tree, called Lic, was itself the mother of men who, according to one account, emerged from a hole at its foot or, according to another account, dropped off its branches like ripe fruits

Whether they are speaking about events which happened *ne walka*, in the beginning or long ago, or about happenings of yesterday or today, God, creative Spirit, is the final Nuer explanation of everything. When asked how things began or how they have come to be what they are they answer that God made them or that it was his will that they have come to be what they are. The heavens and the earth and the waters on the earth, and the beasts and birds and reptiles and fish were made by him, and he is the author of custom and tradition. The Nuer herd cattle and cultivate millet and spear fish because God gave them these things for their sustenance. He instituted their marriage prohibitions. He gave ritual powers to some men and not to others. He decreed that the Nuer should raid the Dinka and that Europeans should conquer the Nuer. He made one man black and another white (according to one account our white skins are a punishment by God for incest committed by our ancestor with his mother), one man fleet and another slow, one strong and another weak Everything in nature, in culture, in society, and in men is as it is because

---

[1] H. C Jackson, 'The Nuer of the Upper Nile Province', *Sudan Notes and Records*, 1923, pp 70–71, V H. Fergusson, 'The Nuong Nuer', ibid , 1921, pp 148–9; J. P Crazzolara, op cit , p 66.

God made or willed it so. Above all else God is thought of as the giver and sustainer of life. He also brings death. It is true that Nuer seldom attribute death—in such cases as death by lightning or following the breach of a divinely sanctioned interdiction—to the direct intervention of God, but rather to natural circumstances or to the action of a lesser spirit, but they nevertheless regard the natural circumstances or the spirits as instruments or agents of God, and the final appeal in sickness is made to him Nuer have often told me that it is God who takes the life, whether a man dies from spear, wild beast, or sickness, for these are all *nyin kwoth*, instruments of God.

In the Nuer conception of God he is thus creative Spirit. He is also a *ran*, a living person, whose *yiegh*, breath or life, sustains man. I have never heard Nuer suggest that he has human form, but though he is himself ubiquitous and invisible, he sees and hears all that happens and he can be angry and can love (the Nuer word is *nhok*, and if we here translate it 'to love' it must be understood in the preferential sense of *agapō* or *diligo* when Nuer say that God loves something they mean that he is partial to it). However, the anthropomorphic features of the Nuer conception of God are very weak and, as will be seen, they do not act towards him as though he were a man. Indeed, such human features as are given him barely suffice to satisfy the requirements of thought and speech. If he is to be spoken about, or to, he has to be given some human attributes. Man's relation to him is, as it is among other peoples,[1] on the model of a human social relationship He is the father of men.

A very common mode of address to the Deity is '*gwandong*', a word which means 'grandfather' or 'ancestor', and literally 'old father', but in a religious context 'father' or 'our father' would convey the Nuer sense better; and '*gwara*' and '*gwandan*', 'our father', and the respectful form of address '*gwadin*', 'father', are also often used in speaking to or about God. God is the father of men in two respects. He is their creator and he is their protector

He is addressed in prayers as '*kwoth me cak gwadong*', 'God who created my ancestor'. Figuratively, and in conformity with Nuer lineage idiom, he is sometimes given a genealogical position in relation to man. A man of the Jinaca clan, for example, after tracing his pedigree back to Denac, the founder of his clan, may

[1] Friedrich Heiler, *Das Gebet*, 3rd ed, 1921, pp 490 seq

go on to say that Denac was a son of Gee, who was a son of *Ran*, man, who was a son of *Ghau*, the universe, who was a son of *Kwoth*, God. When Nuer thus speak of God as their remote ancestor and address him as 'father' or 'grandfather', and likewise when in praying to him they speak of themselves, as they commonly do, as *'gaatku'*, 'thy children', their manner of speech is no more to be taken literally than are those frequent passages in the Old Testament in which Israel is spoken of as the spouse or son of Jehovah Such ideograms are common enough in all religions [1] Also, when Nuer speak of spirits, birds, and twins as *'gaat kwoth'*, 'children of God', they speak in an allegorical sense. Similarly, when children are named after God or one of the spirits of the air, for example, Gatkwoth, son of God, or Gatdeang, son of (the air-spirit) *deng*, all we are to understand from these theophorous proper names is that the child was conceived in answer to prayer or sacrifice. Even in Nuer family and kinship usages the word *gat*, son, does not necessarily, or even usually, signify a son in a physiological sense but a son in one or other of several social senses. That the language is here allegorical is shown by the use of the word *cak* in the expression *'kwoth me cak gwadong'*, 'God who created my ancestor', for *cak* means to create and not to beget. It is also shown by the fact that the word *dieth*, to beget, is not only not used in this expression but is never used in reference to God.[2] It is true that Father Crazzolara records the sentence *'gwandong ce nadh dieth ke diedh nadhe'*, which, as he rightly says, means 'God did not beget men with the begetting with which men are begotten', but he adds that the word *dieth* was only used by his informant because the question he himself had asked required its use.[3] Nuer do not think of God as the begetter of man but as his creator

God is also the father of men in that he is their protector and friend. He is *'kwoth me jale ka ji'*, 'God who walks with you', that is, who is present with you. He is the friend of men who helps them in their troubles, and Nuer sometimes address him as *'madh'*, 'friend', a word which has for them the sense of intimate

---

[1] Rudolf Otto, *The Idea of the Holy*, Eng. trans , 4th impress., 1926, *passim*

[2] Cf the Anuak who use 'to beget' as well as 'to create' of God: *'inica na gho juokki na cuac ji, juok anywol ki nyiee mi detgi da yier'*, 'once upon a time when God came and created people, God begat children with hair on their bodies' (the author's unpublished *Anuak Grammar*).

[3] Op. cit., p 66

friendship. The frequent use in prayers of the word *rom* in reference to the lives, or souls, of men indicates the same feeling about God, for it has the sense of the care and protection parents give to a child and especially the carrying of a helpless infant. So does another word often used in prayers, *luek*, to comfort God is asked to '*luek nei*' to 'comfort the people'. The Nuer habit of making short supplications to God outside formal and ritual occasions also suggests an awareness of a protective presence, as does the affirmation one hears every day among the Nuer, '*kwoth a thin*', 'God is present'. Nuer say this, doubtless often as a merely verbal response, when they are faced with some difficulty to be overcome or some problem to be solved. The phrase does not mean 'there is a God'. That would be for Nuer a pointless remark. God's existence is taken for granted by everybody. Consequently when we say, as we can do, that all Nuer have faith in God, the word 'faith' must be understood in the Old Testament sense of 'trust' (the Nuer *ngath*) and not in that modern sense of 'belief' which the concept came to have under Greek and Latin influences. There is in any case, I think, no word in the Nuer language which could stand for 'I believe'. *Kwoth a thin* means that God is present in the sense of being in a place or enterprise, the *a* being here again a verb 'to be'. When Nuer use the phrase they are saying that they do not know what to do but God is here with them and will help them. He is with them because he is Spirit and being like wind or air is everywhere, and, being everywhere, is here now.

But though God is sometimes felt to be present here and now, he is also felt to be far away in the sky [1] If he hears a whispered prayer, it is spoken with eyes and hands raised to the distant heavens. However, heaven and earth, that is, God and man, for we are justified here in treating the dichotomy anagogically, are not entirely separated. There are comings and goings. God takes the souls of those he destroys by lightning to dwell with him and in him they protect their kinsmen; he participates in the affairs of men through divers spirits which haunt the atmosphere between heaven and earth and may be regarded as hypostasizations of his modes and attributes; and he is also everywhere present in a way

[1] These contrasted feelings are probably common to all predominantly theistic religions and they have often been noted by scholars, e g. by Antonio Anwander in his discussion of *pietà della 'lontananza'* and *pietà della 'vicinanza'* in his *Introduzione alla Storia delle Religioni*, 1932, pp 168 seq.

which can only be symbolized, as his ubiquitous presence is symbolized by the Nuer, by the metaphor of wind and air. Also he can be communicated with through prayer and sacrifice, and a certain kind of contact with him is maintained through the social order he is said to have instituted and of which he is the guardian, a matter I discuss briefly later But in spite of these communications and contacts the distance between heaven and earth is too great to be bridged.

God's separation and remoteness from man are accounted for in a myth recorded by Father Crazzolara which relates that there was not always a complete separation of heaven and earth and that there might never have been but for an almost fortuitous event I did not myself hear Father Crazzolara's version of the myth, and I judge it to be of Dinka origin, partly because it occurs among the Dinka but more because I think it is very probably only current among Nuer to the west of the Nile,[1] which would indicate recent introduction into Nuerland from Dinka sources; but, whether it is Dinka or not, it accords well with Nuer religious conceptions in general. The myth relates that there was once a rope from heaven to earth and how anyone who became old climbed up by it to God in heaven and after being rejuvenated there returned to earth One day a hyena—an appropriate figure in a myth relating to the origin of death—and what is known in the Sudan as a durra-bird, most likely a weaver-bird, entered heaven by this means. God gave instructions that the two guests were to be well watched and not allowed to return to earth where they would certainly cause trouble. One night they escaped and climbed down the rope, and when they were near the earth the hyena cut the rope and the part above the cut was drawn upwards towards heaven. So the connexion between heaven and earth was cut and those who grow old must now die, for what had happened could not be made not to have happened ('aber was geschehen war, konnte nicht mehr ungeschehen gemacht werden') A variant of this myth has been recorded by Captain Fergusson.[2]

[1] This conjecture is strengthened by information from Dr Mary Smith that the story is not known to the Eastern Jikany Nuer. A version current among the Central Nuer is recorded in *The Nuer*, p 230

[2] J P. Crazzolara, op cit , p 68; V. H Fergusson, op cit , pp 148–9.

It is in the light of their feeling that man is dependent on God and helpless without his aid and that God, though a friend and present, is yet also remote that we are to interpret a word Nuer frequently use about themselves when speaking to or about God: *doar*. The meanings of this word given in Nuer–English dictionaries, 'idiot', 'stupid', 'fool', and 'weak-minded', do not adequately convey the sense of the word, especially when it is used to refer to man's relationship to God. Then it means rather 'simple' or 'foolish' or 'ignorant'—'idiot' in the sense the word used to have in the English language and which the word from which it is derived had in Greek. Nuer say that they are just ignorant people who do not understand the mysteries of life and death, and of God and the spirits, and why things happen as they do.

A favourite Nuer expression is '*yie wicda*', 'my head goes round' or 'I am bewildered'. They are at a loss because they are just foolish people who do not understand the why and the wherefore. In saying that they are simple or foolish or ignorant Nuer are not being modest in respect to other peoples, though I have often had the impression that they regard themselves as guileless compared with other peoples, especially compared with the Dinka, whom they regard as cleverer and more cunning than themselves, a difference dramatized in one of their myths. The story, which reminds us of that of Esau and Jacob, is cited by Nuer to explain why they have always raided the Dinka. Nuer and Dinka—the peoples are personified in the myth—were both sons of God, who had promised to give an old cow to Dinka and its young calf to Nuer. Dinka came by night to God's byre and deceived him by imitating Nuer's voice, and God gave him the calf. When God found that he had been deceived he charged Nuer to raid the herds of Dinka to the end of time. In other words, the Nuer may be robbers but the Dinka are thieves Another story relates that God offered men the choice between cattle and rifles. Nuer and Dinka chose cattle and Arabs and Europeans chose rifles. Here both Nuer and Dinka are figured as simple compared to Arabs and Europeans. Nuer regard themselves as having manly virtues exceeding those of other peoples, but compared with them they are artless. However, when they use the word *doar* in a religious context they are speaking of themselves being foolish in comparison with God and in his eyes The same idea is expressed in speaking of themselves as *cok*, small black ants, particularly in their hymns to spirits of the air, that is, they are God's ants, or in other words what a tiny ant is to man, so man is to God. This is a conscious and explicit analogy Thus Father J. Kiggen quotes the phrases '*kondial labne cuugh, ke min kueine ke kuoth*', which I would translate 'we, all of us, have the nature of ants in that we are very tiny in respect to God', and '*kondial gaad cuughni ke kuoth*', which I would translate 'all of us are like little ants in the sight of God'.[1] The same metaphor has been recorded for the Dinka by Archdeacon Shaw.[2] We are reminded of Isaiah's likening of men to grasshoppers (xl. 22).

In speaking about themselves as being like ants and as being simple Nuer show a humbleness in respect to God which contrasts with their proud, almost provocative, and towards strangers even insulting, bearing to men, and indeed humbleness, a consciousness of creatureliness, is a further element of meaning in the word *doar*, as is also humility, not contending against God but suffering without complaint. Humbleness and humility are very evident on occasions of religious expression among the Nuer—in the manner and content of prayer, in the purpose and meaning of sacrifices, and, perhaps most evidently, in their sufferings. Nuer accept misfortunes with resignation. Whatever the occasion of death and other misfortunes may be, whether they be what Nuer call *dung cak*, the lot of created things, or whether they be the result of what they call *dueri*, faults, they come to one and all alike, and Nuer say that they must be accepted as the will of God. The best that can be hoped for is that God will hear the prayers and accept the sacrifices of those who suffer and spare them any extra burden. Nuer do not complain when misfortunes befall them. They say that it is God's will (*rwac kwoth*), that it is his world (*e ghaude*), and—I have often heard Nuer say this in their sufferings—that he is good (*goagh*) When a child dies women lament, but only for a little while, and men are silent. They say that God has taken his own and that they must not complain; perhaps he will give them another child. This is a common refrain with Nuer, especially in their invocations at mortuary ceremonies. They say of the dead man that God has taken him and that he was in the right in the matter, for it was his man, he has taken

[1] *Nuer-English Dictionary*, 1948, p 60.   [2] 'Dinka Songs', *Man*, 1915.

only what was his own. Also, when a byre is destroyed by lightning Nuer tell him that they do not complain. The grass of the thatch is his, and he has a right to take what belongs to him. Likewise if a cow or an ox of your herd dies Nuer say that you must not complain if God takes his own beast. The cattle of your herd are his and not yours. If you grieve overmuch God will be angry that you resent his taking what is his. Better be content, therefore, that God should do what he wishes, seeing not that he has taken one of your cows but that he has spared the others. If you forget the cow God will see that you are poor and will spare you and your children and your other beasts. I cannot convey the Nuer attitude better than by quoting the Book of Job. 'the Lord gave, and the Lord hath taken away; blessed be the name of the Lord' (1. 21).[1]

Father Crazzolara records much the same of the Nuer in this respect as I have done. He says, for example, that if God kills a man or destroys property by lightning, Nuer say that he has only taken what was his, what was his right.[2] God is always in the right, always, as Nuer say, has *cuong*, a word I discuss later. Nuer also say, when some calamity has happened to them, *'thile me lele'*, which means that there is nothing which can be done about it because it is the will of God and therefore beyond man's control.

People comfort a man who has lost cattle by telling him these things, but they find it hard to comfort a youth who has lost his *dil thak*, his favourite ox, for he is young and the ox was perhaps his only ox and has been his companion. He has cared for it and played with it and danced and sung to it. He now sits by himself and pines, and his friends try to cheer him up. They tell him that he must not be tearful or God will be angry: 'God is good, he might have taken you, but he has taken your ox instead.' Here we have a further and very common reflection in adversity. God has been gracious and he has taken something belonging to a man and has spared the man himself. What appears to be misfortune is therefore really fortune Nuer here use the word *gang*, to shield or protect, saying that the thing has shielded the man.

[1] This quotation is also given by Professor and Mrs. Seligman (op cit , p. 230) It was, however, like most of their account of the Nuer, taken from my notebooks I mention this fact because I have found that Professor and Mrs Seligman are often quoted, for example by P. W. Schmidt in his *Der Ursprung der Gottesidee*, as independent authorities This is no fault of Professor and Mrs Seligman, but it makes nevertheless for confusion   [2] Op cit , p 96

I was told that in spite of these encouragements a youth who has lost his favourite ox has to be pressed to partake of its cooked flesh, his friends saying to him 'What? Are they not all the cattle of God? And if he has taken one of them you must not refuse its flesh. Why do you sit moping?' I have also heard it said that if the owner refuses its flesh and puts his spear away in the rafters of his byre, the spear may cut his hand or leg some later day because it was put away as though useless. In any case, in the end no Nuer can resist meat A Nuer once told me wistfully that a man's eye and heart are mournful at the death of his beast but his teeth and stomach are glad. Nuer say that the stomach prays to God independently of the heart.

In taking things God, as we have noted, takes only what is his, but he is compassionate and, as we have also noted, spares a man if he sees that he is poor and miserable (*can*). In talking about these matters with Nuer I received the impression that, while of course they like to be rich, they think it safer for a man not to have too much good fortune. Pride in the number of his children or cattle may cause God to take them away. For this reason Nuer show great uneasiness if their good fortune is so much as mentioned It is proper to praise a man's moral qualities, to say that he is brave, generous, or kind, but it is more than rude to remark on his physical well-being, the size of his family, or the number and quality of his beasts and other possessions, for evil consequences may follow It is what Nuer generally call *yop*. Thus to say to a man, 'Well, you *are* fat', may make him thin; and it is the ambition of every Nuer to be fat, though I have never seen one who achieved it. It is also very bad to praise a cow, especially to remark on its exceptional milk yield, because it may then cease to give milk. I was told that 'only when her husband has married a wife with a cow will a woman praise it', that is, after it has ceased to be her cow. It is also most dangerous to tell a lad who has recently been initiated that the cuts on his forehead are healing well, or indeed to make any allusion to them, because a comment may result in an unhealed spot festering anew. I was often in trouble with Nuer on counts of this kind. I was always reprimanded if I counted children, saying, for instance, 'Let me see, so-and-so has four children, has he not? So-and-so, so-and-so, so-and-so, and so-and-so.' On one occasion I was eating porridge with Nuer and complimented my host on the size of the meal Every-

one was most embarrassed and I was later taken aside by a Nuer
friend and told that I must never make such comments On
another occasion I got into trouble for asking a man in jest, and,
I admit, in bad taste, whether it was food or beer inside him, for
his belly was as tight as a drum I was told that my question
might well make the man sick, and one of those present said that
once a man had remarked to him, 'Well, you are full', and shortly
afterwards he was violently sick. The worst offence is to praise a
baby. In referring to it one should use some such expression as
'*giakeme*', 'this bad thing' When blessing children by spitting on
them, which is the Nuer manner of showing favour to a child,
kinsmen, and more especially kinswomen, utter some opprobrious
remarks, sometimes a string of obscenities, over them.

The idea here is not that of the evil eye (*peth*), though the two
ideas may in some ways resemble one another and also overlap.[1]
In Nuer opinion the evil eye is an act of covetousness or envy,
whereas here, I think, the emphasis is on the danger of rejoicing
in unusual good fortune lest it should be taken away. There is a
feeling that God evens things out, so that if he helps the needy he
may take away from those with superfluity. As I understood their
view it expresses a certain uneasiness at attention being drawn to
possessions lest pride should bring about retribution. That this is
their view is further suggested by a number of their stories which
relate how God punished presumptuousness I mention only one
in this place, a short myth which reminds us of the story of
Elijah and the priests of Baal and which is obviously either taken
from some foreign people or is a fairly recent creation of Nuer
imaginative thought, because it is about the *Turuk*, Turks, and
their rifles. The word *Turuk* means in Nuer, as it does in the
languages of many of the black peoples of the Southern Sudan,
all lighter-skinned northerners with whom they have had dealings
during the last hundred years, that is, Turks, Egyptians, Arabs,
and Nubians of the Northern Sudan, and ourselves and other
Europeans. The 'Turks' compared their rifles to God's thunder,
and there was a trial of strength between them and God. God
made a huge mud image of an elephant and told the 'Turks' to
shoot at it, which they did to no effect. God then brought clouds
and darkness and thunder and lightning and smashed the image

[1] *Yop* is presumably the same word as the Shilluk *yʊop* which Wilhelm
Hofmayr (*Die Schilluk*, 1925, p 221) translates by '*bose Blick*'

to dust and killed many of the 'Turks' as well because they had compared the rifle he had given them to his power. The point of this story is not merely that God was stronger than the 'Turks' but that he was in the right and the 'Turks' were at fault.

This brings me to an extremely important Nuer concept, an understanding of which is very necessary to a correct appreciation of their religious thought and practice. This is the concept of *cuong* This word can mean 'upright' in the sense of standing, as, for example, in reference to the supports of byres. It is also used figuratively for 'firmly established', as in the phrase *'be gole cuong'*, 'may his hearth stand', which has the sense of *stet fortuna domus*. It is most commonly employed, however, with the meaning of 'in the right' in both a forensic and a moral sense. The discussion in what we would call legal cases is for the purpose of determining who has the *cuong*, the right, in the case, or who has the most right; and in any argument about conduct the issue is always whether a person has conformed to the accepted norms of social life, for, if he has, then he has *cuong*, he has right on his side. We are concerned with the concept here both because it relates directly to man's behaviour towards God and other spiritual beings and the ghosts and because it relates to God in a more indirect way, in that he is regarded as the founder and guardian of morality Up to this point I have been describing Nuer ideas about the nature of God. I shall now describe their ideas about what God requires of them.

III

I do not want to suggest that God is thought to be an immediate sanction for all conduct, but I must emphasize that the Nuer are of one voice in saying that sooner or later and in one way or another good will follow right conduct and ill will follow wrong conduct. People may not reap their rewards for good acts and punishments for bad acts for a long time, but the consequences of both follow behind (*gwor*) them and in the end catch up on those responsible for them. You give milk to a man when he has no lactating cows, or meat and fish to him when he is hungry, or you befriend him in other ways, though he is no close kinsman of yours He blesses you, saying that your age-mates will die while your children grow old with you. God will see your charity and give you long life. Those who have lived among the Nuer must have heard, and received, their blessings. My lamented friend Miss Soule, of the American Mission at Nasser, once related to me how a Nuer woman had told her that her husband wished to throw her monorchid child into a river and how she dissuaded him by saying to him 'Maybe if we take care of this baby God will do great things for us' Miss Soule was herself often blessed by Nuer, being told that she would have a long life because she cared for orphans and babies whose mothers were unable to suckle them. I have myself had similar experiences during my illnesses in Nuerland. Men who appeared to be unsympathetic at other times would visit me then and say gently, 'You will drink Nile water', that is, 'You will return to your home'; or 'Well, pray to God and tell him that you have come on a journey to the country of the Nuer and that you have not hit anyone or stolen anything or done any bad thing there, and then he will leave you alone'; or 'It is nothing. You will not die. This is our earth and you shall not die on it Why should you die? You have not wronged us, and you are friend to all our children. It (the sickness) is nothing. If you call on God it will finish. Let it blow there, and there, and there (pointing in different directions), let it go to the ends of the earth.' As these admonitions imply, if a man does wrong God will sooner or later punish him.

The Nuer have the idea that if a man keeps in the right—does not break divinely sanctioned interdictions, does not wrong others, and fulfils his obligations to spiritual beings and the ghosts and to his kith and kin—he will avoid, not all misfortunes, for some misfortunes come to one and all alike, but those extra and special misfortunes which come from *dueri*, faults, and are to be regarded as castigations. The word *duer* means 'a fault', and the verbal *dwir* means 'to be at fault'. Like similar words in other languages (e.g Hebrew, Greek, and German), *dwir* has both the sense of missing a mark aimed at—in throwing a spear, and today also in firing a rifle—and also of a dereliction, a fault which brings retribution. I discuss interdictions in Chapter VII. Here I wish only to observe that not only a sin (a breach of certain interdictions) but also any wrong conduct to persons is spoken of as *duer*, a fault. Any failure to conform to the accepted norms of behaviour towards a member of one's family, kin, age-set, a guest, and so forth is a fault which may bring about evil consequences through either an expressed curse or a silent curse contained in anger and resentment (pp. 165–73), though the misfortunes which follow are regarded by Nuer as coming ultimately from God, who supports the cause of the man who has the *cuong*, the right in the matter, and punishes the person who is at fault (*dwir*), for it is God alone who makes a curse operative. Nuer are quite explicit on this point What, then, Nuer ideas on the matter amount to is, in our way of putting it, that if a man wishes to be in the right with God he must be in the right with men, that is, he must subordinate his interests as an individual to the moral order of society. A man must honour his father and his father's age-mates, a wife must obey her husband, a man must respect his wife's kin, and so on. If an individual fails to observe the rules he is, Nuer say, *yong*, crazy, because he not only loses the support of kith and kin but also the favour of God, so that retribution in one form or another and sooner or later is bound to follow. Therefore Nuer, who are unruly and quarrelsome people, avoid, in so far as they can restrain themselves, giving gratuitous offence. Therefore, also, a man who is at fault goes to the person he has offended, admits the fault, saying to him '*ca dwir*', 'I was at fault', and he may also offer a gift to wipe out the offence. The wronged man then blesses him by spitting or blowing water on him and says that it is nothing and may the man be at peace He thereby removes any resentment he may have in his heart. Nuer say that God sees these acts and frees the man from the consequences of his fault. Similarly, the consequences of faults which are more directly of a religious order, like the breach of an interdiction or the neglect of some spirit, may be avoided by a timely sacrifice, though Nuer say that sacrifice without contrition is of no use. But—and this is the point I want to bring out here—the fact that the consequences of a fault can be stayed by contrition and reparation shows that the consequences of wrong-doing are not thought to be automatic.

That this is so, and there is a moral, and therefore uncertain and alterable, element involved is further shown by another fact. In estimating the likelihood, or degree, of misfortune that may be expected to follow from an act, Nuer take deliberation into the reckoning. They distinguish between *duer* and *gwac*. The word *duer*, as we have seen, means a fault, and it normally implies that the fault was deliberate, though, as will be seen later, this is not always or entirely so. *Gwac* means a mistake, an unintentional error and generally one of no great consequence, one in which a serious breach of religious or moral precepts is not involved, such as an unintentional lapse in manners or a slip of the tongue It implies that the action was incorrect but inadvertent, and the man asks to be excused. In a certain sense, however, in the sense that the act was not deliberate, a more serious fault may be regarded as a mistake, even though it is at the same time a fault, and the fact that it was not a deliberate fault is held to some extent to alter the circumstances. This is very evident in affairs in which damage and compensation are involved, as, for example, in homicide. When a man kills another, how the damage is treated, both with regard to manner and to the amount of compensation demanded, much depends on whether the slaying was premeditated or was the unfortunate outcome of a sudden quarrel or an accident. God also takes deliberation into account in breaches of moral law. Thus it is not thought that children will fall sick if they have incestuous relations in their play 'because the children are ignorant of having done wrong' They know no better Likewise, if two kinsmen have relations with the same girl, which Nuer regard as incest, without knowing that the other was making love to her, 'it is not incest because each was unaware that the other was making love to her'. Again, it is not thought that a man who commits incest with a kinswoman, not knowing her to be a kinswoman, will suffer any serious, or even any, consequences: 'This is not incest because he was unaware of the relationship between them.' If a man who respects hearts or lungs of animals eats them not knowing the nature of the meat he eats, 'this is an accident and his spirit (the spirit of hearts or lungs) knows that it was not done deliberately'. He may get a slight illness, but not a serious one. When I was living on the Sobat river news came to our village that some persons in an upstream village had found some meat and had cooked and eaten it, thinking that it was the flesh of some animal crocodiles had mutilated, and that they had later discovered it to be the flesh of a man whom crocodiles had killed and torn to pieces I was told that these persons would at once have taken *wal nueera*, medicine to cleanse them from pollution, and that while the happening was very disgusting it was unlikely that it would cause death because the flesh was eaten in ignorance of its nature. Nuer say that God may overlook what was done in error Similarly, they say that he will not allow a curse to harm a man who has done no deliberate wrong.

One can make too rigid distinctions between the meanings of words, and while an error or accident is clearly regarded by Nuer as different from a deliberate and premeditated act, the concepts of *gwac* and *duer* shade into each other There is perhaps always an element of the unintentional in the worst fault, and a Nuer who has committed a bad fault is inclined to excuse himself, as we would do, by calling it a mistake, but it is also true that, except in matters of no moment, and although the consequences may not be so severe, a wrong act is always a fault, whether it was deliberate or was due merely to forgetfulness or even involuntary, and may involve liability. Thus the men who in ignorance have relations with the same girl, the man who unknowingly has relations with a kinswoman, and the man who by mistake eats the flesh of his totem have all committed *dueri*, faults, and they cannot be certain that evil consequences will not follow. The effects may be the same as if the acts had been wilful Likewise a man who inadvertently eats from a dish from which a man with whom his kin have a blood-feud has eaten, and a man who appears naked before a kinswoman of his wife (Nuer men normally have no covering), not having noticed her presence, have committed faults. It may well happen that a man does not know he has done wrong till he suffers the consequences of the wrong For example, a man takes a woman for concubine not knowing that she is distantly related to him, and his children by her die. He then makes inquiries and discovers the relationship. He sinned, like Oedipus, in ignorance, but that did not alter what he had done and, like Oedipus, he paid the penalty of his fault. Even the innocent may suffer, as the example I have just given shows Indeed the whole human race suffers death on account of what was no more than a trivial oversight. If man had prevented the hyena and the durra-bird from escaping from heaven there would have been no death. This is the lesson of another story, probably also of Dinka origin, recounted by Father Crazzolara about the origin of death. It makes death follow from a mere blunder or a trifling act of malice. When man was created God took a piece of a gourd vessel and threw it into water to indicate that man would live for ever just as the rind would float for ever on the water He then sent a

[1] Op cit, p 67

barren, or divorced, woman to men to tell them that they would live for ever, but, in delivering her message, she threw, instead of a piece of gourd, a potsherd into the water, and it sank Almost fortuitous though this incident was, what had happened, as we have noted before, could not be made not to have happened. Men have to accept the consequences of actions whether they are deliberate or not.

Hence when Nuer suffer misfortune they ponder how it may have come about, for it follows from what has just been said and from the fact we noted earlier that God is always in the right, that if misfortune comes to a man it is most likely on account of some fault. This is why on such occasions one hears so often in Nuer prayers and invocations the plaint 'what have we done?' or 'what evil have we done?' and why Nuer sacrifices are so often propitiations, expiations, atonements, and purifications. It is therefore probable that suffering usually entails a measure of guilt Nuer search their consciences to discover what fault might have brought it on them, though this is more evident when a misfortune is only pending and may yet be stayed or though it has fallen may yet be mitigated, for if the fault can be determined they will know better what action to take. When the misfortune is complete and their condition can in no way be alleviated they are less interested in its cause and accept its accomplishment with sorrow and resignation

When Nuer suffer they sometimes at once know what is the cause of their suffering because they are well aware of some particular fault They sometimes, as we would say, tempt God by doing what they know to be wrong, hoping that it will not matter very much, such as having relations with a woman which are incestuous but not very incestuous. If trouble comes they know that this is the cause, for they have said that whether the relationship was too close for congress would be decided by any consequences of it. They now discover that it was more serious than they thought. Nuer often neglect their duties to their various spirits. They omit or forget to sacrifice to them or they fail to dedicate cows to them or they use cows dedicated to them for marriage and find that they cannot replace them or do not trouble to do so If a misfortune falls on them they then know that it is due to the anger of a spirit. Often, however, they are in doubt about the cause and confused and bewildered. It may be that the suffering is just something, like death in old age, which had to happen It may be due to a fetish or the evil eye. It may be the outcome of a curse or the anger of a ghost. Nevertheless, Nuer generally appear to feel that suffering is due to some fault of theirs, and it is probable that there is always an element of this feeling in every situation of misfortune, whatever its immediate cause may be thought to be.

IV

I have discussed in a preliminary way the conception Nuer have of God, the ideas and feelings they have about their relations with him, and some of the actions they think bring about divine intervention in human affairs I take these topics up again in succeeding chapters after the notion of Spirit has been broadened by an account of other spiritual conceptions. A brief consideration of some of the commoner expressions used in Nuer prayers may, however, be given now because they are used only when speaking to God.

For obvious reasons Nuer prayers are most commonly heard on public and formal occasions, generally in connexion with sacrifices At any important sacrifice, and sometimes on other important occasions also, Nuer make long invocations, called *lamni*, about the event which gave rise to the occasion, and into these long rambling addresses are every now and again introduced short prayers, mostly petitionary prayers. These what we may call stock prayers are often strung together in strophes in a kind of Pater Noster, such as 'Our father, it is thy universe, it is thy will, let us be at peace, let the souls of the people be cool, thou art our father, remove all evil from our path', and so forth However, there are no set form and order to these prayers, and each petition may be used separately and anywhere and at any time, and not only in invocations but also in private and spontaneous prayer, whether spoken or inward, and as pious ejaculations. If he is in any trouble or anxiety, the head of a Nuer household may pace up and down his kraal brandishing his spear and uttering some of these supplications; or, less formally, he may say them standing or squatting with his eyes turned towards heaven and his arms outstretched from the elbows, moving his hands, palms uppermost, up and down. They may also be uttered, if he says anything at all, in the petition a man on a journey makes to God as he knots grasses together at the side of a path, a practice Nuer call *tuc*. A man may do this because he has knocked his 'bad foot' against a stump in the path, for this presages misfortune, which can be avoided by asking God to let the badness remain in the grass so that the traveller may continue his journey with fortune. Each man has a 'good (auspicious) foot' and a 'bad (inauspicious) foot' and he learns which is which by experience. Nuer tie grass in the same manner to ensure success in any enterprise for which a journey is undertaken, often at the present day when they go to buy or beg something from an Arab merchant. They ask God to let them make a good bargain or that the merchant may make them a gift.[1] Nuer may also utter these phrases of prayer at any time as devout ejaculations, and not only when they are in trouble or desire a boon, for they have told me that they like to speak to God when they are happy (*loc tedh*) and because they are happy, and that they often say a few words to him as they go about their daily affairs

I have already discussed the significance of some of these prayerful words and expressions· 'our father', 'it is thy universe', 'it is thy will', and others. I will now consider the meaning of yet a few others, choosing for the purpose the commonest petitionary phrases. Before doing this I would draw attention to the fact that the petitioner generally uses the first person plural In private ejaculations a Nuer may use such expressions as 'ah, my God', 'ah, God, what is this?', and 'let me journey well', but he will also use the plural pronoun, and in prayers and invocations uttered in public the plural is invariably used: 'let us be at peace', or whatever the expression may be.[2] I draw attention to this because it is not, I believe, just an indication that there are other people on whose behalf the speaker is asking God's favours. It is rather that the occasions on which prayers are publicly offered are generally

[1] Some Nuer have told me that this custom of knotting grasses originated among the Dinka. It is found among some, if not all, the Dinka tribes (R T Johnston, 'The Religious and Spiritual Beliefs of the Bor Dinka', *Sudan Notes and Records*, 1934, p. 126)

[2] There are two pronominal suffixes for the first person plural, *ko* and *ne*, which are respectively exclusive and inclusive For example, '*bako wa*', 'we shall go', includes the speaker and others but not the person or persons spoken to, whereas '*bane wa*', 'we shall go', includes also the person or persons spoken to. In speaking to God Nuer have, of course, to use the exclusive form

such as emphasize by their gravity that, particularly in relation to God, all are members one of another It is of course natural as well as noticeable that close kin stick together in danger and when a wrong has been done to any one of them, but Nuer also quite clearly show that they feel that a misfortune for any member of their community is a misfortune for all, that when one suffers all suffer, and that if each is to be at peace all must be at peace. This feeling of oneness is particularly evident in Nuer prayers, because they are asking to be delivered from suffering, which has a common quality, the more so in that it is suffering in general rather than particular misfortunes of which they speak.

Perhaps the commonest phrase in Nuer prayers, and the one with which they often start prayer, is '*akonienko*'. Literally this means 'let us sleep', but here it should be rendered 'let us be at peace'. The commonest of the Nuer greetings and, when others are said, the first to be spoken is '*ci nien?*' or '*ci nienu?*', literally, 'have you slept?' The saluted man replies to this, as to other greetings, by a grunt of affirmation This is something of a joke among Europeans because Nuer have a reputation with them for being lethargic and lazy; but the question means something rather different from 'have you slept?' It means even more than our 'did you sleep well?' What Nuer understand by the question is rather, I think, 'have you rested?' or 'are you at ease?' The sense of 'ease' is reinforced by the question which generally follows: '*male?*' or '*maleu?*', which can be translated 'are you well?' but is better translated in the same general sense as the first question as 'are you at ease?' or 'are you at peace?'—not, however, so much with the meaning of not being at strife with others as with that of being at peace within. The word *mal* is also used in farewells: '*wer ke mal*', 'go in peace', and '*dudhni ke mal*', 'remain in peace'. It has in the Nuer tongue the sense of 'easy' or 'light', and in other Nilotic tongues it means 'heaven' or 'above' and in its verbal form 'to pray'—images which go with sleep which eases the mind

That Nuer regard being at ease or at peace as having something to do with being in friendship with God is shown by a further question which may follow: '*ci pal?*' or '*ci palu?*', 'have you prayed?' I think that the idea implied here is that being at peace in yourself means being at peace with God as well as with your fellow men. A fourth question asked in greetings is '*ci tol?*', the sense of which is does the smoke rise from your hearth, that is, is everything well with your home? A fifth question sometimes asked is *'ci bagh?'*, 'has it dawned (well for you)?' Not all these questions are always asked, but often two or three of them are, and sometimes more. In the full greeting we therefore get a composite picture of easy sleep and fresh awakening, contentment, prayer, and a smoking hearth, that is, of a person at peace in himself.

This digression was made to explain the meaning of the expression *'akomenko'* in prayer. The phrase is in harmony with some other expressions used in prayer: *'apwonyko pwol'*, 'may we be light', and *'apwonyko koc'*, 'may we be cool'. *Pwony* means 'body' or 'self' and here it means 'self' in the sense of the person as an entire person, body and soul. There is no reason why a Nuer should want to be light or cool in a purely physical sense. What is intended is to ask that the people may be light not only in the sense of physical well-being but also in the sense of *pwol loc*, of being light-hearted or joyful, free from burdens and troubles, and that they may be cool in the sense of not being anxious or worried, cool in the sense of calm. This is shown by a variant which is one of the commonest Nuer prayers, *'a yiegh neni koc'*, which can in this context only be translated 'may the souls of the people be cool', though in other contexts *yiegh* can mean 'breath' or 'life'. Very often the word *thei* is added, *'a yiegh neni koce thei'*, and this gives an emphasis· 'may the souls of the people be very cool'. Obviously Nuer are not asking, unless it be metaphorically, that their breath or life may be very cold. The word *koc* is also used in expressions of good will towards persons, especially in the blessing *'apwonydu koc'*, 'may you be cool', that is, 'may you be at peace'.[1]

The word *koc* can also mean 'soft' or 'tender', and though it is best translated 'cool' in prayers the two meanings may blend. Here again, Nuer clearly do not want to be physically soft. Indeed the expression *'koce thei'* in the physical sense of softness means when applied to men 'to be completely impotent sexually'. The idea of softness is seen in the metaphor often heard in prayers and invocations· 'may we tread on wild rice' *Poon*, wild rice, is, Nuer say, the softest of grasses to the feet, as it is also one of the

---

[1] The symbolism can at once be appreciated by ourselves, especially by those acquainted with the Vulgate and other Latin sacred texts where *refrigerium*, a cooling, is used in the tropical senses of 'consolation', 'mitigation', 'refreshing', and comfort'

tenderest pasture grasses, being sometimes gathered to feed small calves by hand. Nuer speak of life as walking through pastures and they ask for a path that has no hidden dangers, that is, is free from evil, and for softness underfoot, that is, a mind at ease. Hence they petition also *'gwenyi ko kwel gwath me jalko ko'*, 'make clear a way for us in the place where we journey', and *'gwenyi ko gwath'*, 'clear for us a place' Here again the sense is mainly allegorical. The words do not usually refer to any particular place or journey but to the journey through life, and the making clear of the way does not refer only, or even at all, to any particular dangers of travelling through the bush but to all the sufferings and evils which beset the life of man

Peace and deliverance are the key-notes of these petitions. They are seen again in the phrase *'kwoth ngaci rum yieni, romni yieko'*, 'God, thou (who) knowest how to support [or care for] souls, support [or care for] our souls'. The general sense of the prayer is that God should protect those who supplicate him as a parent protects his helpless infant. This desire for peace, deliverance, and protection is summed up in another common petition: *'akoteko'*, 'let us be'. I am not certain whether the verb here is *tek*, to be alive, or, as I think it is, *te*, to be. There is in any case a considerable overlap in meaning between the two words, and in this context there would not be any great difference in meaning between the one and the other, for the sense is: let us go on living and as we are. Nuer are asking for life, but not just life in the sense of living but of living abundantly, free from the troubles and sufferings which make life, as we say, not worth living. That this is the right interpretation is further suggested by another expression frequently heard in prayer, *'akolapko'*, which also has to be translated 'let us be', and here again signifies, and in a deeper moral sense, life in the mode and manner of leading it. The verb is *labe*. It expresses a continuous state and can, I think, only be used of persons. It indicates a particular quality of a person which is part of his nature as that person and is therefore unchangeable, as in the phrases *'labe kuaar'*, 'he is a leopard-skin priest', *'laba Nac'*, 'I am a Jinaca clansman', *'laba ran'*, 'I am a Nuer' or 'I am a man', and *labbo cok'*, 'we are (like) ants [in the sight of God]'.

It will have been observed that these expressions in Nuer prayers, as is the case among other peoples, are often repetitions, but rather in the form of parallelisms than of tautologies, for they are variations of meaning within the same general meaning. Different images are used to express the same general idea, each stressing a different aspect of it.[1]

The distinctive and significant features of Nuer mystical and moral theology cannot be extracted from the short affirmations and petitions which constitute their prayers if these are considered entirely by themselves without Nuer comments on them and without some knowledge of their ritual and of their ideas and values in general, but once these have been delineated they are seen to be summed up concisely in the prayers They are asking God for deliverance from evil, so that they may have peace, denoted by a variety of images with emotional and ideational relatedness—sleep, lightness, ease, coolness, softness, prayer, the domestic hearth, abundant life, and life as it should be according to the nature of the person. As I have explained, Nuer regard the ills they wish to be delivered from as due to faults and they think they can only be avoided by keeping in the right in their dealings with God and men These two ideas, of being in the right and of deliverance from evil, are basic to their religious thought and they are also, of course, complementary. A fuller understanding of these cardinal concepts of Nuer religion can be obtained only by taking into account their attitudes towards other spirits associated with God, their conception of the soul and of sin, and their sacrificial rites.

[1] Archbishop R. C Trench discusses this feature of prayer in his *Synonyms of the New Testament*, 1871, *passim*.

CHAPTER II

SPIRITS OF THE ABOVE

I

In the last chapter I discussed *kwoth*, Spirit, thought of in such a manner—as creator, father, judge, and so forth—that we may say it has a general correspondence to what we understand by God. We now have to consider the problem which arises when we discover that there are besides divers particular spirits each of which is also *kwoth* and that the word has a plural form, *kuth*, by which are indicated a number of such spirits. These spirits are of two categories, those of the above and those of the below. The *kuth nhial*, spirits of the above, are the *kuth dwanga*, spirits of the air or of the breezes, and the *colwic* spirits. The spirits of the air are the most powerful of all the lesser spirits and they are thought of, together with the *colwic* spirits which I discuss later, as being nearest to God. This is expressed in the two ways of referring to them In imagery taken from the physical universe God is symbolized by the sky and the spirits of the air by the air or breezes which are between heaven and earth, and they are also associated with the clouds which are nearest to the sky. In a metaphor taken from the social order God is the father of the spirits of the air and they are his children These spirits, which are greater than the other spirits because they proceed directly from God, might be described as gods or godlings, or as daemons, angels, or apparitors, but though each of these designations may appear suitable from some angle none adequately (perhaps 'daemons' the most adequately) describes their nature I shall therefore speak of them as Nuer do, as spirits of the air.

Apart from certain general linguistic and conceptual difficulties which confronted me in an attempt to gain an understanding of the nature of the different Nuer spirits, and in particular how they are seen in relation to God, there were special difficulties in the case of the spirits of the air. They are much more prominent to the west than to the east of the Nile where I spent most of my time. Another adverse circumstance was the hostility of the

(28)

Government at the time of my inquiries towards prophets of these spirits. Nuer, who at the best of times are reticent when asked about their spirits, were consequently embarrassed and taciturn when the subject was mentioned.

A further difficulty arises from historical considerations All Nuer with whom I discussed the matter said that in olden times they had no spirits other than God and the *colwic*, and that the spirits of the air had all 'fallen' into foreign countries and had only recently entered into Nuerland and become known to them, often in the first instance through the capture or absorption of Dinka, and especially through taking to wife Dinka girls, to whose children they have passed and attached themselves. When speaking of the coming to earth of these spirits Nuer use the word *pean*, to fall, as in the expressions '*ce pen piny*', 'it fell to earth (or downwards)', and '*ce pean nhial*', 'it fell from the sky (or from above)'. To judge from Nuer statements and other evidences, particularly from what we know about their prophets, they did not make their appearance in Nuerland till as late as the second half of last century.

The spirit *deng* is said to have been the first to fall, and it is regarded as the greatest of the spirits of the air. It is also called *deng kwoth*, *deng* son of God, and by its ox-name *dengkur* It is especially associated with sickness, which is very often attributed to it in one or other of its manifestations: *deng* (without qualification), *deng jur*, *deng* of the foreigners (in this context probably the so-called Jur peoples to the south of Rumbek), *deng jaangni*, *deng* of the Dinka, *deng yier*, *deng* of the river, and others It has two sons, *dayim* and *dhol. Deng*, which is said to have fallen to earth among the Dinka, is manifestly the Dinka spirit *deng*, a word which among that people also means 'rain' (it has no such secondary meaning among the Nuer); and *dayim* and *dhol* may likewise be accepted as Dinka conceptions.

Another spirit of the air is *teny*—possibly the same word as that meaning 'sun after rain'—whose ox-name is *dhuorangun*. It is sometimes said to be the *bul*, craftsman, of God who fashions man, occasionally making sport of them by giving their bodies a twist so that they are born deformed. It is said to be a Dinka spirit, and the fact that it is well known to the west of the Nile and is little spoken about among the most easterly tribes supports this view. *Diu* is likewise regarded as a Dinka spirit and is better known to the west than to the east of the Nile. It appears to be associated with a cattle-plague, also called *diu*, and it may have a further association with the sun, but I am uncertain of this, and I must say that this uncertainty may not be entirely due to my ignorance, for in many cases these associations between spirits and natural phenomena are not emphasized by Nuer and are even vague and fanciful ways of giving a bare outline of individuality to the spirits. The spirit *col* has associations with rain, lightning, a river believed to run through the sky, a tree called *nyuot* (*Cordia Rothii*), of which Nuer say that 'God loves it', and the *colwic* spirits who are the souls of those killed by lightning. This spirit is probably a Nuer conception, but then it is hardly conceived of as an individual spirit, but rather as all the *colwic* spirits merged together. *Rang* or *rangdit* and its son *mabith* are both spirits associated with wild animals and hunting, *mabith* having a special association with giraffes; and it may be noted that the word *rang* means also 'a good spearsman', that is, one who shines, for yet a further meaning of the word is 'sunshine' and its verbal form means 'to shine' or 'to dazzle'. In some contexts the word could be translated 'light' The two spirits are said to have come from the country of the *karegni*, the Baggara Arabs, whom the western Nuer used to raid for stock and women; and it is perhaps significant that the Baggara are great hunters of giraffes. Further, Dr. Lienhardt has pointed out to me that the Rek Dinka say that their spirit *garang*, which is also associated with giraffes and is doubtless the same as the Nuer *rang*, came to them from the Twic Dinka who neighbour the Baggara Arabs.[1] The spirit *mani*, whose ox-names are *luthpara* and *bilcuany*, and which is particularly associated with war, is certainly of foreign origin and I believe that it is generally regarded by the western Nuer as having come from somewhere to the north of them It is therefore perhaps worth drawing attention to the belief in a mysterious power called *mani* in northern Darfur[2] The spirit *nai* is asso-

[1] This spirit evidently has today a wide distribution among the Dinka for it is mentioned by Mr Johnson (op cit, p 124) as being regarded by the Bor Dinka as a son of *deng* Mr Johnston says that 'in every respect his attributes are equivalent to those of Satan'

[2] A. J. Arkell, 'Mani Magic in Northern Darfur', *Sudan Notes and Records*, 1936 As Mr Arkell suggests, there may be some connexion between the Darfur *mani* magic and the *mani* magic of the Azande (E E Evans-Pritchard, 'Mani, a Zande Secret Society', ibid, 1931). The word *mani* is almost certainly a loan-word in the Nuer language.

ciated with ostriches. I do not know where it is supposed to have originated.

One of the spirits that are best known throughout Nuerland is *wiu*, a spirit of war and associated with clan spear-names. It is particularly associated with the sacred spear *wiu* of the Gaatgan-kir clan, the dominant clan of the Jikany tribes. *Wiu* is also associated with thunder, '*ce wiu mar*' being equivalent to '*ce nhial mar*', 'it thundered (lightened)'. We may readily accept the Nuer statement that it was made known to them by the Gaatgankir clan, who are acknowledged by all to be of Dinka descent. That the *wiu* spear is of some age and that the Gaatgankir clan have long been indistinguishable from other Nuer in their general culture suggest, in view of Nuer statements that the spirits of the air fell recently, that the spear is older than the spirit, and this may be so, for in the story accounting for the spear there is no mention of the spirit.

A spirit of great interest is *buk*, also called *buk man deang*, *buk* the mother of (the air-spirit) *deng*, and *bungdit*, a Dinka title meaning *buk* the great. This female spirit, known throughout Nuerland, is associated with rivers and streams. It is *kwoth yier*, a river-spirit. Dr. Lienhardt has recorded a song in which it is called 'daughter of fire-flies' and by its cow-name '*kwacwar*', 'leopard of the night', imagery bringing to mind fire-flies and consequently streams, near which they are particularly numerous. Nuer sometimes offer first-fruits of their millet and make libations to it in streams and in times of sickness they may sacrifice animals to it on the banks. They also throw beer and tobacco, and maybe a bound goat as well, into the water as offerings when they take their herds across rivers or engage in large-scale fishing, praying that they may be protected from injury by crocodiles, water-snakes, bones of fish, sharp shells, and lost fishing-spears. On such occasions they may also sing hymns to it, the best known of which I record later. *Buk* is said to have two daughters, also associated with streams, or with particular streams, *candit* and *nyaliep* 'Daughters' is a figure of speech, for I was told that they were once Nuer maidens whom God took and put in the water, where they became spirits *Candit* is said to have once been seized by a man of the Mitnyaal lineage of the Gaatgankir clan on a river bank and to have lived with him till she bore him a child, when she returned to the river. The spirit is therefore revered as the guardian spirit of this lineage They dedicate cows and sheep to it and pour libations of their milk for it into rivers. Since *buk* is in rivers and streams it belongs to the below and I discuss it further in connexion with the tellurian spirits, but as the mother of *deng* it also belongs to the above, though it does not possess men as other spirits of the above do. Nuer explain its being both above and below by saying that as Spirit (*kwoth*) it is in the sky but materially (*pwonyde*) it is in rivers and streams. That *buk* is of Dinka origin is clear both from its being the mother of *deng* and from its Dinka title *bungdit*.[1]

There are other spirits of the air, though I know little about them. I have heard of one called *mar*, probably the same word as that meaning 'to thunder'. Miss Huffman mentions a *cul*, sender of dreams.[2] Father Crazzolara, speaking presumably of the Leek tribe, whose territory, where the Catholic mission is situated, is near the Shilluk kingdom, says that the Nuer have taken over the Shilluk spirit *nyikang*.[3] There are probably others.

Father Crazzolara, though he contrasts fetish spirits and nature sprites with spirits like *nai*, *dayim*, *nyikang*, and *deng*, labels them all *Erdgeister*.[4] In my opinion, on the contrary, these spirits are undoubtedly classed by Nuer in the category of the above, though some are, I concede, regarded as inferior to others, for example *nai* and *dayim*, whom Nuer speak of as *gaat gaat kwoth*, children of the children of God, rather than as *gaat kwoth*, children of God, a usage which indicates that they are more distant from God and belong to the lowest rank of the heavenly beings. That my account is here at variance with that of Father Crazzolara may be due to the fact that the spirits of the air have only the vaguest personalities and lack distinct individualities defined by clear differentiation of attributes, so that Nuer have nothing very definite to say about them. The figures are all more or less alike, and their celestial and other associations are not so much indications of function as a means of differentiation. For the Nuer themselves one spirit of the air is distinct from another really only because it has a different name. For this reason I have written 'it'

---

[1] It is probably common to all the Dinka sections Further evidence of its Dinka origin is the fact, which I have learnt from Dr Lienhardt, that *buk* or *bung* denotes in Dinka black and white markings, like those of the pied crow with which the Nuer *buk* is also associated (p 81)

[2] Ray Huffman, *Nuer-English Dictionary*, 1929, p 10.

[3] Op cit , p 136

[4] Ibid , pp 133 seq

when speaking of them and I have used small instead of capital first letters in writing their names This enables me also to maintain more clearly the distinction between God and other spirits, though strictly speaking, and following the gender of *pneuma*, the neuter is not inappropriate for any conception of Spirit.

II

With the exception of *buk* and *col*, who are of some general interest to all Nuer, the spirits of the air are not conceptions of the same importance for everybody, and in this respect, as in others, they are unlike the conception of God. They have a more general significance than the totemic spirits, which are important only to certain lineages, whereas the spirits of the air are not tied to particular social groups. Nevertheless, a certain spirit of the air is significant for certain persons and families and not for others, because unless it has at some time or other possessed a man or one of his family or forebears he does not feel that he is personally concerned with it.

Possession is generally known by sickness, though in the case of prophets it may also be known by abnormal behaviour Sickness, usually, I think, of a severe and sudden kind, may be diagnosed as being due to a particular spirit and the sufferer may in future, after he has recovered, regard it as one of his personal *kuth*, and then his descendants may continue to revere it. These two ways of acquiring a spirit, by being possessed and made sick and by inheritance, are interconnected, because an inherited spirit often shows that it regards itself as still attached to the family of a man after he has died by causing one of his children to fall sick, and it is likely to be neglected and forgotten if it does not occasionally remind the family of their obligations by troubling them So when Nuer fall sick they may, if they cannot establish the cause, with the aid of a prophet or diviner examine their heredity to discover whether one or other grandparent, very likely a Dinka, may not have had a spirit whom they have forgotten or not thought important and who is bringing their negligence to their notice by the sickness.

Spirits may thus pass in and out of families, be forgotten and then remembered again, and perhaps in many instances forgotten altogether in course of time, or in other instances they may become spirits of small lineages and their families, especially of lineages of Dinka descent. The fact that they are not found as spirits of larger lineages is perhaps further evidence of the late introduction of these spirits into Nuerland.[1] I speak here of ordinary Nuer, many, perhaps most, of whom do not in any case, particularly to the east of the Nile, have any special relationship to one or other of the spirits of the air, though they may have relationships to spirits of other kinds. In the case of prophets, their spirits are most unlikely to be forgotten and pass out of their lines of descent altogether.

Seizure of a man by a spirit may be temporary or permanent. When it is permanent the possessed person becomes a prophet. It will be simpler if I describe temporary possession first. Spirits cause sickness to their devotees and sometimes to others, and illness is often, especially in western Nuerland, attributed to them. If it is thought to be due to a spirit but there is uncertainty which particular spirit is responsible, the relatives consult a prophet or diviner to determine the responsibility, so that sacrifice may be made to the right spirit. They give it *duor*, a thing, as Nuer say,— that is, they sacrifice to it to appease it. The sick man's recovery means that the spirit has released him. If he has not already done so, he then dedicates an animal to the spirit to show it that he is aware of their special relationship, and from time to time he makes sacrifice to it to let it know that he has not forgotten it. Otherwise it may cause trouble again.

I will describe what happened at a ceremony held when a youth called Galuak, of the Leek tribe, was sick on account of his having been seized by the spirit *nai*. This spirit, whom I have only heard mentioned in western Nuerland, has, as I have earlier remarked, a special association with ostriches, to which it is said to be very partial. When an ostrich is killed those who have a special relationship to the spirit tie some of its plumes to the entrances to their byres. When I asked whether *nai* would not be angry at the killing of one of its birds I was told that it cares nothing for the body of the bird, only for its plumes. Prophets of *nai* decorate the shafts of their spears with ostrich plumes. *Nai* seems to be regarded as one of the most inferior of the spirits of the air.

[1] Further evidence is the fact that while people are now often named after the spirits, especially after *deng*, these spirit-names do not occur at the upper levels of Nuer genealogies.

It was this spirit, a particularly dangerous one, that was troubling Galuak. Nuer use the word *kap*, to take hold of or to lay hold
on, to describe the possession of a man by a spirit. It was known
that it was *nai* who was responsible because when the year before
Galuak had a similar sickness a prophet of *nai* had divined that
he was possessed by this spirit. On that occasion his family had
sacrificed goats, but during the past year no sacrifice had been
made or ceremony held in the spirit's honour, an omission of
which Galuak's family now felt very conscious. In the circumstances a return of the spirit to Galuak might have been expected

The same prophet had been sent for from a neighbouring village and was expected to arrive before evening. In the meanwhile
Galuak's kinsmen sought high and low for a beast to sacrifice right
away to *nai*. All animals in the village suitable for sacrifice had
recently been killed in other ceremonies (p. 59) and the kinsmen
were unable to bring back even a goat for their pains. I was told
that *nai* would not, however, kill Galuak in the meantime because
it would see that they were trying to find an animal. The prophet
arrived, as was expected, in the evening and he was accompanied
by two friends. No doubt the matter was discussed in the byre that
night, but no action was taken till the following morning.

In the morning, after a talk in the byre, the persons concerned
went across to the hut of Galuak's mother, Nyadang, and I was
invited to accompany them as a friend of the family. Nhial,
Galuak's brother, was working for me. Here the prophet was presented with five piastres—on his visit the year before he had been
given a war-spear and a fish-spear. He sat with his back to the wall
of the hut, and Galuak and his father, Rainen, sat on a mat facing
him and with their backs to the door, which was closely drawn
against the entrance to the hut The windows had been blocked
with grass so that the hut was illumined only by faint shafts of
light which penetrated round the edges of the door Even this dim
light could not be seen by Galuak and his father, for skins had
been placed over their heads so that they might be in total darkness. Altogether there were, besides Galuak and his father, thir-
teen persons in the hut, sitting with their backs to the wall. The
atmosphere was stifling.

The seance began by the prophet shaking his rattle and singing.
Karlual, one of Galuak's maternal uncles, also shook a rattle
on one side of the prophet and one of the two friends who had

accompanied him to the village shook a rattle on the other side. The instrument is called *jogh*, possibly a Dinka word. It is a bottle-gourd containing seeds, in this instance the seeds of a wild leguminous plant. While the rattles were being rattled and the prophet sang hymns to *nai* the congregation clapped their hands and smacked them on their thighs in accompaniment. Nuer say that they *pat*, clap, or slap, for the spirit.

After about ten minutes' singing Rainen began to have premonitory spasms. It should be noted that it was not the sick youth but his father who became possessed during the seance. A spirit takes hold of an older and experienced man in cases of this kind and uses him as a medium to make its demands known. As the singing, rattling, and clapping continued, Rainen began to twitch and shake from head to foot and then suddenly leapt into the air and fell back on to the floor of the hut where he lay stiff as though in a paroxysm. After lying tense and prostrate for a while he sat up, but shortly afterwards collapsed again. Then for about a quarter of an hour he threw himself wildly about the hut, writhing and twitching as though in agony. He reminded me of a hen which has had its throat cut in the Muslim way, and is thrown on the ground to die. If the people around had not broken most of his falls he might have injured himself. As it was, he complained to me on the following day of the soreness of his arms and legs. Every now and again he barked like a dog. In describing these spasms Nuer say that the spirit wrestles (*kuer*) with the man it possesses.

At the end of a particularly violent seizure, Rainen, who in his exertions had divested himself of the skin over his head, sprang at the prophet, tore his rattle from his hands, and sat

Fig. 1
Pipe

(36)

in front of him, shaking it violently and barking. At this point the prophet called for his pipe, and after lighting it and puffing at it for a while he began to question the spirit *nai* in Rainen, and it answered through Rainen's lips. It was very difficult to follow what the spirit said because Rainen spoke in a jerky, guttural voice very different from his usual voice and he hiccuped and barked a good deal as well. 'The speech of Rainen was wiped out (*woc*). It was pressed down his gullet.' I was, however, able to follow part of what the spirit said. It said that it was *nai* and that it wanted a gift. It had waited till Nhial had returned to the village because it knew that he would be able to provide a gift out of the wages he had received from me, and it had then taken hold of Galuak. It admitted that it had received gifts from Rainen in the past but it now wanted a final gift, and it promised that if it were satisfied now it would trouble Galuak no more. If it needed anything further it would seize another person and get it from him. It pointed out, however, that it was not the only spirit troubling Galuak. The spirit of Luak, Galuak's paternal grandfather, had also taken hold of him. This was *kwoth doar*, a nature sprite, and it was worrying Galuak because the family had not dedicated a cow of their herd to it. Both Galuak's father and mother are of Dinka descent and the family have a number of different spirits attached to them.

It was very noticeable during the ceremony how those present, as is often the case in Nuer ceremonies, chatted among themselves, asked for tobacco, and so on. They evidently, especially the children, enjoyed the spectacle. I was surprised, however, this being the first and only ceremony of its kind I witnessed, at the familiar and off-handed way in which the prophet spoke to the spirit, calling it '*wuta*', 'man'—almost 'old chap'—, bargaining with it about the oblation demanded, and insisting that when the sacrifice had been made it should keep its promise and leave Galuak alone. Galuak himself showed little concern with what was going on. While prophet and spirit were conversing he removed the skin from over his head, walked casually about the hut looking for a pipe, and then filled it with tobacco and sat puffing at it by his father's side. The only part he took in the proceedings was to reply to a question put to him by his maternal uncle, that he had not had sexual relations with a kinswoman. It was thought advisable to make certain that there had been no incest because

(37)

they wanted to be sure that when *nai* and the other spirit had been satisfied there would be nothing further to prevent a speedy recovery. As for Rainen, if his manner of speech was that of a man out of his senses, its content showed reflection and purpose. What he, or the spirit in him, said was aimed at compelling Nhial to hand over his wages for the purchase from government herds of beasts for sacrifices, an object Rainen had been vainly trying to attain for some days previous to the ceremony. Rainen also justified himself, in what the spirit said, for the slaughter of a number of beasts to appease his various spirits, for which his family had criticized him for extravagance. They felt that too much of the family property was being devoted to religious purposes, whereas the spirit made it clear that, far from having made too many sacrifices, he had not made enough. Had he made more, Galuak would not have fallen sick. Religious and personal issues were interwoven in the spirit's declarations.

When the spirit had ceased speaking we left the hut, and Galuak's paternal uncle, Dol, went to chop down a branch of the 'wild date' (*Balanites aegyptiaca*), a tree to which *nai* is said to be very partial, to erect it as a shrine (*riek*) to the spirit near the hut. When it had been erected a clump of *tuat* grass was dug up by the roots and planted at the side of the branch in a hole first filled with water, it being the dry season. A he-goat—by this time one had been procured—was then brought out and the prophet waved his spear, decorated with ostrich plumes, over its back and made a short invocation, telling the spirit that they were honouring it, saying that it would now cease to trouble Galuak, and asking God that the people might rest in peace. He then cut the goat's throat It was later eaten by himself and his two friends. The people of the homestead did not partake of its flesh, but when it had been cooked some children were called from a nearby homestead and given pieces of the meat and told to run back to their home with them The Nuer said of this: '*ca gat kwoth nang cieng*', 'the son of God is taken home'. Finally a *buor*, a mud mound in the shape of an ordinary kitchen windscreen, was erected near the shrine On the following evening Rainen rubbed ashes on the back of a cow of his herd and dedicated it to the spirit of his father By so doing he felt that he had appeased the second spirit which was troubling his son.

The relations between Nuer and their spirits centre in these dedicated cattle, and much of the trouble the spirits cause them is occasioned by failure to devote animals to the spirits or by some fault concerning these beasts. When a spirit is by descent attached, or of its own accord attaches itself, to a family they should devote to it a cow or an ox, generally a cow; and they sometimes, especially at eventide, rub ashes along its back, an act which is in itself a kind of recognition of the spirit, and they may also pour a little milk or beer over the peg to which it is tethered. I do not think that there is any Nuer herd which has not at least one animal dedicated to one or other spirit of the above or of the below, and often there are several, for many families have several spirits and dedicate an animal to each of them. A dedicated beast is often to be identified by metal rings attached to its leather collar. These are ornaments devoted to the spirit and not phylacteries. When a daughter of the family marries, the *kwoth* of one or other parent is given a cow of her bridewealth, being treated in this matter as though it were a kinsman with rights in their daughter. Sometimes the *kuth* of both parents receive cattle at the same marriage, but if a spirit does not get a cow on the marriage of one daughter it will get one on the marriage of one of her sisters.

When a spirit gets a cow, whether it be dedicated to it at a marriage or in its honour on some other occasion, the cow ought not to be disposed of, and should it die it ought to be replaced However, Nuer seem to feel that as long as the spirit has one cow in the herd it will not be angry if a second cow is disposed of. Thus if the spirit gets a cow of a daughter's bridewealth, they feel that there is not the same need to keep the cow previously dedicated to it. Nevertheless, there is always a risk in disposing of any dedicated animal. The male calves of a dedicated cow, or at any rate one of them, may eventually be offered to the spirit in sacrifice. However, it seems to be held that the human owner may dispose of the calves of a spirit's cow for marriage if he explains his purpose to the spirit. If a dedicated cow is driven off with other cattle by persons seeking redress for some injury it will not be kept in the byre of its captors when they realize its character but will either be returned to its owner or will be loosened to wander, lest misfortune should fall on them. When I bought from the Government some cattle which had been taken from Nuer in fines it was pointed out to me by Nuer friends that one of the cows was a *yang kwoth*, the cow of a spirit, and that no good would come of my possessing it. They were not surprised when one night it tore up its tethering-peg and fell into the Sobat river and was drowned. The *Sudan Intelligence Report* of September–October 1934, No. 69, records the interesting case of a man who was ordered by a Government Chiefs' Court to pay a cow in damages to another Nuer. As at the time he possessed only one cow and this was dedicated to a spirit, the Court permitted him to defer payment while he went to obtain a cow owing to him in a different part of the country. During his absence from home on this errand one of the Government chiefs took his cow. The owner was killed by an elephant on his journey and his kinsmen claimed compensation from the chief because they attributed his death to the removal of the cow devoted to his spirit. The milk of a spirit's cow should only be drunk by members of the family It belongs to the spirit and is therefore reserved for the people to whom it is attached. I was first made aware of this rule when on a journey I fell sick in a Nuer village and was compelled to spend a few days there. Being unable to eat solid food, I asked a lad of the nearest homestead if I might have a little milk He said that he was sorry, but the only cow giving milk in his family herd was the cow of his mother's spirit, and he could not let me have its milk without her permission. He later brought some milk and told me that it would be all right for me to drink it as I was sick, but when I could eat again only the children of the home might either milk the cow or drink its milk.

Should a man neglect to dedicate a cow to his spirit when he is in a position to do so, or should he dispose of a beast already devoted to the spirit and not dedicate another to it, sickness is likely to fall on his family or herd. But although Nuer say this, and believe what they say, it is not uncommon for them to use a spirit's cow for bridewealth or some other purpose, hoping that they will soon be able to replace it. They know that they are doing wrong but they think that maybe the spirit, having been informed of their intentions, will understand their difficulty and will excuse their manner of overcoming it, knowing that they mean to keep their promise to give it another cow as soon as they can. But they may not find it easy to procure another cow for some time and the spirit has in the meantime to go without one; or they keep on putting off the replacement because they want to use their cattle for other purposes, and also because they say to them-selves that as no evil has befallen them since they disposed of the spirit's cow it does not matter; or they are just careless and forget-ful. I have known of several cases of men using the cattle of spirits as bridewealth. Then a child of the family died, and then maybe a second child, or some other misfortunes happened to them, and they began to be sorry that they were so casual and summoned a prophet or diviner to confirm that their sufferings were due to the anger of a spirit about the loss of its cow. In one case I heard dis-cussed the spirit *deng* was not appeased even when a new cow was dedicated to it in the place of its cow given as bridewealth, but continued to make trouble for the family. Efforts were therefore made to get back the original cow Unfortunately the man who had received it in the allocation of the bridewealth, the natural father of the bride, had in the meanwhile dedicated it to his own spirit, and he was making difficulties about its return. He did not see why the consequences of a transgression should be passed to him In another case which I had the opportunity to follow, a man had given a cow as his contribution to the bridewealth paid on the marriage of his sister's son This cow calved a female calf in the home of one of the bride's mother's brothers, and then it died there. As the marriage had not been completed, the calf was regarded as having taken the place of its dam A difficulty then arose. The cow had been the donor's spirit's cow and ought never to have left his herd, and subsequent misfortunes in his family were attributed to his having given it away. He therefore pressed for the calf to be handed over to him so that he could give it to his spirit in the place of the beast it had lost. The bride's maternal uncle was not inclined to be helpful, and negotiations had not been concluded by the time I left Nuerland. Had it been the bride's own family who had received the cow they would, for their daughter's sake, have let the man have the calf without argument, on the understanding that he would one day let them have a similar animal in its stead Thus I have known a family who had recently disposed of all their cattle in making a marriage to ask for, and receive, the return of an ox of the bridewealth from the family of the bride when one of them fell sick, so that they might dedicate it to God, to whom it would one day be sacrificed.[1]

[1] Cows are not dedicated to God, only to spirits Oxen are occasionally dedi-cated to God but, in my experience, only on such an occasion as this, when the

To appreciate how Nuer get into such difficulties with their dedicated cattle as I have mentioned we must bear in mind the overwhelming importance of cattle in their lives, that cattle are generally the issue in disputes, and that almost every Nuer owes cattle and has cattle owing to him, debts which are often not settled, if at all, for years and sometimes even for generations. Nuer will go to almost any lengths to obtain cattle to which they think they have a right and to put off the settlement of their own debts. It is not surprising that in these circumstances a man may postpone fulfilling his obligation to a spirit if it is a question of having to choose between the claims of an importunate creditor and of a spirit which, it is hoped, will be satisfied for the time being with the man's good intention; or that to fulfil an unavoidable obligation to a kinsman a man may take a liberty with a spirit which, he hopes, will not take offence at a fault in such compelling circumstances.

Besides dedicating a cow to his spirit and sacrificing an ox, sheep, or goat to it when it is displeased, a Nuer ought now and again to hold a ceremony in its honour. This generally takes place after the harvest has been gathered in and there is plenty of beer. I attended one of these ceremonies in the home of Karlual, who figured in the story of Galuak's sickness which I have just related It was held in honour of *deng*, who is what the Nuer call *kwoth ciengde* or *kwoth goale*, the spirit of his home or of his family. I was told that each of Karlual's numerous brothers holds a like ceremony in turn till it is his turn to hold it again. The ceremony of the year before had been on a large scale and an ox had been sacrificed at it. *Deng* had afterwards told Karlual through the mouth of someone who had become possessed by it that all it wanted this year was some beer, so the ceremony I witnessed was on a smaller scale. It is known as 'the bathing of the cow in beer'.

The ceremony was held in the morning and was very late in starting because those who attended it, or some of them, had first attended a ceremony of the same kind elsewhere in the village, that held by a man called Mokwac for the spirit of his concubine's dead husband When I arrived at Karlual's homestead I found that a gourdful of beer had been placed at the side of a clump of grass at the edge of the kraal. Karlual's brothers and their families

intention is to sacrifice it in the near future, the dedication being in the nature of a consecration for sacrifice and a number of kinsmen and neighbours were present, one of whom, Dhoal, was asked to preside because he was a leading man in the community. He began by pouring some of the beer out of the gourd over the tethering-peg of the cow devoted to *deng* when Karlual shouted to him to wait till they brought him a ladle. When it was brought, he poured a libation with it over the peg. A small son of Karlual was then told to do the same and afterwards to drink what was left in the ladle. Then various kinsmen also poured libations over the peg and all present poured beer into their hands and threw it into the air, an act called *kith*. The people then sat around the gourd and drank the remainder of the beer while they discussed family affairs

All kinsmen who can do so should attend a ceremony of this kind, especially close agnatic kinsmen, for this is an occasion when kin are expected to reveal any resentment they may have in their hearts towards one another. Each tells the others where they have been at fault (*duer*) in speech or act during the past year, and the issues raised are then settled peacably by discussion. A man must not keep a grievance hidden, and if he does not reveal it now he must for ever keep silence. Nuer say that all the evil in their hearts is then blown away. I think that this is the meaning of the throwing of beer into the air. They also say '*giakni dial ba ke bap e yang*', 'all evils (which they have done to one another) will be gathered to (or taken over by) the cow'. All present place ashes on the back of the beast, probably an ox, and it is then cleansed by sprinkling or blowing beer on it However, I did not see this part of the ceremony because owing to the lateness in starting it the beast had gone to pasture with the rest of the herd. I was told that it was performed in the afternoon when the herd returned from grazing.

III

In what I have said so far about the spirits of the air I have been speaking of their relations to ordinary Nuer Sometimes a spirit possesses a man and when he has recovered from the seizure abides with him, giving him powers of healing, divination, exorcism, and foresight. I discuss the functions of these prophets in Chapter XII. Here I give only such information about them as is necessary for an appreciation of the spirits which possess them.

Nuer call such a charismatic person *gwan kwoth*, owner or possessor of Spirit, the name of the particular spirit sometimes being added. as *gwan kwoth deang*, the possessor of the spirit *deng*, or *gwan kwoth mani*, the possessor of the spirit *mani*. He is also referred to as the *guk* of the spirit, a word meaning a leather bag. The prophet is a bag containing the spirit 'Possessor' might seem to be here an inappropriate translation of *gwan* ('father', 'owner', or 'master') since the spirit possesses the man rather than the man the spirit, but the man does own the spirit in the sense that it is in him and gives him spiritual power ordinary people lack.

It appears to be first known that a man has become possessed permanently by a spirit, either without or after sickness, by sustained abnormal behaviour and occasional bouts of frenzy In these states, which are said to occur most frequently in the earlier phases of possession, when the spirit comes, or leaps, upon, or moves the prophet (to use Old Testament expressions) he acts like a madman (*yong*), and Nuer cannot always distinguish for certain at this stage between a prophet and a madman or epileptic (*gwan noka*); but if there is any doubt it is dispelled by the later behaviour of a prophet, for he ceases to prophesy only when possessed in the narrow sense of being for the time out of his mind and gives spiritual guidance when in a normal state to those who ask for it From time to time he may have renewed mantic seizures, but these are regarded by Nuer as only outward signs of a spiritual power which directs his utterances whenever he speaks as a prophet and also when, as sometimes happens, he speaks as a judge and political leader. Nuer conceive of permanent possession of this kind, in contrast to temporary seizure in the form of Spirit-induced sickness and mediumistic trances, as a filling with Spirit as with air. They use the word *gwang* to denote Spirit penetrating or entering into and filling the man. A prophet is a person filled with, or inspired by, Spirit, which controls him as the *Ruah Adonai* controlled the prophets of the Old Testament. The word *gwang*, which has much the same general sense in Dinka,[1] is used for such actions as scraping out a gourd, hollowing out a canoe or mortar, or the burrowing of a hole by a wild beast. Something is hollowed out to allow entry for something else. Dr. Mary Smith tells me that Nuer have told her that when a spirit *gwange ran*,

[1] R Trudinger, *English–Dinka Dictionary*, 1942, p. 216.

fills a man, his character is changed. The man is hollowed out by Spirit to receive it. In this sense *gwang* is complementary to *kwoth*, inspiration to expiration.

Prophets may perform sacrifices on behalf of individuals or of the people of their neighbourhoods in times of sickness, for barrenness, and on other occasions when spiritual aid is required, but the main social function of the leading prophets in the past was to direct cattle-raids on the Dinka and fighting against the various foreigners who troubled the Nuer from the northern Sudan. For the most part the air-spirits are conspicuously associated with war, and Nuer prophets are chiefly regarded as the medium through which God gives orders to fight and victory The spirits accompany the warriors to battle.

Before Nuer set off for any large-scale fighting against strangers their prophets made sacrifice and sang hymns to the spirits of the air while the warriors, kneeling on one knee and with the points of their spears resting on the ground, sang the responses. The same posture is adopted by warriors in making the responses to these songs when they are sung by a song-leader on ceremonial occasions. Also people, generally and perhaps always under a prophet's direction, sing hymns to the spirits on occasions of sickness and of other troubles; though Nuer say that they sometimes sing the hymns, as at dances, 'just to be happy with the son of God'. Unfortunately I did not have the opportunity to record more than a few verses of these hymns

I give below a short hymn to *buk* It is known all over Nuerland and is therefore probably earlier than most hymns. It is sometimes sung at mortuary ceremonies, and it is also sung before fishing battues are begun, on account of the spirit's association with rivers and streams.

> Mother of *deng*, the ants (the Nuer) ransom their lives from thee,
> Mother of *dengkur*, the ants ransom their lives from thee,
> The mother of *dengkur* brings life,
> The mother of *dengkur* brings me life,
> Life is revived
> She brings life and our children play,
> They cry aloud with joy,
> With the life of the mother of *deng*, with the life of the mother of *deng*.

The pied crows are given life and are filled.[1]
Our speech is good, we and *buk*,
Our speech is excellent,
The country of the people is good,
We journey on the path of the *pake*.[2]
We are here, we and *buk deang*,
Buk, mother of *deng*, the ants ransom their lives from thee,
Mother of *dengkur*, the ants ransom their lives from thee.
We give thee red blood.
The ants of *deng* are simple people, they do not understand
    how their lives are supported.
Let all the people of the cattle camps bring tobacco to the
    river.

The general sense of this hymn is that *buk* protects the people
from dangers and gives them life Protection and life are given
them in exchange for oblations of animals (the red blood) and
tobacco. I give the opening verses of another hymn, which appears
to be addressed to both *dayim* and *mani* It is a war hymn,
although I heard it myself at a ceremony in western Nuerland
held in honour of a person killed by lightning.

Stars and moon which are in the heavens,
Blood of *deng* which you have taken,[3]
You have not summoned the ants of *deng* capriciously,[4]
Blood of *deng* which you have taken,
The wing of battle on the river bank is encircled by plumes.[5]
Dayim, son of God, strike the British to the ground,
Break the steamer on the Nile and let the British drown,
Kill the people on the mountains,[6]
Kill them twice,[7]

[1] The pied crow 'is' *buk* (p. 81).
[2] This is not a Nuer word but the Arabic *faki*, a fakir or holy man In Nuer
the word is used for an Arab pedlar or merchant. The use of the word in this
hymn, probably one of the oldest Nuer hymns, is further evidence of the late
introduction of these spirits into Nuerland
[3] Dinka blood on Nuer spears
[4] The spirits which summoned the Nuer to raid the Dinka through the mouths
of their prophets did not summon them in vain. The raid was successful. The
ants are the Nuer.
[5] When warriors are drawn up for battle the prophet runs along the flanks
shouting encouragement to them and waving his spear decorated with ostrich
plumes
[6] The people of the Nuba hills.
[7] Slay them two years in succession

Do not slay them jestingly.[1]
Mani goes with a rush,
He goes on for ever,
The sons of Jagei are proud in the byres,[2]
Proud that they always raid the Dinka.

I do not know the time or circumstances of composition of this hymn, but as it not only exults in defeats of the Dinka and asks for victory over the people of the Nuba hills but also demands the destruction of the British it must be fairly recent and probably dates from the early days of British occupation of the Southern Sudan. Dr. Lienhardt has recorded a hymn about *deng* which vividly suggests the mobility of the spirits of the air and the ubiquity of Spirit. A man says he is tired of the demands made by *deng* and that he will move. But *deng* replies

A man avoiding *deng*
Will find *deng* in front,
On the right he will find *deng*,
On the left he will find *deng*,
Behind him he will find *deng*.

In another hymn he recorded there is a metaphor in which protection of the people by *deng* is compared to the coiling of a python around its young These hymns are, I believe, always the creations of prophets, and Nuer say that they come to them in dreams, unlike ordinary songs or poems which men construct for themselves when idling, as when herding in the grazing grounds. We need not concern ourselves greatly with their word to word meaning. Nuer do not do so, or even know it, and the songs may be sung on occasions which in no way concern the particular spirits they are addressed to and for which the words have no relevance, the songs merely serving to create atmosphere and to express a general sense and intention. I have been told that the hymns sometimes come to a prophet through a drum, called *bul kwoth*, spirit's drum, dedicated to his spirit, which is thought to be in some way immanent in it. These drums, which are beaten at dances held in honour of the spirits to which they are dedicated, are formally dedicated by being rubbed with ashes, in the same

---

[1] Do not trifle with them but strike them hard.

[2] The Jagei are a small group of Nuer tribes; but since the Nuer believe that they were created in their territory the word probably here refers to the Nuer as a whole

way as an animal is dedicated, while a short invocation is made
They are decorated with beads and metal rings. I was told that
now and again, especially after dreams, a prophet rubs his spirit's
drum with ashes, and sometimes also with butter, and asks God
for peace and happiness. A prophet also builds a mud shrine,
called *yik* or, if it is shaped like a windscreen, *buor*, to his spirit,
the largest monument of the first kind being the pyramid of *deng*
in the Lou tribal territory (p. 306).

IV

I now come to the most difficult, and the most important, part
of this survey. How do Nuer conceive of these spirits in relation
to God? I do not attempt yet to make a full analysis of the notion
of *kwoth*, but only to discuss a limited part of it, the nature of the
spirits of the air; though what is said about them has some bearing on the nature of other spirits and of Spirit in general. The
matter is, for us, complex and confusing, and the conclusion I
reached about it, that the spirits of the air are conceived of as
both separate beings and yet also as different manifestations of
God, may at first sight seem to hold a contradiction

We may say to begin with that there is no question of Nuer
regarding these spirits as beings of the same importance as *kwoth
a nhial* Whatever else they may be thought to be they are not
thought of as beings independent of and equal to him. There is
only one God This is evident from a number of facts.

In the first place, it is shown by the way Nuer regard the beliefs
of neighbouring peoples. It creates no problem for them when they
find other peoples approaching God under different titles and in
different ways from their own. Some Nuer, in spite of the general
isolation of the Nuer and their lack of interest in other peoples,
are aware that in religious matters neighbouring peoples differ to
a greater or lesser degree from themselves Some of them know
something of Dinka religious beliefs and ceremonies, and a few of
them are also aware, though Islam has made no impression on
them, that Arab traders have their own form of worship and,
though the influence of the Christian missions has been negligible,[1] that the Christian missionaries and their converts have

[1] In 1940, some years after I had concluded my research, there were 464
Christian Nuer (250 Catholics and 214 Protestants), easily the lowest figure for

theirs. I have found that when one of these Nuer who has had contacts with foreign peoples speaks of their religious beliefs and practices he shows that he does not regard them as having a different God from his own but merely as having a different name for him and a different manner of communicating with him. A Dinka prays to *kwoth a nhial*, whom he calls *nhialic*. Similarly the Muslim or Christian prays to *kwoth a nhial* under other names. Hence, though Nuer have taken over from neighbouring peoples various lesser spirits like the Dinka *deng* and the Shilluk *nyikang*, they have not taken over their deities, such as *nhialic* and *jwok*. The reason for this is undoubtedly that they identify these other deities with *kwoth a nhial*. *Kwoth a nhial*, *nhialic*, and *jwok* are one person who has different titles among different peoples. The Nuer attitude in this matter shows clearly the markedly monotheistic tendency of their religious thought. It is polyonymous, but not henotheistic. The inference we can draw from this in considering the spirits of the air is that they are not thought of as independent gods but in some way as hypostases of the modes and attributes of a single God.

A number of circumstances may have influenced Nuer thought in this matter. One important circumstance is that they have no proper name for God. He is simply *kwoth*, Spirit, and if they wish to distinguish him in speech they can only do so by a qualifying clause. It follows that since the Nuer God has no proper name he cannot be sharply distinguished in the mind from the God of a neighbouring people who is also inevitably regarded by the Nuer as *kwoth* and is therefore easily identified with him, and the titles by which other peoples call God do not present to the Nuer an obvious challenge or any kind of contradiction which might lead to monolatry or to more precise metaphysical definition. It follows also that since the only word in Nuer for God, *kwoth*, means simply 'Spirit' any spiritual being is also *kwoth*. This in itself, apart from the absence of any organized cult and developed political institutions,[1] has allowed easy entrance to foreign spirits. All

any of the major peoples of the Southern Sudan. The missions were then American Presbyterian at Nasser on the Sobat (founded in 1913), Catholic at Yoahnyang on the Bahr al-Ghazal (founded in 1929), and Anglican at Ler to the west of the Nile (founded in 1932) and Juaibor to the east of the Nile (founded in 1936). This information was supplied by the heads of the various missions.

[1] W. Hofmayr, op. cit., p. 160, reports that a Shilluk who erected a shrine to

spirits, whatever their particular names may be, are *kwoth*, and God being *kwoth* also, and having no isolating name of his own, they and he are merged together in the same concept as they are denoted by the same word. It is not that the other spirits form a class with *Kwoth a nhial*, for the nature of spirit, 'like wind' and 'like air', is not such that a clear differentiation of individuals is easy, or even possible to conceive.

Further light is shed on this question by other linguistic evidences. The spirits of the air can be referred to collectively as *kuth nhial*, spirits of the above, in contrast to the *kuth piny*, spirits of the below, but we cannot say of any one of them that it is *kwoth nhial* except in making this contrast and in this sense. Otherwise the phrase can only mean 'Spirit of the heavens', that is, God Also, the particularizing particle *in* when coupled with the adjective *dit*, great, can only be used when speaking of God and is not used when speaking of even the most powerful of the spirits of the air, for which, however, the indefinite particle *me* may be employed.[1] Thus one may say that a spirit of the air is a *kwoth me dit*, a great spirit, compared, that is, with lesser spirits, but *kwoth in dit*, the great Spirit, can only be used of God. It should be noted further that God is always addressed, in a way familiar to ourselves, in the singular and never in the plural. Moreover, it would, I think, be an impossible usage to address God together with one or more of the spirits as '*yen kuth*', 'you spirits'. This could only denote several spirits other than God.

The use of the expressions *gaat kwoth*, sons, or children, of God and *kuth dwanga*, spirits of the air, is a clear indication that these spirits are regarded as something lesser and lower than the Father-God in the sky; and they are not regarded by Nuer, as he is, as creative spirits but as beings that derive from him. Nuer speak of them in a more material and, in spite of their lack of distinct personality, in a more anthropomorphic way than they speak of God. They are spirits, it is true, but they have fallen from above, and though they are in the air they are also in prophets and speak through them, seize men and make them sick, and enter into mediums, wrestle with them, and speak through their lips. They

the Dinka spirit *deng* had to pay the fine of an ox, this being considered an affront to the national cult of *jwok*. It is inconceivable that anything of the kind could have happened in Nuerland.

[1] The same distinction is made in Anuak by use of the particles *man* or *mana* (*ma-in*) and *ma* (*mi, mo*)

regularly have cows dedicated to them and they have their shrines and drums.

Also, the Nuer attitude towards them is different from their attitude to God, who, though he punishes men, is their father and friend. The spirits of the air are not so benevolent, and they are more immediately exacting To the European observer they seem to be greedy, capricious, and hostile, but this is not quite how they appear to the Nuer, for though they demand that animals be devoted to them and animal oblations made, and bring misfortunes on those who neglect these duties, and though, as the hymns to them show, they delight in blood and battle and bring sickness and death, yet they only cause misfortunes to those who in one way or another are at fault. They give victory in war, and they favour those persons and families to whom they attach themselves, but they are jealous spirits who demand tribute from their votaries. The Nuer fear them but they do not feel so much resentful as guilty when they bring sickness on them. They recognize that an angry spirit generally has right on its side, and they seek to make amends so that it will cease to trouble them; and in making amends through sacrifice a bargain is struck in a much cruder and more human way than when a sacrifice is made to God. No Nuer would try to bargain with God as he bargains with a spirit, trying to buy it off as cheaply as he can, and no Nuer would use such familiar terms in addressing God as he sometimes uses in addressing spirits of the air. One reason for this difference is perhaps not far to seek: the spirits of the air are 'owned' by persons and they make their wishes known through men, through prophets who may be ambitious and greedy, and through mediums whose revelations may be coloured by their own interests.

Yet, though one may say all this, the spirits of the air are, nevertheless, being Spirit, also God. They are many but also one. God is manifested in, and in a sense is, each of them. I received the impression that in sacrificing or in singing hymns to an air-spirit Nuer do not think that they are communicating with the spirit and not with God. They are, if I have understood the matter correctly, addressing God in a particular spiritual figure or manifestation They speak to God directly or they speak to God in, for example, the figure of *deng*, whichever mode is most appropriate in the circumstances. They do not see a contradiction here, and there is no reason why they should see one. God is not a particular air-spirit but the spirit is a figure of God. So while in a sacrifice one can say that the oblation is made to *deng* and not to *wiu, manı,* or any other spirit of the air, one cannot say that it is not made to God. The spirits are not each other but they are all God in different figures. Consequently, if one asks a Nuer whether a sacrifice is to God or to a spirit of the air the question makes no sense to him. Nuer pass without difficulty or hesitation from a more general and comprehensive way of conceiving of God or Spirit to a more particular and limited way of conceiving of God or Spirit and back again. This is often very apparent in invocations made at their sacrifices and in what they say in times of sickness and other troubles. Therefore a queston which tries to present a disjunction, an either . . . or, in answer to which either one proposition or the other may be accepted but not both, is not understood

It is in the nature of the conception of Spirit that it can be thought of in this sort of way, that what is distributed in a number of beings is, though different, yet the same and, though divided, yet a whole Therefore, what has been said in this respect about the conception of God in relation to the conception of spirits of the air can also be said of the spirits of the air themselves. *Deng* has several forms but they are all the same *deng*, and *deng* may be in a number of different prophets at the same time, each of whom is *deng*, without *deng* being in any way divided

V

Another sort of spirits which are regarded as spirits of the above in contrast to those of the below are the *colwic*, spirits which were once persons. These persons were struck by lightning or, more rarely, disappeared in a whirlwind, and some Nuer included also persons found dead in the bush without the cause of death being apparent. They are conceived as having been, as we would say, metamorphosed. The human has been changed into the divine *Tie*, soul, has become *kwoth*, spirit Nuer think of these persons as having been 'taken by God into the sky' and they say that there are multitudes of such spirits in the sky. Their names are for the most part forgotten in course of time but a few become tutelary spirits of lineages and are for that reason remembered. Such a *kwoth goal*, spirit of a lineage, is called on for aid, especially, I was told, by a man seeking refuge from enemies pursuing him. Most lineages seem to have at least one *colwic* patron spirit, to which cows are dedicated and their bull calves sacrificed. In their role of patrons of lineages they are similar to the totemic spirits, which I discuss in the following chapter, but they are treated in the present place, and not with the totemic spirits, partly because in other respects they obviously lack what are usually regarded as totemic characteristics, but chiefly because they are spoken about by Nuer as spirits of the above whereas totemic spirits are spirits of the below.

Although each *colwic* spirit, so long as it is remembered, retains its individuality in relation to its family and lineage, all of them are also conceived of as merged in God or in his hypostasis of *col*, the air-spirit of lightning. I have heard it said that *col* is black-haired and that this is the reason for calling a person killed by lightning a *colwic*. This suggestion, which is not entirely satisfactory grammatically, may have been put forward by the Nuer I was conversing with as a piece of *ad hoc* etymology deemed adequate to satisfy my curiosity,[1] but whether this is so or not, the first part of the word, *col*, means 'dark', and the spirit to which the word also refers is a spirit of storms, so in the word *colwic* there is an association of some kind with darkness and the suggestion made to me shows that Nuer are conscious of this.

Many people are killed by lightning, as memorials erected in their honour in villages bear witness, and it is therefore not surprising that Nuer are anxious when violent storms break over their homes and the sky is pierced by flashes of lightning. Then there is silence in the byres and one may see old men throw pieces of tobacco from the doorways into the storm, uttering a simple prayer, such as 'ah God, father, take this tobacco [or they may say "ox"]. I have paid thee ransom (*kok*) father [with this offering].

[1] Miss Soule informed Professor and Mrs Seligman (op cit , p 238) that the expression is *colwec*, '*col* of the village community' Father Crazzolara (op cit , pp 97–98) writes *colwic*, gen *colwec*, but he does not give a literal translation of the expression In my opinion the second syllable of the word is *wic*, gen. *wec*, 'head', and not *wec*, gen *wic*, 'cattle-camp' or 'community'. Dr Marv Smith tells me that she has heard Nuer speak of *coldoor* in reference to a person killed by lightning in the bush (*door*), though *colwic* is also used. On the other hand, some Nuer told her that people killed by lightning are called *colwic* because they do not have their heads shaved after death, as other people do Clearly the syllables which compose the word have no definite meaning for Nuer.

Come to earth gently, do not come with fury to thy grass [the thatched roof]. Come gently to thy grass. No one disputes with thee It is thy universe. It is thy will, thine alone ' Or a man may take a mallet, used for driving tethering-pegs into the ground, lay it in the doorway to his byre, and, after asking God to 'rain well' for it is his universe, throw some ashes into the air in offering. Once when after a heavy storm I told a Nuer that should there be another storm of like severity I would desert my tent and take shelter in his byre he rebuked me, saying 'God does not wish the thunder to come like that again. You should not suggest it.'

When a person is killed by lightning Nuer are resigned. They say that God has struck him with his fire and that as God has taken him there is nothing to be said. God has taken the soul of the man to himself and 'he would be angry if he saw you grieving for the person whom he has taken'. The death is not a punishment for some fault but a mysterious act of divine will, almost what some theologians call an election. All death is ultimately attributed to God, but only in the sense of his being the first and necessary cause which operates through secondary and contingent causes. In the case of a *colwic*, however, God has chosen a particular person for himself and taken him with his own hand. Nuer say that the chosen person has entered into kinship, or friendship, with God [1] For this reason a person struck by lightning does not receive an ordinary burial and the usual mortuary rites are not held for him. I was under the impression, and have elsewhere stated, that, nevertheless, the formal rules of mourning were observed, but Dr. Mary Smith tells me that this is not so, and what she says is more in accordance with what I have recorded above.[2]

A person is usually struck in his byre or hut and the walls of the burnt-out building are broken down over the body, and the

---

[1] In a published note on *colwic* (*Man*, 1949) I have translated a phrase, 'ca mar e kwoth' by 'he has been brought into kinship with God' As written it could mean this, but I now think that I may not have heard the words correctly and that what was said should be translated 'he was struck by God (with lightning)'. However, the idea of kinship, or friendship, with God was also expressed where the context allowed no room for misunderstanding

[2] We find the same idea among the Shilluk. They do not bury or mourn a person killed by lightning. The death is an honour and the family feel that they have made an offering and will therefore prosper (the Rev D. S. Oyler, 'Shilluk Notes', *Sudan Notes and Records*, 1926, pp 58–59). Dr Lienhardt tells me that the Dinka also do not mourn a person killed by lightning

charred remains of the rafters, supports, and thatch are heaped on top of them. If a man is struck in the bush his body is covered with grass and thornwood. Nuer say that it is only the *ring*, the flesh, which they cover up. The *yiegh*, the life, or in this sense the soul, has been taken by God and has become part of him. Sacrifices must be made at once. The people sacrifice to God even if a byre or hut is struck without causing death because the misfortune, being a direct intervention of God in human affairs, is a danger which must be got rid of. They say '*ba luak kier ka del*', 'the byre is expiated with one of the flock'.[1] If a person is killed, his kith and kin feel that they are in grave danger and anyone closely connected with the dead makes sacrifice as soon as he hears of the calamity. The dead man's paternal and maternal kin and his affines bring oxen and sheep and goats to the mortuary mound and sacrifice them there. Even distant kinsmen and unrelated friends and neighbours make sacrifice; and if a girl is killed by lightning her sweetheart will sacrifice an animal. The whole community is involved, and fellow villagers who do not feel that they are sufficiently connected with the dead for animal sacrifice to be necessary throw leaves of the tobacco plant on the mound in silence. It is believed that unless sacrifices are made at once the *colwic* may return bringing death to man and beast. Also, the close kinsmen of the dead are so unclean that relatives and neighbours may not eat or drink in their homes before they have sacrificed; animals must follow the dead before the people can rest in peace. Nuer say '*ca je kir ka det kene rueth*', 'he (the dead man) was expiated with some of the flock (goats and sheep) and oxen'. The sacrifices cleanse the kith and kin and ward off from them further misfortune.[2]

But only immediate danger is warded off by these sacrifices The kin are not yet free from the ordinary contamination of death and they will not be till another ceremony has been performed some weeks or months later. This ceremony resembles the usual *cuol woc* mortuary ceremony held for a person who has died in some other way than by lightning and which I describe later, but Nuer do not call it by that name. Indeed they say, as I have

[1] *Del* means both 'sheep' and 'goat'.

[2] Dr R. G Lienhardt tells me that an ox must be sacrificed on the evening after the death, just before sunset, and that its flesh must be consumed during the night, a rule which obtains for sacrifice only on this occasion. This is perhaps a further association of *colwic* with darkness.

mentioned, that one does not hold a mortuary ceremony for a *colwic*. The difference between an ordinary mortuary ceremony and a ceremony to commemorate a *colwic* would appear to be that whereas in both one purpose of sacrifice is to cleanse the living, another purpose in an ordinary mortuary ceremony, to send the soul of the dead to the ghosts, is lacking in the commemoration ceremony for a *colwic*. The soul of a man killed by lightning is at the moment of death translated to its heavenly home. Nevertheless, it may be that this ceremony is performed not only to cleanse the living and to commemorate the dead but also to fix his soul firmly in the above so that there will be no return to the living, just as an ordinary mortuary ceremony fixes the soul in the underworld of the ghosts.

I had the opportunity in 1936 to witness this ceremony when it was held for a girl called Nyakewa, the daughter of Rwacar, among the western Nuer. During the afternoon the women of the village collected in the garden of the dead girl's home to make beer, for it is the custom on this occasion for the women to work together instead of each in her own home. While they were engaged in making beer rain began to fall and wood ash[1] was thrown into the air and Nyakewa was addressed: 'Sister, wouldst thou spoil our work in this way? It is for thee we do it.' The rain soon passed over, though the sky remained overclouded for the rest of the day. Nuer expect rain to fall on this day, but after they have sacrificed They say 'we have slaughtered cattle for God. The chyme (*wau*) will be watered today by God, and the blood also.'

The ceremony began in the late afternoon in the homestead where Nyakewa was killed, that of her mother Nyaruithni and of her brother Malith, an uninitiated boy. Her *pater*—she had been begotten in adultery by another man during his lifetime—was dead. The ceremony was held in her mother's home and not in her husband's home because, although bridewealth had been paid for her, she had not passed through the consummation ceremony before she was struck by lightning. A fully married woman who is killed by lightning becomes a *colwic* of her husband's lineage and not of her father's lineage Her husband is *gwande*, her owner or master, and they say of such a spirit that she was married with cattle and will not return to her father's lineage—that is, will not

[1] The ash of women's cooking fires, not the ash of cattle-dung of the men's fires of byre and kraal.

be its patron. I have noted that when a widow is killed by lightning at the home of a man with whom she cohabited after her
husband's death her memorial is erected at her husband's home,
though his people invite her lover to attend the commemoration
ceremony.

Lat, son of Pan, the master of ceremonies (pp. 287–9) of
Nyakewa's father's family, made fire ritually with firesticks and
from it were lighted the various fires on which pots were placed
for boiling the beer. The mud supports for the pots were made on
the spot, for one does not use old utensils on these occasions. Since
the ceremony was for a woman a new mud windscreen was constructed. The master of ceremonies then erected a *riek*, a shrine-
stake, in the centre of the funeral mound and planted at the side
of the mound a sapling of the *nyuot* tree. Such a mound and stake
are shown in Mr Corfield's photograph in Plate II.[1] The *nyuot*
tree is, as we have noted, associated with the spirit *col* and also
with rain and with the sky from which rain and lightning come
and to which the soul of the dead person has gone. When planted
in the rains the sapling generally takes root. If it dies they plant
another. Many of the trees one sees in Nuer villages have been
planted in this manner.

Shortly before sunset a procession of about twenty men arrived
bearing in their hands leaves of the tobacco plant and heads of
millet They threw down these offerings near the mound with the
freshly erected shrine-stake in the centre of it. No one comes to the
place of sacrifice empty-handed. The procession was headed by
the master of ceremonies leading a black ox, *a thak ma col* It
should preferably be a black one. This *ma col* sacrificial victim,
col the spirit of lightning, and the *colwic* make a harmony of
darkness (*col*), the darkness of storm. Before the ox was sacrificed
men came from all directions leading oxen and castrated he-goats
and wethers. The father of the dead girl's husband brought an ox,
as did one of her maternal uncles. Among those who brought he-
goats and wethers were the girl's mother, one of her maternal
aunts, one of her maternal uncles, several of her father's kinsmen,
and the man who had begotten her brother in adulterous congress

---

[1] This is almost certainly a *colwic* shrine, but it is more elaborate than most
and the offerings of tobacco seen at the base would not be seen at shrines in
other parts of Nuerland The photograph was taken among the eastern Jikany
Nuer who border the Anuak, great cultivators of tobacco.

with her mother, for her brother had also been begotten in adultery, though by a different man from the man who begat her. The black ox was speared near the funeral mound and the other oxen and the sheep and goats were speared immediately afterwards. I have not known sheep and goats to be speared in any other sacrifices. The usual mode of sacrifice for them is by cutting the throat. Dr. Mary Smith tells me that they are speared on this occasion to symbolize the instantaneous death of a *colwic* by lightning. As soon as a goat or sheep fell it was cut in half through the belly. The oxen were also cut up unskinned, for one does not use the hides of animals sacrificed for a *colwic*, as one uses those of most sacrificial beasts, for sleeping on or for women's skirts. The head, hooves, some of the entrails, and part of the skin of the black ox were placed at the foot of the stake or hung on it. The chyme of the animals was collected and placed at the foot of the stake, and their tethering-cords were hung on it. Most of the flesh of the black ox went to the girl's father's lineage, on whose behalf it was sacrificed, but some went to collateral lineages, some to women of the father's lineage married to men of other lineages, and some to the girl's maternal uncles I did not inquire how the other animals were divided but it may, I think, be assumed that in each case the animal was mostly consumed by the paternal kinsmen of the man who brought it to the sacrifice

At dawn on the following morning the dead girl's senior maternal uncle sacrificed a bull on behalf of the maternal kinsfolk. It was first castrated in his byre because animals are not sacrificed entire. The uncle made a short invocation before spearing it. The meat of this animal was divided between the dead girl's own family, her maternal uncles, and various other relatives on the mother's side who were present. A man representing the mother then sacrificed an ox at the mound on behalf of the family. However the flesh of these sacrificed oxen may be divided according to rights of kinship, all present must receive pieces of meat, even though they be unrelated persons, because all must taste the meats of sacrifice to show the *colwic* that they do not reject or disregard (*cany*) it. The last sacrifice I witnessed was of a goat by a brother of the husband of the dead girl's mother's sister, on behalf of this maternal aunt, but I was told that more sheep and goats were slaughtered on subsequent days and that in all more than twenty animals were sacrificed. These were in addition to

PLATE II

Shrine for person struck by lightning

those which had been killed immediately after Nyakewa had been struck by lightning. As the husband of one of Nyakewa's maternal aunts was killed at the same moment as herself while he was on a visit to her village many animals of the village had also to be sacrificed on his behalf in his own village The flocks of the village were so depleted that there was no suitable beast available for sacrifice in a case of serious sickness which occurred in the village shortly afterwards (p. 35) The number of beasts sacrificed is an indication both of the seriousness of the event which occasioned the ceremony and of the wide circle of persons it affected.

When the sun was high in the heavens on this second day of the ceremony the beer was drunk, though it had not properly fermented. The old men poured some on the sacred stake while uttering a few words. I heard one of the maternal uncles say 'Nyakewa, we have no kinship with God. Thou hast kinship with him now. See, thy mother remains here; do not let the spirits trouble her.' Towards the end of the beer-drinking the people sang hymns to spirits of the air to the accompaniment of hand-clapping.

Later the waste products of the beer were heaped around the base of the stake on top of the tobacco leaves and millet heads and parts of the sacrificed beasts. The dead girl's ox-tassels, her horn spoon, her butter-gourd, and two lumps of tobacco were tied to the stake. These things were said to belong to God, for the girl's soul was now with God. They had become holy and could not be used by man. Finally the cooking stones and pots used in the beer-making were neatly arranged around the heap of offerings. I was told afterwards: 'Nyakewa has altogether departed from us who are men and has become Spirit (*kwoth*). Henceforward we will invoke her name in battle as we brandish our spears.' About a year after this ceremony kinsmen gather again at the shrine to drink beer and to sprinkle (*kith*) some of it into the air as an offering.

Sometimes a *colwic* spirit seizes a member of its family or lineage, in the same way as a spirit of the air may seize a man, and makes him sick. When he recovers he makes a small mound-shrine (*yik*) in his homestead and this then takes the place of the original shrine at the home of the person killed by lightning. Some of the dead person's ornaments may be inserted into the mound of the new shrine and others hung on the stake erected in

(59)

it and on the low fence enclosing it. Occasionally the spirit, again as the spirits of the air may do, enters into (*gwang*) a man to abide with him He then becomes a *guk col*, a prophet of *col*, and the spirit of lightning speaks through him to the people. Or he may be called a *gwan colwec*, the owner of a *colwic*. There is no clear distinction here between the spirit *col* and the *colwic* spirits, *col* being a collective representation of the *colwic* spirits in general.

The *colwic* is a conception which appears to be, unlike many of their religious conceptions, not only native to the Nuer but at one time also peculiar to them;[1] and it is one of unusual interest. Its significance cannot be altogether perceived at this stage of our inquiry, but certain features of it may be remarked upon.

In that a *colwic* is a spirit which dwells in the sky and can fall and enter men it is like the air-spirits which also have their abode in the above and fall and enter men, but there is an important difference between the two conceptions. The spirits of the air derive, or proceed, directly from God but the *colwic* spirits were once human beings, created things Consequently, whereas the spirits of the air are *gaat Kwoth*, sons of God, the *colwic* spirits are not, at any rate in the same sense. In the one case God descends to man, in the other he takes man up to him.

Apart from the fact that the spirits of the air and the *colwic* spirits both dwell on high there is in another respect something common to the two conceptions. In discussing prophets it was observed how Spirit in the form of spirits of the air can enter into men, the human being expelled, as it were, and the divine taking its place. There is in the idea a suggestion of the natural man being changed into the spiritual man In the *colwic* conception we have again, though in a rather different form, this idea of the soul in exceptional circumstances being transmuted into Spirit. I emphasize this aspect of the belief because, as will be seen more clearly later, it is essential to an understanding of Nuer religious thought that the conceptions of 'soul' and 'spirit' should be distinguished

[1] Dr Lienhardt tells me that the *colwic* of the Rek Dinka is a very different conception. It is an evil spirit of the bush The Dinka probably borrowed both the idea and the word from the Nuer and they seem then to have quite changed its meaning in assimilating it to their own notions, especially to their *macardit* conception The Twic Dinka conception is nearest to the Nuer one (Fr A Nebel in P W. Schmidt, op cit, p 161) Twic country is coterminous with that of the Bul Nuer

and kept apart. The distinction is made very clearly in what Nuer say of a *colwic*—that he is a person who has become Spirit. They say of him that '*coa kwoth*', 'he has become Spirit'.

Having become Spirit the soul of the dead person is now not only a spirit but, as a spirit, part of God, who is all Spirit, and also, when Nuer think of the manner and instrument of death, of God conceived of in his hypostasis of *col*, the spirit of lightning. We are here faced with the problem I have been discussing with regard to the spirits of the air and which I discuss again in more general terms in Chapter IV Each *colwic* spirit is a quite distinctive being, bearing, if it is remembered and revered, the name it had on earth as a person, so that one can say that a sacrifice is made to one particular *colwic* and not to another. But, here again, one cannot say that sacrifice is being made to a *colwic* spirit and not to God or to God in the figure of *col*. The argument developed in reference to the spirits of the air holds also for the *colwic* spirits. The relation of these spirits to God is not a disjunction, an either . . . or, but a conjunction, a both . . . and. A *colwic* is itself and it is also God.

We may develop the argument a bit further. If a *colwic* is God it is God thought of with reference to a particular family or lineage It is true that, as we have seen, in relation to the awesome event, the death by lightning, all who had any social connexion with the dead person are involved, but when the ceremonies I have described are over they cease to be. Afterwards only members of the spirit's family and lineage are concerned with it. A *colwic* which has become the patron of a lineage is not revered by members of other lineages. It has significance for that lineage alone. Hence there is here an important difference not only between a *colwic* spirit and Spirit comprehensively conceived of as God but also between a *colwic* spirit and a spirit of the air The spirits of the air are much more general and mobile conceptions. Though they may be of direct concern only for those persons, families, and lineages to which they have attached themselves they may attach themselves to any person, family, or lineage and indirectly, through the political role of their prophets, they can be of importance for local communities. The *colwic* spirits, on the contrary, are confined within the narrow limits of families and lineages. They cannot attach themselves to persons who are not members of their own families and lineages. We begin to see how the conception of Spirit is refracted by the social structure, and this will be more clearly seen when an account has been given in the next chapter of the totemic and totemistic spirits, which are also patrons of lineages, families, and persons and of significance only for those lineages, families, and persons to whom they stand in a tutelary relationship.

CHAPTER III

SPIRITS OF THE BELOW

I

Nuer speak of *kuth piny*, spirits of the below or of the earth, in contrast with the *kuth nhial*, spirits of the above or of the sky, which I have so far been discussing In a certain sense all spirits of the below are thought to have fallen from above, and inevitably so, because the above is the abode of Spirit. In one way of thinking about them they are conceived of as being still in the above, though they are also conceived of as immanent in creatures and things on earth, and they are then opposed in thought to the spirits of the above. It might be urged that much the same could be said of the spirits of the air for they are also conceived of as immanent in their prophets on earth. But they can easily be thought of, once people are familiar with their names, quite independently of the persons in whom they manifest themselves. The spirits of the below, on the contrary, can hardly be dissociated in the mind from their earthly appearances, for it is only by reference to them that they are known at all. Moreover, Nuer evaluate the two kinds of spirit quite differently. The spirits of the air are not only 'of the above' but also 'great spirits'. Those of the below are not only 'of the below' but also 'little spirits', and Nuer do not hold them in high esteem.

The spirits of the below can be classed into a number of separate categories, what I am calling totemic spirits, totemistic spirits, nature sprites, and fetishes. This classification is made partly for descriptive convenience but it also in part rests on a Nuer classification Although they describe all alike as *kuth*, spirits, and, in contrast with the spirits of the above, *kuth piny*, spirits of the below, they have separate class names for the last two categories, *bieli* and *kulangni*, and the fetishes are also *wal*, medicines. Consequently *kuth piny*, when not being used inclusively to point a contrast with the spirits of the above, generally refers specifically to the totemic and totemistic spirits. I describe these sorts of spirits first, using 'totemic' in the classical sense of

(63)

the word to denote a relationship between a social group and a natural species or a class of objects and 'totemistic' when the relationship tends to concern individuals rather than social groups. The distinction is not, however, a vital one and need not therefore be rigorously maintained, and such being the case, the word 'totem' may serve to denote the species or class in both instances The same species, that is to say, may be the totem of a lineage (a totemic relationship) or of individuals (a totemistic relationship). I use the expressions 'totemic spirit' and 'totemistic spirit', as the case may be, to designate the *kwoth* of the species or class which is totem to a group or individual. Nuer distinguish between the spirit and the creature in which it may be said in some sense to make its appearance, for example, between the lion-spirit and the lion It is to the spirit and not to the creature that Nuer devote cattle of the bridewealth of their daughters and to which they make sacrifice Before discussing this problem further I give some examples of relationships between lineages and the natural species they are said to respect and from which they sometimes take their spear-names and honorific titles

Some lineages respect lions. One of them, the *Leng* lineage of the Jinaca clan, say that the lion is their totem because their ancestor Gilgil was born twin to a lion. When they sacrifice to the lion-spirit, they are said to take a leg of the victim into the bush and leave it there, calling on the lions to come and eat their share, which I have heard described as the share of the *jibuthni*, the people of a collateral lineage (p 287) I fancy that what is meant is that a token piece of meat is thrown into the bush and that it is spoken about as a leg. It is said that if a man who has the lion for totem injures a lion he may beget a son with nails like claws. I was told of a man that he took a spear belonging to a member of the Leng lineage, a neighbour of his, and killed a lion with it, and that shortly afterwards another lion killed a number of beasts of the Leng man's herd. It was proposed that the people should go out to hunt the animal, but after discussion it was decided that it would not be just to do so because the lion had right (*cuong*) on its side. Instead, the man who had killed the first lion with the spear of its totemic kinsman compensated him for the loss of his cattle and a sacrifice was made to the lion-spirit. After compensation and atonement had been made the second lion gave no more trouble My friend Cam of the village of Yakwac on the Sobat river was born of a woman of the Leng lineage and has, moreover, married a wife to the name of his maternal uncle and begotten children to him by her; so, though he is not himself a man of the Leng lineage, he has intimate ties with it, and he lives with its members. His brother told me how one day Cam killed a lion which he believed to be killing his cattle, for, his brother commented, 'Cam has no sense at all'. He returned from his successful hunt bending his fingers like claws and crouching as though he intended to spring on the people around him. A sheep was at once sacrificed to the lion-spirit, and Cam composed himself. While I was living in a cattle camp at the same village of Yakwac, which is occupied by part of the Leng lineage in the dry season, a girl of the lineage was taken hold of by the lion-spirit and had hysterics. Her family sacrificed a sheep to the spirit and dedicated a cow to it, for the seizure was thought to have been due to their failure to dedicate a cow to it earlier; and the girl was restored to her normal self. The Thiang lineage of Kurmayom village, also in Lou country, are another lineage whose totem is the lion, and they told me that they would not kill lions unless the lions first killed their cattle, for then the lions would have done wrong (*dwir*) and they would be in the right (*cuong*) in retaliating. This lineage has *mut luony*, spear of lion, for its spear-name. Another friend, Rainen of the Leek tribe, told me that he used to respect lions because his paternal grandfather's mother had been born twin to a lion in Dinkaland (she was a Dinka), the lion twin having run away into the bush. He said, however, that he had ceased to respect them when they began to eat his cattle. He conceded that the lions which ate his cattle were small lions from Dinkaland and not the large lions of Nuerland, but he felt he had been wronged by lions as a body and now refused to respect lions of any kind. He said '*ce theak thuk*', 'the respect is finished'. The same man told me that in the past, before lions began to eat his cattle, he had sometimes tied up a goat in the bush for them, and they had taken it. In the terminology I am using he had a totemistic relationship to lions. I have no certain knowledge that any mammalian species besides the lion is the primary totem of a Nuer lineage. The waterbuck, as will be seen later, is a secondary totem of a large clan.

A considerable number of lineages respect reptilian species. The large lineage of the Lak tribe who are known as *cieng* Gangni respect the monitor lizard The story is told that long ago some people of *cieng* Gangni were dying of thirst on a journey. They were wandering, light-headed with thirst and the heat of the sun, when they saw a monitor lizard in a *thep*-tree (*Acacia verugera*) They intended to kill it but it escaped them and following it brought them to water, to which, being a water creature, it naturally made. Ever since, their descendants have respected the lizard and dedicated cows of their herds to the lizard-spirit. I was told that if there is one of them present when a Nuer of a different clan kills one of these lizards, as apparently sometimes happens, he throws a bead or some grass on to its body to make recompense (*ba je col*), because he saw his totem killed. I was told also that should a man of *cieng* Gangni knowingly eat of its flesh he would die, while should he eat of it unknowingly he might fall sick or become crazy. Nuer also say that should a man who respects the lizard harm it he may beget a child with deformed legs resembling the legs of the lizard. The *cieng* Gangni also respect the *thep*-tree for the reason given in the story I have related and, though why I do not know, the *keac* tree (*Crataeva religiosa*) and *pak*, the Dead Sea apple (*Calotropis procera*). One of their spear-names is *mut thep*, the spear of the *thep*-tree, and one of their honorific titles is *gat thep*, son of the *thep*-tree.

There are a number of lineages in different parts of Nuerland who respect crocodiles and dedicate cows to the crocodile-spirit, the Cany major lineage of the eastern Gaajak being one of the largest The reason given for the totemic relationship is a twin-birth of an ancestor with a crocodile's egg, the egg having been placed in a stream. I was told that a twin-birth of this kind may occur at any time in a lineage which respects the crocodile. Members of these lineages are said sometimes to milk the cows dedicated to the crocodile-spirit and to pour the milk into a stream in which there are crocodiles One of their honorific clan-names may be *nya nyanga*, daughter of the crocodile. It is said that should a man who respects crocodiles harm one of the reptiles without cause, or eat its flesh, he may beget a child with a rudimentary arm resembling a crocodile's leg; and I was told of a woman of one of these lineages who ate crocodile flesh, thinking that it was turtle flesh, and afterwards bore a child so deformed that it had to crawl on its belly. Those who respect crocodiles enjoy a special immunity from their attacks and I have been assured by old men when about to wade through crocodile-infested streams that I need have no fear, because people whose totem was the crocodile lived nearby, and they contrasted the benevolence of their local crocodiles with the savagery of crocodiles in other districts. When once I remarked to a Nuer about a man fishing far out in the Sobat river, in a place I knew to be infested with crocodiles, that I thought he was taking a big risk, my companion simply replied 'maybe he respects crocodiles'. I have also been told that men of these lineages call the reptiles out of the water and stroke them. There can be no doubt that people who have the crocodile for totem are regarded by other Nuer as having some control over them. They are summoned by their neighbours to perform a rite to prevent crocodiles from attacking them or their flocks and herds when streams and rivers must be crossed. The *gwan kwoth nyanga*, the person who possesses the crocodile-spirit (who has the crocodile for totem), bends a metal bracelet till the ends overlap and binds them in this position with grass, and then presses the bracelet into the river mud, calling on *gwandong*, grandfather or ancestor (in this context, the crocodile-spirit), to let the people pass over in safety. This operation closes the jaws of the crocodiles while people and cattle are in the water. He may also, on certain occasions, as when a stream is being fished, bind a goat and push it under weeds and reeds into the stream for the crocodile-spirit at the same time as performing the bracelet rite; and it is said that he must then sit on the bank and abstain from drinking water while people are still in the stream.

A large number of small lineages in Nuerland respect snakes. All those whose descent I was able to trace are of Dinka origin Some respect *nyal*, the python. Those I have asked about their totemic affiliation have told me that a python was born as twin to their ancestor. When they sacrifice to the python-spirit they take a goat to the edge of the stream and there kill it, in imitation of the python's killing of its prey, by blocking its mouth and nostrils and bouncing on its belly till it suffocates. They throw a piece of the sacrificial meat into the stream and another piece towards the land. They boil the rest of the meat, taking care that no soup of the boiling is spilt, and eat it. A senior man then sharpens a new cattle-peg and, after driving it into the ground and winding grass round it, pours some of the blood of the goat at its foot, asking the python-spirit to take its 'cow' and let the people be at peace. They complete the rite by building a small mound of ashes as a shrine (*yik*) to the spirit I have seen goats with what the Nuer call *ma nyal*, python-like, markings dedicated to the python-spirit in kraals. A Lou tribesman told me that when he was a boy a python entered his father's kraal and paid particular attention to a goat dedicated to its spirit, and his father gave it milk in a gourd and rubbed its scales with butter. All Nuer say that if any snake enters the homestead of a man who respects that species he will offer it milk and rub its scales with butter, but I have not seen this done. They say that a snake which has been treated with these courtesies may enter the byre and sleep there and, when it wakes, crawl among the cattle in the kraal, paying friendly attention to the cow or beast of the flock dedicated to its spirit. A man who respects pythons respects also bees, because Nuer consider their markings to be like those of the python, and will not kill them or eat their honey.

Another snake respected by a large number of small lineages of Dinka descent is *lualdit* or *rir*, which I believe to be the tree cobra. A Nuer of the Leek tribe told me how this totem had come into his family, and his story has some interest in that it illustrates the way in which a lineage may acquire a totem His father was digging a hole in which to plant a support to a new cattle byre when he scooped up a cobra with the earth in his hands. In his fright he killed it with a digging-stick Later he fell sick and the form of a cobra appeared to him in a dream and told him that it wanted a *duor*, a gift, so he sacrificed an ox to the cobra-spirit and dedicated a cow to it. His sons now respect the cobra, and their descendants may continue to do so. During my first expedition to Nuerland one of my Zande servants was chased into my tent by one of these cobras and I was forced to shoot it Later in the day a man of the cattle camp where I was residing came to complain that I had killed his *kwoth*, totem, when I might easily have sent to ask him to remove it from my tent. He demanded compensation, which I made with a lump of tobacco. Some people say that if you can kill a cobra without it seeing you, you will find *wal*, medicine, inside it. If it sees you it will spit out the medicine before you can kill it Those who respect the cobra respect also the little red soldier ants, here again apparently on account of a resemblance of colour.[1] When bitten by them they do not slap them on their

[1] Dr Lienhardt tells me that a beast dedicated to the spirit of cobra should

PLATE III

Sacrifice of ox by suffocation

bodies and kill them as other Nuer do, but they carefully remove them and place them on the ground. When my camp in the eastern Jikany country was overrun by these insects and I tried to drive them out with fire, some men whose totem they were protested, and they requested me not to harm the ants. When a man sees his totem being harmed he feels it an obligation to make a formal protest and he may ask for a gift to remove the offence, but he does not make it occasion for a quarrel Miss Ray Huffman relates (in a letter) how many years ago she and a fellow mission-ary, Mr. Adair, killed a cobra just outside the Nasser mission compound The people of the homestead where it was killed showered grain on its body to cover it 'so the god in it would not be angry with them for letting it be killed'. However, I should record Mr. Jackson's statement that a dispenser of Malakal hospi-tal, presumably a lad of some foreign people, 'was travelling with a party of pedlars [presumably Arabs] and killed a snake which he came across. Although only a boy he was at once attacked by the Nuer of the Longaish section and beaten into unconsciousness.'[1]

Some lineages, also of Dinka origin, have the spitting viper, *thatut*, for totem. I have been told that there are some Nuer who respect the snakes called *gur* and *dengcek* (the puff-adder), and it is possible that other snakes are totems. The small Cuor lineage of Dinka descent in Leek tribal area have the serpent *lou* for their totem. This huge, and presumably imaginary, creature is said to frequent streams and to have a comb like that of the crested crane and hair on its head which waggles from side to side as it swims in the water. Members of this lineage say that their ancestor was sleeping in a hut with his wife and small child when one of these serpents came through the doorway and lay across them. The wife woke up and swooned at the sight of it. Later the man woke up, and finding his wife unconscious, but without seeing the serpent, promised God an ox for her recovery Afterwards he saw the serpent and dedicated a cow to that serpent-spirit, and his descendants have respected the *lou* ever since. One of them, a man called Dol, told me that he once speared a *lou* by mistake, think-ing that the movement he saw in the water was that of a fish, and was brought home prostrated He recovered after sacrifice had been made.

be a brown beast calved of a brown beast The snake is called *lualdit* on account of its brown (*lual*) colour   [1] Op cit , p. 167

I have been told that there is a small lineage, called Waloak, in, eastern Gaajok country who respect tortoises. There is a curious story accounting for their adoption of this totem. A man of the lineage had his cow taken by a man of a neighbouring village and his repeated requests for it to be returned to him were unavailing One day when he was going to the river he found a tortoise and wrapped it in a sheepskin. He continued on his way, and as he was passing the village of the people who had taken his cow, he took the opportunity of once more asking for it. They refused his request, but at that moment the tortoise poked its head against the skin pressing it outwards The man bent over it and told it to be quiet as it would get its share that day Again he asked for his cow and again it was refused, and once more the tortoise wriggled in the skin and was told to be quiet. The people of the village then became frightened because they thought that the man had some powerful medicine in the sheepskin and that, if they did not give his cow back to him, they might die with their children and cattle; so they surrendered the cow. The mention of medicine suggests a recent origin for the story.

Some lineages respect birds The Jibegh of western Nuerland respect the ostrich and will not use its feathers as ornaments. Their spear-name is *mut wuot*, spear of the ostrich. It is said that ostriches will not eat the millet of members of this clan. I once met a man with only three toes, stocky and undeveloped, to one of his feet. I was told that his maternal grandmother had the ostrich for totem, and that on the day of her daughter's marriage one of the bridegroom's people, as is the custom, threw a spear at her mud windscreen. She took the spear as her right and on examining it found that part of the shaft was bound with ostrich-skin. When her daughter bore a son he was deformed as I have described. The ostriches—or, rather, the spirit of ostrich—had stamped the likeness of an ostrich on the child

Some small lineages of Dinka origin respect cattle egrets. One such lineage are the Rial of western Nuerland. I also met Lou tribesmen who have the cattle egret for totem and I was present when some of them sacrificed a goat to the cattle egret-spirit on the bank of the Sobat river, not because anyone was sick, which is a common occasion of sacrifice to a totem-spirit, 'but just because they think of (*tim*) it'. This spirit is said to be a river-spirit because they sacrifice to it at the river's edge, near which cattle egrets are generally to be seen

I am uncertain whether the many little species of birds the Nuer class together as *kec*—weaver-birds (the Sudan dioch), finches, and others, known collectively in the Sudan as durra-birds—are rightly regarded as the totem of lineages or whether the spirit associated with them is possessed by individuals and not by groups. It may be that only the son who takes on the ritual functions of a *gwan keca* or *gwan kwoth keca*, an owner of durra-bird or an owner of the spirit of durra-bird, respects these little birds, and not all his sons or all members of his lineage, but I believe that they are respected by small lineages of Dinka and Anuak descent and therefore include them in the list of Nuer totems. The Nuer class, as we do, all these little birds together because they feed together on millet seed. They may be seen to rise in swarms from the millet gardens and, whilst in most years Nuer pay little attention to them, they are in some years so numerous and destructive that the entire crop is threatened. It is then necessary to protect it by posting boys, sometimes on plat-forms erected for the purpose, to scare them off. The owners of the threatened gardens may also summon a man who respects the birds to induce them to depart. He takes some stems of millet of different varieties from each of the gardens of the village and, carrying this bundle, heads a procession of the villagers to where the gardens meet the bush. There he utters an invocation over the goat, telling the birds that it is their cow and exhorting them to turn towards the bush where they will find plenty of grass seed to eat, for that is the millet of the birds. He tells them that the people have come out of their village to greet (*lor*) them with a 'cow' (goat) and requests them to leave the millet alone. When he has sacrificed the goat to the durra-bird-spirit he places the millet he has gathered on the ground with their heads facing the bush to show the birds the direction in which it is desired that they should go. I was told that the carcass is left in the bush. On the occasion on which I was present an expert had been brought from some distance to perform the rite, and a local man, who also respected the birds and could therefore have performed it, felt slighted, and was said to have threatened that next year he would cut stalks of millet before the harvest was ripe. Nuer often cut stalks of unripe millet to chew, but a man who has these birds for totem must not do so lest he cause the birds to devour the crop.

Plants are respected by some lineages. They may not cut them or burn their wood. The large Gaanwar clan respect the *nyuot*-tree (*Cordia Rothii*) and the *koat*, tamarind, tree. The ancestor of this clan fell from heaven holding a branch of the *nyuot*-tree in his hand or, some say, he descended from heaven by, or on to, a *nyuot* near which was a small tamarind.[1] Members of this clan call for aid on *kwoth nyota* or *kwoth kota*, the spirit of these trees. The *nyuot*, a branch of which is often erected in the homes of Gaanwar as a shrine to this spirit, is associated with rain on account of the humidity of its leaves even in the dry season The verbal form of the word, *nyot*, means 'to drizzle'. Members of the clan may therefore be called on to bring rain in time of drought. This they do by placing a sprig of the tree in water, sacrificing an animal, and calling on the spirit of the clan, which is the spirit of the tree, for rain. It is, we may suppose, on account of their connexion with water that the clan have as additional totems the waterbuck and the fish *nyiwar*, *cur*, *lam*, *yiau*, and *gwejual* and can also speak of their spirit as '*kwoth puoara*', 'spirit of our waterbuck', '*kwoth lameda*', 'spirit of our *lam* fish', and so on I have been told that women of this clan will not eat the meat of a cow which has died calving, but I do not know, the reason for this abstention. The scattered Jwal clan share some of the Gaanwar totems. They seem at one time to have formed a single clan with the Gaanwar. The Jingop and Keunyang lineages of western Nuerland respect the *ngop* tree, the sycamore or wild fig (*Ficus Sycomorus*), and speak of '*kwoth ngoapna*', 'spirit of our fig-tree', to which they dedicate cows in their kraals, as is usual where there is a totemic relationship. The largest clan in Nuerland, the Gaatgankir of the Jikany tribes, respect gourds Their ancestor was found in a gourd (*kir*). They will not cut or step over the stems of gourds or prepare them to serve as utensils, for they must not handle a gourd which still contains its pulp and seed Nevertheless they use them as utensils for the same purposes as do other Nuer. The clan is of Dinka origin, though it now counts as a Nuer clan. Other plants respected by lineages, usually of Dinka descent,

---

[1] Some variants of the story of his appearance on earth are recorded in *The Nuer*, p 230

are the *thep*-tree, papyrus, the *kwel*-tree (*Ficus platyphylla*), and *lel*, the dom palm.[1]

Some lineages respect rivers and streams The ancestor of the Juak lineage of western Nueiland, of Dinka descent, is said to have come out of a big lagoon called *gwol*, so his descendants are known as Juak *jigwol* and the honorific titles of their sons and daughters are *gat* and *nya gwol*, son and daughter of (the lagoon) *gwol*. They respect all rivers and streams, and when a man of the lineage intends to cross a river he throws a bead into the water calling on his 'grandfather' (the river-spirit) to accept the offering and bring him in safety to the other side A woman of the lineage will not take off her skirt when crossing a river as other women do, and unmarried girls, who are naked, place a few wisps of grass round their loins before entering the water I was told that were a married woman to forget and step into the water naked, and were then to remember her obligation, she would return to the bank and pull off a bead or tassel from her skirt and throw it into the water, telling the river-spirit that she had not purposely offended it and asking it to accept her offering in atonement. The Gaatiek clan also respect rivers, and the Nile in particular because God brought their ancestor out of it. Being *jiyier*, river-people, they respect also the *gwot yier*, papyrus and will not cut it. Their spear-names are *mut kier* and *mut yier*, spear of the Nile and spear of the river, and their honorific names are *gat* and *nya bar*, son and daughter of lagoon. They dedicate black cows to the Nile-spirit and they sometimes pour a libation of milk from these cows into rivers. When people are taking their families and cattle across rivers they milk one of the black cows dedicated to the river-spirit into a black snail-shell, which a man of the clan then turns upside down at the river's edge and keeps pressed into the mud while the people and herds pass over This keeps the jaws of the crocodiles closed In virtue of their relationship to rivers certain senior members of the lineage may also perform a rite for the safety of those

---

[1] Mr. H C. Jackson, op. cit , p 165, records that one of the clans of the Bul tribe respect the tree called in Arabic *duruba*, because their ancestor hid in this tree when fleeing from avengers. It is called *rir* in Nuer and is probably to be identified with *Pseudocedrela kotschyi* Professor and Mrs Seligman, op. cit., p. 213, say that the *kac* tree is respected by the Bul Nuer because their miracle-working ancestor used to sit under it, and by the Jidiet clan because their ancestor was killed with clubs made of its wood They do not on this occasion tell us the sources of their statements

taking part in fishing battues. Such a man is called *gwan biedh*, owner of fish-spear, and *kuaar juaini*, priest of grass, because he protects the people by winding grass round the point of a fishing-spear which he then drives into the earth. He also fills a snail-shell with mud and presses it into the mud of the river, and he bends and binds together the points of a metal bracelet and stamps it into the mud. He may also bind a goat and place it in the river as a sacrifice to the river-spirit, which he calls on to protect the people against the dangers of the water. I was told that he must not himself take part in the fishing, but must sit on the bank and abstain from drinking water. He can also heal wounds caused by fish-spears by spitting in them. The Gaatiek clan is probably of Dinka origin.

The Nyanding river in the eastern Jikany country is the totem of a small lineage of Anuak descent who live on its banks. It is said that once upon a time the river-spirit asked for a bride, and a girl was decked for marriage and thrown into it by her father Juac, whose name means 'grass' in Nuer. This girl who was sacrificed to the river-spirit (*ca je kok yir*) was called Nyanding. I was told that 'she was not drowned, the river took her', and that she became part of the river-spirit. The present 'owner' of the river, Monytuk Joak, a man of this lineage, told me that each year he binds a goat and throws it into the river. He also protects people taking part in large-scale fishing by treating a bracelet and a shell in the manner I have described. When a girl of the lineage is married, a male goat and a female goat are paid as part of the bridewealth. The male goat is sacrificed to the river-spirit and the female goat is dedicated to it.

Some Nuer lineages respect cattle with certain markings. The Kwok lineage of western Nuerland and their kinsmen among the Atwot people (a section of the Nuer who have to a large extent adopted Dinka culture) will not keep in their herds an animal with *ma reng* markings, that is an animal which has a coloured back but is otherwise white. If one is calved by their cows they

FIG. 2
Girl's
dancing-
stick

(74)

exchange it, or give it to one of their affines. When I asked whether this might not compromise the daughter or sister to whose husband it was given I was told: 'They have gone over to another lineage (*gol*), they are not your people any longer.' It is related—the theme of the story is widely distributed among the Nilotic peoples —that a man of the lineage went to bathe in a stream and placed his bead-strung girdle on the bank, where a *ma reng* cow came and looked at it while he was bathing. The man saw the cow near his girdle, but he did not see a kite swoop down and carry the girdle away in its claws; so when he discovered that it had disappeared he thought that the cow had eaten it, and he killed the animal and examined the contents of its stomachs in vain. Later someone found the girdle a long way off, where the kite had dropped it, and brought it to its owner, who was then sorry that he had killed the cow. Moreover, the owner of the cow uttered a conditional curse (*biit*) against him, saying that the spirit of cattle with *ma reng* markings would dog his footsteps and would kill him and his descendants were they ever again to drink the milk of cattle with *ma reng* markings, use their dung for fires, or clean their teeth with the ashes of their burnt dung.

The Gaagwong lineage of the Gaatgankiir clan respect cattle with *ma cuany* markings—an incongruous patch of colour in the middle of one of the common markings. The Jimem, or at any rate one of their lineages, the Jiruet, said to be of Dinka origin, also respect *ma cuany* cattle, and they are respected by all monorchids, to whom all cattle with this peculiarity are thought to be dangerous. This Jimem lineage also respect monorchids, both human or animal, and they have *mut tora*, spear of monorchid, for their spear-name.

The Jikul clan respect the hides of cattle. As far as I am aware, they sleep on them as do other Nuer, but it is said that they refrain from beating a hide to get the ashes of their dung fires off it, as other Nuer do, and shake it instead. The ancestor of this clan is believed to have fallen from the sky, wrapped in a fawn-coloured ox-skin, into a pool of water. Hence their spear-name is *mut kuli*, the spear of the hide, and their honorific titles are *gat* and *nya yan*, son and daughter of fawn-coloured, and *nya kuli*, daughter of hide. I have heard it said that a man of this clan will not eat heads of cattle and will not accept compensation in cattle for adultery with his wife. I was also told that should a man of the clan beat an ox-hide his next child might be born without teeth in the gums of the upper jaw as a cow is without upper incisors. A further observance said to obtain in the clan is that their women may not cross a marshy shallow without first kicking some water out of it. People say that the Jikul are *jikwoth*, God's people, in that they are an augury in war, for if a man on the side they are supporting in a fight should be the first to be wounded their party knows that it will be defeated and should retire, whereas if a man of the other side is the first to be wounded they know by this that they will be victorious and should press forward When a girl of the clan is married a cow of her bridewealth goes to the hide-spirit, and if she is later divorced this cow remains with her parents as indemnity for the hides the people sat on during the marriage negotiations Mr. B A Lewis tells me that when he suggested holding a dance in a village mostly occupied by a Jikul lineage in the Lak tribe he was asked to make a present to the chief man of the community in compensation for the beating of the tympanum of the drum.

The Jikoi clan respect rafters (*koi*) and rope used in the building of byres and huts They use them for building but they will not use those of an old habitation for fuel. It is related that in ancient times men of this clan tried to build a byre which would reach to the clouds Other people said that this could not be done because the clouds were far away, and there was much argument on the matter during the building God in the sky heard the argument and was angered at the presumption of those who wanted to build a byre to reach the heavens, and he sent down lightning and destroyed the builders

I have mentioned all Nuer totems of which I have certain knowledge and I now say a few words about totemistic relationships before discussing some of the chief features of Nuer totemism and its significance for an understanding of their conception of Spirit. In Nuerland one often finds that individuals respect classes of things not respected by other members of their lineages or even by their close kin. There are people, probably all or mostly of Dinka origin, who refrain from eating certain parts of beasts. entrails, heart, liver, kidneys, spleen, head, and hooves In those few cases I have inquired into, the association was said to have come about through a misfortune connected with the parts abstained from For example, people who abstain from eating hearts are, at any rate often, those who have had some heart trouble and have been cured by massage by a man who respects hearts They now respect hearts themselves and can cure others Again, a man told me that he would not eat liver because a forebear had burnt himself when roasting liver and had died of the burns. I was told, and it is highly probable, that these abstentions do not last for more than a generation or two In the same way some people—here again they are said to be Dinka or of Dinka descent—respect certain diseases, or rather their symptoms. These are people who have suffered from the diseases, have been cured by others who respect them, and can now treat sufferers in their turn. I believe that usually, if not invariably, this is a relationship between an individual and a disease and that the respect is not shared by his kinsmen or descendants. Among the diseases recorded by Miss Soule[1] or myself which people respect are *kerker*, a yaws condition, *weth*, also a yaws infection of some kind, *rieny*, convulsions in infants, *gueng*, an abscess, *tanglok*, tubercular abscess, *lih*, hipjoint disease, *kor*, myalgia of the lumbar region (p. 185), and *thiang*, dysentery (pp 187–8). I discuss later totemistic relationships of individuals to totems of female forebears

II

It is essential to an understanding of Nuer totemism that it should be appreciated that Nuer respect the natural species or class of objects because they regard them as being in some manner emblems or representations of Spirit. A European observer may easily be led astray by a Nuer speaking of his totem, as he ordinarily does, as his *kwoth*, but he means no more by this than that the totem in some special way belongs to a spirit which also makes itself known to him concretely in that species. Doubtless, as the spirit is only known in and through the species, spirit and species can never be wholly dissociated, but Nuer quite explicitly distinguish between them. Those who respect species say that it is the spirits of their totems and not the creatures themselves that they call on for aid, that they sacrifice to, and that they dedicate beasts to; and when we speak about the spirit of a totem it must be understood that what is meant is the spirit for which the totem

[1] *Some Nuer Terms in Relation to the Human Body*, a pamphlet published by the American Mission, Nasser, 1931

stands as a material emblem, for when Nuer speak of 'their spirit'
they refer to men and not to the creatures. Hence Nuer speak of
'spirit of lion' or 'spirit of crocodile' and not 'spirit of lions' or
'spirit of crocodiles'. Nuer have explained to me the distinction
between totem and totemic spirit by comparing the relationship
of a man to his totem with that of their leopard-skin priests to
leopards Leopard-skin priests respect leopards, they said, but only
in the sense that they will not kill them: 'there is no spirit (*kwoth*),
they respect (*thek*) only its body (*pwonyde*)'. It is by reference to
the contrasting terms *kwoth*, Spirit, and *pwony*, creature, that
Nuer most clearly indicate the difference between totemic spirit
and totem. Therefore, though totemic spirits are classed as *kuth*
piny, spirits of the below or of the earth, people sometimes went
out of their way to explain to me that it is not the species themselves, the material things one can see, that they pray and sacrifice
to but the spirits associated with them, and to emphasize further
the difference between the species and the spirits they added that
while the species are creatures on the earth the spirits are with
God in the sky. Thus I was told by a man who respects lions '*jale*
lony pwonyde piny, cu kwothde jen a nhial', 'the lion in its body
(as a creature) walks on the earth, while its spirit is in the sky', and
by a man who respects pythons '*nyaal jale piny bang enene, ka*
kwothde, ne fadiet ka ulengdit, te nhial', 'the python just crawls
on the earth so, but its spirit, which is *fadiet* or *ulengdit*, is in the
sky'. The man who respects pythons further said that the python-
spirit is the maternal uncle of the air-spirit *deng*. Moreover, somewhat to my surprise, Nuer spoke to me, or to others in my presence, about totemic creatures, even of their own totems, not only
without deep feeling or high regard but even disparagingly and
as though they were ashamed of them, especially where the totem
was known to have a Dinka origin.

The distinction between totemic species and the spirits figured
in them is further apparent in the common designation of the
totemic spirit by a name different from that by which the natural
species is called. Thus in the quotation I have just given the
speaker says that *nyal*, the python, is on earth while its spirit
which is called *fadiet* or *ulengdit* is in the sky. Similarly a lion is
lony but the lion-spirit is referred to not only as *kwoth luony*,
spirit of lion, but also by its particular names *joo* and *cuar* (Dinka
names for lions); the *cuur* fish-spirit has the name *kwong*; the

spirit of spitting viper (*thatut*) has the name *rol*; and the tree cobra-spirit (*lualdit*) has the name *fajook*. It is clear also in stories of how the ancestor of a lineage was aided by the totem that Nuer are thinking not so much of the animal as such aiding him as of Spirit making itself known to the ancestor in the creature and helping him through it. Nuer further distinguish between totem animal and totemic spirit when the animal harms a man who respects it and he retaliates by harming the animal. It is not the spirit he complains against but the animal, which is here regarded as separate from the spirit and incurring liability simply as a creature. On the other hand, when a totemic spirit seizes one of those to whom it stands in a spiritual relationship and causes him sickness, the sickness is attributed to the spirit and not to the totemic species, a member of which obviously has not seized him. We have also to remember that so far as it can be said that it is thought that a spirit is in a totemic creature it is not thought to be in any particular members of a species but in all of them. It is not a question of *a* spirit being in *a* creature, but the idea of Spirit being associated with a certain creaturely form, a question discussed further in Chapter V.

The words I have translated 'respect' and 'to respect' are *theak* and its verbal form *thek*. As the words are used in other connexions as well as in reference to totems I leave full discussion of their meaning till a later chapter. Here it is sufficient to say that a Nuer shows respect for his totem by refraining from hurting it in any way and above all from eating it, if it is edible; by paying it some courtesy of recognition if he meets it; by formal expression of regret, such as throwing grass on its body, should he find it dead; and by an expression of disapproval, for no more than that seems to be required of him, should someone injure it in his presence. The respect is reciprocal. As we have seen, lions should refrain from killing the cattle of those who respect them, crocodiles should not injure those who respect them, and ostriches should not eat the millet of those who respect them It will be noted that Nuer respect the totem and not the totemic spirit I do not think that the word *thek* can properly be used of Spirit, except so far as it is identified with a totemic or other appearance, for it implies that the object of respect is something knowable to the senses and can therefore be avoided or treated with special concern.

Can any conclusions be reached about the nature of the things which are objects of respect? The totemism of any people involves the selection of certain natural objects to the exclusion of others Nuer totems are certainly an odd assortment· lion, waterbuck, monitor lizard, crocodile, various snakes, tortoise, ostrich, cattle egret, durra-birds, various trees, papyrus, gourd, various fish, bee, red ant, river and stream, cattle with certain markings, monorchids, hide, rafter, and rope; and, if we were to include totemistic objects, parts of beasts and some diseases. Taking them as a whole we may say that there is no marked utilitarian element in their selection. The animals and birds and fish and plants and artifacts which are of most use to Nuer are absent from the list of their totems. The facts of Nuer totemism do not, therefore, support the contention of those who see in totemism chiefly, or even merely, a ritualization of empirical interests [1] Nor in general are Nuer totems such creatures as might be expected, on account of some striking peculiarities, to attract particular attention. On the contrary, those creatures which have excited the mythopoeic imagination of the Nuer and which figure most prominently in their folk-tales do not figure, or figure rarely and insignificantly, among their totems.

It is too broad a question to ask why animals, birds, reptiles, and trees should have become symbols for Nuer of the relation of Spirit to lineages. Any answer would have to be in very general terms because they have been common religious symbols among many different people at many different times We may, however, note that most, though not all, Nuer totems are in a general way highly regarded by all Nuer, and not only by those who respect them, on account of religious associations of one kind or another which have nothing to do with totemism as such. Thus all Nuer have friendly feelings towards all birds and do not harm them because they are—some more than others—symbols of Spirit and loved by God, though Nuer may also be influenced in this matter by their belief that twins are birds, so that all twins respect all birds. Ernst Marno noted nearly a century ago that Nuer will not eat birds[2] and Mr. Jackson, speaking of this avoidance, remarks

[1] e g B Malinowski, *Science, Religion and Reality*, 1926, pp 24 and 43 seq , A R. Radcliffe-Brown, *Fourth Pacific Science Congress*, vol iii, 1929, pp. 295–309 Émile Durkheim protested against such interpretations (*Sociology and Philosophy*, Eng trans by D. Pocock, 1954, p 86)

[2] Ernst Marno, *Reisen im Gebiete des Blauen und Weissen Nil*, 1874, p 349

that 'one explanation put forward for this abstention is that the
bird can fly in the skies and is accordingly in communication
with the Great Spirit'.[1] The *jakok in rol*, the pied crow, a bird
which frequents Nuer homesteads, is especially favoured because
it is the bird of the female spirit *buk*, the mother of *deng*. Nuer
say that 'everyone respects the pied crow', and one sometimes
hears it spoken of as *kuaar*, priest. Nuer can therefore readily
entertain the idea of a bird being the totem of a lineage, being,
that is, an emblem of Spirit conceived of in relation to a lineage.
Also, whilst I would hesitate to say that all Nuer have a high
regard for snakes, it can be said that they do not go out of their
way to harm them, whether they belong to lineages which respect
snakes or not. They leave them in peace unless they are threatened
by them or suddenly afraid of them. All Nuer seem to regard
them as being in some sense manifestations of Spirit, so that, here
again, it appears natural to those who do not respect them that
other people should do so. Some of the more important totems are
trees. To all intents and purposes, and so far as any question of
showing them respect or otherwise is concerned, this means trees
of certain species when they grow on village sites, and no Nuer,
and not only those who respect them as totems, would injure trees
growing near their homesteads. Nuerland is for the most part
treeless savannah country, and trees which give shade, such as
sycamores and to some extent the tamarind, are rare. Nuer have
a feeling that those which give them shade in their sun-baked
homes have grown there by a special dispensation of God Their
being there at all is a manifestation of Spirit, and all the more
so if, as is sometimes the case, they have grown from saplings
or cuttings planted as shrines to spirits. Here again, therefore,
people can easily understand that such trees are regarded by some
lineages as material manifestations of a special relationship of
Spirit to themselves.[2] Rivers and streams also have a general spiritual significance for all Nuer because they are associated with *buk
man deang*, which is the spirit of all rivers It is *kwoth pim*, the
spirit of water. Nuer say that '*yier e kwoth neini dial*', 'rivers are
the spirit (totem) of everybody'. Again, monorchids are for all a

---

[1] H C Jackson, op cit., p. 169.
[2] It may be noted that the Nuer word for tree, *jath* (pl. *jen*), is probably the
same word as the generic term for totem in Dinka, *yath* (pl *yeth*) (P. A Nebel,
Dinka Grammar, 1948, p 170)

sign of spiritual activity, as is also the birth of a calf with *ma cuany* markings.

We may conclude that Nuer totems tend to be creatures and things which for one or other reason easily evoke the idea of Spirit in any Nuer and are hence suitable symbols for Spirit in relation to lineages; and then the image of the symbol may become through association linked with other images, leading to additional totems. The Gaanwar clan have a special connexion with rain, which is a symbol of Spirit in its special relationship to their clan. The *nyuot*-tree is a secondary symbol which, on account of its peculiar appearance and habits, is associated in the Nuer mind with rain. The waterbuck and several species of fish are further symbols linked to the *nyuot*-tree as secondary totems because, we may presume, they also, in their different ways, are associated with water. An interpretation of the totemic relationship is here, then, not to be sought in the nature of the totem itself but in an association it brings to the mind Similarly those who respect bees respect them not because they are bees but because their colour resembles to Nuer eyes the python, and it is probably the same with soldier ants and the tree cobra.

As we have seen, in their totemic relationships it is Spirit rather than the totems in which Nuer are interested. In so far as they are interested in the totems themselves it is not in their intrinsic nature but in their character as symbols through which Spirit manifests itself to human intelligence Consequently, since the totemic attitude is neither derived from, nor primarily directed towards, the things as they are in themselves but the things as representing and manifesting Spirit, Nuer would not be at all surprised at anything being, or becoming, a totem. Anyone may at any time suddenly find himself in a totemistic relationship to some class of objects, and if for one reason or another his descendants trouble to remember and maintain the relationship, then that class becomes the totem of a lineage. Let us consider how Nuer think of totemic relationships coming about

I have had frequent occasion to remark that those who respect a totem are Dinka or of Dinka origin, and our discussion of the whole problem of Nuer totemism is complicated, as was our discussion of the spirits of the air, by the fact that Nuer regard their totems as having for the most part come from the Dinka. I have often heard true Nuer say that when you find that a man respects reptiles and such things as parts of animals and diseases you may be sure that he is a Dinka or had a Dinka mother or grandmother, and I have found this to be so. Hence true Nuer tend to despise many totems, especially reptilian totems, as something Dinka. They say that the *kuth* of Nuer lineages are spirits of the above and not earthly spirits. 'If a true Nuer (*gat dila*) respects (*thek*) a totem (*kwoth piny*) it is because of a maternal link (*cieng mandongni*).' The word *thek* is here used in reference to *kwoth* because it is identified in thought with some hypothetical material appearance which, since it is not specified, cannot be designated. What this statement means is that while true Nuer clans and lineages do not commonly respect things of nature, and especially not things that creep and crawl, an individual may respect them out of regard for a Dinka mother or grandmother. It is supported by the evidence I have recorded, and it may be further noted that those whole clans in Nuerland who respect natural species are generally either of Dinka origin, like the Gaatgankir, or of a peculiar mythological, and therefore possibly foreign, origin, like the Jikul and the Gaanwar. It is also to some extent supported by the common Nuer explanation of a totemic relationship between a lineage and a natural species as having come about through the ancestor of the lineage and a member of the species being born twins. This is a common Dinka explanation of totemic associations[1] Moreover, the names of totemic spirits, such as *joo*, *cuar*, *fadiet*, *ulengdit*, and *fajook*, are Dinka words. Personally, I consider the great majority of lineages found in Nuerland today with totems to be of Dinka origin. The important point, however, is not so much that they are Dinka lineages as that Nuer regard totems as something Dinka. They have nevertheless become fully incorporated into Nuer religious thought.

In spite of what Nuer say about totems being Dinka they also think of those of clans or large lineages as having come down to them from their ancestors of ancient times. They became attached to certain lines of descent so that not all lineages of the same clan necessarily have the same totems They were divided up (*dak*) among the different lines of descent Nuer say that the '*ring kukien*', 'the meats of their sacrifices', spread out along the lines

[1] C G and B Z Seligman, op. cit, pp. 142–51 The Seligmans were writing about the eastern Dinka Dr. R G Lienhardt tells me that the western Dinka have the same belief

of descent. Other totems were added later. 'The spirits of their sacrifices (to which they sacrifice) entered into the generations of descent (*kath*) ' This might happen in various ways, some of which I have described. An animal or plant, or rather Spirit in and through an animal or plant, helps a man in trouble, and so forth. The commonest aetiology is twin-birth of a man and a member of a natural species. Twin-birth is so stock an explanation of totemic affiliations among the Nuer that when asked why a certain lineage respect a certain species they often, if they do not know any story accounting for the association, say at once and without reflection that it must be because of a twin-birth of this kind. It is only when it would be totally unreasonable that a Nuer rejects this as a likely explanation In discussing totemism with some Nuer on one occasion one of them told me that he had heard that there were people who respect fire. When I asked whether this meant that a man and fire had been born together my question was greeted with derision· 'How, now, could a woman carry fire in her womb?'

Strange though it may seem to us, Nuer claim that twin-births of men and animals have taken place not only in ancient times but also in recent generations. They may take place even today and occasion no surprise I had not been long in Nuerland when one morning my Nuer servant Nhial came in some excitement to tell me that a woman of his village, where we were staying, had given birth to a hippopotamus and a male child, both dead It was too late to see what happened, but I was told that the hippopotamus had been placed in a nearby stream and the child, being a twin and therefore in Nuer eyes a sort of bird, had been placed in a tree. In answer to my questions, I was further informed that it was uncertain whether the family would on account of what had happened respect hippopotamuses in future, though had the child lived he and his descendants would certainly have done so The reason given for this particular twin-birth was that the woman's husband had killed several hippopotamuses and they had revenged themselves on him by stamping their likeness on one of the twins (*ca gat cal e rau*). In this case, therefore, one is in doubt whether what was taken to the stream was regarded as a hippopotamus in the full sense or not, for animals can stamp their likenesses on a human foetus; but at least the incident shows us how the totemic mentality of the Nuer inclined them at once to

(84)

perceive the form of a hippopotamus in what we would have regarded merely as a monstrosity, and it enables us to understand better why, since the past is justified in the present, they do not reject as beyond the bounds of possibility the stories of their ancestors having been born twins to animals

The story I have related introduces us to another way in which Nuer think that a totem might enter a family and perhaps in certain circumstances become a totem of its descendants, though I have no evidence of a totemic relationship actually being established in this way. The hippopotamuses caused the child to resemble (cal) themselves I was told that similarly a man who has killed several elephants might beget a child with crooked mouth and nose and thick legs. The whole race of sheep is said to have been acted on in this manner by the koat-tree, because they make a habit of eating its shoots. When a lamb is born its legs are doubled up like the roots of the tree. Women refrain from eating the bulyak or puff-fish, a remarkable creature which when irritated inflates itself like a balloon, because by doing so they might cause their children to be born with abnormally distended bellies. When Nuer see a fish-eagle swoop on to the water and carry away a fish in its claws they sometimes run after it shouting, to cause it to drop its prey, but should a pregnant woman eat a fish dropped by an eagle her child might be born with deformed arms resembling the wings of the eagle or with twisted feet resembling its claws If parents who respect tortoises pass a tortoise without some gesture of recognition their child may be born with tiny eyes like those of a tortoise. Other examples of a foetus being stamped with the likeness of a totem have been cited earlier in reference to some similar human fault in behaviour towards the totem and this would seem to be regarded as the most usual cause of an abnormality of this kind, though Nuer think that a new totemic relationship might start in the same way. I think, both because in most cases it is in an established totemic relationship that a creature is said to stamp its likeness on a foetus and also because it is more in accordance with Nuer ideas about Spirit and also about animals, that we would certainly be right to say that when Nuer speak of creatures acting in this way they are thinking of Spirit doing so in the guise of the creatures. The very fact of the abnormality is evidence of the action of Spirit. Consequently, should a man on account of such an event in his family respect a species of creatures his first act would be to dedicate a beast of his herd to Spirit in the form and of the name of that species. Thus Spirit through its new attachment to whatever the natural species may be becomes in relation to that man and his family a new spirit of the below with its own distinctive material form different from the material forms of other spirits, and with a name derived from the natural species distinguishing it from other spirits with names derived from other species.

There are other ways in which Nuer say that a man may acquire a totemistic relationship to a natural species, though they also say that it is only rarely that the relationship is maintained by his descendants. They have told me that a man may become seized or possessed by a spirit associated with some creature, the seizure or possession being known by sickness and its diagnosis by one or other form of divination, and that he may afterwards respect it. In practice this is only likely to happen when the particular spirit has been the spirit of some forebear of the sick man. He and his relatives may cast their minds back to any such past affiliations when reflecting on what might be the cause of the sickness People acquire totemistic obligations through affinal and maternal links. A man respects his wife's totems, at any rate to the extent of not eating or otherwise harming them shortly before having congress with her and during her pregnancies; and a woman respects her husband's totems. Nuer generally respect their mother's totems, but not always A man said to me, in speaking of a totem of his mother's lineage, 'it is not shared by us, she was married into another lineage' (the speaker's own lineage). Nuer have assured me that a wife's totems will not persist in her husband's line of descent. Her sons' sons may respect them, but this is unlikely unless the spirits of the totems cause them sickness, and then they will generally be forgotten. Consequently, totems, other than those which belong to lineages and go with agnatic descent, enter into families for a generation or two and then go out of them again. But they may return. I once had an interesting discussion with some Nuer about a baby with deformed legs. My informants, who were not related to the child, held that the deformation must have resulted from one of his parents, who should have respected the monitor lizard, having killed or eaten this reptile. They made this deduction from the resemblance they saw between the legs of the child and those of the lizard. When I protested that surely a man would not kill or eat a creature he respects, I was told that 'it may be that a man is a fool and kills his *kwoth* deliberately'. Here we are to understand by *kwoth* a totem deriving from some maternal affiliation and not the totem of the man's own lineage I was also told that it sometimes happens that a man does not know all the classes of objects he ought to respect or is uncertain about them. 'His father was forgetful and did not trouble to dedicate a cow to it (the spirit) or think of it at all, though he did not eat it (the totem). Then the son is forgetful too and one day they forget all about it and have no recollection of it at all.' Nuer also told me that it may happen that a boy is brought up among his mother's people and is not told by them about totems which have come into his father's family from Dinka women. In other words and in our way of speaking, people have totemistic relationships to the totems of persons with whom they have affinal and maternal links and these totemistic relationships are forgotten in course of time by their descendants, who may then be reminded of them by sickness I do not think it could ever happen that a man could be ignorant of the totem of his own lineage, for I have found that children of under six years of age know it; or that a man would deliberately harm it.

Nevertheless, though a spirit associated with a natural species is most likely to seize persons who have some past connexion with it, any striking event, and particularly any sickness or other unfortunate event, might, Nuer think, bring about a totemistic relationship which could persist till it had hardened into a totemic one. The event is evidence of the action of Spirit and the conception of Spirit may become particularized by reference to the specific cause of misfortune in relation to the person or persons who have suffered it. Thus, as we have noted, a man may suffer from a disease and, after recovering from it, respect it. The disease was taken to be a manifestation of Spirit and the man who suffered it afterwards has not only the general relationship everyone has to God but also a particular relationship to God in his refraction as a spirit of the disease.

A totemistic, and potentially totemic, relationship may come about with regard to some class of objects through a man or a member of his family suffering any kind of misfortune. A man was killed by a fishing-spear and his children now respect fishing-spears. Another man was killed by the bite of a snake and his children now respect this species of snake. Mgr. Mlakic records how a Nuer who has a tree for his totem told him that one of his ancestors had died from being pricked by a thorn of that tree Anything may thus become a totem. Mgr. Mlakic also recounts how a Nuer refused to accept a milleme coin the Father offered him because a boy of his family, when playing with a milleme, got it into his ear and died. The family now respect millemes.[1] A youth, a friend of mine in western Nuerland, had recently acquired a respect for speckled vultures. The Nuer consider it a misfortune if a speckled vulture, a hooded vulture, a Goliath heron, a maribou stork, or an egret settles on the crown of a byre or dwelling-hut. '*Theke ke, cike de nyur wi tie*', 'they (the birds) respect them (byres and huts), they ought not to settle on their crowns'. If this happens a goat is sacrificed and the bird is asked why it should settle on a habitation. It is requested to accept the offering and take itself and all badness from the homestead. Nuer say that the bird is *kwoth*, Spirit, but, here again, they do not mean that the bird is in itself Spirit but that it is a form in which Spirit is beholden. Nuer know that the bird is *kwoth* only through its unusual behaviour. The man to whom I have referred went some years ago with a party of men to find a cow which had died in the bush. When they found it, some speckled vultures rose from the carcass and one of them settled on the man's head This caused great consternation because its settling on the man's head showed the presence of Spirit. As soon as the party reached home a goat was sacrificed and left in the bush for the vultures to eat From that time the man respected vultures. One day he told me that the night before he had dreamt of this incident and had early that morning visited a female diviner (*tiet*) to find out whether his dream presaged anything bad for him. She assured him that no harm would come to him as the vulture-spirit had been sacrificed to (*ca kir*) in the first place. If it had not been satisfied it would have caused him sickness long ago. All he need now do, she said, was to cut a piece off a goat's ear and tell the vultures that it was his gift to them. This he had at once done. I do not know of any lineages which have the vulture as their totem, but it became a totem for this man by its action of alighting on his head. Since such an event is regarded by Nuer as a manifestation of Spirit, through the happening there came into being for this man a

[1] Op cit

(88)

vulture-spirit. It must be said, however, that it does not follow that because a thing has caused or presaged a misfortune it will be respected. Thus, to give a single example, I was told that a hippopotamus bit a pregnant woman in the belly. She died, but her child, a male, lived. When I asked whether his descendants respect hippopotamuses I was told 'no, why should they when a hippopotamus killed their grandmother?'. Any number of examples could be cited of persons being killed or injured—by lions, crocodiles, spears, and so on—without a respect relationship being brought about thereby between the cause of the misfortune and the man who suffered it or his descendants. For this to happen it would seem that the event must have extraordinary features. Even then, as the case of the pregnant woman shows, a totemic relationship does not inevitably arise.

However a totemic relationship may be thought to have come about in the first instance, it seems very natural to Nuer that it should typically be a relationship between a lineage and a whole species or class, for they speak of natural species, on analogy with their own social segments, as lineages, so that the relationship between a lineage and a totemic species is for them on the pattern of what they call a *buth* relationship—that is a relationship between collateral lineages with a common ancestor. The animal world is spoken of in terms of the pattern of their social world, in terms of *cieng*, community, and *thok dwiel*, lineage. There is the community of the *jiciengngang*, the growling folk of tooth and claw such as the lion, the leopard, the hyena, the jackal, the wild dog, and the domesticated dog. A lineage of this carnivorous community are the mongooses, which divide into a number of smaller lineages of little animals: the brindled mongooses, the white-tailed mongooses, the serval cats, the civet cats, the genets, &c Another what the Nuer also call *bab*, collectivity or class or kind, are the graminivorous animals: thiang, white-eared cob, gazelle, buffalo, bushbuck, waterbuck, hare, cow, sheep, goat, &c. The *nyarecjok*, the feetless people, are the lineages of snakes. The big and miscellaneous community of the *jiyier* or *ciengbalangni* are the river people, the people who hate to be away from streams and marshes: crocodiles, monitor lizards, the many kinds of fish, the marsh birds (such as herons, darters, shoe-bills, fish-eagles, snake-birds, the mouse-coloured pelican, and the large lineage of geese, duck, and teal), and the Anuak and Balak Dinka peoples, who for the most part are without cattle and are riverain cultivators and fisher-men. The birds are of two main classes. The *gaat kwoth*, the children of God, or the *jiciengkwoth*, the people of the community of God, are such birds as the speckled vulture, the hooded vulture, the white pelican, the pied crow, the black crow, the glossy ibis, the sacred ibis, the crested crane, the goshawk, and the dove. The *jiciengnyadiet*, the community of birds, count as *gaat nyiet*, sisters' sons, to the children of God, and are hence of the category of *gaat nya kwoth*, sons of daughter(s) of God. It includes guineafowl, francolin, finches, swallows, weaver-birds, wagtails, bats, &c. Some birds, as we have seen, belong to the river people Birds of which Nuer think little, such as the guineafowl, the francolin, and some of the marsh birds—the most earth-bound birds—are described by them as being *jaang*, Dinka or of Dinka descent, again on the pattern of their own society. The same idea is expressed by saying that they are *gaat nya dila*, sons of daughter(s) of a person of true or aristocratic descent. *Dil*, in the wide general sense of the word on which the analogy is based, denotes a true Nuer as distinct from someone of Dinka origin, and to say that a lineage are sons of daughters of a *dil* implies that agnatically they are of Dinka origin. The same idea is expressed in a different metaphor by figuring the birds as children of *deng* the air-spirit, for Nuer think of it as a Dinka spirit.

In saying that certain birds are children of God and that others are children of his daughters Nuer are, as I have earlier explained, speaking in poetic metaphors. A bird is not regarded literally as a child of God any more than another bird is regarded literally as a Dinka The metaphor is, however, somewhat more complex than it appears to be at first sight, because, as we shall see, spirits are represented in a similar genealogical configuration, suggesting a symbolic correspondence between the scale of birds and the scale of spirits which fits in with the positions both occupy in space.

III

After some account has been given of the other spirits of the below we will be better placed to view the conception of Spirit as a whole. and the place of totemism in the entire system of Nuer religious thought will then be more clearly seen. Here, only some conclusions are presented, and in a preliminary way.

I discussed in Chapter I Spirit conceived of, in its most comprehensive and transcendental sense, as God, the father and creator in the sky. In Chapter II I discussed the spirits of the air, Spirit conceived of under more particular forms and which falls from above and seizes and enters into men, and through them is associated with political activities. These spirits of the air also sometimes become spirits of lineages. This refraction of Spirit by the social order was even more evident in our discussion in the same chapter of the *colwic* spirits, which are God, or Spirit, in a particular and exclusive relationship to lineage groups. We find the same refraction of Spirit by the social order in the totemic spirits, which are Spirit in a more immanent and material form, beholden in creaturely appearances. Each of the totemic spirits is Spirit in a particular relationship to a lineage, which expresses its relation as an exclusive social group to God in the totemic refraction by respecting the creature which stands as a material symbol of the refraction The imprint of the social order on the conception of Spirit is very evident in the totemic beliefs and observances of the Nuer. And we see in the totemistic spirits the conception of Spirit refracted to the level of the individual, who besides his general relationship to God, which he shares with all men, and his totemic or *colwic* or air-spirit relationship to God in virtue of his membership of a lineage, may as an individual have a special relationship to God as revealed to him in one or more particular modes and forms.[1]

In his account, soon to be published, of Dinka religion Dr. Lienhardt uses the word 'emblems' to denote the species and classes of objects respected by Dinka lineages. The word could appropriately be used in reference to the species and classes which are objects of respect by Nuer lineages, and perhaps more suitably than the word 'totems', for what I have described is certainly not what we are accustomed to think of as totemism. Nuer respect the creatures not for themselves—their relationship to them is only secondary—but because they are symbols. But if the totems are

[1] Much the same conclusion was reached about Dinka totemism by Mr. R T. Johnston He says of the *jok*, totemic or totemistic spirits, of the Bor Dinka that 'to not a few people their *jok* is a Bain Deng, apparently conceived of as either an emanation of Deng Dit, i e. Nhialich himself, or as God in special relation to the individual' (op cit , p 126) The same point is discussed at length, and with much illustrative material, by Dr Lienhardt in his forthcoming book on Dinka religion

symbols or emblems what are they symbols or emblems of? They are not, at least primarily, diacritical signs of social differentiation. Lineages are distinguished by names of ancestors and spear-names and honorific titles and not by totems. Even though the spear-names and honorific titles may sometimes contain a reference to totems, lineages are not thought of, at any rate primarily, as people who respect certain species and classes. Also, many lineages have no totemic affiliations, and those who have them tend to be thought of as at one time not having had them and of having at some point in time and through some event acquired them; and Nuer also tend to think of them as something they got from the Dinka. Further, many lineages have the same totem, and were Nuer to think of the unity of a lineage and its distinction from other lineages in terms of totems we would expect to find that respect for the same totem would be a bar to intermarriage, but it is not so. People with the same totem intermarry if there is no kinship between them. Nor can the totems be adequately described just as symbols of Spirit Crocodiles, bees, and ants are not symbols of Spirit to people who do not respect them—they kill and eat crocodiles, they eat honey, and they destroy the ants without qualms. Totems are therefore to be described as symbols of particular relationships rather than of Spirit; relationships, that is, between lineages, or it may be families or individuals, and God figured by the symbols in relation to those lineages, families, or individuals.

It is not that the members of a group see themselves as a group through a totemic class of objects which are then further conceptualized collectively as a spirit of the class, but rather that the conception of Spirit, which is in itself quite independent of the social structure, is broken up along the lines of segmentation within the structure. It is not that the members of a group see themselves as a group through a totemic relationship to millemes which are then conceptualized as a spirit of millemes, but rather that the conception of Spirit as manifested in the death of a child from a milleme getting in his ear is given a social dimension in accordance with the lineage and kinship principles of the Nuer. The people concerned did not first think that they had a special relationship to millemes, on account of something intrinsic to these coins, which they expressed in the notion of Spirit. They had first the conception of Spirit and it was a quite fortuitous event which, interpreted in the light of that conception, brought about a religious connexion between men and millemes.

Consequently, we are once more faced with the problem of the one and the many Just as it can be said that a man is sacrificing to one of the air-spirits and not to another, or to one *colwic* spirit and not to another, but it cannot be said that he is sacrificing to a spirit of the air, or to a *colwic* spirit, and not to God, so it can be said, for example, that a man is sacrificing to lion-spirit and not to crocodile-spirit, but it cannot be said that he is sacrificing to lion-spirit and not to God. Nuer do not conceive of lion-spirit as something separate from God but only as separate from other and like refractions in which God is figured to groups as their patrons Lion-spirit is thought of as Spirit in a tutelary relationship to a particular social group It and God are the same thing differently regarded.

It will be observed, however, that the conception of Spirit is here more strictly limited and bound to persons and things than is the case with the spirits of the air, and even, with regard to things, of the *colwic* spirits. The totemic and totemistic spirits are recognized only within the range of the lineages or persons who respect the totems, and they are tied to the totems. In these respects they are unlike the air-spirits. The air-spirits are recognized by all and, though they are thought to have established direct relations only with certain persons and groups, they may enter into relations with any persons and groups. They are here, there, and everywhere. And they are not in anything in the sense that the totemic spirits are in the totems. Nuer themselves perceive this difference and make this evaluation. It is because the spirits of the air are superior that they are in the category 'of the above' and it is because the totemic spirits are inferior that they are in the category 'of the below'. That they place the totemic spirits on a lower plane of religious thought is shown also in their position in the genealogical representation of Spirit, to be discussed in the next chapter, and in two other ways I mention here. Firstly, it is shown in the marked tendency we have noted to look upon, we may even say to look down upon, totemic observances as something Dinka, and in the corresponding condescension, almost contempt, sometimes expressed for the totemic creatures Secondly, it is, I think, shown in the fact that though totemic spirits may *kap*, seize, members of lineages which respect their species and make them sick, or Spirit may seize men and make them sick through objects which then become on this account totems representing spiritual refractions, the totemic spirits do not, to my knowledge, *gwang*, inspire, men. Inspiration comes from above in the divine hypostases, the spirits of the air, or, less commonly, in the *colwic* spirits, and not from the totemic spirits, which have a fixed external relationship to members of lineages, visibly represented in the relationship of their members to the creaturely species. Consequently one does not find prophets who are the mouthpieces of totemic spirits, only men who have, in a rather vague way, what we may call totemic familiars, which I discuss in the next section.

We are faced also with a new problem, the relation of Spirit to things, the problem of religious symbolism. I discuss this in Chapter V, but it may be noted here that, as I have observed, the spiritual significance of totems is not intrinsic. They are thought of by Nuer as having acquired spiritual significance through events which they have interpreted as divine interventions for better or for worse in human affairs. There is nothing intrinsically spiritual about monitor lizards or rafters. Were it so, all Nuer would respect them They became totems for certain lineages because Spirit aided men through a lizard and destroyed men on account of rafters. The relation of Spirit to things derives therefore from its relation to men. The problem of religious symbolism and the problem of the one and the many are two sides to a triadic relationship of Spirit to men through things.

IV

There are a number of other sorts of spirits classed by Nuer with the totemic and totemistic spirits in the category of *kuth piny*, spirits of the below or of the earth. I discuss them briefly because for the most part Nuer themselves attach little importance to them and regard them as being something of almost a different order from Spirit in other forms.[1] However, were I to leave them out of my account altogether I would risk impeachment for a selection of the facts or the suppression of some of them. And this would be fair, for if one is to define the meaning of a word or

[1] Some further information about them is to be found in my article 'The Nuer. Tribe and Clan', *Sudan Notes and Records*, 1935, pp 68 seq.

a conception one has at least to consider all the situations in which it appears in a people's speech or thought.

We have observed that a totemic or totemistic spirit sometimes gives a man certain powers over the totemic species The rites these people perform might be classed, according to some definitions of the term, as magic, but in the Nuer classification, which is the one we have to follow if we are to delineate their thought and not our own, we are still concerned with a relationship between man and *kwoth*. Nevertheless, with diviners, leeches, owners of nature sprites, and owners of fetishes we are on the periphery of the conception of Spirit, where it becomes more and more embedded in the psychical and material.

Those who practice various forms of divination and leechcraft are known, as in other Nilotic languages, as *tiet*. Their powers come from some minor spirit, which is not, as I understood the Nuer, regarded as entering into and possessing a *tiet*, as spirits of the air and *colwic* possess men, but as having an external relationship to him. We may speak of Spirit so conceived of in relation to the exercise of his special powers as his familiar. If he did not have this familiar he would not be able to perform his functions, which are thought of as petty revelations of Spirit acting in an indirect manner through some traditional device.

The familiar spirits of these specialists may be totemic spirits, such as those of the tree cobra or the lion, but there may be no way of referring to them except in relation to the functions of the specialists, as the spirit of this or that kind of specialist Nevertheless, they are always thought of on the pattern of the totemic and totemistic spirits, so that there is really little difference, except in manner of speech, beween any *tiet* and such a person as performs rites to control crocodiles or durra-birds. Indeed, anyone who is credited with special powers over nature might be described as a *tiet*, which has the general sense of a person with such powers, a cunning man, so that, for example, the fact that a man has been able to acquire a wife with an unusually small payment of cattle suggests to Nuer the likelihood of his being a *tiet* However, the word is generally used only for the skills I am about to mention, and a person with other but similar powers derived from a totemic or totemistic relationship who is not so called is spoken of as *gwan kwoth*, owner of a spirit (of whatever it may be). In either case, the familiar may be inherited from father to son

_ The best-known sort of *tiet* is the *tiet gwent*. He divines by throwing mussel shells on the convex surface of a gourd and studying the way they fall By this means he answers such questions as whether a man will find a lost cow, have success on a journey, or slay a victim in a blood-feud, and whether, if he is on a journey, all at home is well. While engaged in throwing the shells he speaks to his familiar spirit, which is associated with the gourd, perhaps being regarded as in it during the seance Another sort of specialist of this order is the *tiet dala* I was told that some of his functions are to aid a man to recover cattle by performing a rite to make the herdsmen inattentive, to aid a man to recover a runaway wife, to win female favours, to exact vengeance in blood-feud, and to avoid enemy spears in fighting Another sort is the *tiet me ngwet*. She—all I heard of were women —is a leech who removes objects from the bodies of sick persons which have been put there by a *peth*, a witch or possessor of the evil eye. Another sort is the *tiet me monye dholi*, a leech who massages constipated children with his spittle. Other sorts of *tiet* treat barren women, impotent men, and sick calves; and there may be yet others with minor skills.

Nuer do not highly regard these people and have small confidence in them. They are little men and women who perform their petty rites for the benefit of their immediate neighbours and for inconsiderable rewards. They never achieve social prominence, far less tribal renown, and their possession of special powers is not likely to be known outside their own village or its immediate vicinity. But, apart from this, they are regarded as being in themselves something very humble and of quite a different class and order from the prophets, who, whether they achieve great renown or not, are inspired by spirits of the above, whereas these diviners and leeches and other specialists of the same order merely have little spirits of the below as familiars. Were this not to be made clear there would be a danger that Nuer religious ideas and practices might be viewed in false perspective, for they are not all of the same significance for Nuer. Some are important and some are unimportant, and they are of different kinds and of different orders. It was because this was not appreciated by British administrators that the role and nature of the prophets was very largely misunderstood and their treatment of them ill-considered (pp. 303–7). Nuer do not regard all manifestations of Spirit as of equal value, nor do they accept all claims to spiritual guidance at their face value.

Nuer also class among the *kuth piny*, the tellurian spirits, certain nature sprites they call *bieli*, and also certain fetishes or spirits of 'medicines'. I give only such a brief and condensed account of these notions as is sufficient to indicate their nature. It is unnecessary to discuss them at length for Nuer regard them, like the practices of their diviners and leeches, as so low a manifestation of Spirit as to be almost something of a different kind.

Nevertheless, here again, some reference to them must be made because they are spoken of as *kuth*, spirits. Moreover, the nature sprites are spoken about, and in some respects are treated, as having some resemblance to the spirits of the air, though much inferior to them, being associated with things, material objects in which they are manifested and to which they are in a sense bound; although it must be emphasized that it is not the things themselves which are regarded as Spirit. This is clear from the fact that the spirits are thought to become attached to, or detached from, them. Their presence in objects and processes is known by luminosity or phosphorescence. We see here again the implicit metaphor, which runs through Nuer religion, of light and dark, associated with sky and earth; and the word *biel* is probably the same as that meaning 'colour', which for Nuer is not an absolute abstraction but a relationship of light and dark shades.

One of these sprites is the *biel pam*, the meteorite-sprite, also called *biel pauka*, ash-sprite. It is, I believe, the same as that called *biel nhial*, sky-sprite, and *biel mac*, fire-sprite. Like all the nature sprites, it can be purchased from its owner (*gwan bila*)—for a goat or two in the first place I was told that he does not hand over the meteorite itself but a small gourd containing ashes of cattle-dung —hence the name ash-sprite. The purchaser hangs this from the porch of his byre and sacrifices a goat to the sprite, telling it that he will one day dedicate a cow to it and asking it to fall. The gourd of ashes remains in the byre till a meteorite falls. When it does so, the man anoints it with butter and makes a sacrifice, and he then lays it on the floor at the back of his hut. One day '*be macde dop wi pam, be cu pet*', 'it (the sprite) lights its fire on the surface of the meteorite, and then it burns (shines)'. When the man sees this light he sacrifices a goat and makes beer and gives a feast at which the assembled people clap their hands and sing hymns to the sprite in the manner I have described when speaking of the spirits of the air. He must then give the man from whom he purchased the sprite some cattle to get him to invoke it, asking it to assist the purchaser and not to harm his family, for spirits of this kind are regarded as dangerous for the families of their possessors. They may protect their owners and bring them good fortune, but they are also liable to turn on members of their families and kin if they are not frequently offered gifts. The new owner now hangs the meteorite in a gourd in his hut and hangs also near it offerings of butter, ashes, and tobacco in other gourds.

Similar sprites are the *bieli yier*, river-sprites. They are found, under the name *biel roa*, hippopotamus-sprite, in some hippopotamuses, and also in certain fish, *rec car*, *ludh* (lung-fish), *lek*, and *ril*.[1] Nuer declare that '*cike mat*'. 'they have congregated'. in certain hippopotamuses. It is said that if a man kills one of these animals he will see a light on its head, and that afterwards the sprite will seize him. He breaks the skull of the animal with an axe and takes out the brains and boils them, rubs a little of the boiled brains on his forehead and right arm, and eats the rest of them. Shortly afterwards he falls sick, and if his surmise that it is the sprite which has made him sick is confirmed by a prophet, or by a possessor of this or another kind of sprite, a hand-clapping and hymn-singing ceremony is held, in the course of which the sick man becomes dissociated and the sprite speaks through his lips, saying what it is and what it wants A sacrifice is then made and the bones and chyme of the victim are placed near the entrance to the man's hut and a mound of ashes is piled over them, forming a shrine (*yik bila*), into the top of which a branch of the *nyuot*-tree is stuck. The sprite then leaves the man, but he continues to pay it attention from time to time, dedicating an animal to it and making it offerings, and his children may continue to do so after his death. Other *bieh* are the *biel jiath*, tree-sprite, *biel real*, termite mound-sprite, and what is sometimes called *kwoth juaini*, spirit of grasses, which manifests itself in a will-o'-the-wisp coming from rotting swamp vegetation and is perhaps the same as *kwoth doar*, spirit of the bush. Dr. Howell speaks also of a *biel rir*, cobra-sprite, and a *biel loi*, cattle peg-sprite, connected with

---

[1] For identifications of some of the fish mentioned in this chapter see Sabet Girgis, 'A List of Common Fish of the Upper Nile with their Shilluk, Dinka, and Nuer Names', *Sudan Notes and Records*, 1948, pp 122–5

the fertility of cows.[1] These various sprites seem to have much the same character as that of the meteorite-sprite and to be treated in a similar way.

A collection of hymns sung to nature sprites might tell us much more than I have recorded about them, but I took down only one specimen,[2] which begins·

> Biel, you love a cow in the heavens,
> Son of the master of deng, you love a cow in the heavens,
> Say if you want a brown cow,
> Say if you want a white cow,
> The cow of biel deang is a cow which will calve.

I quote these lines because, whatever their precise meaning may be, if they have one, they bear the unmistakable imprint of Dinka influence and therefore support the conclusion I reached on other grounds, mainly on the fact that these sprites are little heard of in eastern Nuerland, that the bieli have been taken over by the Nuer from their Dinka neighbours. The sprite is represented as the son of the Dinka spirit deng and the word I have translated, following Dr. Lienhardt's usage, 'master' in the second line is bany, which must in this context be a Dinka word.

Likewise, and even more surely, the fetishes, with which the bieli are sometimes classed, may be considered to be of foreign origin and to have been introduced fairly recently into Nuerland. At the time I was living there they were rarely found among the most easterly tribes and those who possessed them there had journeyed to the west of the Nile to purchase them. All Nuer whom I consulted were unanimous that the fetishes are foreign and new, those of the Lou tribe saying that they first began to hear of them in the time of the initiation period of the Dangunga age-set, roughly some 50 years ago The Nuer got them from the Dinka, but it is highly probable that the Dinka first got them from the Sudanic so-called Jur peoples (Beli, Sofi, Gberi, Mittu, and Lori).[3] The Nuer have tried, not entirely successfully, to assimilate

---

[1] P. P. Howell, 'Some Observations on "Earthly Spirits" among the Nuer', Man, 1953

[2] Others have been recorded by Father Crazzolara, op cit., p. 146, and Dr Howell, ibid.

[3] The conclusion that they come from the Jur is based partly on what Nuer say and partly on a number of ethnological considerations arising out of my earlier research—much still unpublished—among the Jur and neighbouring peoples. It gains support from a note by Capt V. H Fergusson ("'Mattiang Goh"

these Sudanic medicines, which represent something quite alien to their traditional way of thinking, to their conception of Spirit.

The Nuer word for what I have called fetishes is *kulangni*, and they often use this plural form even when they are speaking of a particular fetish. They are what the Nuer call *wal*, a word which means in its widest sense 'plants' but in a special sense, as here, what are usually spoken of as 'medicines' in writings on African peoples—magical substances. The fetishes are so called because they are pieces of wood, though Nuer distinguish them from ordinary magical substances by calling them 'medicines which talk'. By this they mean that the spirits in them talk, because, here again, Nuer can conceive of the spirits as separate from the material substances in which they have their abode.[1] What has been said earlier about air-spirits and totemic spirits must be said also about nature sprites and fetishes The same spirit is in a number of different luminescences or bundles of wood.

Like the nature sprites these fetishes bear some resemblance, especially in the manner by which men communicate with them, to the spirits of the air. Nuer have tried to assimilate them to an earlier model of Spirit, and this is indicated metaphorically by calling both types of spirits *gaatnyadeang*, children of daughter(s) of *deng*, a Nuer way of saying both that they are Dinka and that they are spirits of a very inferior order. There are quite a number of fetishes. *mathiang, ngo, macar, darguk, mabor, malual, maluil, maluth, goucien*, and others.[2] The names of several of those I have mentioned are colour-names the white one, the black one, the brown one, &c.

Fetishes are amoral in their action. They are acquired in the first instance by purchase, though they may later be inherited,

Witchcraft', *Sudan Notes and Records*, 1923, pp 112–14) in which he says that an Agar Dinka first got this kind of medicine from the Jur about the year 1902 Writing in 1923 he says 'To-day it is universally used throughout the entire Eastern and Rumbek District and many Dinka are enriching themselves by introducing it into the Nuer Country '

[1] Capt Fergusson (ibid , p 112) also notes that the substance is 'merely a visible sign' of Spirit.

[2] Father Crazzolara (op cit . p. 136) divides them into the *kulang* type, which speak through men, and the *gah* type, chthonic beings which speak from the earth Dr Howell (op cit) makes the same division, though he would agree with me that '*kulangni*' can be, and commonly is, used to cover both I am ready to accept a formal division into these two types but I cannot agree with Dr. Howell's opinion that the *kulang* type is of Nuer, and the *gah* type of Dinka, origin. I am fully convinced that both are of foreign origin

for private ends and personal aggrandizement. They are highly dangerous, not only to those who are at enmity with their owners, but also to their owners' families, kin, and neighbours if they do not receive sufficient attention. When they seize people death follows rapidly on the first symptoms, which are said to be generally violent pains in the abdomen sometimes combined with blood in the faeces, unless steps are at once taken to appease them and, in the case of enemies, their owners also. Therefore a *gwan kulangni*, an owner of a fetish, whom I shall speak of as a wizard,[1] is much feared by those with whom he disputes and by those around him. Some wizards ape prophets by growing little beards and they sometimes thread beads on the hairs and can be identified by this mark.

I have only known one of these wizards, a man called Bul in Lou tribal country. I was living in his village, Kurmayom on the Sobat river, when he returned home with a fetish he had acquired on a visit to western Nuerland, it was said from the Jur people. The whole village was in a state of alarm, so much so that, finding my previously friendly relations with the villagers severed, I thought it best to leave it. A goat was sacrificed on his arrival and I was told that offerings of porridge, milk, and tobacco would have been placed on the ground near the fetish, which is said to 'eat' (*cam*) the 'souls' of these things (*tiethdien*), its owner later consuming their substance. Though everyone was nervous and anxious about what might happen, I was told on this and on other occasions that a man who has acquired a fetish may be welcomed in his village, its people feeling that, if it is placated, it may be a protection for them and a useful weapon against outsiders, and one hears men of the village speaking of '*waldan*', 'our fetish'; but none the less my impression was that they would much rather be without it.

A wizard uses his fetish to avenge what he regards as injuries (others may not regard them as such), to obtain cattle which he considers to be owing to him (others may not think so), and in general to make himself a person of importance. Nuer told me that European administration has made it easier for men to acquire and exercise these powers. They said that when fetishes

[1] They have a resemblance to the *ba'al ōb*, 'wizards that peep and mutter', of the Old Testament, the *ob* being a familiar spirit which seemed to speak either from beneath the ground or out of the stomach of the diviner, and to the Greek daemon (W Robertson Smith, *The Prophets of Israel*, 1895 ed , pp 202 and 421)

first appeared in Nuerland their owners ran the risk of being killed by avengers if it was thought that they had been responsible for people's deaths, and that therefore a man belonging to a numerically weak community would not own a fetish. It is some-times known that a wizard has caused a man's death by his falling sick after a dispute with him. If, however, a man falls sick and only suspects that his sickness may be due to a fetish he confirms whether this is so by getting a diviner to reveal the cause, or he may summon a friendly wizard to determine it, and if it prove to be a fetish, which fetish. I have not seen this operation but I was told that the friendly wizard shakes a gourd-rattle while the people rock their bodies, clap their hands, and sing hymns to the fetish till the sick man enters into a dissociated state. The wizard then questions the spirit in the sick man and it reveals to him its name. The wizard also questions his own fetish-spirit, which is in the rattle during the seance and answers by grunts his questions about the sickness, such as what sacrifice is required and whether the patient will recover if it is made The sickness may be caused by the fetish of a kinsman which wants attention, or it may be due to some wizard having pointed his *wal* in the sick man's direction to kill him If the name of a fetish is not revealed by these procedures it is thought that the sickness must be due to some other cause and not to a fetish at all. If the responsible agent is found to be the fetish of a kinsman the sick man's family placate it by dedicating a beast to it and by sacrificing to it—'they send them (the *kulangni*) back (to where they came from) with a "cow"'. A little of the boiled meat of the sacrifice is minced and thrown as an offering to the spirit to the four points of the com-pass The rest is divided between the wizard and the people of the home. If it is the fetish of an enemy, sacrifice is made, I believe to the fetish of the wizard who has conducted the seance, and after-wards he goes to the enemy wizard and asks him to desist. I was told that the enemy wizard may either deny responsibility or give some reason why he has pointed his fetish at the man who has fallen sick and promise that he will call it off if his wrong is set right. Should his victim die he must sacrifice a sheep or a goat, a rite known as *laka wangkien*, the washing of their (the fetish's) eye, and said to be equivalent to the rite of incising the arm of a homicide.

When a wizard dies his fetish is likely to be put aside, but if so, it is expected that before long the spirit will seize a member of his family or kin, causing him sickness, and announce through his lips that it is offended at neglect. They then give it offerings of food and tobacco, and when the sick man has recovered he respects (*thek*) the fetish, as its previous owner did when he possessed it, and makes it offerings from time to time. Or a son, brother, or wife may just take over the dead man's fetish without it first causing sickness, but they are not likely to do this if they are young Young people prefer to be free from such ambiguous encumbrances.

What I have recorded about these fetishes is no more than hearsay It is possible, nevertheless, to reach some general conclusions about them and about the Nuer attitude towards them. It is easy to observe that Nuer feelings in the matter are either hostile or ambivalent. They fear and dislike the fetishes and are afraid even of those of their kin, perhaps most afraid of those, and they seem to be confused and bewildered about the whole question of fetishes. This is understandable in that here is something that has entered into Nuerland with the reputation of being mobile and of having lethal powers, attributes which the Nuer can only think of in terms of their own culture as Spirit in some form or other, and yet it is used for private ends that they regard with disfavour sufficient to consider that homicide caused by it requires vengeance. Those men with whom I was best acquainted among the eastern Nuer spoke harshly against these fetishes and would gladly have seen the end of them. I do not myself know the circumstances in western Nuerland, but Father Crazzolara says that there is much hostility to them there also, and also great confusion concerning them, for new fetishes frequently appear, they become well known in one district and are unknown in others, and they wax and wane in popularity [1] We would doubtless be right in seeking for an explanation of the anxiety Nuer express lest their fetishes may turn on themselves and of their emphasis on the almost insatiable greed of fetishes for offerings, which are moreover of the lowest kind (such as porridge) and presented to them in the most materialistic way, in their perception that spiritual powers are being used for selfish ends. It would not be going beyond Nuer feelings on the matter to speak of their fetishes as evil spirits.

[1] Op cit, pp 133 seq

Indeed, the fetishes seem only to have been placed in the category of Spirit by the logical necessity of assimilating the powers attributed to them to some model the Nuer already possessed. They are also of the category of *wal*, medicines, which sharply differentiates them from Spirit proper, but since they can reveal their wants and wishes in speech, move about, and kill people, they seem to Nuer to fall between the two categories. It is to be remarked that the *kulangni* and the *bieli*, which are closer to totemic representations of Spirit, are generally referred to by these names and not, like the totemic spirits, as *kuth*, as though by distinction of name they were being marked off from the other spirits. It should be stressed also, in this connexion, that the fetishes, and to some extent the nature sprites, are spoken of in the plural, as when we speak of angels, devils, goblins, and fairies, showing that they are conceived of as having less individuality than other spirits.

It remains only to say a few words about medicines which do not talk, the ordinary *wal*, magical substances which have an efficacy in themselves and do not derive their power from Spirit. Coming to the Nuer from Zandeland, where everyone is a magician and medicines are legion and in daily use, I was at once struck by their negligible quantity and importance in Nuerland, and further experience confirmed my first impression. I mention them chiefly for the reason that their rarity and unimportance are highly indicative of the orientation of Nuer thought, which is always towards Spirit.

In speaking of Nuer magic we are faced with the same historical problem that I have mentioned earlier, for all Nuer with whom I have spoken on the subject have said that medicines were almost entirely lacking—only a few are thought to be old—in the days of their fathers and that most of the few medicines they now possess have been taken over from neighbouring peoples. My own view is that ethnological evidences support their statements, but the point that is important for us here is rather that Nuer regard medicines as something foreign and strange. They think easily in terms of Spirit but not in terms of medicines, the idea of which as it obtains among their Sudanic neighbours they seem scarcely able to grasp.

Nuer medicines of today are mostly of the nature of talismans for fortune—in hunting, fishing, courting, and travelling. I did not find that Nuer had much faith in them. Medicines are also used, sometimes as infusions, to protect a person from, or cure him of, sickness brought about by breach of an interdiction. There are also medicines, or people say there are, against the evil eye, monorchids, children conceived by suckling mothers, and fetishes. Nuer also have a few simples for treating common ailments, such as constipation, throat and lung complaints, fevers, and swellings, and for treating sick cattle. These medicines are thought to be efficacious only in very small matters or as secondary to the performance of a religious rite. No *wal* is of any use, at any rate by itself, as protection against the consequences of a serious breach of an interdiction or in any violent sickness Only prayer and sacrifice are then of avail; and this holds, Nuer who know anything about them think, for European medicines—quinine, for example, as well as for their own.

CHAPTER IV

SPIRIT AND THE SOCIAL ORDER

IT is evident from what has been said in earlier chapters that Nuer have a number of quite different spiritual conceptions It is no less evident, on the other hand, that we are dealing with a single conception, for all the spirits are *kwoth*. This problem of unity in diversity confronts students of the religions of many peoples

The great variety of meanings attached to the word *kwoth* in different contexts and the manner in which Nuer pass, even in the same ceremony, from one to another may bewilder us Nuer are not confused, because the difficulties which perplex us do not arise on the level of experience but only when an attempt is made to analyse and systematize Nuer religious thought. Nuer themselves do not feel the need to do this. Indeed, I myself never experienced when living with the Nuer and thinking in their words and categories any difficulty commensurate with that which confronts me now when I have to translate and interpret them. I suppose I moved from representation to representation, and backwards and forwards between the general and particular, much as Nuer do and without feeling that there was any lack of co-ordination in my thoughts or that any special effort to understand was required It is when one tries to relate Nuer religious conceptions to one another by abstract analysis that the difficulties arise.

We have seen that Nuer use the word *kwoth* either in the sense of God (as defined in Chapter I) or in the sense of one or other spirit of the above or of the below (as defined in Chapters II and III) When Nuer pray to God, though often looking to the sky as they do so, they usually address him simply as *kwoth*, Spirit, the 'who is in the sky' being understood or expressed in gesture On the other hand, the word may be used for some particular spirit —an air-spirit, a totemic spirit, and so forth—without its being indicated by name, it being understood in the context that this particular spirit is referred to. Thus Nuer may say, for example when speaking of the spirit of lion in reference to a certain lineage, '*e kwothdien*', 'it is their spirit'. They also speak of a *gwan kwoth*, possessor of a spirit, and of a *yang kwoth*, a spirit's cow, without

specifying which spirit they have in mind. Those who are aware
of the circumstances will know which particular spirit is being
referred to. Those who are not aware of them will only know that
the man possesses one or other spirit and that the cow belongs to
one or other spirit, without knowing which one.

Since God is *kwoth* in the sense of all Spirit and the oneness of
Spirit, the other spirits, whilst distinct with regard to one another,
are all, being also *kwoth*, thought of as being of the same nature
as God. Each of them, that is to say, is God regarded in a particular way, and it may help us if we think of the particular spirits as
figures or representations or refractions of God in relation to particular activities, events, persons, and groups.

That the diverse spiritual figures of Nuer thought are to be
regarded as social refractions of the idea of God will be understood
better if some examples are given of the problem in action. The
ceremony I am about to describe concerned a *nin diet*, a delayed
homicide. When a man has been wounded and recovers but dies
some months, or even years, later his death may be attributed to
the wound he received and compensation for homicide exacted.
A blood-feud is unlikely to break out in these circumstances, for
the killing may generally be regarded as accidental and, in any
case, a long period of time has elapsed between the act and its
consequence; and fewer, some twenty, head of cattle are demanded
than for a straight killing, though the number seems to vary in
different parts of Nuerland and is probably everywhere reached
by negotiation between the parties, both of whom are anxious to
reach a settlement as soon as possible. In the ceremony I witnessed,
which took place in western Nuerland, the first and final rites of
an ordinary homicide were combined, the slayer being cleansed of
the blood and peace between the parties being made at the same
time, and it took place after only some of the cattle had been paid

It was held because a man of the Jikul clan had wounded a man
of the Lual lineage with a fishing-spear some years before, and he
had just died The fact that he had been wounded by a fishing-
spear was important because among the western Nuer less compensation is paid for a killing by fishing-spear or club than for a
killing by fighting-spear, for it is less likely to have been premeditated. Apart from the slayer himself, there were no Jikul present
at the ceremony, which on their side was conducted by their
traditional allies the Ngwol lineage and in a Ngwol village. The

absence of Jikul and the holding of the ceremony in a village of a
third party made it easier for the Lual to be conciliatory.

After some drinking of beer, a sure sign that a settlement was
certain, the people sat in the sun to watch proceedings. The heat
was so intense that from time to time boys were told to place fresh
cattle-dung on the ground so that those delivering addresses could
stand in it now and again to cool their feet One of them inter-
rupted his narration to ask God to send a shower of rain to cool
him, and the downpour which closed the proceedings was regarded
as an answer to his request. The ceremony began with the castration of the young bull to be sacrificed. A Ngwol man then drove a
stake into the centre of the kraal and tethered the ox to it, and
many of the men present threw ashes over its back—a rite I discuss
later. Then lengthy invocations, taking over three hours to deliver,
were spoken by a Lual man, a Ngwol man, and a leopard-skin
priest of the Keunyang lineage, the dominant lineage of the area
in which all these lineages have their villages. I give only the gist
of what they said because most of it little concerns the question we
are considering

Each speaker began his address by calling out his clan spear-
name. He delivered his address walking up and down the kraal
brandishing his spear. Most of what was said was addressed to the
audience, who entered into lengthy arguments with the speakers
about the matter in hand, besides carrying on conversation among
themselves. But in the midst of their harangues the speakers frequently addressed *kwoth* by one or other title and explained to
Spirit so addressed the circumstances which had brought the
people together.

The Lual representative, who made the first speech, besides
addressing *kwoth*, Spirit, and *kwoth a nhial*, Spirit who is in the
sky, called on '*kwoth wicda, kwoth ngoapna*', 'spirit of our home
or community (literally, cattle camp), spirit of our fig-tree', the
fig-tree being the totem of his lineage. He began with a long
account of the history of the lineage of the man responsible for
the death with interminable references to past disputes, threatening that if ever the Jikul or the Ngwol fought his people again the
Lual would exterminate them, to all the events which led up to
the quarrel in which the dead man had been wounded, and to
cattle which had been paid or promised in compensation for the
homicide and the further cattle which were being demanded.

Among his observations he accused the Ngwol of having buried a living ox with some beads and a spear to kill the Lual, and this provoked a violent argument in which the Ngwol part of the audience retorted that the Lual had buried a dog alive in a byre to kill them (I do not know whether such practices ever really occur).

The Ngwol representative then delivered a rambling address He often mentioned *kwoth* in it, though not, so far as I heard, with any particular specifications. His chief point was that the Jikul were paying compensation in cattle for the dead man and that if the Lual reopened the quarrel it would be to their disadvantage, the Jikul being fully able to look after themselves if it came to fighting again. He then, from the Jikul angle, repeated the whole history of the affair, a recapitulation which stirred up involved controversy with the Lual men present. In these invocations grievances, both real and imagined, are made public, not with the purpose of complicating the issue or inflaming passions, but because it is the rule of such gatherings that everything a man has in his heart against others must be revealed and no bitterness kept secret.

Finally, the leopard-skin priest, whose function is to cleanse a killer and to perform rites to terminate a blood-feud, rose and addressed the assembly. In his invocation he frequently, in addition to speaking to *kwoth* and *kwoth a nhial*, called on '*kwoth riengda*', a phrase which literally means 'spirit of our flesh' and which refers to the spiritual source of sacerdotal power. He told the slayer that as some of the cattle had already been paid and the remainder were about to be paid he might go abroad without fear of vengeance. He told the kinsmen of the dead man that if they started a feud their spears would miss their mark and that they would do well to take the cattle and settle the affair for ever He warned the kinsmen of the slayer not to try and hide their cattle, that is, send them secretly to the kraals of distant kinsmen and then say that they had not the wherewithal to meet their obligations He, also, recapitulated the whole history of the quarrel, from the point of view of an impartial onlooker and mediator.

At the end of his address he speared the ox and those present rushed in, as is the custom on this occasion, to obtain what they could of the carcass, hacking and slicing, waving their spears, and shouting. It was a scene of great confusion. When things had quietened down the leopard-skin priest cut off some of the hair of the head of the man who had occasioned the death: 'the blood which entered into his body is purged (*riem me ce wa pwonyde ba woc*), other hairs will grow (*bi miem ti okien dony*), the blood is finished (*ce riem thuk*)'.

The ceremony I have described is typical in form of Nuer religious ceremonies. What I want here to draw attention to in it are the different titles mentioned in the invocations: *kwoth*, Spirit, without further designation, *kwoth a nhial*, Spirit who is in the sky, *kwoth wic(da)*, spirit of the home, *kwoth ngoap(na)*, spirit of the fig-tree, and *kwoth rieng(da)*, spirit of the flesh (the virtue of the leopard-skin priests), and there may have been others which I did not hear. Besides these titles such expressions as *gwandong*, grandfather, and *kwoth gwara*, spirit of our fathers, were used. At other ceremonies at which people of different families and lineages from those concerned in this particular ceremony have been represented I have heard references in invocations to a variety of other spirits—totemic spirits, *colwic* spirits, and spirits of the air. How are we to interpret Nuer thought about the nature of Spirit as it is expressed in such ceremonies as the one I have described?

In this particular ceremony several groups were opposed to each other, and the leopard-skin priest was acting in his priestly capacity as mediator between them and to conclude a settlement by sacrifice. The persons who made the invocations therefore appealed to, or spoke about, God not only as God but also as God in his special relation to the groups they represented, and in the case of the leopard-skin priest to God in his special relation to the priestly function as well as to a particular priestly lineage. The circumstances may be compared to a war between European powers in which each prays for victory to the God of its fathers, Lord of its battle-line. Those engaged in the struggle do not believe that two distinct deities are being appealed to. That this is the correct interpretation of the Nuer material is shown by a number of observations, one of the most significant being the fact that although the invocations were made to different titles they were all made over the same victim and this same victim was offered up by all the parties concerned This appears to me to be proof that the sacrifice was made to one and the same being. Another significant observation is the fact that in situations in which no sectional interests are at stake but where men approach God simply as men and in the context of their common humanity, as, for example, when furious storms are raging, in times of severe drought and famine, or when a man is seriously ill, then God alone, or in certain circumstances one of his hypostases by which he is figured in relation to some particular natural phenomenon, is addressed and he is not, as it were, divided by a variety of titles along the lines of the social structure. This may also be to a large extent the case even where different social groups are involved, so long as they are not antagonistic but have a common interest and intention. I give one such illustration.

A youth in a village where I was residing was badly wounded in the shoulder by a spear in a fight with a man of the next village. His antagonist had not intended to kill him and the people of the two villages were on good terms, so his kinsmen at once sent the spear with which the wound had been inflicted to the injured youth's home with expressions of regret and wishes for a speedy recovery. The elders of the wounded lad's home bent the point of the spear and placed it point downwards in a pot of cold water. This was done to lessen the pain of the wound, especially when it was washed, and to cool the inflammation. Next morning the wounder's village sent us a deputation, leading a goat for sacrifice. By this further indication of their regrets and of their willingness to pay compensation at once should the lad die they anticipated a blood-feud. It was hoped in any case that the danger of death would be obviated by the sacrifice of the goat The wound would, as the Nuer put it, 'be finished with the goat'.

Before the animal was sacrificed the visitors consecrated it by rubbing ashes on its back. It was then tied to a stake opposite the hut of the wounded youth's maternal grandmother and an invocation was delivered over it by a man called Lel, a leopard-skin priest and also a prophet, who had been summoned from a distance to officiate, partly, I think, because his presence would give greater importance, and therefore perhaps efficacy, to the ceremony and partly because it would be a further insurance for a peaceful outcome to the incident. His address was largely taken up with reiterations that the youth would not die and with giving to God and the people a lengthy and detailed account of how the accident had occurred. He sacrificed the goat at the conclusion of his speech. Our home party then brought forward a wether and it was also consecrated with ashes Afterwards a man of the home poured a libation of water over its tethering-peg as a prelude to delivering an oration. He told the story of the accident all over again and commented on it to God in this vein: 'ah God! We call on you about this wound There is no enmity between us [the party of the injured youth and the party of the spearer]. This wound came of itself [they do not attribute it to the spearer because it was an accident and also because the youth will not die and so there will be no *thung*, debt of homicide]. Throw the badness away with this cow [they call a sheep or goat a 'cow' in sacrificial contexts]. Let the wound heal. Ah God! it is only a headache [it is not a sickness of any importance—they speak of the most ghastly wounds in this way], let it be finished, let it go right on [heal without complications]. Let it be removed from the man's body. Let us be at peace.' Another man of the home party also made an invocation in much the same language· 'Friend (*maadh*), God who is in this village, as you are very great we tell you about this wound, for you are God of our home in very truth. We tell you about the fight of this lad. Let the wound heal. Let it be ransomed [with the sheep]'; and so forth. A representative of the visitors now said a few words to the same purpose and the sheep was then sacrificed. The meat of both sacrifices was eaten by the people of the home after the visiting deputation had departed; and also the carcass of a third animal, another wether, which the people of the home later sacrificed after three of them had made further invocations over it in much the same vein

In this ceremony Spirit was addressed simply as *kwoth* and no designated refractions were mentioned, and when on such occasions Nuer speak to, or about, *kwoth* without differentiating specifications they are, as I have explained, speaking to, or about, Spirit in the comprehensive conception of God the creator and the sustainer of life. This is often the case in their sacrifices, and it is the same when they pray for peace and deliverance from evil.

That emphasis is given to the refractions when a social group, acting as such and marking itself off from other groups, makes a sacrifice on behalf of itself or of one of its members in virtue of his membership of it, and that they are then to be regarded as diverse exclusive representations of God by which he is figured to the groups concerned in a special way as their patrons is evident also from other considerations. It is clear that totemic spirits of lineages are Spirit conceived of in a tutelary relationship to the

PLATE 1

Movement in wedding dance

lineages. The *colwic* spirits are also Spirit in a tutelary relationship to the families and lineages to which they belonged in the
flesh before they were metamorphosed into spirit Also, the spirits
of the air may have a tutelary relationship to families and lines
of descent, and where their attachment is more to an individual
prophet he has public functions through which the spirit becomes
patron of local and political communities. Totemic spirits may
also, though in a rather different manner, have a secondary significance for political groups through the association of dominant
lineages with tribal sections. Likewise, though to a lesser extent,
nature sprites are Spirit in a tutelary relationship to families; and
even fetishes, though of a rather different complexion, are Spirit
in a tutelary relationship to individuals, and sometimes to local
communities to which these individuals belong The attachment
of all these spiritual figures to social groups is indicated in various
ways, most noticeably in ceremonial and in payment of cattle to
them at marriages.

That these spiritual conceptions lack autonomy and are rightly
regarded as social refractions of God is further shown by the fact
that *kwoth*, without any distinguishing name, can become associated with any social group or office. Thus, as we have seen, Nuer
speak of the *kwoth* of a leopard-skin priest, 'the spirit of the flesh',
and they speak also of '*kwoth muonde*', 'the spirit of his (the
priest's) earth' (pp 291–2). This is no particular *kwoth* but is
Spirit seen in relation to priestly powers and functions. Likewise
they speak of *kwoth cuekni*, the spirit of twins, to which sacrifices
are made at the birth of twins and to which a cow of the bridewealth of the sisters of twins is dedicated. Here again, this is not
thought of by Nuer as some particular spirit which has an existence
and name of its own but as God in a special relationship to twins,
or rather to the event of a twin-birth. Another example is the
way in which they speak of the *kwoth* of an age-set, the tutelary,
nameless, spirit which protects the members of the set and avenges
wrongs done to men by their age-mates This cannot be a distinctive spirit in its own right as it were, if only because the sets pass
in turn into oblivion and are replaced by others It is rather God
thought of in relation to a particular set, just as he is also the
separate, while still being the same, guardian spirit of the other
sets. He is both the one and the many—one in his nature and
many in his diverse social representations.

Moreover, though God is God of all men he is not only conceived of, in the various totemic and other representations we have considered, as the special patron of descent, and sometimes of local, groups, but each family regards him, without specific differentiation of title, as having a particular relation to itself; and he may be spoken about in terms of a particular household, hamlet, or village community. One hears Nuer say in invocations, as in the one I have just recorded, 'God who is in this village', or 'God who is in this home'. When a Nuer builds a byre he holds a small ceremony before its central support is erected. Beer is prepared, and before the people drink it the master of ceremonies or the owner of the byre pours a libation of it to God and the ghosts at the entrance to the byre and in the centre of it, where the hearth and shrine will be, and asks God to give peace and prosperity to the home, its people and its cattle. They think then of God looking after their home in a special way, of being particularly attached to it so that he then becomes, as it were, in a special sense the family's God, a household God The shrine, a forked post, is the altar of God within the home, God of the hearth, as well as being associated with any of his particular representations—totemic, *colwic*, air-spirits, &c —in which he may stand in a tutelary relationship to the lineage or family of the owner of the homestead, and also with the ancestral ghosts. He is spoken of in this domestic representation as *kwoth rieka*, God of the post (shrine). Further, every member of a Nuer lineage, whether or not it has totemic or other specifically designated spirits, will in invocations speak of '*kwoth gwara*', 'spirit of our fathers', or in reference to the name of the ancestor of the lineage or clan, just as the Old Testament speaks of 'the God of our fathers' or 'the God of Abraham, Isaac, and Jacob' Similarly one hears the leopard-skin priests address God as '*kwoth Geaka*', 'spirit of Gee'. Gee was the first leopard-skin priest from whom all the leopard-skin priests derive their powers, so that the expression refers to God figured as patron of priests; though it also has a wider, national, sense, for Gee was also the ancestor of the most important Nuer clans.

Apart from the use of names or titles as diacritical signs to indicate an inclusive or exclusive relationship to God, Nuer make the same distinction grammatically through their inclusive or exclusive pronominal suffixes. These particles are rather complicated when they are attached to family and kinship terms, as in reference to God as 'father', and it is perhaps sufficient to say that they enable the speaker to indicate whether he speaks to Spirit as 'Spirit of our fathers' in the sense of Spirit in relation to his lineage alone or in the sense of Spirit in relation to everyone He can thus stress the unity of all present in relation to God or their separateness as social groups in a distinctive relationship to him as such.

The ambiguities which seem at first to be so puzzling a feature of Nuer religion are, at least to some extent, resolved by considering in this way their religious ideas in relation to their social order, for in all societies religious thought bears the impress of the social order. Given the segmentary political and lineage structure of the Nuer it is understandable that the same complementary tendencies towards fission and fusion and the same relativity that we find in the structure are found also in the action of Spirit in the social life. Just as, for example, two lineages are distinct and opposed groups in relation to one another at one level of segmentation and are a single unit at a higher level of segmentation, so Spirit as conceived in relation to these segments must be divided at the lower level and undivided at the higher level. It is intelligible, therefore, that in its relation to the segmentary social order the conception of Spirit is broken up into diverse refractions, while in relation to nature and man in general the many become again the one.

In the light of what has been said above it is not surprising that any number of new spirits may come into existence without disconcerting the Nuer, either being borrowed from neighbouring peoples or derived from some unusual experience. We have good reason to believe that the spirits of the air, the fetishes, and, at any rate for the most part, the totemic spirits have been introduced, some of them very recently, into Nuerland, and probably the same is true of the nature sprites.[1] I think it can be assumed—I do not see how it can have been otherwise—that there have always been different representations of *kwoth* among the Nuer, and if this is so the old, or traditional, religion must have consisted,

---

[1] Many of these spirits are probably new not only for the Nuer but also for the Dinka Even those which can be shown to have some antiquity in Dinka culture, e g *deng*, may be supposed, since they are not found among most other, or all other, Nilotic peoples, to have come into existence after the dispersal of these peoples took place. Complicated philological issues are raised by these questions

as far as the notion of Spirit is concerned, of the conceptions of God, of God figured to specific social groups by grammatical indications or by reference to their names, of *colwic* spirits, and of some totemic spirits

The taking over of new spiritual conceptions from neighbouring peoples may have been partly fortuitous, but I would suggest that it may also in part be accounted for by reference to recent Nuer history. During the last hundred years the Nuer have absorbed a great number of Dinka and have also been brought into closer contact, directly or indirectly, with other peoples of the Southern Sudan and also with Arabs and ourselves. This provided opportunities for borrowing foreign ideas. But it may be suggested that not only was the opportunity there, but also the need. Nuer statements lead us to suppose that certain social developments were taking place at the same time. They say that their clans and lineages were being broken up by expansion, and were incorporating into their stocks Dinka lines of descent, besides assimilating politically Dinka communities—hence the Dinka totems in Nuerland today; that prophets emerged who directed large-scale raids on the Dinka and defence against the 'Turks' (the Arabs and the British)—hence the Dinka and other foreign spirits of the air; and that the peace and administration imposed on them by the government of the Anglo-Egyptian Sudan have given protection to those who wish to pursue private gain and vengeance—hence the introduction of fetishes and their spread. Ethnological evidences support what they say, and we can add that it is in accord with the logic of the Nuer conception of Spirit that it should be represented by figures corresponding to these new social phenomena. Dr. Lienhardt tells me that since I was last in Nuerland the number of spirits has increased and that they have spread widely and freely. This is what we would expect to follow further social disintegration (p. 309).

God may thus be figured in numberless ways in reference to social groups and to persons, and in relation to effects which are significant for them; and in none of them has the figure any sharply defined individuality. This is fairly easy to understand when we are dealing with refractions which are referred to simply as *kwoth* of a group and without distinguishing name or title; but it may fairly be asked whether those spirits which are named can adequately be thought of as refractions and are not rather to be regarded as quite independent conceptions. We must distinguish here between class names and individual or personal names. The reason why Nuer divide the spirits into kinds, spirits of the above, spirits of the below, *colwic* spirits, *bieli*, and so forth, is that they regard them as different sorts of manifestation of Spirit and of varying degrees of importance. This is a matter I discuss later. It is rather the individual names with which we are immediately concerned.

The reason why some of the refractions have distinguishing names is, I think, mainly a matter of ownership. We have seen that, in the sense already defined (p. 44), Spirit can be owned by persons. Now, no one in this sense owns God, but all the various spirits may be owned by persons; and it may be said that the most distinctive naming of them is where individual ownership is most marked, in the case of the spirits of the air and the fetish spirits, which have proper names and ox-names. A prophet who is inspired by Spirit has in the logic of the situation to give it a name which distinguishes it as his particular spirit from the spirits of other prophets of his neighbourhood who are his rivals for renown and influence, for the attachment here is to individuals who build up through it a personal following, and not, at least primarily, to social groups. When a spirit falls from above and enters into a man who becomes its prophet it attains individuality by revealing through the prophet what it is called—its name; and when a person becomes possessed for the first time the immediate endeavour of his neighbours is to get the spirit to reveal its name when he is in a dissociated state. The spirit gets its name, the *numen* gets its *nomen*, by being owned by the person it possesses and to whom, by possessing him, it brings power and prestige. Fetishes are also owned by individuals who compete, though in a different way from prophets, for prestige and power against one another, so they must have distinguishing names. Thus it is through the name that ownership is established. The individuality is, in a sense, that of the person and not that of the spirit, the spirit getting its name through him.

The conclusion we have reached is that the conception of *kwoth* has a structural dimension. At one end Spirit is thought of in relation to man and the world in general as omnipresent God. Then it is thought of in relation to a variety of social groups and activities and to categories of persons to political movements connected with prophets, and in a special relation to warfare, as spirits of the air, to descent groups as *colwic* and totemic spirits, and to a variety of ritual specialists as totemic, totemistic, and similar spirits. At the other end it is conceived of more or less in relation to individuals in a private capacity as nature sprites and fetishes. God figured as common father and creator is patron of all men; figured in spirits of the air he is patron of political leaders, figured in *colwic* and totemic spirits, and also in unnamed refractions, he is patron of lineages and families; and figured in nature sprites and fetishes he is patron of individuals. I give only a general indication of the main lines of social demarcation between the various types of refractions, and I do not discuss exceptions and overlappings.

This impress of the social structure on Nuer religious thought is to be marked also in the natural and moral attributes of the different types of spiritual refractions. Mighty celestial phenomena, and great and terrible happenings, such as plagues and famines, and the moral order which concern all men are attributed to God, while processes and events which do not have so general a range of impact tend to be attributed to whichever particular refraction or type of refraction the situation and context evoke Likewise the refractions tend to decrease in the degree of universality, stability, and morality attributed to them the smaller the social space to which they refer. I give a brief indication of this tendency, illustrated by a few examples.

God is everywhere; he is permanent and changeless in his relation to the constant elements in the natural and moral orders, he is one, and he is all-powerful, just, and compassionate. The spirits of the air are in particular persons and places, and even when their prophets are politically important persons they have a limited spread of influence; they have fallen from the clouds in recent times and their renown depends on the personal prestige of their prophets and on political circumstances, both of which are unstable factors and may be ephemeral, they are multiple, though compared with lesser spirits they are few in number, and they are unpredictable, and even capricious and ill-intentioned. The *colwic* and totemic spirits are restricted to certain lineages and families; they became tutelary spirits of these groups at certain points of time and many are sooner or later forgotten; they are numerous; and compared to the spirits of the air they are unimportant. The nature sprites and fetishes are for the most part acknowledged only by the persons who own them and by their immediate kin The fetishes certainly, and the nature sprites probably, are very recent introductions, and they enter into relationships with persons and families and are forgotten by their descendants The sprites flit here and there, come into homes, and then return to the bush. The fetishes are bought and sold and pass from hand to hand. Their reputations wax and wane with those of their owners. They lose ground and are replaced by others. Both alike are potentially inexhaustible in number Though some fetishes are feared, neither they nor the sprites are highly regarded and the fetishes are in general disapproved of. On the other hand, the lower down the scale of Spirit we descend and the more it can be said to be owned the more prominent do cult features appear. God is approached in simple prayer and sacrifice. The spirits of the air receive more elaborate ceremonial attentions, into which enter hymns, possession, and divination Cult features are also prominent at the level of the *colwic* and totemic spirits. The most regular ritual attention appears to be given to the fetishes, which receive frequent offerings from their owners and in the most material form.

In relating the configuration of Nuer religious thought to the structural order of their society I am, of course, relating abstractions to one another by a method of sociological analysis. It is not suggested that the Nuer see their religion in this sort of way. Nevertheless, the structural configuration we abstract by this process is of the same design as the symbolic configuration in which they think of their various *kuth* The various spirits in their symbolic configurations occupy the same positions in relation to each other as they do in the structural configuration we perceive through sociological analysis.

In a typically Nuer way they represent the interrelationship of the spirits in a genealogical metaphor. God is the father of the greater spirits of the air, and the lesser of them are said to be children of his sons, of his lineage. The totemic spirits are often said to be children of his daughters, that is, they are not of his lineage, which is the Nuer way of placing them yet lower in the spiritual scale. The fetishes (and possibly also the nature sprites) come lowest of all in the representation of children of daughters of the air-spirit *deng* Another way of indicating this spiritual hierarchy is in terms of descent values in their political connotation. The spirits of the air are *diel*, true or aristocratic spirits, the totemic spirits are *jaang*, Dinka-like spirits, and the fetishes are *jur*, despised foreigners. It has earlier been noted that a similar metaphorical evaluation in terms of genealogical and social status is made by Nuer in their classification of birds (p. 90).

The interrelationship of the spirits is represented also in the symbolism of height or space, or more accurately in the relation of sky to earth. The spirits, as we have noted, are those of the above and those of the below. God is symbolized by the sky and the spirits of the air by the atmosphere, the clouds, and the breezes, the lesser ones being nearer to the earth than the greater ones. The totemic spirits as spirits are above and as creatures are below. The nature sprites may also be thought of as having a dual existence. The fetishes are the most earthly of the spirits, some of them speaking from beneath the ground. Implicit in this symbolic configuration is also an evaluation in terms of light and darkness, ranging from celestial brightness to subterranean darkness.

We see, and in their own way of looking at the matter Nuer see, degrees of immanence in this symbolic configuration. The cosmological representation of Spirit, and in particular the dichotomy between heaven and earth, the spirits of the above and those of the below, is further indicated by the mode and manner of appearances, the forms in which Spirit is manifested to humans. At one end there is pure Spirit, transcendental being which is everywhere and in nothing particular, Spirit as it is in itself, God. God is seen only in the works of his creation and he speaks only in the language of inner spiritual experience. The spirits of the air, on the other hand, and sometimes also the *colwic* spirits, appear to men in their prophets, through whom they are known and speak. Then Spirit is manifested in totemic species, which are mostly creatures, and at the farther end in things, the natural things associated with sprites and the magical substances which are the outward appearances of fetishes, which are Spirit in its lowest and most material form, Spirit which 'eats' offerings and which is bought and sold. Nuer themselves draw these comparisons, and it is evident from their observations that they themselves perceive that they are dealing with Spirit at different levels of thought and experience, Spirit in itself, Spirit in persons, Spirit in beasts, and Spirit in things. Moreover, I think we may conclude further that they perceive these different levels of immanence also as levels in time. This is implied in the genealogical representation of Spirit, for father must come before children and children before grand-children; and possibly also in its spatial representation in the fall-ing of spirits from above in a succession of descents at points in time. But it is also explicit in Nuer statements of the order in which their various spirits appeared among them. God was always there, then at various points of time *colwic* spirits, spirits of the air, totemic spirits, nature sprites, and fetish spirits appeared on the scene, the fetish spirits being the most recent arrivals.

These refractions correspond, as we have noted, with different levels of social activity, but an interpretation in terms of social structure merely shows us how the idea of Spirit takes various forms corresponding to departments of social life. It does not enable us to understand any better the intrinsic nature of the idea itself. The varying degrees of immanence in which the con-ception is expressed show us that the different social levels at which Spirit is manifested are also different degrees of religious perception. Spirit is sometimes perceived, intellectually and intui-tively, as one, transcendental, pure Spirit and at other times, in relation to human affairs and interests, as one or other of a great number of figures through which it is made known, in varying degrees of materialization, concretely to human intelligence Nor is it, even with strict reference to a purely structural interpretation of the conception of Spirit in Nuer society, simply a matter of social levels, for, as we have seen, God is also experienced un-refracted at all levels, down to the individual; so that a structural interpretation explains only certain characteristics of the refrac-tions and not the idea of Spirit in itself. I have only tried to show that, and how, that idea is broken up by the refracting surfaces of nature, of society, of culture, and of historical experience.

This way of looking at the Nuer conception of Spirit gives us a model by reference to which we can reduce the bewildering variety of their spirits to some sort of order in our own minds, and research could be carried deeper on the lines I have indicated. But the value of the model for our present inquiry is limited, for it does not help us to understand the specifically religious facts any better The analysis made in this chapter is from the outside, and were I writing about Nuer social structure this is the feature of their religion it would be most necessary to stress But in a study of religion, if we wish to seize the essential nature of what we are inquiring into we have to try to examine the matter from the inside also, to see it as Nuer see it, to examine how they differentiate at each level between one spirit and another. Naturally, they do not differentiate between them in sociological terms, but rather by grammatical distinctions, by references to descent, and by names of one sort or another. However, were the distinctions purely verbal, inevitable confusion, we may assume, would result. But the words are linked to visible objects which enable the mind to hold them, and so keep them apart. There is not the same need of visible symbols in thinking of God. Signs are indeed required, for it would be difficult otherwise to think about him at all, but what is one and has none like it does not require concrete diacritical differentiation. Where, on the contrary, there are a number of like representations they can only be kept apart by concrete differentiation, some thing which brings the name and the idea it stands for to the mind. In the case of the spirits of the air this requirement is provided by the prophets they possess, in the case of *colwic* spirits by the persons who have become such, in the case of the totemic spirits by the creatures they are beholden in, in the case of the nature sprites by luminous objects, and in the case of fetishes by the substances they are in, or attached to. This differentiation of spiritual forms through their identification with material phenomena presents us with a very difficult and delicate problem in religious thought. If what distinguishes one spiritual form from another is an object, we have to consider whether the object is the spiritual form or in what sense it may be said to symbolize it.

CHAPTER V

THE PROBLEM OF SYMBOLS

In the last chapter I discussed how the Nuer conception of Spirit is figured in different ways to different persons and categories and groups. In this chapter I consider the material forms in which Spirit manifests itself or is represented. God is, properly speaking, not figured in any material representations, nor are almost all the spirits of the above, though both God and his supra-terrestrial refractions may reveal themselves in signs. But the spirits of the below are represented in creatures and things. Our problem chiefly concerns these spirits of the below. It can be simply stated by the question: What meaning are we to attach to Nuer statements that such-and-such a thing is *kwoth*, spirit? The answer is not so simple.

There are several ways in which what we would render as 'is' is indicated in the Nuer language. The one which concerns us here is the particle *e*. It is used to tell the listener that something belongs to a certain class or category and hence about some character or quality it has, as '*e dit*', 'it is a bird', '*gat nath e car*', 'the Nuer is black', and '*Duob e ram me goagh*', 'Duob is a good man.' The question we are asking is what meaning or meanings it has for Nuer when they say of something '*e kwoth*', 'it is Spirit' (in the sense either of God or of a divine refraction).

Nuer do not claim to see God, nor do they think that anyone can know what he is like in himself. When they speak about his nature they do so by adjectives which refer to attributes, such as 'great' and 'good', or in metaphors taken from the world around them, likening his invisibility and ubiquity to wind and air, his greatness to the universe he has created, and his grandeur to an ox with widespread horns They are no more than metaphors for Nuer, who do not say that any of these things is God, but only that he is like (*cere*) them. They express in these poetic images as best they can what they think must be some of his attributes.

Nevertheless, certain things are said, or may be said, 'to be' God —rain, lightning, and various other natural—in the Nuer way of speech, created—things which are of common interest. There is here an ambiguity, or an obscurity, to be elucidated, for Nuer are

(123)

not now saying that God or Spirit is like this or that, but that this or that 'is' God or Spirit. Elucidation here does not, however, present great difficulties.

God being conceived of as in the sky, those celestial phenomena which are of particular significance for Nuer, rain and lightning, are said, in a sense we have to determine, to be him. There is no noun denoting either phenomenon and they can only be spoken of by verbs indicating a function of the sky, as 'ce nhial deam', 'the sky rained', and 'ce nhial mar', 'the sky thundered'. Also pestilences, murrains, death, and indeed almost any natural phenomenon significant for men are commonly regarded by Nuer as manifestations from above, activities of divine being. Even the earthly totems are conceived of as a relationship deriving from some singular intervention of Spirit from above in human affairs. It is chiefly by these signs that Nuer have knowledge of God. It might be held, therefore, that the Nuer conception of God is a conceptualization of events which, on account of their strangeness or variability as well as on account of their potentiality for fortune or misfortune, are said to be his activities or his activities in one or other of his hypostases or refractions. Support for such a view might be found in the way Nuer sometimes speak of one or other of these effects. They may say of rain or lightning or pestilence 'e kwoth', 'it is God', and in storms they pray to God to come to earth gently and not in fury—to come gently, it will be noted, not to make the rain come gently.

I do not discuss this ontological question here beyond saying that were we to suppose that such phenomena are in themselves regarded as God we would misunderstand and misrepresent Nuer religious thought, which is pre-eminently dualistic It is true that for them there is no abstract duality of natural and supernatural, but there is such a duality between kwoth, Spirit, which is immaterial rather than supernatural, and cak, creation, the material world known to the senses. Rain and lightning and pestilences and murrains belong to this created world and are referred to by Nuer as nyin kwoth, instruments of God.

Nevertheless, they and other effects of significance for men are διοσημία, signs or manifestations of divine activity; and since Nuer apprehend divine activity in these signs, in God's revelation of himself to them in material forms, the signs are, in a lower medium, what they signify, so that Nuer may say of them 'e *kwoth'*, 'it is God'. Rain and pestilence come from God and are therefore manifestations of him, and in this sense rain and pestilence are God, in the sense that he reveals himself in their falling. But though one can say of rain or pestilence that it is God one cannot say of God that he is rain or pestilence. This would make no sense for a number of reasons. In the first place, the situation could scarcely arise, God not being an observable object, in which Nuer would require or desire to say about him that he is anything. In the second place, the word *kwoth* does not here refer to a particular refraction of Spirit, a spirit, but to Spirit in its oneness, God, and he could not be in any way identified with any one of his manifestations to the exclusion of all the others. A third, and the most cogent, reason is that rain is water which falls from the sky and pestilence is a bodily condition and they are therefore in their nature material things and not Spirit. Indeed, as a rule, rain is only thought of in connexion with Spirit, and is therefore only said to be Spirit, when it does not fall in due season or falls too much or too violently with storm and lightning—when, that is, the rain has some special significance for human affairs This gives us a clue to what is meant when Nuer say of something that it is God or that it is a spirit of the air, as thunder may be said to be the spirit *wiu* or a prophet of the spirit *deng* may be said to be *deng*—especially as Nuer readily expand such statements by adding that thunder, rain, and pestilence are all instruments (*nyin*) of God or that they are sent by (*jak*) God, and that the spirit *deng* has filled (*gwang*) the prophet through whom it speaks. In the statement here that something is Spirit or a spirit the particle *e*, which we translate 'is', cannot therefore have the meaning of identity in a substantial sense. Indeed, it is because Spirit is conceived of in itself, as the creator and the one, and quite apart from any of its material manifestations, that phenomena can be said to be sent by it or to be its instruments. When Nuer say of rain or lightning that it is God they are making an elliptical statement What is understood is not that the thing in itself is Spirit but that it is what we would call a medium or manifestation or sign of divine activity in relation to men and of significance for them What precisely is posited by the hearer of any such elliptical statement depends on the nature of the situation by reference to which it is made. A vulture is not thought of as being in itself Spirit, it is a bird. But if it perches on the crown of a byre or hut Nuer may

say '*e kwoth*', 'it is Spirit', meaning that its doing so is a spiritual
signal presaging disaster. A lion is not thought of as being in itself
Spirit, it is a beast. But it may, on account of some event which
brings it into a peculiar relation to man, such as being born, as
Nuer think sometimes happens, as twin to a human child, be
regarded as a revelation of Spirit for a particular family and lineage. Likewise, diseases, or rather their symptoms, are not thought
of as being in themselves Spirit, but their appearance in individuals may be regarded as manifestations of Spirit for those individuals. Spirit acts, and thereby reveals itself, through these creatures.
This distinction between the nature of a thing and what it may
signify in certain situations or for certain persons is very evident
in totemic relationships A crocodile is Spirit for certain persons,
but it is not thought to be in its nature Spirit, for others kill and
eat it. It is because Nuer separate, and quite explicitly when questioned about the matter, spiritual conceptions from such material
things as may nevertheless be said 'to be' the conceptions, that
they are able to maintain the unity and autonomy of Spirit in
spite of a great diversity of accidents and are able to speak of
Spirit without reference to any of its material manifestations.

So far I have been mostly speaking of the conception of God
and of those of his refractions which belong to the category of the
sky or of the above. With two possible exceptions,[1] we cannot say
that the things said 'to be' these spirits are material symbols or
representations of them; at any rate not in the same sense as we
can speak of things being symbols of those lesser refractions of
Spirit Nuer call spirits of the earth or of the below, in which
God stands in a special relationship to lineages and individuals—
such diverse things as beasts, birds, reptiles, trees, phosphorescent
objects, and pieces of wood. These lesser refractions of Spirit,
regarded as distinct spirits in relation to each other, cannot, unlike
the spirits of the air, easily be thought of except in relation to the
things by reference to which they derive their individuality, and
which are said 'to be' them.

When, therefore, Nuer say that the pied crow is the spirit *buk*
or that a snake is Spirit, the word 'is' has a different sense from what
it has in the statement that rain is Spirit. The difference does not

---

[1] The spear *wiu* may be said to stand for the spirit *wiu* (pp 31 and 241), and
the pied crow may be said to stand for the spirit *buk* which is the most terres-
trially conceived of among the greater spirits (pp 31–32 and 81).

merely lie in the fact that *kwoth* has here a more restricted connotation, being spoken of in reference to a particular and exclusive
refraction—a spirit—rather than comprehensively as God or Spirit
in its oneness. It lies also in the relation understood in the statement between its subject (snake or crow) and its predicate (Spirit
or a spirit) The snake in itself is not divine activity whereas rain
and lightning are. The story accounting for a totemic relationship
may present it as arising from a revelation of divine activity, but
once it has become an established relationship between a lineage
and a natural species, the species is a representation or symbol of
Spirit to the lineage. What then is here meant when it is said that
the pied crow 'is' *buk* or that a snake 'is' Spirit. that the symbol
'is' what it symbolizes? Clearly Nuer do not mean that the crow
is the same as *buk*, for *buk* is also conceived of as being in the sky
and also in rivers, which the pied crow certainly is not; nor that a
snake is the same as some spiritual retraction, for they say that the
snake just crawls on the earth while the spirit it is said to be is in
the sky. What then is being predicated about the crow or snake in
the statement that either is Spirit or a spirit?

It will be simpler to discuss this question in the first place in
relation to a totemic relationship When a Nuer says of a creature
'*e nyang*', 'it is a crocodile', he is saying that it is a crocodile and
not some other creature, but when he says, to explain why a person
behaves in an unusual manner towards crocodiles '*e kwothdien*',
'it (the crocodile) is their spirit', he is obviously making a different
sort of statement He is not saying what kind of creature it is (for
it is understood that he is referring to the crocodile) but that what
he refers to is Spirit for certain people But he is also not saying
that the crocodile is Spirit—it is not so for him—but that certain
people so regard it. Therefore a Nuer would not make a general
statement that '*nyang e kwoth*', 'crocodile is Spirit', but would
only say, in referring to the crocodile, '*e kwoth*', 'it is Spirit', the
distinction between the two statements being that the first would
mean that the crocodile is Spirit for everyone whereas the second.
being made in a special context of situation, means that it is Spirit
for certain persons who are being discussed, or are understood, in
that context. Likewise, whilst it can be said of the crocodile that
it is Spirit, it cannot be said of Spirit that it is the crocodile, or
rather, if a statement is framed in this form it can only be made
when the word *kwoth* has a pronominal suffix which gives it the

meaning of 'his spirit', 'their spirit', and so forth; in other words, where the statement makes it clear that what is being spoken of is Spirit conceived of in relation to particular persons only. We still have to ask, however, in what sense the crocodile is Spirit for these persons.

Since it is difficult to discuss a statement that something which can be observed, crocodile, is something more than what it appears to be when this something more, Spirit, cannot be observed, it is helpful first to consider two examples of Nuer statements that things are something more than they appear to be when both the subject term and the predicate term refer to observable phenomena.

When a cucumber is used as a sacrificial victim Nuer speak of it as an ox. In doing so they are asserting something rather more than that it takes the place of an ox. They do not, of course, say that cucumbers are oxen, and in speaking of a particular cucumber as an ox in a sacrificial situation they are only indicating that it may be thought of as an ox in that particular situation; and they act accordingly by performing the sacrificial rites as closely as possible to what happens when the victim is an ox. The resemblance is conceptual, not perceptual. The 'is' rests on qualitative analogy. And the expression is asymmetrical, a cucumber is an ox, but an ox is not a cucumber.

A rather different example of this way of speaking is the Nuer assertion that twins are one person and that they are birds.[1] When they say 'twins are not two persons, they are one person' they are not saying that they are one individual but that they have a single personality. It is significant that in speaking of the unity of twins they only use the word *ran*, which, like our word 'person', leaves sex, age, and other distinguishing qualities of individuals undefined. They would not say that twins of the same sex were one *dhol*, boy, or one *nyal*, girl, but they do say, whether they are of the same sex or not, that they are one *ran*, person. Their single social personality is something over and above their physical duality, a duality which is evident to the senses and is indicated by the plural form used when speaking of twins and by their treatment in all respects in ordinary social life as two quite distinct individuals. It is only in certain ritual situations, and symbolically,

[1] I have given a more detailed account in 'Customs and Beliefs Relating to Twins among the Nilotic Nuer', *Uganda Journal*, 1936.

that the unity of twins is expressed, particularly in ceremonies connected with marriage and death, in which the personality undergoes a change. Thus, when the senior of male twins marries, the junior acts with him in the ritual acts he has to perform; female twins ought to be married on the same day; and no mortuary ceremonies are held for twins because, for one reason, one of them cannot be cut off from the living without the other. A woman whose twin brother had died some time before said to Miss Soule, to whom I am indebted for the information, 'Is not his soul still living? I am alive, and we are really children of God'

There is no mortuary ceremony even when the second twin dies, and I was told that twins do not attend the mortuary ceremonies held for their dead kinsfolk, nor mourn them, because a twin is a *ran nhial*, a person of the sky or of the above. He is also spoken of as *gat kwoth*, a child of God. These dioscuric descriptions of twins are common to many peoples, but the Nuer are peculiar in holding also that they are birds. They say 'a twin is not a person (*ran*), he is a bird (*dit*)', although, as we have just seen, they assert, in another sense, that twins are one person (*ran*). Here they are using the word *ran* in the sense of a human being as distinct from any other creature. The dogma is expressed in various ways. Very often a twin is given the proper name *Dit*, bird, *Gwong*, guineafowl, or *Ngec*, francolin [1] All Nuer consider it shameful, at any rate for adults, to eat any sort of bird or its eggs, but were a twin to do this it would be much more than shameful It would be *nueer*, a grave sin, for twins respect (*thek*) birds, because, Nuer say, birds are also twins, and they avoid any sort of contact with them. The equivalence of twins and birds is expressed particularly in connexion with death When an infant twin dies people say '*ce par*', 'he has flown away', using the word denoting the flight of birds. Infant twins who die, as so often happens, are not buried, as other infants are, but are covered in

---

[1] That the names, at least all those I have heard, are taken from birds lowest in the scale of Nuer reckoning requires comment, especially in view of the argument I later develop. It may be due to the Nuer habit of speaking of their relation to God—the birth of twins constitutes such a context—by comparing themselves with lowly things On the other hand, it may be simply in keeping with the logic of the analogy Twins belong to the class of the above but are below; just as guineafowl and francolin belong to the class of birds, which as a class is in the category of the above, but are almost earthbound.

a reed basket or winnowing-tray and placed in the fork of a tree, because birds rest in trees. I was told that birds which feed on carrion would not molest the bodies but would look at their dead kinsmen—twins and birds are also said to be kin, though the usage may be regarded as metaphorical—and fly away again. When I asked a Nuer whether adult twins would be buried like other people he replied 'no, of course not, they are birds and their souls go up into the air' A platform, not used in the normal mode of burial, is erected in the grave and a hide placed over it. The body is laid on this hide and covered with a second hide. Earth is then carefully patted over the upper hide instead of being shovelled in quickly, as in the burial of an ordinary person. I was told that the corpse is covered with earth lest a hyena eat it and afterwards drink at a pool, for men might drink at the same pool and die from contamination (nueer).

It is understandable that Nuer draw an analogy between the multiple hatching of eggs and the dual birth of twins. The analogy is explicit, and, through an extension of it, the flesh of crocodiles and turtles is also forbidden to twins on the ground that these creatures too, like birds, lay eggs. Miss Soule once had a girl twin in her household who refused fish for the same reason—the only case of its kind known to either of us. But the analogy between multiple births in birds and men does not adequately explain why it is with birds that human twins are equated when there are many other creatures which habitually bear several young at the same time and in a manner more closely resembling human parturition. It cannot be just multiple birth which leads Nuer to say that twins are birds, for these other creatures are not respected by twins on that account. The prohibition on eating eggs is clearly secondary, and it is extended to include crocodiles and turtles— and by Miss Soule's girl fish also—not because they lay eggs but because their laying eggs makes them like birds. Moreover, it is difficult to understand why a resemblance of the kind should in any case be made so much of. The multiple hatching of chicks is doubtless a resemblance which greatly strengthens the idea of twins being birds, but it is only part of a more complex analogical representation which requires to be explained in more general terms of Nuer religious thought. A twin, on account of his peculiar manner of conception is, though not Spirit himself, a special creation, and, therefore, manifestation of Spirit; and when he dies his

soul goes into the air, to which things associated with Spirit belong
He is a *ran nhial*, a person of the above, whereas an ordinary person
is a *ran piny*, a person of the below. A bird, though also not in itself
Spirit, belongs by nature to the above and is also what Nuer call,
using 'person' metaphorically, a *ran nhial*, a person of the above,
and being such is therefore also associated with Spirit It cannot,
of course, be determined for certain whether a twin is said to be
a person of the above because he is a bird or whether he is said
to be a bird because he is a person of the above, but the connexion
in thought between twins and birds is certainly not simply derived
from the multiple birth similitude but also, and in my view
primarily, from both birds and twins being classed by Nuer as
gaat kwoth, children of God. Birds are children of God on account
of their being in the air, and twins belong to the air on account of
their being children of God by the manner of their conception
and birth.

It seems odd, if not absurd, to a European when he is told that
a twin is a bird as though it were an obvious fact, for Nuer are not
saying that a twin is like a bird but that he is a bird. There seems
to be a complete contradiction in the statement; and it was precisely on statements of this kind recorded by observers of primitive peoples that Lévy-Bruhl based his theory of the prelogical
mentality of these peoples, its chief characteristic being, in his
view, that it permits such evident contradictions—that a thing
can be what it is and at the same time something altogether different. But, in fact, no contradiction is involved in the statement,
which, on the contrary, appears quite sensible, and even true, to
one who presents the idea to himself in the Nuer language and
within their system of religious thought. He does not then take
their statements about twins any more literally than they make
and understand them themselves. They are not saying that a twin
has a beak, feathers, and so forth. Nor in their everyday relations
with twins do Nuer speak of them as birds or act towards them as
though they were birds. They treat them as what they are, men
and women. But in addition to being men and women they are of
a twin-birth, and a twin-birth is a special revelation of Spirit; and
Nuer express this special character of twins in the 'twins are
birds' formula because twins and birds, though for different
reasons, are both associated with Spirit and this makes twins, like
birds, 'people of the above' and 'children of God', and hence a bird

L

a suitable symbol in which to express the special relationship in which a twin stands to God. When, therefore, Nuer say that a twin is a bird they are not speaking of either as it appears in the flesh. They are speaking of the *anima* of the twin, what they call his *tie*, a concept which includes both what we call the personality and the soul; and they are speaking of the association birds have with Spirit through their ability to enter the realm to which Spirit is likened in metaphor and where Nuer think it chiefly is, or may be. The formula does not express a dyadic relationship between twins and birds but a triadic relationship between twins, birds, and God. In respect to God twins and birds have a similar character.

It is because Nuer do not make, or take, the statement that twins are birds in any ordinary sense that they are fully aware that in ritual relating to twins the actions are a kind of miming. This is shown in their treatment of the corpse of a twin, for, according to what they themselves say, what is a bird, the *tie* or *anima*, has gone up into the air and what is left and treated—in the case of adults platform burial being a convenient alternative to disposal in trees—as though it might be a bird is only the *ring*, the flesh. It is shown also in the convention that should one of a pair of twins die, the child who comes after them takes his place, counting as one of them in the various ceremonies twins have to perform and respecting birds as rigorously as if he were himself a twin, which he is not. The ceremonies have to be performed for the benefit of the living twin and their structure and purpose are such that there have to be two persons to perform them, so a brother or sister acts in the place of the dead.

This discussion of what is meant by the statement that a twin is a bird is not so far away from the subject of totemism as it might seem to be, for the stock explanation among the Nuer of a totemic relationship is that the ancestor of a lineage and a member of a natural species were born twins. The relationship of lineage to species is thereby made to derive not only from the closest of all possible relationships but also from a special act of divine revelation; and since the link between a lineage and its totem is the tutelary spirit of the lineage associated with the totem it is appropriate that the relationship should be thought of as having come about by an event which is a direct manifestation of Spirit.

However, an examination of the Nuer dogma that twins are

Windscreen

birds was made not on account of totemic relationships commonly being explained in terms of twinship but because it was hoped that it would be easier to understand, in the light of any conclusions reached about what is meant by the statement that a twin is a bird, what Nuer mean when they say that some totemic creature, such as the crocodile, is Spirit. Certainly there is here neither the sort of metaphor nor the sort of ellipsis we found in earlier statements. Nor can Nuer be understood to mean that the creature is identical with Spirit, or even with a spirit, Spirit conceived of in a particular totemic refraction They say quite definitely themselves that it is not; and it is also evident, for Nuer as well as for us, that a material symbol of Spirit cannot, by its very nature, be that which it symbolizes. Nevertheless, though crocodile and Spirit are quite different and unconnected ideas, when the crocodile is for a certain lineage a symbol of their special relationship to God, then in the context of that relationship symbol and what it symbolizes are fused. As in the case of the 'twins are birds' formula, the relation is a triadic one, between a lineage and a natural species and God.

There are obvious and significant differences between the creature–Spirit expression and the cucumber–ox and bird–twin expressions. Cucumber, ox, man, and bird are all things which can be known by the senses; but where Spirit is experienced other than in thought it is only in its effects or through material representations of it. We can, therefore, easily see how Nuer regard it as being in, or behind, the crocodile. The subject and predicate terms of the statement that something is Spirit are here no longer held apart by two sets of visible properties. Consequently, while Nuer say that totemic spirits and totems are not the same they sometimes not only speak of, but act towards, a totem as if the spirit were in it. Thus they give some meat of a sacrifice to the lion-spirit to lions, and when they sacrifice to the durra-bird-spirit they address also the birds themselves and tell them that the victim is for them Nevertheless, they make it clear in talking about their totems that what respect they show for them is on account of their representing the spirits associated with them and not for their own sake.

Another difference is that whereas in the cases of the cucumber-ox and twin–bird expressions the equivalence rests on analogies which are quite obvious even to us once they are pointed out—

the cucumber being treated in the ritual of sacrifice as an ox is, and twins and birds both being 'children of God' and also multiple births—analogy is lacking in the creature-Spirit expression. There is no resemblance between the idea of Spirit and that of crocodile. There is nothing in the nature of crocodiles which evokes the idea of Spirit for Nuer, and even for those who respect crocodiles the idea of Spirit is evoked by these creatures because the crocodile is a representation of Spirit in relation to their lineage and not because there is anything crocodile-like about Spirit or Spirit-like about crocodiles. We have passed from observation of resemblances to thought by means of symbols in the sort of way that the crocodile is used as a symbol for Spirit.

We are here faced with the same problem we have been considering earlier, but in what, in the absence of analogical guidance to help us, is a more difficult form. The difficulty is increased by Nuer symbols being taken from an environment unfamiliar to us and one which, even when we familiarize ourselves with it, we experience and evaluate differently. We find it hard to think in terms of crocodiles, snakes, and fig-trees. But reflection shows us that this problem is common to all religious thought, including our own; that a religious symbol has always an intimate association with what it represents, that which brings to the mind with what it brings to the mind. Nuer know that what they see is a crocodile, but since it represents Spirit to some of them it is for those people, when thought of in that way, also what it stands for The relationship of members of a Nuer lineage to Spirit is represented by a material symbol by which it can be thought of concretely, and therefore as a relationship distinct from the relationships of other lineages to Spirit. What the symbols stand for is the same thing. It is they, and not what they stand for, which differentiate the relationships. There results, when what acts as a symbol is regarded in this way, a fusion between Spirit, as so represented, and its material representation. I would say that then Nuer regard Spirit as being in some way in, or behind, the creature in which in a sense it is beholden.

The problem is even more difficult and complex than I have stated it, because we might say that what are fused are not so much the idea of Spirit and its material representation as the idea of Spirit and the idea of its material representation. It is rather the idea of crocodile than the saurian creatures themselves which

stands for Spirit to a lineage. If a Nuer cannot see Spirit he likewise in some cases seldom, if ever, sees his totem; so that it is no
longer a question of a material object symbolizing an idea but of
one idea symbolizing another. I doubt whether those who respect
monorchid bulls or waterbuck often see a member of the class or
species, and children in these and other cases must often be told
about their totemic attachments before they have seen their
totems. There must also be Nuer who respect dom palms who
live in parts of Nuerland to the east of the Nile where this tree
does not grow [1] Indeed, I feel confident that one totem, the *lou*
serpent, a kind of Loch Ness monster, does not exist, and if this
is so, a totem can be purely imaginary. As this point has some
theoretical importance for a study of totemism I draw attention
to a further significant fact. Nuer do not speak of the spirit of
crocodiles, lions, tamarind-trees, and so on, but always of the spirit
of crocodile, lion, and tamarind-tree, and they would never say
that crocodiles, lions, and tamarind-trees were somebody's spirit
but always that crocodile, lion, and tamarind-tree was his spirit
The difference in meaning between the plural and singular usage
is not, perhaps, very obvious in English but it is both clear and
vital in Nuer. It is the difference between crocodiles thought of as
they are seen in rivers and crocodiles thought of as crocodile or as
the crocodile, as a type of creature, crocodile as a conception. The
point I am making is exemplified by the story already recorded
(p. 65) of a man who gave up respecting lions because they killed
his cattle. He still regarded lion-spirit, Spirit in the representation
of lion, as a spirit connected with his family But if a totemic
relationship may be an ideal one, and has always something of
the ideal in it, I would still say that Nuer regard Spirit as being

---

[1] Dr Lienhardt tells me that a number of lineages in western Dinkaland
respect creatures which no longer exist there A Dinka who travelled with him
to other parts of the Southern Sudan was astonished when he first saw his totem,
an elephant Nana Kobina Nketsia IV of Sekondi permits me to say that the first
time he saw his totem, the buffalo, was last year in a film at Oxford. Professor I
Schapera tells me that the ruling family of the senior tribe in the Bechuanaland
Protectorate, the Kwena, have been living for a hundred years in a region where
their totem, the crocodile, is unknown (see also what he says in *The Tswana*
(International African Institute), 1953, p 35, and Hugh Ashton, *The Basuto*,
1952, p 14) Other examples could be cited It may help us to appreciate the point
better if we consider the nearest parallels in our own country. When we think of
the lion as our national symbol we do not think of the mangy creatures of the
African bush or in zoos. Nor does it incommode us that there are no unicorns
and never have been any.

in some way in, or behind, totemic creatures when they think of them as representations of Spirit.

This must be all the more so with the other spirits of the below, the *bieli*, nature sprites, and the *kulangni*, fetishes. In general much of what has been said in this chapter about the totemic spirits applies to these other spirits also, but there is one important difference. In the statement 'crocodile is their spirit' both terms of the proposition can be thought of quite separately and are indeed so presented in the statement. This is partly because the crocodile is Spirit only for some persons and not for others, and also because, even for those for whom it is Spirit, it also exists in its own right as a reptile and may be so regarded by them without the idea of Spirit being involved. The reptile can be said to be Spirit only because it is something which may represent it and is, therefore, different from it. But in the case of a luminescence, such as will-o'-the-wisp from rotting swamp vegetation, the appearance can scarcely be represented in thought apart from what appears in it. It does not seem to be regarded, as rain may be, as a manifestation of Spirit through a medium which can be said to be sent by, or to be an instrument of, Spirit, but as an emanation of Spirit or as Spirit itself revealed in the light, a theophany like the burning bush in Midian. Nuer speak of it sometimes as the spirit's fire, and of its fire burning. Nor is it, as a crocodile may be, regarded as a representation of Spirit which, being apart from what it represents, can be said to be what it represents. On the contrary, whilst the lights are easily kept apart in the mind from the things on which they are accustomed to appear—swamp vegetation, hippopotamuses, meteorites, and other objects—they are not themselves conceived of as other than Spirit in the form of *bieli* and under that name. They are not something that is thought to exist in its own right but can be said to be Spirit. They are in themselves Spirit, in however lowly a form. Consequently, though they have a special significance for those persons who have acquired a relationship to the *bieli* spirits, they are Spirit also for those not directly concerned with them. Rain and crocodiles are created things with which Spirit may, or may not, be associated, according to circumstances and persons, but a will-o'-the-wisp is a property of Spirit, fractionally conceived of as a spirit of a special kind, and it cannot be thought of in terms other than of Spirit.

So when a Nuer says of a light in the bush that it is Spirit the problem we have been considering has changed its form and, at least on first consideration, seems to elude, if not altogether to escape, us For us the light is a gas arising from swamp vegetation, so that the statement that it is Spirit is of the same kind as the statement that a crocodile is Spirit; and whatever meaning might be attached to the one would be the same for the other But we cannot say that they are statements of the same kind for Nuer. For them, whereas the crocodile is a thing conceived of separately from Spirit, even though in a certain sense and for certain people it may be said to be Spirit, the phosphorescence is a descent of Spirit in the form of light on to something which is not in any way said to be Spirit, such as a hippopotamus, and on which it may appear at certain times and places and not at other times and places. So we are no longer asking what sense it has for Nuer when one of them says of a thing, which is not for them in itself Spirit, that it is Spirit. We are asking what sense it has for them when one of them says of a thing which has no meaning for them other than an emanation of Spirit that it is Spirit. In the case of the crocodile what is perceived is the reptile, and in certain circumstances it may be conceived of as Spirit for certain persons In the case of the *bieli* what is perceived may indeed be said to be just light but it can only be conceived of as Spirit, for it has no other name which differentiates it from any other sort of light or fire than *bieli*. When, regarding such a light, Nuer say 'it is Spirit' they are no longer saying that something is something else but are merely giving a name to what is observed; so that here 'it is Spirit' belongs to the same class of statements as 'it is a crocodile', and it might be held that the question we have been examining does not properly arise. Nevertheless, this is not entirely the case, as I will explain later.

What has been said of the lights of the nature sprites can be said also of the little bundles of wood in which the *kulangni*, the fetish spirits, have their abode, but for a different reason. A bundle of wood in which a fetish spirit has its abode is not a symbol of spirit, as a crocodile may be. Nor is it, like the *bieli*, a visible appearance of Spirit. It is a thing where a particular spirit abides. Nevertheless, it must be difficult for a fetish-owner to regard the bundle as being just anything which serves as a lodging for the spirit. It is before the bundle that he makes his offerings and it is the bundle he points at an enemy he wishes the spirit to harm.

Moreover, the bundles are fashioned solely as habitations for spirits and have no significance other than is derived from this purpose and use. Hence when Nuer say of a fetish-bundle that it is Spirit they are not saying that something which also has for them a separate meaning as something in itself, which is other than Spirit, is something else, namely Spirit, but that something which has no meaning of any kind outside its being an abode and a material sign of Spirit is Spirit. So the fetish-bundles cannot easily be thought of, as can rain or crocodile, either in terms of Spirit or in terms of their purely material natures, but only in terms of Spirit.

But though in the case of both the lights and the bundles there seems to be a more complete and fixed fusion between things and Spirit than in the case of the totems, the problem of something being something else is still present, though in a more complex, and also a more obscure and roundabout, form. Here again, although it can be said of a light in the bush or of a fetish-bundle that it is Spirit, the statement cannot be reversed. It cannot be said of Spirit that it is the light or the bundle, for that would mean to Nuer that Spirit in its oneness, conceived of as God, is entirely in the light or the bundle, which would make no sense to them. In the statement that the light or bundle is Spirit what, therefore, has to be understood by Spirit is a refraction of Spirit, or a spirit. But, even so, the 'is' is not one of identity, for though a phosphorescent light is a nature sprite exhibiting itself and is not conceived of as anything else, the nature sprite may be thought of independently of the light; and though the fetish-bundle may be a meaningless object except in relation to the fetish-spirit which occupies it, the spirit which occupies it can be thought of independently of it. When the light is no longer visible the *biel* sprite is none the less present for certain people as their sprite, which is Spirit in relation to them as an idea quite apart from its sporadic appearances as a light. A fetish-spirit takes its abode in a fetish-bundle of wood and it may leave it; and it is also present for certain people as Spirit in relation to them as an idea quite apart from its material home. In either case the spirits are thought to come, or at some time to have come, from above to earth and to be independent, as Spirit, of any material forms. Consequently the same nature sprite or fetish-spirit can be in different lights or in different bundles at the same time, just as an air-spirit can be in different prophets at the same time or a totemic spirit can be in any number of members of a species at the same time.

There is a further fact to be taken into consideration. When Nuer speak of lights in the bush or of fetish-bundles as Spirit they normally would not use the generic word for Spirit, *kwoth*, or even its plural and fractionary form *kuth*, spirits. They would say of them that they were *bieli* or *kulangni* So whilst it is true that *bieh* and *kulangni* are *kuth piny*, spirits of the below, the fact that they are given distinctive class names and that consequently it is possible for Nuer to explain them by saying that they are Spirit or that they are spirits attached to certain persons shows that though they are regarded as Spirit or spirits they are also somehow regarded differently from the way in which Spirit is usually regarded So the problem here is further complicated by a third term being understood in the statement about something that it is something else· the light is *bieli*, and the *bieh* are Spirit; the bundle is *kulangni*, and the *kulangni* are Spirit This added complication may be supposed to be due to the fact that though these spirits cannot be said to be identical with things they are more closely bound to them than is the case with other, and higher, spiritual conceptions; and the more Spirit is thought to be bound to visible forms the less it is thought of as Spirit and the more it is thought of in terms of what it is bound to In other words, there are gradations of the conception of Spirit from pure unattached Spirit to Spirit associated with human, animal, and lifeless objects and more and more closely bound to what it is associated with the farther down the scale one goes. This scale of Spirit, as I have explained earlier, is related to segmentation of the social order and is represented by Nuer by levels of space as well as by levels and degrees of immanence. So when Nuer say of something that it is Spirit we have to consider not only what 'is' means but also what 'Spirit' means. Nevertheless, though the sense of '*kwoth*' varies with the context, the word refers always to something of the same essence, and what is being said, directly or indirectly, in the statements is always the same, that something is that essence.

We can make some contribution towards a solution of the problem in the light of this discussion. When Nuer say of something '*e kwoth*', 'it is Spirit', or give it a name of which it can be further said 'that is Spirit', the 'is' does not in all instances have the same connotation It may be an elliptical statement, signifying that the thing referred to is a manifestation of Spirit in the sense of God revealing himself in instruments or effects. Or it may be a symbolical statement, signifying that what in itself is not Spirit but represents Spirit to certain persons is for these persons Spirit in such contexts as direct attention to the symbolic character of an object to the exclusion of whatever other qualities it may possess. Or it may be a statement signifying something closer to identity of the thing spoken of with what it is said to be, Spirit. The statements never, however, signify complete identity of any-thing with Spirit, because Nuer think of Spirit as something more than any of its modes, signs, effects, representations, and so forth, and also as something of a different nature from the created things which they are They are not able to define what it is, but when it acts within the phenomenal world they say it has come from above, where it is conceived to be and whence it is thought to descend. Consequently Spirit in any form can be detached in the mind from the things said to be it, even if they cannot always be so easily detached from the idea of Spirit.

I can take the analysis no farther; but if it is inconclusive it at least shows, if it is correct, how wide of the mark have been an-thropological attempts to explain the kind of statements we have been considering. Anthropological explanations display two main errors. The first, best exemplified in the writings of Lévy-Bruhl, is that when a people say that something is something else which is different they are contravening the Law of Contradiction and substituting for it a law of their own prelogical way of thinking, that of mystical participation.[1] I hope at least to have shown that Nuer do not assert identity between the two things. They may say that one is the other and in certain situations act towards it as though it were that other, or something like it, but they are aware, no doubt with varying degrees of awareness, and readily say, though with varying degrees of clarity and emphasis, that the two things are different. Moreover, it will have been noted that in the seemingly equivocal statements we have considered, with per-haps one exception, the terms cannot be reversed. The exception

[1] I refer to his earlier writings, in particular *Les Fonctions mentales dans les sociétés inférieures* (1910) and *La Mentalité primitive* (1922) The second part of his last book, *L'Expérience mystique et les symboles chez les primitifs* (1938), which took account of modern research, is a brilliant discourse on the problems we have been discussing

is the statement that twins are birds, because it can also be
said that birds are twins. That a hatch of birds are twins is a statement, to which we also can give assent, which does not derive
logically from the statement that twins are birds but from a
perception independent of that proposition; so it does not concern
our problem. Rain may be said to be God but God cannot be said
to be rain; a cucumber may be called an ox but an ox cannot be
called a cucumber; and the crocodile may be said to be Spirit but
Spirit cannot be said to be the crocodile. Consequently these are
not statements of identity They are statements not that something is other than it is but that in a certain sense and in particular
contexts something has some extra quality which does not belong
to it in its own nature; and this quality is not contrary to, or incompatible with, its nature but something added to it which does
not alter what it was but makes it something more, in respect to
this quality, than it was. Consequently, no contradiction, it seems
to me, is involved in the statements.

Whether the predicate refers to a conception or to a visible
object the addition makes the subject equivalent to it in respect
to the quality which both now have in common in such contexts
as focus the attention on that quality alone. The things referred to
are not the same as each other but they are the same in that one
respect, and the equivalence, denoted by the copula, is not one of
substance but of quality. Consequently we cannot speak here, as
Lévy-Bruhl does, of mystical participation, or at any rate not in
his sense of the words, because the two things are not thought to
be linked by a mystical bond but simply by a symbolic nexus.
Therefore, what is done to birds is not thought to affect twins, and
if a totem is harmed the spirit of that totem may be offended but
it is not harmed by the harm done to the totemic creature.

That the relation between the thing said to be something else
and that something else it is said to be is an ideal one is indeed
obvious, but anthropological explanations of modes of primitive
thought as wide apart as those of Tylor, Max Muller, and Lévy-
Bruhl, are based on the assumption that though for us the relation
is an ideal one primitive peoples mistake it for a real one; and
those anthropologists who sponsor psychological explanations
often make the same assumption. This is the second error. If my
interpretation is correct, Nuer know very well when they say that
a crocodile is Spirit that it is only Spirit in the sense that Spirit is

represented to some people by that symbol just as they know very well that a cucumber is only an ox in the sense that they treat it as one in sacrifice That they do not mistake ideal relations for real ones is shown by many examples in this book: the identification of a sacrificial spear with that of the ancestor (p 240), the identification of man with ox in sacrifice (p. 262), the identification of a man's herd with that of the ancestor of his clan (p. 258), the identification of sickness and sin in a sacrificial context (pp 191–2), and the identification of the left hand with death and evil (pp. 233–6). It is shown also in the symbolism of many of their rites, where their purpose is expressed in mimicry (pp. 231–2).

I think that one reason why it was not readily perceived that statements that something is something else should not be taken as matter-of-fact statements is that it was not recognized that they are made in relation to a third term not mentioned in them but understood. They are statements, as far as the Nuer are concerned, not that A is B, but that A and B have something in common in relation to C. This is evident when we give some thought to the matter A cucumber is equivalent to an ox in respect to God who accepts it in the place of an ox. A crocodile is equivalent to Spirit only when conceived of as a representation of God to a lineage Consequently, though Nuer do not mistake ideal relations for real ones, an ideal equivalence is none the less true for them, because within their system of religious thought things are not just what they appear to be but as they are conceived of in relation to God.

This implies experience on an imaginative level of thought where the mind moves in figures, symbols, metaphors, analogies, and many an elaboration of poetic fancy and language; and another reason why there has been misunderstanding is that the poetic sense of primitive peoples has not been sufficiently allowed for, so that it has not been appreciated that what they say is often to be understood in that sense and not in any ordinary sense. This is certainly the case with the Nuer, as we see in this chapter and in many places elsewhere in this book, for example, in their hymns In all their poems and songs also they play on words and images to such an extent that no European can translate them without commentary from Nuer, and even Nuer themselves cannot always say what meaning they had for their authors. It is the same with their cattle- and dance-names, which are chosen both for euphony and to express analogies. How Nuer delight in playing with words is also seen in the fun they have in making up tongue-twisters, sentences which are difficult to pronounce without a mistake, and slips of the tongue, usually slips in the presence of mothers-in-law, which turn quite ordinary remarks into obscenities. Lacking plastic and visual arts, the imagination of this sensitive people finds its sole expression in ideas, images, and words.

In this and the last chapter I have attempted to lay bare some features of the Nuer conception of Spirit. We are not asking what Spirit is but what is the Nuer conception of *kwoth*, which we translate 'Spirit'. Since it is a conception that we are inquiring into, our inquiry is an exploration of ideas. In the course of it we have found that whilst Nuer conceive of Spirit as creator and father in the heavens they also think of it in many different representations (what I have called refractions of Spirit) in relation to social groups, categories, and persons. The conception of Spirit has, we found, a social dimension (we can also say, since the statement can be reversed, that the social structure has a spiritual dimension) We found also that Spirit, in the Nuer conception of it, is experienced in signs, media, and symbols through which it is manifested to the senses. Fundamentally, however, this is not a relation of Spirit to things but a relation of Spirit to persons through things, so that, here again, we are ultimately concerned with the relation of God and man, and we have to consider not only what is the God-to-man side of the relationship, to which attention has so far mostly been given, but also the man-to-God side of it, to which I now turn.

CHAPTER VI

SOUL AND GHOST

I

RELIGION is the reciprocal relation between God and man. Our study of Nuer religion is therefore a study not only of this people's conception of *kwoth*, God, but also of their conception of *ran*, man, and of the relation between the two conceptions. They stand to each other as opposites, symbolized in the opposites of sky and earth; and this is one of the salient contrasts of Nuer thought. I have already discussed the ideas they have about God, and I now propose to discuss some of their ideas about man. We can perhaps best start this discussion by considering what happens at death when man disintegrates into his three component parts, *ring*, flesh, *yiegh*, breath or life, and *tie*, intellect or soul.

Nuer say that a man who does not fear death summons his family and closest kin to his death-bed, but all who are not grave-diggers leave his homestead immediately he is dead, and the grave is dug and the corpse buried as quickly as possible and without ceremony. Usually only two or three people dig the grave and these are senior kinsmen, or sometimes kinswomen. A member of a man's age-set must not dig his grave, and all children and young people keep away from the homestead, even those nearest to the dead, such as his sons and younger brothers, however grieved they may be at their loss. They may weep but they do not attend the burial, for death is an evil thing and only those who must get rid of the corpse should go near the grave. Men do not wail, and if women wail it is not for long, just a little as soon as the person has died and again shortly before he is buried to let the neighbours know of the death and burial I have never witnessed a burial and it was with difficulty I obtained a description of what happens. Death is a subject Nuer do not care to speak about.

The shaft is dug near the left-hand side (as one faces it) of the dead man's hut or, if he dies in camp, his windscreen This is the *kwi giakni*, the side of evil. The grave is dug to the depth of a

man's chest as he stands in it. Nuer say that were a man to be
buried in a shallow grave and his corpse to be scratched up by
hyenas he would haunt those responsible. The head of the corpse
is shaved and all ornaments are removed from the body before
burial A man goes to the grave as naked as he was born A woman
is buried in her loin skin, closely drawn between the legs. The
legs of both sexes are flexed and one arm is placed under the
head and the other over it as the corpse lies on its right side on
a strip of ox-hide. Another strip of ox-hide is placed over it and
pieces are also placed over the ears to prevent earth entering them.
I believe that in western Nuerland a man is buried facing east and
a woman facing west, but in eastern Nuerland both sexes are
buried facing west. Nuer have told me that this is because the
eastern Nuer came orginally from the west and that it was in
western Nuerland that their ancestors were created, but, as will
be seen, they also associate the passage from birth to death with
the movement of the sun across the sky. The grave-diggers heap
the earth they dig around the edge of the shaft, five heaps for a
man and four for a woman. When filling the shaft they sit or
stand with their backs to it and scoop the earth back with their
hands, at first slowly and then quickly, from each heap in turn.
When the earth is above the level of the ground they beat it down.
The small hump which is left is stamped down a few days later
so that there is then no sign of the grave, unless it is an old
woman's grave, when her pipe or neckrest or cooking-pot may be
placed on it. Graves are not places of cult and are not long remembered. I have never heard a man speak of the grave of an ancestor
or kinsman. The dead man's hut continues to be occupied after
the women have beaten it inside and outside with wild rice. Persons killed by lightning, twins, and holders of certain ritual offices
have special modes of burial (pp. 54–55 and 129–30).

   When the burial is completed the master of ceremonies of the
dead man's family dips a handful of wild rice in water and
asperses the grave-diggers with it. They then go to the nearest
stream to wash themselves. They may not drink water before
they have been aspersed and have washed lest they die of the
consequences (nueer). A few days later the master of ceremonies
sprinkles all the people of the homestead and close kin who live
nearby in the same manner and sacrifices an animal to God, an
ox if the dead man had a large herd, otherwise one of the flock,

in front of the dead man's hut. He also addresses the ghost and tells him that he has been taken away and must turn his face to the ground and not trouble the living 'friend, this (beast) is yours (for you) Now turn yourself to the ghosts Turn yourself away from us. Death was not made by us in old times, it was made by God, friend. Do not trouble your people with bad dreams but regard us favourably. God has not entirely destroyed you, for there are those who come after you; you have children left behind you ' If the family have no animal to sacrifice the master of ceremonies sacrifices by cutting in two a wild cucumber. 'The half of the living, the half of the children, the right half, remains outside, being placed in the thatch of the hut. The half of the dead man is thrown into the bush ' With it is thrown out of the village the contagion of death. They say of this sacrifice *'ba kier piny ka del'*, '(the dead man) is expiated in the earth with a goat', and that the badness goes into the earth with the blood and the chyme.

Members of the family mourn till the mortuary ceremony has been held some months after death. They shave their heads after the burial but then they do not shave them again, neither do they treat the hair with ashes nor depilate their bodies, till the period of mourning is ended. They also remove all ornaments, and the closest relatives wear a *dep luath*, a mourning cord of grass, around their waists and necks. There are no prescribed food and sex abstentions during the period of mourning though I was told that close kin may abstain from sexual relations for a few days after death 'because they are sad and thinking of their dead friend' Less closely related persons and the wives of kin show their respect by leaving their hair untended but for a shorter time, perhaps only a month or so. When people are in mourning they do not attend dances People do not mourn for a small child, for 'a small child is not a person (*ran*). When he tethers the cattle and herds the goats he is a person. When he cleans the byres and spreads the dung out to dry and collects it and carries it to the fires he is a person.' A man will not say that he has a son till the child is about six years of age. A small child is buried by old women and without sacrifice.

Four to six months after burial the mortuary ceremony is held It is known as *wocene cuol* or *cuol woc* because its purpose is to wipe out (*woc*) the debt (*cuol*) which Nuer feel to be due on account of the death. They seem to feel that there is some mis-

fortune hanging over them and that the death may be only part
of it. It is necessary to clear off the whole debt before any further
evil comes to them. Otherwise people may cut their feet when
fishing, pierce their feet when hunting, cut themselves with spears
when dancing, or indeed meet with almost any misfortune, even
death. Nuer also feel that if the dead is not appeased by this
ceremony he may return in anger to fetch the living, especially
his wives and children, and the cattle.

I have only once witnessed this ceremony, rather early in my
study of the Nuer, and I have supplemented my account of what
I then saw with statements made to me later. The ceremony was
held at Dini in the Lou tribal area for the ghost of an important
old man called Lam. When I arrived at the dead man's village
towards evening the people had just sacrificed an ox outside his
kraal. This sacrifice had been for Tutthiang, Lam's father, for it
was known that Lam had intended before he died to sacrifice this
animal in his father's honour. Next morning, before sunrise, an
ox and a cow and its bull-calf were speared at their tethering-pegs
in Lam's kraal. People watched to see how they fell; because if a
sacrificed animal falls over cleanly on its side, especially if it falls
on its right side, it is a good omen and shows that the ghost is
content, whereas if it falls on its head or totters about before falling it is a bad omen. It is regarded as important that a cow still
giving milk should be sacrificed for the ghost of an old man who
had a position in his community lest he should feel that sufficient
sacrifice had not been made. To kill a cow in milk is the greatest
sacrifice a Nuer can make. An animal must be sacrificed for each
wife of the dead by one of her sons or by some kinsman on behalf
of her hut. If the ceremony is for a young unmarried man his
favourite ox should be sacrificed. A cow should be sacrificed for
a senior woman if the herd is large, and a male calf for a young
woman. However, there are no hard and fast rules about the
matter. The people of the home should sacrifice what they can
afford, cattle if possible, but a goat or sheep if they cannot obtain
at least a male calf, which is unlikely, because a man can generally
borrow one from a neighbour.

At Dini after the cattle had been killed they were skinned and
the meat apportioned to the various categories of kin. It is an
absolute rule, however, that no member of the ghost's age-set
may partake of the meat of animals sacrificed at his mortuary

ceremony, and I was told that it is dangerous for them even to smell the cooking meat. Everyone then moved off to sit in front of a hut to listen to the commemorative orations, which are also invocations; and here were spread out on the ground the ghost's possessions, his fighting-spears and fishing-spears, his beads, his metal arm-rings, his ostrich-shell girdles, his pipe, and, since his son was senior government interpreter in the district, his clothes and whistle, articles not possessed by ordinary Nuer. At the side of these were placed the heads and hides of the cattle which had just been sacrificed. The people sat with their backs to the now rising sun and facing the direction of the setting sun because 'death follows the setting sun'. Nuer say that 'the west is the side of death, the east the side of life', and the verb *kwony* in their language means both 'to bury' and 'to set' (the sun). When they sacrifice an ox for a sick man they hope it will fall towards the east The master of ceremonies (pp. 287–9) of the ghost's family made the first commemorative oration, after throwing some tobacco towards east and west. As he spoke he walked up and down in front of the people brandishing the spear with which the animals had been sacrificed. He commenced his address (*lam*) by shouting out his ox-name. He must also have shouted out his clan spear-name, though I have not recorded it in my notebooks.

I did not take down his address at the time but I was told later that a master of ceremonies speaks in this wise· 'God, now thou hast given us badness, or is it simply the lot of creation? [Is the death thou hast sent us a special evil designed for us or has the dead man merely suffered what soon or late comes to all created things?] Now thou hast taken so-and-so [he names the dead man], now he has become one of thy people, turn about and take him right away. We who are left in the world, give us peace. Let his children who remain in the world be at peace He is not finished, his children will carry on his name. In the future they will bear his name. Let no further evil befall us ' The master of ceremonies is now speaking to the ghost: 'So-and-so, my brother [or 'my father' if he was a much older man], now thou art one of God's people. Do not forget us, let it be thy habit to speak [on our behalf] to thy father [God]. When we go into the bush let us tread on wild rice [avoid all dangers and troubles]. Let us beget children. May all evil be taken away from us now, and may we remain in peace.' The master of ceremonies again addresses God: 'God, and you ghosts! Thou, God, madest man and thou also madest death. [Thou hast said] thou, man, I made thee only that thou mightest perish. God, it is thy world Thou hast shown us death this year. Now we here, we go about with this debt, there has been no laughing with happiness for us this year, thou hast given us mourning. God, turn about and take away the man thou hast taken. Breathe on us with favourable breath (*ku ko ngok ni yiegh me goagh*). Thou hast taken this man, take also this ox of his together with him.' He addresses the ghost once more 'and thou, so-and-so, art thou now in the great cattle camp [community] of the dead? Where art thou, our father? Where are all the people of our home? Eh! It is the camp to which we all go at last. We who remain in the world, may we be at peace. May the children thou hast left behind thee rest in peace. Thou who hast gone before do not close thine eyes to us. Thou art a person of God. May there be nothing further bad for us to see.'

The master of ceremonies spoke for a long time in this vein and when he had finished five senior kinsmen made similar orations, one after another, the six addresses taking over four hours to deliver. The kinsmen harangued the ghost. They told him that when his daughters were married he would receive the finest cows of their bridewealth. They asked him to be a good ghost and not to trouble his kinsmen. They frequently admonished him to turn away from them (*ku ro du rit*). They wanted the ghost to look away from them and not to trouble them. His kinship (*mar*) was now with God and not with men. This request to turn away, made to both God and the ghost of the dead man, is a constant refrain in mortuary ceremonies. In a text given by Professor Westerman, the translation of which I have slightly emended, the speaker says on such an occasion, 'Oh God, why dost thou pursue us? Why dost thou pursue us? Turn thyself away, take this thy man and go; let him be sufficient; do not look at us again! In what are we at fault?' And also 'Oh God, take thy cow! And thou [the dead man] turn away! Turn thy face away into the bush! Do not look at us again! We have given thee thine own things, but then leave us alone!'[1] The kinsmen at Dini also told the ghosts that if they must give them something bad they should give them hunger and not sickness and death. They pointed out to the dead man that his age-mates were present to honour him. They implored God

[1] Op cit, pp. 117-18

(149)

that they might sleep quietly and their souls be 'cool' (*koce thei*)
Their remarks also contained many reflections on life and human
destiny and the transience of all living things, and they recounted
the deeds of the dead and reiterated that he had left sons to carry
on his name and lineage Speakers and listeners also stated any
grievances they had in their hearts towards kinsmen, for any of
the kin of the dead man who bears a grudge against a relative
must now declare it If he does not do so now, he must for ever
keep silence This is an occasion for amicable settlement of family
and kinship quarrels. Thus at this ceremony the senior wife of
Mayan, the eldest son of the dead man, complained that her cow
had been given by her husband to his second wife. A wife of the
dead man who had gone to live with another man, taking her
daughter with her, said that she wished now to live at her dead
husband's home, and cattle of her bridewealth which had been
returned were sent back again to her people on the day of the
ceremony.

A part of the ceremony I did not see, for it was taking place
elsewhere during these orations, was the preparation of porridge
and beer. The master of ceremonies makes three new clay fire-
stones, places on them a new pot, and pours water into the pot.
He then puts out the old fire in the dead man's homestead, throws
its ashes and fire-stones into the bush, and starts a new fire under
the pot. He begins the mixing and stirring of the porridge. When
the women have cooked the porridge he ladles it out with a new
gourd-ladle into a new gourd-dish. All the utensils are new for the
occasion. The porridge and a pot of beer were now carried to
where we were sitting, and as each of the later speakers rose to
make his speech he dipped a gourd-ladle into the pot of beer and
poured a libation to the ground.

When the last speech was finished everyone stood up and the
master of ceremonies dipped wild rice into a gourdful of milk and
aspersed the people with it He did this many times till everyone
had been aspersed He then sprinkled the dead man's possessions
and poured what was left of the milk at the side of a tethering-peg
over the dung which had been spread out to dry, and knelt down
and kneaded the milk with the dung. I was told that the cattle
and huts were also aspersed with milk I believe that milk is only
used in this rite if the dead man was, like Lam, 'a man of the
cattle' (pp. 300–2). In the case of a leopard-skin priest water

mixed with blood is used For ordinary people water is used Then
butter was brought out in a small gourd and was smeared on the
backs and chests of those present and on the dead man's spears.
Those who were wearing mourning cords came forward and the
master of ceremonies cut them from their waists and necks and
carried them into the bush and threw them away. Afterwards
the porridge was distributed and eaten.

The master of ceremonies now began to divide up the dead
man's possessions. He gave the tobacco to a woman of the dead
man's household and his spears to a younger son He gave half the
skin of the sacrificed ox to the eldest son and he took the other
half for himself as his right. The rest of Lam's possessions were
tied in a bundle for future distribution among his wives and sons.
The people then washed themselves. At a mortuary ceremony
there is a feeling of pollution and the need to cleanse men and
things. The dead man's goods were also washed. I left at this
point, while the meat of the sacrifices was still being cooked

The rites were concluded shortly after sunrise on the following
morning. Two men stretched a goat on its back and a third, acting
on behalf of Lam's eldest widow and the mother of his dead son
Deng, cut it in two with a spear from throat to tail. Even the tail
was carefully severed in twain and to complete the division the
head was split in two with an axe. While the carcass was being
halved in this way an old man and the senior widow pulled at
it on one side and Lam's sons pulled at it on the other side till
with laughter and cheering it fell apart. The old man and the
senior widow ran with their half, the left or bad half, into the bush
and threw it there, while the sons carried their half, the right
or good half, to the hut outside which the sacrifice had been
made. The old man carefully collected half the chyme of the goat
and deposited it with the bad half in the bush Lam's eldest son
collected the other half and placed it with the good half of the
goat. They express in this manner the departure of evil from the
home, where people may now rest in peace. The left half which
was carried away represents death and misfortune and the right
half which was left in the home represents life and prosperity.
Nuer say also that with the bad half go all the secret enmities
between the dead and the living and any resentment and guilt
there may have been between them For example, one of the sons
may have quarrelled with his father and his father may have

nourished secret resentment in his heart, or a son may have had relations with one of his father's wives and not confessed his guilt. I was told that the bad half of the goat was eaten by persons unrelated to the dead man and the good half by members of his family

Lam's goods which had been tied up for later distribution on the first day were now brought out again and divided among members of the family by the eldest son assisted by the master of ceremonies and some senior kinsmen. The clothes, beads, and ostrich-shell girdles were given to Lam's wives. His series of metal arm-rings was broken up and the rings distributed among the men and boys of the family.

The ceremonies were concluded by all the people shaving their heads. On this account the mortuary ceremony is often spoken of as the *mut*, the cutting The cutting of the hair of the kin symbolizes the cutting off of the dead from the living just as in the marriage ceremonies the rite, known by the same word *mut*, by which the bride's hair is shaved off, symbolizes the cutting of the ties between her and her family and kin The mortuary ceremony is one of deep 'silence and sadness', the marriage ceremony one of 'happiness and laughter'. They also say of the dead man *ca je mut*, he has been cut off (by this ceremony). It is clear from the orations and actions of the mortuary ceremony that part, perhaps the main part, of their purpose is to cut the dead from the living The dead man has to be given the full status of ghost and persuaded to accept it so that he will remain as a ghost and not try to return to the living with the taint of death on him. This is the constant refrain of the invocations. 'Now you ghosts, you are finished with us, you are the people of God, you are the people on the other side.'

That this is one of the main purposes of the ceremony is further shown by a curious observation I made in western Nuerland. There was living in a village there an unhappy-looking man of unkempt appearance, called Gatbuogh This man had some years before gone on a distant journey and had not been heard of for a long time. Then there came to his village news of his death and in course of time the mortuary ceremony was held for him. He later returned home and was living in the village at the time of my visit He was described as *joagh in tegh*, the living ghost. I was told '*ca tiede mut. ce tiede wa kene tie yang kel. ce te ni ringe*

PLATE VI

Riek shrine

cunge', 'his soul was cut off. His soul went with the soul of the (sacrificed) ox together. His flesh alone remains standing.' His soul, the essential part of him, had gone and with it his social personality. Although people fed him he seems to have lost such privileges of kinship as pertain to the living and not to the dead. I was told that he could not partake of sacrificial meat because his agnatic kinship (*buth*) had been obliterated (*woc*) by the mortuary ceremony. A neighbour said to me 'he lives in our village with Baranyai but we do not count him a member of it because he is dead. The mortuary ceremony has been held for him.'

There were doubtless points I missed in the mortuary ceremony I witnessed and possibly some I did not hear about in later discussions with Nuer. A feature I did not observe but which, I was later told, is common, was the singing of hymns to the spirits of the air, in particular the hymn to *buk* which I have recorded earlier. These hymns are not an integral, and therefore essential, part of the ceremony and their meaning is in no way related to the matter in hand. They are in keeping, however, with the religious character of the rites and enhance it.

In conclusion I should say that Mayan told me at Dini that he would later cut the ears of the bulls of his dead father's herd and that this is always done when the dead man was a person of age and social importance. The cattle would then prosper. For such a man another ox may be sacrificed some months later. The master of ceremonies again prepares porridge for those who gather to honour the ghost, and the senior kinsmen again make speeches to God and to the dead man and to all the ghosts of the lineage. Before the animal is speared all the people, men, women and children, bring ashes of cattle-dung and rub them on the ox. I discuss the meaning of this act in later chapters. The meat is distributed to all present, and also the porridge and the beer, which has been prepared in advance. An ox sacrificed in this manner to honour a dead man is known as *thak bar* or *thak joka*. A man may at any time decide to honour his father in this way and Nuer sometimes set apart an ox or an old bull (*tut jookni*) for their dead fathers, as Lam had done for his father Tutthiang, and await a suitable occasion for sacrificing it, as when they see their fathers in dreams and know that they want something An ox so set apart cannot be disposed of but must be kept in the herd till it is sacrificed.

II

Two main questions arise from the account I have given of ceremonies connected with death: In what way do Nuer conceive of the disintegration of the person at death and how do they regard those who have departed? I discuss these two questions in turn, but I must say at the outset that Nuer are neither very clear nor very explicit in what they say about the matters they concern.

As I have said, Nuer avoid as far as possible speaking of death and when they have to do so they speak about it in such a way as to leave no doubt that they regard it as the most dreadful of all dreadful things. This horror of death[1] fits in with their almost total lack of eschatology Theirs is a this-worldly religion, a religion of abundant life and the fullness of days, and they neither pretend to know, nor, I think, do they care, what happens to them after death

When a man dies the flesh, the life, and the soul separate themselves out. The idea of *ring*, flesh, presents no difficulties. All creatures have *ring*, and it is what, when a man dies, is committed to the earth. *Yiegh*, life, is a more difficult concept, especially as, as will be seen, its meaning overlaps with that of *tie*, soul—they are different aspects of what in a living man is a single whole. *Yiegh* means both 'breath' and 'life'. In the sense of 'life' it may mean, according to the context, either mere life, what is common to man and all living creatures, or it may include the intellectual and moral faculties as well. At one end the meaning is much the same as *tegh*, life, in contrast to *liagh*, death, and at the other end it approximates to *tie*, the soul A man's *yiegh* may be stronger or weaker according to circumstances. When he is drunk he is partly dead, and also when he is ill. Sleep is also a partial death, the death, Nuer say, for which people do not mourn. When a man is dying the life slowly weakens and then it departs from him altogether, and Nuer say it has gone to God from whom it came. Nuer ideas on this matter are relatively simple and also easy for us to understand. Life comes from God and to him it returns.

[1] Horror of death is probably the reason for the great reluctance with which Nuer discuss dreams, even impersonally and with reference only to stereotyped interpretations, for these only too often are prognostications of death· as when a man dreams of death, or of a fish called *rec ma car*, black fish, or of a turtle walking about which the dreamer fails to catch

Tie corresponds to the *anima* in scholastic writings and presents many of the difficulties of that word. It would appear to be that part of the *yiegh* which embraces the intellectual and moral faculties of man, his rational soul as distinct from his mere life as a living creature [1] It is used in varying contexts in a variety of senses and might sometimes be translated 'cleverness', 'wisdom', and 'disposition', but the English word that best covers its general sense is 'soul' It is true that sometimes 'life' is a more appropriate rendering than 'soul', just as *yiegh* may sometimes be more suitably translated 'soul' than 'life', but when this is so it is the psychic life rather than the animal life that is to be understood The essential difference, in spite of mutual overlap, between the two conceptions is clearly to be seen in the already related case of Gatbuogh. He ostensibly had breath and life (*yiegh*), but what made him a person (*ran*), his soul (*tie*), had departed. Hence, although he was described as 'a living ghost' he was also said to be 'dead'. It is to be seen also in the Nuer dogma about twins, that they are one person. Ostensibly each has his independent individual life, but they have a single soul and are therefore one person The distinction also emerges at death. The *yiegh*, the life. returns to God at the moment of death, so we may suppose—and Nuer remarks on the whole lead us to the same conclusion—that what survives death in an independent, if shadowy, existence as a ghost or shade is the *tie*, the soul. I return to this aspect of the matter later.

Associated with the *tie* is the *tiep*, the common Nilotic word for a shadow or reflection. In Nuer it may simply mean 'shade', as the shade of a tree, and also the reflection of anything in water. When used for the human shadow it might sometimes be translated 'soul', though in its general sense *tiep* cannot be equated with *tie* and when it is used in a context where we might expect *tie* to be used it would seem to be in the sense of an external representation or symbol of the soul There may be here a merging of ideas, but Nuer are nevertheless fully aware that a man's shadow is only a reflection visible at certain times and in certain circumstances

[1] Psychical functions are associated with the head and the heart The head is the seat of intelligence and will and by synecdoche stands for the whole person, especially when a pronominal suffix is added The heart is similarly used as a periphrasis for the personal pronoun when a man's affections, emotions, or sentiments are referred to (Cf. Aubrey R Johnson, *The Vitality of the Individual in the Thought of Ancient Israel*, 1949, pp 77–88)

and is not an integral part of him. They do not attach any importance to it and there are no beliefs and practices connected with it. They presumably see an analogy between a man's shadow and his soul, the shadow being the best way they can find to figure the sort of thing the soul might be. The analogy may derive from the idea of ghosts being shadowy replicas of the living. The fact that other creatures and things have shadows does not lead Nuer to say that they have souls; and since they have no souls, in their case the shadow does not at any time have a figurative meaning.

Nuer hold no decided opinions about the nature of the soul, which does not surprise us in view of their lack of interest in what happens after death, or of how there comes to be one They know that the foetus begins as a result of the male sperm entering into the womb. The child is begotten (*dieth*) by man. But it is also created (*cak*) by God, so it appears that they think of conception as a product of this combination of human and divine action. But it does not necessarily follow that because a man is alive he has a soul. Gatbuogh was alive. So when we observe that Nuer do not mourn or hold a mortuary ceremony for a dead child, it suggests to us that either they do not think of a small child as having a soul or they regard it as immature. It is only when he begins to take part in activities of the social life that he is said to be a person (*ran*), and Nuer sometimes indicate that the sign of having become a person is the removal of the second lower incisor teeth, which is done when the child is about seven or eight years of age. On the other hand they speak of infant twins having one soul. Clearly they hold no definite opinion about the matter.

Though Nuer would not themselves bring the ideas of flesh, life, and soul so neatly together, we can see that taken together they are covered by the concepts of both *pwony* and *ran*. *Pwony* means the whole creature, the individual or the self, what is one man and not another '*Pwonyda*' is 'myself' and '*pwonyda pany*' is 'my very self'. *Ran* is what we may describe as 'the person', the social being as distinct from the individual creature Its plural form *nath* is the word Nuer use to distinguish themselves from other peoples. They are *nei ti nath*, people (in the general sense of the word) who are people (in the sense of persons as Nuer think of themselves). *Pwony* is, as it were, the total organism, *ran* the total personality. As I have explained, a small child is the one but not the other, and twins are two *pwony* but a single *ran* (p. 128). However, the idea of the soul, as we have noted, seems to be attached chiefly to the concept of *ran*, to belong to the representation of a developed social being. An animal has, or is, a *pwony*, but it is not a *ran*, except in a purely figurative sense.

Nuer do not attribute souls to creatures other than man except perhaps cattle and elephants They speak of the *tie* of a man at his mortuary ceremony going together with the *tie* of the sacrificed beast away from the living to wherever the ghosts may be, and since in sacrifice, especially in piacular sacrifice, there is an identification, discussed in a later chapter, between man and ox, it is understandable that, at any rate in sacrificial contexts, Nuer should speak of the souls of cattle. But though Nuer imply in relation to sacrifice that cattle have souls, they have no clearly formulated belief to that effect, and I am not sure that they would agree to the proposition if it were put to them as a question unrelated to sacrificial intention. Nevertheless, it may be supposed that since Nuer sometimes speak of an ox's *tie* they think that cattle have in some degree intelligence and will and a personality that survives death, however vague it may be.[1] Moreover, they speak of the ghosts as herding cattle in wherever it is they have their abode. That Nuer reflect on this question, and also that they are undecided about the answer to it, is shown by the fact that Dr. Smith, so she tells me, has often been asked by Nuer whether she thinks cattle have souls.

Though I have never heard Nuer speak of an elephant's *tie*, that it is thought to have one is implicit in the belief that if the rules about the division of the tusks of a slain elephant are not observed the dead beast may *gwor*, track down, those responsible (Dr. Lienhardt tells me that in Dinka the word means 'to take revenge'). *Gwor* has here, therefore, the same sense as *cien*, haunt. Also, Dr. Howell states that the man who first speared a slain elephant, and is therefore by a convention regarded as responsible for its death, has to have his right arm incised by a leopard-skin priest before he can eat or drink just as if he had slain a man, and a beast is sacrificed in the one case as in the other. He says

[1] That a cow in a kind of way can be thought of as a person is suggested by other facts. A rite is performed to separate twin cows, which are hence, unlike other beasts, regarded till then as being one, as human twins are A rite is also performed, to prevent the calf sickening, when the first milk of its dam is taken for human consumption. See also Chap X.

further that when the tusks are removed they are first buried under the floor of a cattle byre before being cut up for distribution among such persons as have rights in them, and that when they are buried a sacrifice, called *kirpiny*, is made, the name of the sacrifice being the same as that made when a man is buried.[1]

The only occasions on which I have heard Nuer speak of creatures, other than cattle, or things having a *tie* was when they were discussing offerings of food and tobacco to fetishes, and in this case the usage was clearly metaphorical just as was their use of the word *cam*, to eat, in the same connexion *Cam* is often used in a metaphorical sense to indicate that something is being appropriated, as when it is said of a man, usually a man with the evil eye or someone connected with the Government, that '*came nath*', 'he eats the people', that is, he takes something from, or exploits, the people. Nuer know very well that a fetish does not really eat the offerings. They only suppose that it in some way appropriates them, and since the offerings are obviously not materially appropriated they are more or less obliged to use the only available analogy and to speak of the fetish taking their 'souls'. Nuer do not attribute souls to food and tobacco, or to any other things. They are merely using the word in an attempt to explain their use in a very special and peculiar situation.

I have discussed this question partly because it was necessary to do so to make clear that in Nuer thought the soul is something essentially human which man has in addition to life, which he shares with other creatures, and partly because it is of some theoretical importance. In the light of the discussion it will be seen that the so-called animistic theory of religion, chiefly associated with the name of Tylor, cannot be sustained for the Nuer; since they are not animists and there is no evidence that they ever have been. But there is a further and more decisive reason for rejecting it. It supposes that the conception of Spirit derives and has developed from that of the soul, whereas in Nuer thought *kwoth*, Spirit, is something of quite a different nature from *tie*, soul. The soul is part of man and a created thing. Spirit is extrinsic to man, operating on him from outside him, and invasive. Nuer express the difference in nature between the human and the divine, between soul, or ghost, and Spirit when they say that 'God

[1] P P Howell, 'A Note on Elephants and Elephant Hunting among the Nuer', *Sudan Notes and Records*, 1945, p. 100.

is a person of the above (*ran nhial*)' and that man, or ghost, 'is a person of the below (*ran piny*)'. The difference, and the contrast, is clearly seen in the Nuer belief that the soul of a person struck by lightning is changed into Spirit. It is evident also in the way they speak about their prophets and about sick persons. They say that Spirit comes from above and enters into them or takes hold of them. Since, therefore, Spirit and soul are conceived of as of different natures, the conception of Spirit cannot be derived from a development of the conception of soul. On the contrary, it is precisely because God and man are thought of as quite different sorts of being that Nuer can think of themselves in relation to God and that God can be represented in different ways to different persons and social groups. Therefore it is necessary, if we wish not only to avoid confusion but also to seize upon the essential content of Nuer religious thought, that we should speak of the 'soul' and not of the 'Spirit' of man and of the 'ghosts' and not of the 'spirits' of the departed.

It follows from the Nuer orientation towards Spirit that they are little interested in the ghosts of the dead, so long as they cause no trouble. When people 'disappear'—Nuer avoid using the word 'die'—only one thing is certain, that they have departed for good. 'They dwell apart, they have become ghosts.' It is taken for granted that people have some sort of existence after death, though Nuer do not presume to know where they have it or what kind of life it is that they lead. Sometimes they say that they may be under the earth and live a life like that they lived when they were on earth amid their cattle and dung fires in villages and camps. This seems to be the general opinion and it is perhaps strengthened by the discovery, when digging wells, of goats' dung and fire-stones deep down in the earth, for I have heard Nuer say that maybe these belong to the ghosts. But Nuer also say of a dead man *'ce mat ka kwoth'*, 'he has joined God', and *'ce tiede wa nhial, ca ringde kwony'*, 'his soul has gone above, (only) his flesh was buried'. One often hears also the idea expressed that the dead have lost their relationship to the living and have therefore no further claims on them for attentions and services, and that they have instead 'become kin to God' or have 'become God's people'. Sometimes Nuer say that since the dead are near to God they can intercede with him on behalf of their families and relatives. However, no one supposes he can know where is the *wec indit*, the great community (of the departed) which all, each in his turn, must join, or what it is like.

It is possible that the apparent contradiction between being under the earth and being with God in the sky arises from the vagueness of the concept of *tie* and in particular from the absence of any dogma that it is the *tie*, soul, which becomes a *joagh* (pl., *jook*), ghost. It is perhaps important that Nuer always speak of the *joagh* of the departed and never of his *tie* when speaking of his survival as a person. They speak of the 'ghosts' of the dead and not of the 'souls' of the dead. This distinction would seem to allow both for the idea of the dead leading some sort of existence in the Nuer sheol as shadowy replicas of the living and also at the same time for the idea that their souls are taken on high by God. They cannot say anything more definite about this question of what is conceived to survive, or how or where.

There is a further question: when does a man become a ghost? Here again there is no formal doctrine to help us. We have to draw conclusions from what seems to be implicit in the mortuary rites As we have seen, they not only close the period of mourning and cleanse the home and the kin from the pollution of death but also send the dead man away to join the ghosts and cut him off formally and finally from the living Only when that has been done can his property be taken by his heirs and his widows cohabit with those with whom they have decided to live. It follows that the dead must be thought to be in some way still among the living till he is dispatched by these rites to the community of the ghosts.[1]

The word for ghost, *joagh*, is found in various forms in all the Nilotic languages. In most of the Shilluk–Luo group of languages it means 'God' or 'Spirit'. In some of the Nilotic languages, including Nuer, the word is either the same as, or is closely related to, that used to denote plagues, pestilences, murrains, and indeed any serious sickness, and, this being so, it is perhaps wise to point out that such calamities are not thought to come from the ghosts but from God· '*ce jok ben piny*', Nuer say, '*ca kam piny e kwoth*', 'the murrain came to earth, it was given to earth by God'. In Nuer

---

[1] Robert Hertz ('Contribution à une étude sur la représentation collective de la mort', *L'Année sociologique*, vol x, 1907, reprinted in *Mélanges de sociologie religieuse et de folklore*, 1928) was the first to draw attention to the universality of this idea and to show the great variety and complexity of its forms

the word *joagh* also means 'back' or 'behind' and this cannot be fortuitous, not only because in Dinka the word for a troublesome ghost, *cien*, likewise also means 'back' and 'behind', but also because it is a common Nuer refrain in speaking to, or about, the ghosts that they should have their backs to the living, the Nuer way of saying that they should keep away from the living. If they return to the living, except when summoned as witnesses on formal occasions, it is only to cause trouble, to fetch the living to join them in the place of the dead or to punish them for faults and shortcomings. We have already noted how pronounced is this apotropaic motif in the mortuary rites, and especially in the invocations spoken at them, the speakers frequently adjuring the dead *'bi rodu rit'*, 'turn thyself about'. They ask the dead to turn away from the living, to turn his back on them. Father Crazzolara notes the same sentiment He says that the dead are buried with their backs to the huts and their faces to the bush and that a dead man is addressed. 'turn thine eyes to the bush, do not turn them to the home'. He comments that this means that the dead man must not regard the doings of the living, for he might see something which offends him and draw another person after him to death [1] The living do not want the dead to take any interest in their lives. The dead had best look after their own affairs and let the living look after theirs That the ideas of 'behind' and of 'the ghosts' are related is further shown by the fact that Nuer sometimes use the phrase 'to go behind' as a euphemism for 'to go to the ghosts' and hence 'to die'

It is consistent with the idea of the ghosts being turned away from the living so that they do not see their affairs that the ghosts are relatively unimportant in Nuer religious thought and practice, even the troublesome ones, which I discuss later; and they are in the ordinary course of affairs seldom mentioned But though Nuer pay them little attention they cannot entirely ignore them, for there are some occasions when they are directly concerned with what is happening and their relationship to the living has to be emphasized, occasions of collective sacrifice (pp. 198–9). such as their funeral and mortuary ceremonies, settlement of blood-feuds started on account of their violent deaths, and the marriages of their children. Occasionally also dutiful sons honour their memory by sacrifice, especially if they have had vivid dreams

[1] Op cit, p 173.

of the departed On such occasions Nuer usually have a definite ghost in mind, but in contexts in which the lineage as a whole is involved they may speak of *jook dial*, all the ghosts (of their lineage), though I have seldom heard them do so; and the reason for this is that when, on ceremonial occasions, Nuer speak of a lineage as a collectivity to which both dead and living belong they speak in terms of Spirit rather than of ghosts, of '*kwoth* which created our ancestor', rather than of the ancestor himself, and of '*kwoth* of our fathers', rather than the fathers themselves. The conception of the ghosts is subordinated to that of Spirit.

Nuer do not pray (*pal*) to the ghosts, which have no power in themselves to grant requests. On such occasions as I have mentioned they may invoke (*lam*) them, but even when they do this the ghosts take second place to God in some such phrases as '*kwoth, yene jook*', 'God, thou and the ghosts'. Even when beasts are reserved for them, Nuer do not formally dedicate them to the ghosts as they do to their spirits, and though they sacrifice on certain occasions on their behalf or in their honour or memory, I do not think that it can be said that sacrifice is ever made to them, at any rate not to them by themselves, for it may be that in those sacrifices in which God and the ghosts are invoked together Nuer think of the sacrifice being to both. Even if this is so, the victim is consecrated to God and not to the ghosts Likewise, though the ghosts are associated with the *riek* or post-shrine which elderly men erect in their homes, it is a shrine firstly to God as God of the hearth and in whatever further refractions he may be figured as the guardian of the family and lineage. It is therefore called *riek kwoth*, God's shrine, and not *riek jookni*, ghosts' shrine. There is no cult of the dead, and their graves, not being marked, are soon forgotten unless a tree happens to spring from the tomb, when it may be named after the man buried there A man's memorial is not in some monument but in his sons.

Dead persons, though for the most part only men, are remembered in their names, and this is a matter of great importance both for the Nuer themselves and also for an understanding on our part of their sentiments. Every man likes to feel that his name will never be forgotten so long as his lineage endures and that in that sense he will always be a part of the lineage. Consequently, Nuer do not so much think of the ghosts of their forebears as being those members of their lineage who are in the home of the dead, but rather as names numbered, as it were, in the archives of the lineage. They think of the dead continuing in this way in the living. It is to ensure the survival of the dead in their names, Nuer say, that they have the customs of the levirate, widow-concubinage, and ghost-marriage.

I have discussed these practices at length elsewhere,[1] and here it is only necessary to show their connexion with the matter under discussion. Nuer practise the true levirate. Widows are neither remarried nor inherited but continue till death to be married to their dead husbands to whose names they continue to bear children begotten by their dead husbands' brothers, with whom they have in certain circumstances an obligation to live If, however, for one or other reason, a widow does not choose to live with one of her dead husband's brothers she may cohabit with any man she pleases, but all children such a widow-concubine may bear to her lovers count as children of her dead husband The custom of ghost-marriage further ensures that every man must have a son who will be called after him '*gat* so-and-so', 'son of so-and-so'. If a man dies without a male heir and without leaving a widow to bear him male heirs it is a paramount duty for his near kin to marry a wife to his name before they take wives in their own names In theory at any rate, therefore, every man has at least one son and through this son his name is forever a link in a line of descent This is the only form of immortality Nuer are interested in They are not interested in the survival of the individual as a ghost, but in the survival of the social personality in the name

The memory of a dead man is thus kept alive by its being constantly on people's lips through the favoured patronymic usage during the lifetime of his children and afterwards in the recitation of a line of descent This is why at a mortuary ceremony Nuer stress that a man who has died is not entirely finished. 'His children will carry on his name.' A dead man's name is also on people's lips in reference to bridewealth cattle. If a man has a right to cattle in the division of a girl's bridewealth he does not lose that right at death Indeed, if he is dead he not only retains the right but his claims are given precedence, as being 'the right of a ghost', over those of the living These cattle are *ghok jookni*,

---

[1] 'Some Aspects of Marriage and the Family among the Nuer', *Zeitschrift fur vergleichende Rechtswissenschaft*, 1938 (reprinted in *Rhodes-Livingstone Papers*, No XI, 1945), also *Kinship and Marriage among the Nuer*, 1951, chaps III and IV

'cattle of the ghosts', and they must be handed over to his sons, at once if they are adults, and later if they are children. It is a grave fault for a kinsman to take advantage of the minority of children to use the cattle of ghosts for his own purposes. The rights of the dead in bridewealth cattle derive not only from the fact that it is their kinswoman who is being married but also from the feeling Nuer have that a line of descent is attached to its herd. Whatever individual may have control over the herd it is thought of as being in a vague general sense owned by the ghosts who once tended it, for though the animals change the herd is felt to have a sort of continuity. This is partly why the ghosts are addressed in invocations at weddings. It must be explained to those on the bridegroom's side that the cattle are leaving the herd so that a girl of another lineage may come into the family to bear sons who will continue their own lineage; and it must be explained to those on the bride's side that she is being married with cattle which will enable her family to acquire a wife who will bear sons to continue their lineage.

The great importance attached to the maintenance of a dead man's name and the privileges and obligations of the living which derive from their relationship to him—*ciek joka*, ghost's wife, *gat joka*, ghost's son, and so on—give sharp individuality to the dead; and it is interesting to note that in the Nuer language the word for the departed has singular and plural forms, unlike many languages in Africa and elsewhere, which, like the Latin *manes*, can indicate only a collectivity. It is possible that we are to seek in the desire for survival of the self in the name—not just survival in the children—the reason for the fact that Nuer do not, at any rate in normal circumstances, care to call a son by the same name as his father and even show aversion at the suggestion that one might do so. Were father and son to bear the same name they would be likely in course of time to become merged in the recitation of a genealogy. I think Nuer realize this. However, it would be necessary, were such an interpretation advanced, to account for the fact that some of the other Nilotic peoples have no objection to father and son bearing the same name, the Anuak for instance, and Dr. Lienhardt tells me that it is also the case among the Dinka.

III

When a ghost comes to trouble the living it is said to *cien* them. It is useful to discuss this concept in the light of another, that of *but*, to curse,[1] because the two are closely connected, the ability of a ghost to harm being the *post mortem* operation of the projective power of the psyche, the power to harm another through the mind and the heart.

The curse of certain persons in Nuer society is believed to be effective if they have been wronged. If they utter curses without due cause (*cuong*) the curses will either be ineffective or harm the speakers of them. A man curses another by uttering an invocation (*lam*)—which in this context is an imprecation—over, or about, him, and Nuer distinguish different kinds of curse by reference to the relationship of the persons implicated in it—*but gwan*, the curse of a father, *biit nara*, the curse of a maternal uncle, *biit kuaara*, the curse of a leopard-skin priest, and so forth. Some of these curses are regarded as weightier than others.

The curse of father or mother is serious. A man may curse his son for constant disobedience and for meanness, especially for refusing him meat. Indeed, any old man may curse a youth for refusing him food, because both in a general sense and in terms of the age-set system all youths are sons to the aged, but his curse would not be as weighty as that of the true father. 'A father's curse is to hunting, to fishing, and to hoeing, but he will not curse him (his son) to cattle.' The youth may then miss his mark in hunting, fishing, and war, and his crops may fail. He may also injure himself in these occupations, or suffer one of the many possible misfortunes that beset a traveller, both in the literal sense of mishaps to one on a journey and in the figurative sense of evils that face a man on his journey through life, which the Nuer, who have a liking for meiosis, speak of collectively as 'thorns'. At its worst the curse of a father or mother may be a *biit liagh*, a curse which results in death. However, 'a father will not curse his son to cattle', because the cattle belong to the lineage and if he caused them to die he would only be harming himself and his kinsmen and ancestors.

---

[1] A *but* is a curse in the sense of consigning a person to misfortune and not in the sense of swearing at a person, which is *kuith* or, where there is a joking relationship, *leng*

A mother may curse her son for neglect, especially when she is old and must rely on others for support, or for divulging her hiding-place to her husband if he is angry with her and seeks for her to chastise her. A mother's curse may have the same effects as a father's curse, but it is thought that, in addition, it has the particular effect of preventing the son from begetting male children. A mother's curse may thus injure the lineage, and in this respect her curse is more like that of the mother's brother than that of the father. I have also been told that a mother may, because she loves a son who has wandered to a distant country, curse him mildly so that he may suffer some minor sickness which will put him in memory of his home and cause him to return to it

The curse of a mother's brother—at any rate that of a mother's uterine brother—is also greatly feared by Nuer, for he, unlike the father, may curse a man 'to cattle', so that he loses his entire herd Nuer seem to regard it as the worst of all curses and they recognize it as a strong sanction behind the demands of their mothers' brothers, where these are just. A sister's son who fails to carry out certain duties or who fails to observe certain interdictions concerning his mother's brother may develop a disease called *keth nara* (disease of the *nar*, mother's brother), which may be fatal Nuer describe it as '*cere ke but*', 'like to a curse'. People say that the curses of father, mother, and mother's brother are the worst, though that of a paternal grandmother is also said to be bad, and it is said that the curse of an eldest child is feared by his parents, especially his mother, and by his maternal uncle, in certain circumstances a sister's son, especially the eldest son of the sister, may curse his maternal uncle's herd The only other kinsfolk of whom I have been specifically told that they may curse a man, in the sense that one may speak of a curse of the kinship category in which they stand, are the father's sister and the mother's sister, and Nuer say that these are very small curses and they do not therefore give them much thought; but a person standing in any social relationship to another may curse him if he has been wronged by him. However, the more distant the relationship the less effective the curse, because the less the obligation and therefore the less the wrong

A run of misfortunes may be attributed to the curse of one of these relatives I tell one story in illustration. Luak, a man of the Leek tribe, refused to stay at home and help his father Thicjok to herd the cattle and hoe the gardens, but spent his time attending dances and courting girls. He wandered about the country having a good time, and when he returned home it was only for a meal. He would be off again next morning. One day his father, in exasperation, cursed him, saying that he would never have a wife and children and would live to a great age to lament that he had no sons of his own in whom he would be remembered but only children he had begotten by the wives of other men. So it happened. Luak never married, though he begat two sons by a widow-concubine. When he died he left ten head of cattle with instructions that Dol, the second of his natural sons, was to marry with them a wife to his name, so that he might have sons called after him. That year all the ten animals died of rinderpest; so that people said that the curse on Luak went on acting after his death. The father's curse was here not in the first instance 'to cattle' but 'to sons', although in the sequel its purpose could only be achieved by the death of the cattle. Dol told me that, as he has now enough cattle, he would like to marry a wife to his genitor's name but fears to take steps to do so lest the cattle die. He had decided that it would be prudent to marry first a wife for himself and then, if ever he has again enough cattle, to make a second marriage in the name of his natural father.

Other specified curses among the Nuer are those of the *ric*, the age-set, and of certain religious personalities, the *kuaar muon*, the priest of the earth (the leopard-skin priest), the *wut ghok*, the man of the cattle, and the *guk*, the prophet (Chapter XII). If a man wrongs a member of his age-set, as by committing adultery with his wife or by not assisting him when attacked by strangers or when wounded, the wronged man may utter an imprecation, saying 'as if we did not look at this sun together' (when lying on their backs awaiting the cutting of the marks of manhood on their foreheads), and Nuer told me that it may well have lethal consequences. A leopard-skin priest can curse a man who obstructs him in the exercise of his functions as peacemaker in fighting and feud. On account of his mystical connexion with the earth his curse is believed to be particularly harmful to the crops, though it may cause other misfortunes as well. In his imprecation he may forbid the man he curses to plant in his earth and tell him to beget his children in the tree-tops and herd his cattle in the sky. The *wut ghok* has ritual functions in connexion with cattle and his curse is said to be feared because it may injure the cherished herds. It may also cause a man diarrhoea whenever he drinks milk. Much of the influence exercised by the Nuer prophets who were so prominent in recent times was due to the fear their curses inspired.

A *biit*, in a conditional form, is often cited by Nuer as a mythological explanation of some custom. Somebody in past times cursed certain persons if ever they or their descendants should do certain things. I give a few examples. A member of the aristocratic lineage of the Karlual section of the Leek tribe will not live in the country of the Lang tribe. The explanation is that once upon a time a Karlual aristocrat and a Lang aristocrat together speared a buffalo, which charged and knocked down the Lang man and began to worry him. He called out to the Karlual man to spear the animal again, but the Karlual man did not do so, fearing that he might injure his companion. Before Lang (tribes are personified in myths) died he cursed Karlual, saying that if ever a member of the dominant clan of Karlual settled in Lang country he would die. Another story is about the Riaagh lineage, who are a branch of the Keunyang lineage, the dominant lineage in the Karlual country referred to in the story I have just related. It concerns their relations with the Ngwol lineage of the same tribal section who are said to be descended from a man of this name who was a foundling adopted by Keunyang. Riaagh had a newborn child and the mother was so busy looking after it that she often let her fire out and rekindled it by borrowing a brand from the fire of Ngwol's wife One day Ngwol fell sick with smallpox and sent word to Riaagh that his wife was not to come to his home again for fire as he was ill. Riaagh did not believe him and sent his wife again to borrow fire. A fight ensued and Ngwol killed Riaagh. Riaagh's mother then uttered a curse, saying that the descendants of Ngwol would suffer misfortune if ever they were to eat out of the same pot as the descendants of Riaagh or to sit near their cooking-pots. If today a Ngwol man sits near a Riaagh pot there will be a quarrel. The Keunyang lineage figures in another myth of this kind. If a man of this lineage crosses the Gazelle river to settle among the collateral lineages of Deng and Cuaagh, or a member of either of these two lineages crosses the river to settle among the Keunyang, the settler builds his byre without an entrance of the usual form. This custom is said to date from the time when the Deng and Cuaagh lineages first crossed the river to settle to the north of it, leaving the Keunyang in what had been their common home to the south of it. Quarrels ensued and Keunyang uttered a *biit* making it a condition of any future settlement. Yet another story relates how Jwal and Gaawar (clans, like tribes, are personified in myths) went fishing together. Jwal lacked a pot in which to cook his catch and he asked Gaawar to lend him his pot, but Gaawar refused, so Jwal had to do the best he could with a gourd plastered with mud. To mark this meanness he uttered a *biit* saying that if a member of either clan were to take shelter during rain under the same roof as a member of the other clan lightning would destroy them both. I have heard people shout to a member of one of these clans who had entered a hut for shelter from a storm to get out as there was a member of the other clan present. This story may be connected with the association of the Gaawar clan with sky and rain. There are a number of such stories relating to inter-clan relations which probably mirror actual or historical local and political interrelations which lie outside the present discussion.

A *biit* of a rather different kind is that relating to certain girls called *kuony*, who are said to be dangerous to their husbands. It is said that a girl of this name was affianced by her brothers to a man with some unpleasant complaint. She refused to marry him and was often beaten by her brothers on this score, because the man had many cattle. Eventually she gave way and married him, but then she refused to cohabit with him. Her husband eventually died of his complaint and the girl was left alone in his home, and lions and hyenas came by night and ate the cattle and beasts of the flock, as there was no man in the home to defend it. So she uttered a curse over her kinsmen, saying that in future daughters of their lineage would always bring death to their husbands. I have met *kuony* girls in western Nuerland, where it was pointed out to me that their husbands, as I could see for myself, had died young. However, this does not seem to prevent men from marrying them, and I was told that they are regarded as unusually attractive.

There are also many examples of a *biit* in Nuer just-so stories explaining how animals acquired their characteristics and habits. The giraffe has what looks like a hollow in the top of its head. When his mother died giraffe asked shrewmouse to lend him a hoe to dig a grave in the earth to bury her, but as shrewmouse refused to let him have a hoe he had to bury her in his head. As a result of this incident giraffe and shrewmouse uttered conditional curses, giraffe saying that if ever a shrewmouse crossed a path he would die, and shrewmouse saying that if ever a giraffe ate grass he would die. This is why one never sees a shrewmouse on a path unless it be dead,[1] and why one never sees a giraffe eating grass, only the leaves of trees. The mother of goat, in another story, borrowed a knife from the mother of hyena and lost it. The mother of hyena cursed her, saying that in future her descendants would eat goats wherever they found them. This is the reason why goats are always pawing the ground. They are still looking for the lost knife of the mother of hyena. Another story relates how man lent his running-powers to ostrich and ostrich refused to return them It is because man then cursed the race of ostriches that today men sometimes hunt them for their feathers and lions kill them for meat. Shoebills eat fish and blue herons eat frogs and other small creatures of marsh and shallows. The reason for this is that *bany*, the shoebill, and *ngok*, the blue heron, were sons of one father and because *ngok* neglected an uncle's duties to *bany's* children when their father died, *bany's* mother cursed him and his descendants. Yet another of many such stories relates how the village mouse, after having taught men how to beget children, taught women how to bear them In return for this service woman uttered a *biit*, saying that village mice would share the food of the home with its mistress. This last story introduces us to a further sense of the word *but*, an invocation which is a blessing and not a curse, for a man can *biit* a person to good fortune, as woman did in the case of mouse, instead of to bad fortune. In my experience this sense is rare.

The curse is undoubtedly a powerful sanction of conduct, largely because it is not thought necessary that a wronged man should utter it aloud for misfortune to follow. He has only to think it. Such an unspoken curse Nuer call a *biit loac*, a curse of the heart. Indeed, it would seem that he need not expressly formulate a curse in his mind at all. a mere feeling of resentment arising from a genuine grievance being sufficient to cause injury to the person who occasioned it Thus I was told that if a man is killed by his wife's brother and the wife laments his death, her sorrow and sighs are themselves a kind of *but*. God hears them and will cause

[1] Cf the old belief in England that a shrew cannot cross a footpath and live

the slayer to become a wanderer on the face of the earth and to
die in the midst of his wanderings. He becomes one of the *jibiet*,
the cursed ones, and what Nuer also call a *gwan giakni*, a man
possessed by evil An action by itself may bear evil fruit without
anyone saying or doing anything to make it bear. Nuer say that
'it is like a *biit*' A man who kills another finds all the strength
gone out of him. The infringement of a religious interdiction
carries its own penalty, for the interdiction is 'like a *biit*'. For
example, misfortune will fall, if only in that the cuts of manhood
on his brow will not cicatrize, on a lad who during the period of
seclusion after initiation has contact with the cattle.

Though the word *biit* may not often be used with the sense of
blessing it is sometimes so used, and as the idea of blessing has
some importance in Nuer thought a few words may be devoted
to it before making some concluding remarks about curses [1] An
older person blesses a younger one by spitting on his head. The
spittle (*ruei*) has, as in other parts of Africa, a special virtue
and is said to benefit the *yiegh*, the life, of the person who
receives it. I was told that this is particularly done by a man's
parents when he returns from a long journey, and one man said
that it is then done so that the ghosts, who may have forgotten
their kinsman, may know him again. A mother also blesses a
son about to set out on a long journey by taking his middle
finger in her hand, spitting on him, and saying something like
'friend, my son, you will journey on this earth, you will go
round [avoid] all thorns [troubles]'. She may also take some soot
from the bottom of a pot and mix it with butter and daub this
paste on the soles of his feet, under the knees, and on thighs, chest,
and head. Spitting figures as a blessing in various other contexts.
If a woman does not conceive, her father's kin spit into a gourd
and rub her belly with the spittle, asking God that she may conceive. If she does so, the child may be named *Ruei*, Spittle, or
Nyaruea, Daughter of Spittle. The spittle of a prophet is considered
to be especially efficacious in curing barrenness When a leopard-
skin priest arbitrates between two parties and gives a decision in
favour of one of them, that man may hand his spear to the priest,

---

[1] Another word which sometimes has the sense of blessing is *puth*, but, though
it sometimes has this sense, it is most commonly used in reference to the making
of a gift to in-laws and is then, as in most other contexts, best translated 'to
honour'

who returns it to him after having first spat on it When a father has agreed to his son's initiation the boy goes to a member of his father's age-set and this man plucks out a tuft of the boy's hair, spits on it, and brushes it against the boy's face and head. This is the blessing of the father's age-set A leech massages a sick person with his spittle. Mr. B. A. Lewis records that when the Gaawar tribe chose a certain Bwoogh Kerpel to lead them across the Nile to conquer fresh lands from the Dinka the people lifted him on high so that God might see that he had been chosen, and they gave him a gourdful of milk to drink into which they had all spat.[1] In all these examples—and others could be given—there is the idea of blessing. However, a blessing can be given without spitting Any person can bless another (pp. 16–17), but the blessings of those whose curses are most effective are also the most effective.

It is important to note that, as with curses, blessings are thought to be effective only because God makes them so. Just as a curse is an imprecatory prayer (for if God is not formally addressed in it it is understood that it is his affair), so a prayer is implied in a blessing. It is a benedictory prayer. Hence (and here again as with curses), a man can be aided merely by a person thinking well of him, bearing him in sweet recollection (*tim*) without formally blessing him. He blesses him in his heart, and just as God sees a man's just resentment for a wrong and the resentment then has the force of a curse, so he sees the love and the love has then the force of a blessing So when a Nuer says '*ba ji tiem*', 'I will think of you', he means that he will think fondly of you and so blesses you. A good action in itself may bring fortune to a man. God sees it and it becomes, Nuer say, like a *biit* for good, just as he sees a bad action and it becomes a *biit* for ill.

The religious significance of cursing and blessing lies in a dominant motif of Nuer religion, that of *cuong* in opposition to *duer*, right in opposition to wrong. A person's curse of another is only effective if he is in the right and the other is in the wrong. There must have been damage or negligence, and in Nuer reckoning this implies a social relationship of some kind between the two persons, such as, in fact, is bound to exist between any persons so involved in Nuer society It is when the obligations of a relationship have not been observed that a curse can act, its effectiveness increasing with the closeness or social significance of the relation-

[1] B. A. Lewis, 'Nuer Spokesmen', *Sudan Notes and Records*, 1951, p 81

PLATE VII

Youth and boy

ship, and it can be quieted by reparation to the wronged person
In an account of Nuer religion what is here important is that the
curse is only effective, Nuer say, because God sees that one man
has right and the other wrong and allows it to act. It seems to the
observer therefore that the curse, like the blessing, has its own
psychic power, but that Nuer relate it to a set of moral rules of
which God is conceived of as guardian and judge The power of a
curse or a blessing thus lies ultimately not with man, who is only
the medium, but with God. God's role is not merely permissive,
for, as we have noted, a wrong itself may, through the sufferings
and lamentations of the wronged persons, bring retribution to the
wrongdoers without their taking any action in the matter themselves. This is why also Nuer say of the infringement of a religious
interdiction, in which no immediate question of wrong to another
may arise, that it has a certain similarity to a *biit*. Formally the
two ideas are quite distinct, and Nuer see a similarity between
them only because in both cases there is a fault which is punished
by God, in the first case indirectly and in the second directly.
Consequently we are once again faced with the Nuer idea of faults,
which necessitates a fuller discussion than I have so far given to it
but which is also more appropriately treated separately in the next
chapter.

The concept of *cien*, to which I now turn, has certain similarities
to that of *biit*, especially to the silent curse, 'the curse of the heart'.
Nuer think that it bodes ill for those who have wronged a man if
he dies with resentment in his heart, for he will then take ghostly
vengeance on them from the grave.

The word *cien* is found in one form or another, and with common elements of meaning, in all the Nilotic languages. In Nuer it
means the vengeance, generally producing sickness or other misfortune ending in death, taken by an aggrieved ghost on the living,
and in its verbal form the taking of such vengeance Nuer regard
it as a most serious matter if a man dies with a legitimate grievance
in his heart, for while it may be possible to make amends to a
living man for a wrong done to him and thereby rid oneself of his
biit, it is often impossible to make peace with the dead. Fear of
cien undoubtedly, if we are to believe what Nuer say, makes them
avoid, at any rate sometimes, persistently denying men justice
lest they take their wrongs to the grave and from there seek
settlement.

I give some examples of the kind of circumstances in which *cien* acts. A man haunts his kinsmen because he was slain and they neither avenged him nor exacted compensation in cattle for his death. When a man slays a close kinsman 'they [may] say "do not spear him, let him die of *cien*"'. After a while he becomes distracted and his ears ring. He loses his wits and takes to wandering alone in the bush and to sleeping there by himself at night. or he wanders to a distant country and lives there haunted 'Nuer have no sense. A man may slay even his mother's son in anger. Well, he haunts him from the grave He [the living man] sits moping. For two or three days together he refuses food He wanders by himself in the bush. Then he sickens and dies.' A man may kill another secretly when they are alone together in the bush and tell no one of the deed. Then the dead man's ghost will pursue him from the grave. I was told of a case of this kind among the eastern Jikany in which the slayer married some two or three years after his crime. His first child died, then his second child, then his third child; and 'he remained childless like an impotent man' He consulted a diviner, who wormed out of him that 'he had something in the earth', a euphemism for the body of his victim. On the diviner's advice he confessed and paid compensation for the life he had taken Nuer told me also that a man who has witnessed a killing, though he had no part in it, yet if he keep silence, will suffer misfortune because 'it is like as though he had hidden the [dead] man'. A man who commits serious incest, such as one who has carnal relations with a woman and then with her daughter, and so causes the death of the daughter, will be haunted by her ghost. The ghost will summon him to the land of the dead, saying '*ban wa jogh*', 'let us go behind' [to the *jookni*, ghosts]. A girl who is married to a man she detests and commits suicide may take vengeance from the grave on her kin who forced her to marry him However, those Nuer whom I questioned were not in agreement in this case, some holding that the girl would not have *cuong*, right, and could not therefore harm her kin A man who knows that his son had congress with his wife may keep silence, hoping that the son will confess and ask his forgiveness, but the son also keeps silence, even when he sees that his father is dying, so the father takes his resentment with him to the grave and punishes him from there. A man who has not been properly buried may haunt his kin. However, a man who has suffered any injustice may take ghostly vengeance Nuer say also that a ghost watches over his kin and punishes those who commit some grave fault, especially that of depriving his young sons of the cattle of his herd or of their sisters' marriages When a father or other close kinsman summons a man from the grave to join him in death Nuer use the word *tul*, which has the sense of 'to punish', to describe his action as well as the word *cien*; and they may also use the verb *be*, with the sense of sending for, or coming to fetch, or returning to get something.

An appreciation of two considerations arising from what Nuer say about ghostly vengeance gives us a further understanding of their ideas about the dead. The dead are thought to have the same feelings as when they were alive. They are resentful of injustice and bear malice to those who have wronged them. It stands to reason therefore—and this is the second consideration—that it is only those who have recently departed who avenge themselves on the living, for it is only they who can have been wronged by them Nuer do not think of *cien* in connexion with ancestral ghosts but only in connexion with those who have recently become ghosts It would appear that a man can still take vengeance even after he has been dispatched to the community of the ghosts by the mortuary rites, but a dead man seems to be most dangerous and his living kinsmen the most vulnerable the less the lapse of time after his death, and consequently in the period between death and the mortuary ceremonies. Those nearest to the dead are those who are most likely to be affected, for though a man can *cien*, just as he can *but*, anyone who has done him an injury, what has been said of the *but* can be said of the *cien*. the closer the relationship of the persons concerned the worse both the offence and its consequences. Curses and ghostly vengeance are thus two sides to the same idea and in general they have the same social incidence

To stop the effects of *cien* it is necessary to make sacrifice to God and, where possible, reparation to the ghost for the wrong done to him. Sacrifice without reparation is of no avail Nuer say that it may temporarily wipe out (*woc*) the *cien* from the body of the haunted man, but it will return if he does not make amends Therefore, when he makes sacrifice he tells God 'I am sorry, I have erred; take thy cow and let the *cien* leave me.' Nuer say that God is to understand that such an expression of contrition implies the intention to make reparation, if this is possible.

As Nuer speak about *cien* it has, therefore, the sense of an injustice crying out for vengeance. The essence of the concept is the notion of a wrong unrighted, of a grievance which demands, and rightly demands, redress. Even a living man who has no other way of getting justice may say to the man who has wronged him *'ba ji cien'*, 'I will haunt you', meaning that though he cannot get justice now he will get it after he is dead. Nuer say that he may express this threat not in words but by looks. As in the case of the *biit*, so with the *cien*, it is God who makes the ghostly vengeance to work. Nuer say that the wronged ghost exacts vengeance by making his cause known to God, who sooner or later punishes the wrongdoer.

The moral action of *biit* and *cien*, which have a similarity to certain ideas of sin discussed in the next chapter, is in this respect very different for Nuer from the exercise of psychical and physical powers which have no moral foundation and are therefore not thought to involve divine judgement and intervention and are only thought of in connexion with Spirit, if at all, so far as all that happens in the world can ultimately be said to happen because God allows it and can be appealed to to change the course of events. I refer to the evil eye (*peth*); ghouls (*roth*); the danger of pregnant women (*ther*) and to a lesser extent of their husbands, an idea some of the eastern Nuer have taken over from the Anuak; the danger of women who commence menstruation in the dry season month of *pet* (*koc mai*), the danger of a child after two or three of its elder brothers and sisters have died at, or shortly after, birth (*jul*); monorchids (*tor*), a child conceived while its mother is still suckling (*mok*); and menstruation, which is dangerous for the cattle—no woman may drink their milk at this time. If Nuer are in danger from any of these influences they may pray and sacrifice to God, but if they do so their prayers and sacrifices are mixed up with all sorts of other and different sets of ideas and they deal with the situation mainly by magical rites which would be both inappropriate and ineffective where Spirit is concerned. They therefore cannot properly be included under the rubric of religion and so lie outside the scope of this book. They are mentioned only in order that their relative unimportance may be emphasized. That in itself is of significance. Perspective would be lost were it not understood.

CHAPTER VII

SIN

I

NUER do not think of the relation of man to God as one of soul, as a separate entity, to Spirit but as one of the whole man to Spirit. The state of the conscience, as we would call it, may be one element in the relation but peace of mind is very much bound up with welfare of body and estate. This is evident from the way they regard the breach of an interdiction which is thought to bring into operation directly, and often almost immediately, spiritual sanctions. We may speak of such a breach as sin.

Sin with the suffering it brings about is central to the study of Nuer religion. If God was thought by Nuer merely to have created man and then to have ceased to interest himself in human affairs there would be no point at all in their paying any attention to him and sacrifice would be a meaningless act. It is because Spirit constantly manifests itself to men and intervenes in their enterprises and affairs that we have the subject of this book, a religion. I draw attention again to the paradox I mentioned in Chapter I, of God being far away in the sky and yet present with men on earth; but we now see that it might better be described as an intuitive understanding of the relation between God and man. God is far removed from man in that man cannot ascend to him. He is very near in that he can descend to man.

Nuer, like other people, want it both ways. They want God to be near at hand, for his presence aids them, and they want him to be far away, for it is dangerous to them. It is particularly dangerous in such situations and relationships as are marked off by religious interdictions.

One of the more important interdictory concepts is that of *thek*, a word we have had occasion to consider earlier in connexion with totems. It has a sense which I translate 'to respect', the word 'respect' being used throughout this book only where Nuer would use *thek*. The word has a similar, but perhaps wider, range of meaning among the Dinka.

Nuer use it for the attitude and behaviour expected of a man towards his wife's parents and to a lesser extent her other kinsmen also. He expresses his respect particularly by abstaining from eating in their homes and from appearing naked before them A newly married woman respects her husband's people, especially his parents. She is circumspect in her relations with them, avoiding the parents as far as is practicable. Until her first child is born she may not eat in the home of her husband's parents—that is to say, in her husband's home. Newly wedded husbands and wives respect one another. In public each treats the other with marked reserve and they will not eat together, or even see each other eat or drink, till some time after their first child is born. Of the many European habits which are strange to Nuer the one I have heard them speak of with the greatest disapproval is that of a man eating with his wife in public Husband and wife also respect each other's name by avoiding its use. Sweethearts display similar behaviour. The respect a husband shows to his wife's parents and her respect for his parents is shared in varying degrees by the kin on both sides and for varying periods of time. I need not discuss details here. It may, however, be noted that avoidance with regard to food and drink between affines which is likely to have altogether lapsed, except in the case of the husband's avoidance of his wife's parents, and to have been relaxed even in his case with time and the birth of children, is demanded with extreme vigour should the wife bear twins. Then the paternal and maternal kin of the twins are for a short time in the position of parties to a blood-feud. They may not, under penalty of death (*nueer*), eat or drink or share a pipe together until sacrifices, the meat of which is divided between them, have been made.

There are also avoidances concerning bridewealth cattle which derive from these relationships of respect relating to marriage. A bride respects the *ghok lipe*, the cattle of her betrothal. These are the cattle her future husband hands over in earnest of his intention to marry her, and they count as the first payment of her bridewealth. She will not drink of their milk, lest she harm the cattle by doing so, till after the ritual consummation of the union, and possibly not even then, for I was also told by some Nuer that while she is still newly wedded and has not yet borne a child (*ciek ma kau*) she abstains from the milk of the cows her husband's people have paid for her. Likewise, even when a husband can drink milk in the home of his parents-in-law they avoid offering him milk from the cattle he has paid them. Further, if there is a divorce and the bridewealth cattle are returned to the husband's people they sacrifice a goat before they drink of their milk.

Nuer 'respect with regard to food' unrelated people (*nei ti gwagh*) of the opposite sex, especially if they are unmarried and possible sweethearts. They will not eat with them or even see them, or be seen by them, eating and drinking, and food must not be mentioned when they are both present. The sexes, unless they are kin, avoid each other in the matter of food. Nuer feel so strongly about this avoidance that I was obliged to observe it strictly myself.

Another situation in reference to which one hears the word *thek* is homicide. I discuss it in greater detail in Chapter XII A man who slays another respects water—he may not drink—until a priest has made sacrifice and cut his right arm. Then until the blood-feud is closed by payment of cattle and by sacrifices the kin of the slayer and the kin of the slain may not eat or drink from vessels from which the other has eaten or drunk. They respect the vessels and the food and water of the other party. Even to use the same vessels at the home of a third party who is in no way connected with the feud may entail the most serious consequences. A third party may cause death to one side or the other by eating or drinking with both.

Another use of the word *thek*, which, as always, contains the idea of avoidance, is in reference to burial and to mortuary sacrifices. Those who bury a corpse respect water—they may not drink —until they have been cleansed. Members of a dead man's age-set abstain from the meat of the cattle sacrificed at the ceremony held to close the period of mourning for him They are said to respect the meat. It has been noted earlier (p 55) that people may not eat or drink in the homes of close kin of a person struck by lightning before they have sacrificed. Another use is in connexion with the eldest child of a marriage He respects the spoons of his parents and the sleeping-hide of his mother. He is careful not to eat with the first or sit on the second. Were he to do so he might cause the mother to be barren and injure the father, himself, and the cattle. A man is also said to respect his as yet unconceived children by abstaining from congress with his wife when she is menstruating[1]

[1] He is not said to *thek*, respect, his wife when she is menstruating He

and while she is suckling an infant, for a child born of union in these forbidden periods is a child of misfortune A woman in her periods respects the milk of cows; she may only drink goat's milk at this time. Nuer also use the word *thek* to refer to the prohibition on men milking cows Men respect the cows with regard to milking. Milking is done only by women and boys It can happen, however, that on journeys there are no women or boys present, and in these circumstances men may milk the cows on condition that each gets another to milk his cows for him I learnt in 1936 that a youth, Tot, who in 1931 had been a member of my household, had died as a result of having milked a cow at night in the byre of his home and drunk the milk.

One of the commonest uses of *thek* is, as we have seen, in reference to totems. A man respects his totem by refraining from harming it in any way (pp 64 seq) The respect is mutual and the totem should refrain from harming those who respect it We have also noted earlier (p 129) the respect relationship between twins and birds. The word is also used for the attitude of a man towards his fetish.

Thek has, therefore, in all its contexts of usage a sense of deference, constraint, modesty or shyness, or a mixture of these attitudes It seems often to carry as part of its load of meaning a feeling of embarrassment which is entirely lacking in the ordinary behaviour of Nuer towards persons and nature The behaviour associated with it is formalistic and includes always avoidance and abstention, though it will have been observed that these need not be absolute. A man does not in any way avoid his cows except with regard to (*ke kwi*) milking them.[1]

The purpose and function of these respect relationships are

observes or honours (*luth*) the days of her indisposition On the other hand, *thek* may be used to speak of a woman being in her periods, it being understood that what she respects are the cattle. The word can thus be used as a polite euphemism for 'to menstruate'.

[1] While a man does not respect a cow dedicated to a spirit, Dr Smith tells me that he can be said to respect it with regard to milk and marriage Only members of his family may drink its milk and it must not be used for marriage, unless in either case the spirit gives its consent Dr. Lienhardt tells me that a man can also be said to respect such a cow with regard to urine, in that he does not use it for domestic purposes As I was not aware of these particular usages of the word *thek* I can only record this information without discussing it A breach of the prohibitions would certainly involve liability (pp 39-40) but it would not be classed as *nueer*.

evident. They are intended to keep people apart from other people or from creatures or things, either altogether or in certain circumstances or with regard to certain matters, and this is what they achieve Some of them have important secondary functions in the regulation of the social order—for example, those which determine behaviour between affines and between parties to feuds, but we need not now inquire why they concern certain persons, things, and situations and not others, nor what these persons, things, and situations have in common. We are concerned only with the fact that a violation of the prohibition is to a greater or lesser degree a fault which in many cases brings disaster to the transgressor.

Failure to show respect when there is a *thek* relationship is more than a breach of decorum. It entails to a greater or lesser extent religious sanctions. It is true that in some cases, as, for example, to be seen naked by a mother-in-law, the breach is chiefly regarded as one of good manners which, since the offence was at the worst one of negligence, can be made up for by presenting the offended person with some small gift. But even here a religious sanction is not entirely lacking, because it is believed that failure to respect the parents-in-law may injure the children, and this would ultimately be attributed to God. Nuer say that were a man's nakedness to be seen often by his wife's parents his children might go blind. However, it is not the sight of the genitals in itself which is thought to cause injury so much as the disrespect in not observing the convention. That this is so may be seen from the fact that though Nuer near the American mission at Nasser, Dr Mary Smith tells me, now often wear shorts, they continue to wear as well and over them when they visit their parents-in-law the wild cat's fur traditionally worn on such occasions. We may surmise that the convention is felt by Nuer to have also a moral significance from the violent indignation I have witnessed in female relatives of wives at exposure by husbands in their presence although they were not their mothers-in-law and the exposures were entirely accidental The violence of their complaints would have been out of proportion to the offence were it merely a matter of etiquette. To see inadvertently an unrelated person of the opposite sex eat, or accidentally to be seen eating by the same, is perhaps the lack of respect nearest to a simple, though serious, breach of manners, but Nuer nevertheless give the impression of believing that some misfortune may follow from it

Nuer speak of these conventions with regard to nakedness and eating as *theak ma tot*, minor respect. That they do not think of them as faults of the same order as breaches of the other rules of respect—*theak ma dit*, major respect—is also shown by the fact that though all the rules are alike referred to as *thek* they do not speak of a breach of either the nakedness or the food convention as *nueer*,[1] the word, the verbal form of which is *nuer*, which they use when speaking of breaches of some of the other rules and the consequences of them. We have earlier met the word in reference to eating human flesh (p. 19) and to drinking from a pool contaminated by a corpse (p. 130). A breach of the more serious rules of *thek* is likely to cause death to the breakers or their children or cattle, especially if the breach was wilful. I was told that *nueer* is a sickness of the whole body which generally begins with violent vomiting, but probably any serious sickness following the breach of a *thek* taboo would be described as *nueer*. Sometimes the offender's life can be saved by timely action, and his recovery is thought to be likely if his offence was unintentional. Sacrifice is made to God and in certain circumstances an infusion of cleansing medicines may also be drunk.

The attitude Nuer call *thek* is thus different from mere avoidance of doing things considered to be unbecoming. Failure to conform to *thek* prohibitions involves the culprit in something more than *puc*, shame, and its counterpart *cany*, a word which has the general sense of 'to despise'. Any conspicuous breach of morality or decorum is shameful in Nuer eyes, as when a man steals or is rude to his father. It is shameful—to give another example—for a man, especially if he is unmarried and is courting girls, to eat birds or eggs. Only a *bar*, a poor man without cattle, would eat them. I was frequently taunted by Nuer on this score: 'are you not a man that you eat such little things?' Nuer also regard the eating of most wild fruits as contemptible and they think it both disgusting and shameful to eat carnivora, monkeys, zebras, most reptiles, and all insects. The breach of a *thek* rule may be shameful and despicable, but when it is spoken of as *nueer* it is also sinful.

There are, as will be seen, prohibitions with religious sanctions

---

[1] It should perhaps be made clear that the word *nueer* has nothing to do with 'Nuer', the name of the people 'Nuer' is not the name by which the people refer to themselves but is what foreigners call them

which do not form part of respect relationships and are, therefore, not called *thek*, but *thek* is the most important Nuer category of interdiction. An infringement of the other prohibitions is not usually spoken of as *nueer*, though Nuer nevertheless say that all such infringements are like *nueer*, which is a standard by which they judge, and to which they tend to assimilate any serious breach of an interdiction with religious sanctions. Before discussing these we may, therefore, note that the most prominent feature of the worst forms of sin is that it kills; and it is significant that the word *nueer* means in Dinka 'to destroy' and 'to kill',[1] a sense it also often has in Nuer when the consequences of sin are being referred to.

Except in the case of a breach of the weaning interdiction, which is discussed further later, and in that of a rare breach of the milking interdiction, the transgressions so far mentioned are unwitting offences. It must be rare indeed that anyone transgresses in these ways knowingly and deliberately. The transgressions we shall now consider are generally deliberate actions.

If *nueer* is the most important of Nuer sin concepts the one most frequently spoken of is *rual, incest,* which Nuer say is '*cere ke nueer*', 'like *nueer*', and they may use the verbal form *nuer* when speaking of its consequences, for example, '*ce nyiman nuer*', 'he brought death to his sister' (by having congress with her). It should be noted that Nuer say this, and also that they sometimes liken both *nueer* and *rual* to *biit*,[2] a curse and a prohibition of which a conditional curse is sanction, because their doing so shows that though there are different words for different sorts of fault they are also thought to have something in common. They all destroy and they are all also, in one way of thinking of them, conceived of as pursuing, or tracking, the transgressor to disaster.

I have given elsewhere[3] a fairly lengthy account of Nuer prohibitions on intermarriage and on extra-marital congress, so the subject may be treated briefly here and with reference only to such features of it as are relevant to a discussion of religion. Nuer

[1] P. A. Nebel, *Dinka Dictionary*, 1936, p 119

[2] Indeed in some cases it is not easy to say whether an act should be described as *nueer* or as a sort of *biit*, e g a girl drinking the milk of her bridewealth cattle or an eldest son using his parents' spoon '

[3] 'Nuer Rules of Exogamy and Incest', *Social Structure*, edited by Meyer Fortes, 1949; E E. Evans-Pritchard, *Kinship and Marriage among the Nuer*, 1951, chap ii

use the word *rual* for incestuous relations, and it can also be used
for the consequences of them These, generally certain forms of
yaws or syphilis, though they may be any kind of misfortune, are
more or less grave according to the closeness of the relationship
between the persons concerned. Nuer think that if they are very
closely related death may follow, possibly within a few days, while
if they are very distantly related nothing untoward may happen.
In cases of serious incest the penalty may fall not only on the
partners to the offence but also on their nearest relatives, particularly on their children. The greater the danger of punishment the
more likely and the more expeditiously will the act be followed by
sacrifice and the more valuable will be the thing sacrificed When
the incest is considered to be very slight, what Nuer call a *rual ma
tot*, small incest, *wal ruali*, incest medicine, an antidote which
some people are said to possess, may be thought adequate protection, and if it is deemed wise to make sacrifice, a cucumber or a
pendulous fruit of the sausage tree is considered a sufficient offering. When the offering is a cucumber it is cut in two and then the
left half is thrown away and the contents of the right half are
squeezed into water and drunk by the partners to the act If the
fruit of the sausage tree is the offering it also is cut in two. I have
several times seen youths in western Nuerland, where this tree is
commoner than to the east of the Nile, cutting down its fruits for
the purpose, and it is interesting to note that the Dinka call the
tree *rual*, the Nuer word for incest If there is incest with the wife
of a close kinsman her sleeping-hide may be cut in two. In cases of
major incest the antidote is not thought to be sufficient protection,
nor a vegetable offering a sufficient sacrifice, and a goat or sheep,
and in the most serious cases an ox, must be sacrificed without
delay, and a leopard-skin priest should conduct the ceremony.
The beast is slaughtered by being cut vertically in twain from
head to tail, and afterwards the guilty persons drink incest
medicine infused in the gall of the victim. All these cuttings are
spoken about as *bakene rual*, the cutting, or splitting, in two of
the incest

One hears much about incest among the Nuer, and sacrifices to
cleanse parties to it are frequent One reason for this is that the
prohibition on sexual congress covers a very wide area of social
relationships. The more important categories covered by it are
clanship, close cognation, close natural kinship, close kinship

through adoption, and close affinity. It is also incestuous for a man to have carnal relations with the daughter of an age-mate and for two closely related persons of the same sex to have congress with a person of the opposite sex, even though that person is unrelated to them. A further reason is that Nuer regard incest as a venial offence if the partners are distantly related, and young men certainly often take the slight risk involved. It is easier to understand why incest outside the family and nearest kin is not infrequent if we consider it also in a general setting of sex relations. Nuer do not object to girls having love affairs before marriage so long as they are reasonably discreet in them and give their favours to youths with cattle, who may at least be supposed to have what we call honourable intentions, and little opprobrium attaches to adultery, of which they speak light-heartedly and without disgust or shame.

Nevertheless, adultery (*dhom*), besides being a wrong done to the husband by infringement of his rights, is a further wrong to him in that he is polluted. A husband who discovers his wife *in flagrante delicto* may obtain summary justice by spear or club. Otherwise he demands compensation in cattle, and if the two men are members of the same local community he is likely to receive it. In addition to the cattle paid in compensation, the adulterer hands over to the husband an ox called *yang kula*, the ox of the (husband's) sleeping-hide. This is paid to protect the husband from the consequences of the adultery, known as *kor*, a concept of which one also hears much in Nuerland. *Kor* is a condition brought about by a man having congress with his wife after she has been unfaithful to him. All three persons are polluted, but if sickness results it falls on the husband, and it is most likely to fall on him if the adultery took place in his home. This sickness is also called *kor*, though it may be referred to as well as *juei kula*, sickness of the hide, or, on account of its symptoms, *juei letka*, sickness of the loins. I was told that it may prove fatal, though Miss Soule says that it is myalgia of the lumbar region. Nuer told me that they learnt about *kor*, as they learnt about so many of the ideas discussed in this book, from the Dinka and that it was also from that people that they took over a preventive and curative treatment of it, *wal kore*, *kor* medicine, the tip of a buffalo's horn which is burnt, and its smoke inhaled. Their statement that the concept is a Dinka one is supported, among other evidences, by the fact that the word *kor* has no further meaning in Nuer whereas in Dinka it is the verb for 'to commit adultery'.[1]

Adultery medicine is probably used only as a precaution and perhaps in addition to sacrifice if a man falls sick and the symptoms suggest *kor*. The main safeguard and remedy is sacrifice, and in cases where the adulterer is known he hands over the *yang kula* for this purpose. It is generally conducted on behalf of the husband by some religious functionary, perhaps a leopard-skin priest or a man who respects *kor* (a man who has himself at some time suffered from it and has recovered), in the presence of the families and friends of the parties involved. He or another person first invokes God that the sick man may recover Immediately the ox has fallen the adulterer and his friends take hold of its head and forelegs, and the husband and his wife and friends of their family take hold of its hindlegs while the man who is conducting the rite cuts the carcass in two through the loins [2] The *yang kula* is sacrificed to wipe out the pollution whether the husband falls sick or not. That it has this significance is shown by the fact that when, for reasons I have set forth elsewhere,[3] in the event of a child being born of adulterous congress the cattle paid in compensation, or others in their stead, are returned to the adulterer, the *yang kula*, if it has not yet been sacrificed, remains with the husband for that purpose. and if it has been sacrificed he is under no obligation to return another ox in its place; and by the fact that if the husband forgoes compensation, as he may do if the adulterer is a close agnatic kinsman and neighbour, the *yang kula* must be paid to protect him from evil consequences. It is not part of the *ruok*, the compensation, but is handed over in addition to it, and for a different purpose. Even the cattle of compensation are tainted for the husband. He keeps them away from his own cattle, putting them in the care of a friend or kinsman well away from his own homestead, and he rids himself of them as soon as he can, either by marrying with them or by giving them to one of his brothers for the same purpose. I was told that above all he would

---

[1] P A. Nebel, op cit, pp 13 and 88 The noun form *akor* means 'adultery'

[2] Dr Mary Smith tells me that if a man suffers from *kor* and the adulterer is unknown the officiant holds the forelegs while someone else cuts through the carcass (of a sheep) She says that in the part of Nuerland she resides in the idea of *kor* is no longer prevalent.

[3] 'Some Aspects of Marriage and the Family among the Nuer', *Zeitschrift fur vergleichende Rechtswissenschaft*, 1938, pp. 332–4.

not drink their milk and that should he even tread on their dung he might cause grave injury either to himself or to his cattle Likewise, a man will not accept as bridewealth for his daughter cattle paid to her husband in compensation for adultery she has committed. This is a shocking idea to Nuer, who say that it is like incest.

The pollution may spread (*dop*) beyond those directly concerned in it. The adulterer, the husband, and the wife are dangerous to anyone they come into contact with who has an open sore, for the *kor* may enter him through it. One day at a wedding a youth was trying to reconcile his desire to watch the dancing with the need to hide an open wound from the eyes of those who might cause it to fester, by watching the dance from the shelter of maize plants. I heard his mother shout to him in reprimand 'there you stand in the maize where people can see you. Is *ther* (p 176) a good thing, and is *kor* a good thing, that you thus expose yourself?' It is largely from fear lest an adulterer or adulteress or cuckold might see them that lads are so closely secluded while they still have open wounds on their foreheads after initiation. Adultery may also cause a wife who has been partner to it to suffer in childbirth, and if she finds the pains of labour grievous she will make known to the midwife any adulterous acts she may have committed. The sin and its consequences become less by being confessed.

Another dangerous influence is that brought about by a man having congress with his wife while she is nursing a child Responsibility rests with the husband, 'for this is an affair of men, and it is not a woman's business to deny her husband access'. As has been noted, this is an offence that comes within the category of *nueer*, but the specific name for it is *thiang*. This word denotes the act itself, the consequences which follow from it, and the rite performed to ward off the consequences. Since children are not weaned till they are about three years old it might be thought that husbands must often give way to temptation, but one seldom hears of a wife becoming pregnant before her child at the breast is weaned, and Nuer themselves say that it is uncommon. I cannot say whether a husband who commits the offence would generally perform the prescribed rites unless the pregnancy of his wife made it common knowledge. In the only cases I have come across action was taken when it became evident that a nursing mother was pregnant. I was told that it was then taken to ward off the serious danger of dysentery, perhaps causing death, her condition threatens to the child she is suckling. The infant is laid at the side of a small termite mound, and a person who respects *thiang*—in this sense the sickness which results from a breach of the inter-diction—circles a handful of burning grass over it, and also holds the child over the flame.[1] A dog is then brought and the child is placed on its back They cut a piece off the dog's ear and it is released and runs off 'taking the *thiang* with it'. Finally a goat is sacrificed and a piece cut from one of its ears is tied with the piece of the dog's ear round the child's neck. Nuer say that in this way the dangerous influence of the abnormality (*buom*) is wiped out (*woc*) The rite is performed by old women, though it is a man who sacrifices the goat. The old women eat the sacrificial meat. On the occasion on which I witnessed it all the older women of the cattle camp ran, shouting, out of the camp, each carrying a child which she placed on a small termite mound so that, I was told, the *thiang* might go into the mound. All the small children of the camp were treated in this way because the husband whose conduct had brought about the situation had eaten and drunk from the same vessels as others in the camp, and had smoked tobacco from the same pipes as they, so that the *thiang* might have spread (*dop*) to the other families in it and endangered all the infants of the community. At the end of the rite the husband and wife wash in a stream to cleanse themselves from their uncleanness A child born in these circumstances is regarded as dangerous (p. 176).

II

In using the word 'sin' to refer to the ideas I have been discussing we have to be more than usually on guard against thinking into Nuer thought what may be in our own and is alien to theirs. From our point of view the ethical content of what the Nuer regard as grave faults may appear to be highly variable, and even altogether absent. A fault of inadvertence, though it may not

[1] Both the word *thiang* and the rite I describe have probably been taken over from the Dinka I cannot prove that this is the case but it is strongly suggested by this totemistic relationship some people have to the sickness caused by a breach of the prohibition (p 77) Dr Mary Smith, who kindly inquired into the matter on my behalf, tells me that the Nuer at her mission say that the word is a Dinka one

have such serious consequences as a deliberate fault, may nevertheless, as I pointed out in Chapter I, entail grave consequences; and most of the acts Nuer class as *nueer* would seldom, if ever, be committed deliberately. Moreover, the sinful act may bring misfortune not only to the persons who committed it but also to persons who are, as we think of it, in no way responsible. It is not the adulterer but the injured husband who is likely to be sick, or it may be some person with a sore who is quite unrelated to either who suffers. It is not the husband or his nursing wife who suffers if he has congress with her but their child, and possibly also children of other parents. Likewise, incest may harm relations of the partners to the sin who are not even cognizant of it. Nuer show deep insight with regard to both inadvertence and the incidence of consequences of sin.

It is difficult also for the European observer to understand why Nuer regard as grave faults, or even as faults at all, what seem to him rather trivial actions. That incest and adultery are regarded as faults and, in the sense we have given to the word, sins, he can understand, but not a man milking his cow and drinking the milk, or a man eating with persons with whom his kin are at blood-feud. I can only say that these rules make sense when viewed in the total context of Nuer social life as interdictions arising out of basic social relations. I have discussed these relations in two earlier volumes. Here we have to take them as given. We are interested not in the structural aspect of the interdictions but in the religious sanctions which uphold them; and we have to note that the force of the sanction is in ratio to the strength of the prohibition. The sin lies not so much in the act itself as in the breach of the interdiction. Consequently Nuer can give no reasons for the acts being bad other than that God punishes them. Consequently also, sins do not arouse indignation, as some quite minor fault may do. The consequences of incest may arouse hostility on the grounds of damage (p. 300), but I have only heard Nuer express indignation about incest as such when it is with the closest kinswomen, and even then they condemn the man's folly rather than the man. Acts of the kind they call *nueer*, with the exception of the suckling interdiction, are, as I have said, almost invariably unwitting offences. Nuer do not, therefore, though they fear the consequences, blame the man. They are sorry for him. In cases of incest with distant relatives and of intercourse with a suckling mother they tend to take the view that it is scarcely for them to censure a man whose desires have got the better of him. When there is adultery, the husband may be indignant and demand compensation for the injury done to him, but Nuer do not become indignant at the idea of adultery. The essential point is that such faults as we are considering are, wholly or in part, conceived of as offences against God, and Nuer think that it is he who punishes them. It is God's *cuong*, right, rather than, or as well as, man's, that has been violated. The man who commits them, therefore, places himself, and possibly others too, in danger by having done something which brings Spirit into action in the affairs of men.

This danger is a condition which to some extent appears to be regarded as physical, the threatening misfortune, usually sickness, which results and is the outward manifestation of the sin being already in the man before it manifests itself. He is contaminated by his act This is why medicines, aspersions, fumigations, and other modes of expulsion and cleansing are used in addition to the atoning act of sacrifice. This is more than mimicry. The pollution is substantival. That the sin is felt to be attached to the man is further expressed by two words of great significance, *dop* and *woc*. *Dop* means to catch alight, the spreading of a flame or fire. It is also used to describe a man catching a disease, yaws for example, from another and the spreading of an epidemic or murrain, such as smallpox or rinderpest (Nuer are aware that such diseases are spread by contact); and it can likewise refer to anything spreading, as a fight developing out of a quarrel and people other than the principals becoming involved in it. The general idea is that of a person catching something from another, an infection, whether it be a disease, a quarrel, or a bad habit. In our present context the word means that the uncleanness which results from sins may pass to others closely related to those who are directly concerned in them. They also are in danger. *Woc* is used in a number of contexts in which the sense is getting rid of something, especially by wiping it out. It is the ritual ones which more particularly concern us The first cut across the forehead at initiation is called the *woc dhol*, the wiping out of boyhood. The final rites of marriage are said to wipe out maidenhood. As we have noted, the mortuary ceremony is called *col woc*, the wiping out of death and mourning with their association of debt. The word is also used in reference to sacrifices made on account of a transgression. Sacrifice is said to *woc*, wipe out, *nueer*, *rual*, *kor*, and *thiang*, and indeed any *duer*, fault. The transgressor is healed by the blotting out of his transgression. God turns away, as the Nuer put it. He does not regard it any more, so it ceases to be. When used in reference to sacrifices made on account of sins the word has thus the sense of expiation, and it is interesting that the same word which Nuer use for wiping out a transgression means in Dinka 'to err', 'to sin', and 'offence'.[1] We have in the words *dop* and *woc* two ideas which throw much light on the way Nuer regard sins and sacrifices made in consequence of them. Sin, as has been noted, is something which destroys and which tracks down. Two other characteristics of it are now revealed. It can spread and it can be wiped out by sacrifice But though sin is regarded as bringing about a condition of the person which is contagious, the uncleanness is not simply a physical impurity which can be washed or purged away It is also a spiritual state which can only be changed by sacrifice; and not even sacrifice is sufficient by itself to change it, only sacrifice which carries with it the will and desire of the sinner. What gives emphasis to the physical quality of the condition is the fact that the consequences of sin, which in a sense form part of it, are physical. This brings us to a very important matter, the identification of disease with sin.

Nuer may speak, as we have seen, of the consequences of a sin by the same word (in which the interdiction is also implied) as they use when they speak of the sin itself. *Rual* is incest, and it is also syphilis and yaws. *Nueer* is a breach of certain interdictions, and it is also the violent sickness which follows the breach. *Thiang* is a breach of the weaning interdiction, and it is also the dysentery the breach causes Different diseases have different names, it is true, but if the sin which brought the sickness about is known it is spoken of by the name of the sin. The particular form of the sickness, the particular consequences which have resulted from the sin, are of secondary interest. Had the man suffered from a different ailment it would have been from the same cause Therefore one may say that where there is a state of sin such sickness as it appears in is a symptom of the sin, or even in a sense is the sin. Even where there has been no breach of a specific interdiction, and there is consequently not the same verbal identification, any sickness tends to be regarded as the operation of Spirit on account

[1] J. C Mitterrutzner, *Die Dinka Sprache*, 1866, p 303; Trudinger, op cit , p 298

of some fault on the part of the sick person or of someone closely
related to him, and it may simply be said to be *kwoth*, meaning
that it is the action of Spirit. A sickness may always be a sign of
some fault. No attempt may be made to discover whether there
has been a fault or not or what the fault, if any, was, but Nuer
think that a man would not be sick if there had been no error,
though the thought is not always expressed.

Since sickness is the action of Spirit therapeutic treatment is
sacramental. The sickness is only a symptom of the spiritual condition of the person, which is the underlying cause of the crisis;
and it can only be cured by expiation—sacrifice—for the sin which
has brought it about This, then, is a further characteristic of sin
It causes physical misfortune, usually sickness, which is identified
with it, so that the healing of the sickness is felt to be also the
wiping out of the sin. When Nuer say that sacrifice wipes out the
giak, the badness or evil, they do not just mean that the sickness
will depart but also that what may have caused it will be no more
When a serious sin has been committed sacrifice is made before
there are any signs of sickness.

So far we have been discussing certain definite ideas and conventions. Certain violations of specific interdictions are held to be
divinely punished and these have special names, *nueer, rual*, and
so forth. But they are covered by the general term *dueri*, faults
That term covers also breaches of any social convention. There is,
therefore, no convenient terminological distinction in Nuer which
we can follow in translation to mark off faults of the kind we have
been considering and have called sins from faults of some other
kind Moreover, God is regarded as the guardian of the social
order and his intervention as a possible sanction for any rule of
conduct. We cannot, therefore, make an absolute distinction between what we have called sins and other faults. We can only say
that the religious sanction is more severe, and more definite, and
tends also to be more exclusive, in the case of the faults we have
been discussing than in cases of other faults.

A *duer*, fault, of any kind may, as we have earlier noted, bring
about divine punishment It may do so through the action of a
curse or of ghostly vengeance, and as in such cases God is thought
to be the arbiter the fault involves to some extent the idea of divine
intervention and consequently the need for sacrifice. and a misfortune may be attributed to a curse of the living or to anger of the

ghosts and hence to injuries done to them. It may do so through
fetishes, though, as we have noted, there is some ambiguity and
confusion about their morality. Particular calamities are not otherwise attributed to specific breaches of custom, and I have never
seen or heard of sacrifices performed on account of such breaches
Serious sickness, the commonest occasion of sacrifice, in all cases
I have examined, was attributed, when attributed to anything, to
an infraction of one of the interdictions we have been discussing,
to seizure or possession by a spirit, generally seizure on account of
neglect of obligations to it, to ghostly vengeance, or to a fetish, and
not simply to failure to observe the social code. But we have to bear
in mind that when there is sickness not attributed to some specific
cause sacrifice is, nevertheless, performed to cover any or all unknown causes and that among such causes may be moral faults
which have caught up with the sick man in his sickness, and this
is so because God has taken notice of them

Consequently, such moral faults as meanness, disloyalty, dis-
honesty, slander, lack of deference to seniors, and so forth, cannot
be entirely dissociated from sin, for God may punish them even if
those who have suffered from them take no action of their own
account. Nuer seem to regard moral faults as accumulating and
creating a condition of the person predisposing him to disaster.
which may then fall upon him on account of some act or omission
which might not otherwise and by itself have brought it about.
This is further suggested by the custom of confession at certain
sacrifices, when it is necessary to reveal all resentments and grievances a man may have in his heart towards others This may be
rather a peculiar kind of confession, that of other people's shortcomings, but the point is that the faults together with the feelings
they have engendered are placed on the victim and flow away into
the earth with its blood.

But though the notion of *kwoth* is as ubiquitous as the air to
which it is likened and may be evoked in relation to any question
of right and wrong there are differences between its association
with such sins as incest or eating with persons with whom one is at
feud and its association with faults which have a moral or legal,
rather than a religious character, such as lack of deference to an
elder or refusal to pay a debt When an action of the first kind,
which is definitely and wholly of a sinful character, has been committed it is likely, if it is thought to be a serious transgression, to

lead to sacrifice before any effects follow from it. This would not happen in the case of faults of the second kind. Also, if sacrifice is not made and the act is followed by sickness Nuer know that the sickness is a result of that sin. They start, as it were, from the sin and reason from it to the sickness. But if there is no known and specific sin they start from the sickness and reason that maybe it results from some fault or faults In the first case, the linking up of the two events is precise; and sacrifice is made to expiate the known sin to stay its consequences. In the second case it is vague. Sacrifice is made to get rid of the sickness and whatever it is which has brought it about, for though the cause may not be determined it is, as it were, contained in the sickness For some reason not known God has sent, or allowed, the sickness, and the evil manifest in it must be got rid of by sacrifice. The difference is one of emphasis or of direction. In the one case the emphasis is on the actions from which one looks forward to the sickness which, when it comes, is identified with them In the other case the emphasis is on the sickness and one looks backwards from it to faults which might have brought it about, even if one makes no attempt to discover what they were. An effort may be made to link up the effect with a cause, a wrong done to the living or the dead, but generally people are content to let it go that there must be something wrong somewhere or there would not be the sickness And this something wrong may be some fault or faults or it may be nothing in particular. It may be nothing more than what we would call natural evil, what happens to man because he is man, or just human folly. I have often been struck in listening to Nuer myths and folk-tales with the way God is figured in them when man wants to do something foolish. He lets him do it, and when he is made to speak he says something like what we would render by 'all right, have it your own way' Man is given the choice, and if he chooses wrongly he must put up with the consequences.

Nevertheless, though there is this feeling that wrongful actions may be punished by God, it would lead us entirely astray were we to try to equate sin with breaches of custom and convention. I have already noted that Nuer do not express indignation at sin and that what they get most indignant about is not thought of as sin. Nuer do not reason that incestuous congress with a kinswoman is bad and therefore God punishes it but that God causes misfortune to follow it and therefore it is bad It is bad not in itself but in its consequences. Furthermore, we must note that the conditions in which an interdiction, a breach of which is *nueer*, arises may in no way come about through the breaking of a social regulation. Homicide is not forbidden, and Nuer do not think it wrong to kill a man in fair fight. On the contrary, a man who slays another in combat is admired for his courage and skill. Nevertheless he places himself and his kinsmen in a state of grave spiritual danger. Certainly no one is blamed for the birth of twins, the parents being thought to be most fortunate, but it brings about a precisely similar interdiction Consequently, we are not primarily concerned with people's morals, whether according to Nuer ideas they are good or bad people, but with their spiritual condition, though good or bad conduct may affect this condition.

When there is sin a man's spiritual state is changed. I have spoken of him then as polluted, contaminated, or unclean. We now see that the pollution, contamination, or uncleanness is Spirit itself acting on the man on account of the violation of some interdiction Nuer themselves say this when they simply remark of the sickness that it is *kwoth*. As we regard the matter from the outside, we see that the ethical significance of sin lies in the violation of the interdiction. The interdiction itself may have no ethical significance, only a spiritual one. It may be some trifling injunction, like not drinking water. The circumstances in which spiritual danger attaches to certain events, circumstances in which Spirit is present and threatening, can be said to be good or bad only in the sense that they are fortunate (as the birth of twins) or unfortunate (as death) for the persons concerned. But if notions of sin are not just a rationalization of social convention neither are they just a rationalization of chance. The question whether the circumstances are fortunate or unfortunate is not really a relevant one. Nuer have the idea of luck (*bang*), but it does not arise here. Fundamentally in this context it is not a matter of being lucky or unlucky, or of being good or bad.

We shall see later how this double aspect of Spirit, what aids and what harms, what sustains and what destroys, is represented in the rite of sacrifice. In the present place we need only note further that it has some bearing on the question of the one and the many which we have earlier discussed. The idea of Spirit as the holy with whom it is extremely dangerous for man to be in contact is only absolute where God is concerned, and in such situations as have been discussed in this chapter. It is not absent in his refractions—prophets are treated with reserve as containers of Spirit, totems are avoided as creatures in which Spirit appears to man, and the objects associated with nature sprites and fetishes are not handled by others than their owners—but though Spirit in these forms is dangerous there is no feeling of the lethal contamination of it which derives from the idea of it being something so wholly different from what is human as to be incompatible with it. In them Spirit is not in its entirety and it is also, as it were, filtered through material things. Man can then possess it and use it for his own purposes; but what he then possesses, as Nuer would be the first to recognize, is not God but *deng, teny, colwic, kwoth nyanga, kwoth nyota, biel roa, mathiang,* and so forth.

CHAPTER VIII

SACRIFICE

I

WE have seen how Nuer regard Spirit and creature as things of different orders and standing conceptually in opposition, and that Spirit is always, though it may aid him, dangerous to man. It is in the light of these observations that the most typical and expressive act of Nuer religion, the turning to God in the rite of sacrifice, is to be viewed and understood. It is an enactment of their most fundamental religious conceptions. Nuer, as we have seen, cannot say, because they do not know, what God is, but we shall at least learn from their sacrifices more of what they conceive man's relationship to him to be.

I speak here only of bloody sacrifice. I exclude from the discussion cereal and other offerings. People sometimes place heads of the first maize and millet in the thatch over the entrance to their byres as a thank-offering to God, though this is not obligatory. They also sometimes throw grain into streams as an offering to the spirit *buk*. I exclude also the casting away of lumps of tobacco, beads (especially a woman's offering), or some other small piece of property in minor troubles or anxieties, when there is a sudden danger for which immediate action has to be taken and there is no time for formalities, or when a man is in the bush and cannot lay his hands on a beast or even a cucumber. The suppliant asks God to take the offering and spare him. I exclude also the offering of beer or milk, poured in libation, often at the foot of a tethering-peg, probably a peg to which a beast dedicated to some spirit is tied, by a very poor person who cannot afford animal sacrifices. On the other hand, I include as coming within the sense of bloody sacrifice offerings of cucumbers, for they are consecrated and immolated as surrogates for oxen.

Nuer sacrifice on a great many occasions· when a man is sick, when sin has been committed, when a wife is barren, sometimes on the birth of a first child, at the birth of twins, at initiation of sons, at marriages, at funerals and mortuary ceremonies, after homicides and at settlements of feuds, at periodic ceremonies in honour of one or other of their many spirits or of a dead father, before war, when persons or property are struck by lightning, when threatened or overcome by plague or famine, sometimes before large-scale fishing enterprises, when a ghost is troublesome, &c.

When we examine this variety of occasions we see that Nuer sacrifices fall into two broad classes. Most sacrifices are made to prevent some danger hanging over people, for example on account of some sin, to appease an angry spirit, or at the birth of twins, or to curtail or to get rid of a misfortune which has already fallen, as in times of plague or in acute sickness. On all such occasions Spirit intervenes, or may intervene, for better or more often for worse, in the affairs of men, and its intervention is always dangerous Any misfortune or grave danger is a sign of spiritual activity. Such sacrifices are made for a person or persons and not for social groups and they involve ideas of propitiation, expiation, and related intentions. As they are the most common and the most specifically religious sacrifices I shall devote chief attention to them. There are other sacrifices which accompany various social activities, mostly of the *rites de passage* kind, such as initiation, marriage, and death We cannot make an absolute distinction between the two sorts of sacrifice. A sacrifice of the *rites de passage* kind may contain elements of meaning characteristic of the other type. Sacrifices in marriage ceremonies—at betrothal, at the wedding, and at the consummation—are the best examples of the second type. A sacrifice to ward off the consequences of serious incest is a good example of the first type. A sacrifice to end mourning is an example of the blending of the two. It is a routine sacrifice in a *rites de passage* context, but it is also intended to get rid of the contamination of death and any evil there may be in men's hearts. For the purpose of discussing the meaning or meanings of sacrifice it is necessary to make the distinction, even if there is some overlapping. I shall speak of the one type as personal sacrifice and of the other as collective sacrifice These terms draw attention to the formal distinction between sacrifices offered for persons and those offered on behalf of social groups, but we shall see that they differ also in intention, the first having primarily a piacular intention, and the second a confirmatory one; or, to use Hubert and Mauss's terms, the first are sacrifices of 'désacralization' (they make the sacred profane, they get rid of Spirit from man) and the second

PLATE VIII

Consecration

are sacrifices of 'sacralization' (they make the profane sacred, they bring Spirit to man).[1]

This chapter is mostly devoted to a discussion of personal sacrifices but I say something of the collective ones before giving exclusive attention to them The primary purpose of collective sacrifices, and also their main function, is to confirm, to establish, or to add strength to, a change in social status—boy to man, maiden to wife, living man to ghost—or a new relationship between social groups—the coming into being of a new age-set, the uniting of kin groups by ties of affinity, the ending of a blood-feud —by making God and the ghosts, who are directly concerned with the change taking place, witnesses of it. The ceremonies are incomplete and ineffective without sacrifice, but sacrifice may be only one incident in a complex of ceremonies, dances, and rites of various kinds, which have no religious significance in themselves. Its importance lies in the fact that it sacralizes the social event and the new relationships brought about by it It solemnizes the change of status or relationship, giving it religious validation. On such occasions sacrifice has generally a conspicuously festal and eucharistic character.

Collective sacrifices thus have a marked structural character. Sacrifices may be made on behalf of whole communities, as in times of epidemic, but they are then made for a great number of individuals. Here, however, we are dealing with something rather different, with sacrifices made on behalf of social segments, lineages, and age-sets, which are concerned as whole groups, sometimes in relation to groups of like order. This is why they have to be performed by specially appointed representatives of the groups concerned or by public functionaries, as is explained later.

It is indicative of Nuer religious thought that these sacrifices performed as part of social activities are concerned with relations within the social order and not with relations between men and their natural environment. We are often told in accounts of African peoples that their sacrifices are concerned with weather, rain, fertility of the soil, seed-time, fructification, harvest, and fishing and hunting. Generally no rite of any kind is performed by Nuer in connexion with these processes, certainly no regular and obligatory rite; and if in certain circumstances one is performed,

[1] H Hubert and M Mauss, 'Essai sur la nature et la fonction du sacrifice', *L'Année sociologique*, vol. ii, 1899, pp 89 seq

as before large-scale fishing, it is rarely a sacrifice, and if it is
a sacrifice it is not regarded as either necessary or important. All
this may be due to some extent to lack of interest in agriculture
and hunting, but it is also because Nuer take nature for granted
and are passive and resigned towards it. They do not think that
they can influence it to their own advantage, being merely ignorant
folk. What happens there is the will of God, and that has to be
accepted Hence Nuer are little interested in ritual for bringing
rain and even consider it presumptuous to think of asking God for
rain before sowing. This mentality is illustrated in one of their
stories which relates how death came to a girl who asked that the
setting of the sun might be delayed till she had finished her work.
Nuer rather turn their eyes inwards, to the little closed social
world in which they live, they and their cattle. Their sacrifices are
concerned with moral and spiritual, not natural, crises.

II

We have now first to ask to whom sacrifices are made. This
brings us again up against the problem of the one and the many.
When a sin is expiated or pollution is wiped out by sacrifice it is
made to God alone. Likewise in major calamities, such as plagues
and murrains Also when a person is struck by lightning, in connexion with death, and in cases of sickness not attributed to a
specific cause. We are here dealing with circumstances common
to all men and with universals—with the moral law which is the
same for all men, with effects of common interest and concern,
and with dangers and misfortunes which fall on each and all alike.
Sacrifices may, however, be made on some occasions to one or
other spirit, for example, to a spirit of the air before battle or when
it is thought to have brought about sickness in a man or if it is
feared that it may do so; or to a totemic or other spirit of the below
in circumstances already mentioned in earlier chapters We are
here dealing with something more particular and specific, the
relation of certain persons to Spirit figured to them, and not to
others, in one or other special form as a spirit. Nevertheless, as I
have earlier explained, these spirits may be regarded as hypostases,
representations, or refractions of God, and in the already defined
sense in which this is so we can say that a sacrifice to any one of
them is a sacrifice also to God. The cause of sickness, or of any

misfortune, is always thought to be, either immediately or in the last resort, Spirit, which in some circumstances may be more specifically defined as a certain spirit. Furthermore, when sickness is attributed to an air-spirit, for example *deng*, whether the patient recovers or not is thought to rest with God, that is, with Spirit in the comprehensive sense which includes *deng* as one manifestation of it. The two representations may thus be separated in the mind in relation to cause and cure, but they are fused in the sacrificial act. If, therefore, it can be said that, in this sense, God is sacrificed to in all sacrifices, it must be added that in particular circumstances connected with particular persons or social groups Spirit conceived of in some lower form may be dominant. This inevitably affects to some extent the character of the rite.

Spirit conceived of as God does not seize people and make them sick as some air-spirits and earth-spirits may. They exact a special tribute which God does not demand, a payment for special protection and favour, and this can hardly fail to affect the meaning of the sacrificial act. We have to take this fact into consideration, and it complicates our problem. To avoid ambiguities and obscurities at this stage I shall take sacrifice to God as my model and describe that, and then state later what modifications and qualifications are required when sacrifice is made to a spirit.

In the case of collective sacrifices, which, for reasons already given in Chapter IV, may be to Spirit in some totemic or other refraction, the changes in social status and relations they serve to bring about involve the ghosts, who are usually little or not at all concerned in personal sacrifices. At collective sacrifices they may therefore be invoked together with God in some such formula as 'God, thou and the ghosts'. Since the matter has been discussed earlier I need only say here that the sacrifices are made to God, even on those occasions which most directly concern the dead. The ghosts must be summoned as witnesses and the matter must be explained to them because it concerns them, but they are only witnesses as the living are, and what is explained to them is explained to the living also. Even when sacrifice is made at a mortuary ceremony or when a man commemorates his dead father it cannot be said that the victim is sacrificed to the ghost. It is sacrificed for the dead man, but the life of the victim is given to God and not to the ghost.[1] Even when a ghost is troublesome and

[1] Dr Lienhardt tells me that this is also the case for the Dinka, it is probably

sacrifice has to be made to pacify it the victim is consecrated to God and not to the ghost. It is to God that expiation for the wrong done to the ghost must be made. What is made to the ghost is reparation, where this is possible. It follows from all that has been said about the Nuer notion of faults, and it will be seen that it also follows from the whole character of the sacrificial act, that it is only to Spirit that sacrifice can be made.

Our second question is, What is sacrificed? The sacrificial animal *par excellence* is an ox, and in important social ceremonies, such as weddings and those held for settlement of feuds, the victim must be an ox Oxen are also sacrificed in times of general calamity, sometimes when people are dangerously ill, and occasionally to spirits. A barren cow may take the place of an ox. Bulls are only sacrified in one of the rites closing a blood-feud, and occasionally, though only old beasts, in honour of a dead father. Except in these instances a male victim must be a neuter. If it is not, it is castrated before the rites begin. Fertile cows are only sacrificed at mortuary ceremonies, and then only for senior persons, as a tribute to their position in the community It does not matter what is the colour of the victim, though in certain sacrifices there is a preference for beasts with certain markings

However, Nuer have not large herds and could not afford to slaughter oxen on every occasion of sacrifice, so, except on such occasions as the slaughter of an ox is obligatory, they generally use wethers and castrated he-goats as surrogates. Female and stud beasts would not be used if young males were available. This means in practice that it is one of the flock that is sacrificed when there is sickness and on most other occasions, and a poor man may use one of these animals where a rich man might use an ox. The ritual procedure is the same whatever the animal may be. It is of no significance that oxen are speared through the heart while the other beasts generally have their throats cut with the spear

The animal, whatever it may be—cow or ox or bull, ewe or wether, nanny-goat or castrated billy-goat—is spoken of in invocations and in any sacrificial context as '*yang*', 'cow'. This word, like our 'cow', denotes in ordinary usage any bovine animal of any age and of either sex or, when used more exclusively, a female and, still more exclusively. an adult female. When translating what

so for the Shilluk as well (C G. and B Z. Seligman, op. cit., pp. 97–98, where several authorities are cited).

Nuer have said in sacrifices or about them I have preserved their sacrificial idiom. It must be understood, therefore, that in this context the word 'cow' seldom refers to a cow but almost always, when the victim is an animal, to an ox, a wether, or a castrated he-goat. In a sacrificial context Nuer also always speak of a cucumber-victim as *'yang'*, 'cow'.

Should for some reason no beast be available Nuer may instead, or as a temporary expedient, sacrifice a small trailing knobbly

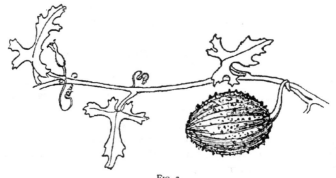

FIG. 3

Cucumis prophetarum (Crowfoot)

cucumber called *kwol*, or *kwol yang*, cow's cucumber (*Cucumis prophetarum*) which grows wild on cultivated sites.[1] If necessary, animal sacrifice is made later, when a victim can be acquired. Nuer also sacrifice this cucumber in minor anxieties, as when they have bad dreams or have committed petty incest. It is treated as though it were an animal victim. It is presented and consecrated, an invocation is said over it, and it is slain by the spear, being cut in half along its edge. The left, or bad, half is then thrown away and the right, or good, half is squeezed and its juice and seeds rubbed on the chest and forehead of the officiant and maybe on others present. This half is afterwards put in the thatch over the entrance to the byre, or sometimes to the dwelling-hut. In cases of petty

---

[1] I have described it in some earlier accounts as 'a yellow tomato-like fruit'. This is probably the Nuer *kot* (*Solanum incanum*) and not their *kwol* (*Cucumis prophetarum*): *vide* Grace M. Crowfoot, *Flowering Plants of the Northern and Central Sudan*, n.d., Nos. 34 and 129. I am indebted to Dr. Lienhardt for the correction of this unfortunate error.

incest a fruit of the sausage tree (*Kigelia aethiopica*) may be cut in half, though I am uncertain whether this constitutes a sacrifice *in sensu stricto*.

We have discussed to whom sacrifice is made and what is sacrificed. We have now to ask by whom it is made, and when and where. We have first to distinguish between the person (or social group) on whose behalf it is made, whom we may speak of as the sacrificer, though with some danger of misunderstanding, because he may not take an active part in the rite performed on his behalf, and those who act on his behalf, the actors in the drama.[1] There may be a number of these. Several people may take part in the consecration and several men may deliver invocations. One man may present the victim, another consecrate and make the invocation over it, and yet another slay it. Nevertheless, there are always one or more prime actors, those who make the consecrations and invocations, which, rather than the actual killing, constitute for Nuer the main acts in the series of rites making up a sacrifice; and we may therefore speak of anyone who, after consecrating the victim, makes an invocation over it as the officiant. There may be several of them In certain sacrifices, particularly those of the collective kind, whoever else may invoke God, one or other particular functionary either must do so or it is thought highly desirable that he should do so. I discuss in Chapter XII the sacrificial roles of these various functionaries in Nuer society. Normally any senior man, usually the head of the family of the sacrificer, can officiate at personal sacrifices. He would generally be one of the sacrificer's paternal kinsmen but it would not matter if he were not The sacrifice is to God and not to ghosts, and it therefore does not matter who officiates. A youth would not officiate if there were an older man present, but this is a matter of social convention only· there is no ritual bar to his acting. Women do not sacrifice. They may assist in the act of consecration with ashes and they may pray, but they do not make invocations or slay victims. Neither the·sacrificer nor the officiant has to be in a state of ceremonial purity. This is an idea entirely unknown to Nuer.

It is obvious that in the collective sacrifices the rites must have to some extent a determined place in the whole social activities of

---

[1] Hubert and Mauss, op cit, pp 48 seq, make the distinction by using 'sacrifiant' and 'sacrificateur' A word corresponding to 'sacrifiant' is not so easily formed in English.

which they form a part, though Nuer are not usually particular
about the exact moment of their execution. For example, an ox
must be sacrificed at a betrothal ceremony and it is usually slaughtered towards the end of the dancing in the evening, but it does
not matter if it is sacrificed on the following morning instead.
Personal sacrifice may be made at any time if a sudden crisis arises.
If it is not acute, people may delay sacrifice till they have discovered its cause with the aid of a prophet or diviner if they sus-
pect that it may be due to something particular, perhaps some sin
or the anger of some spirit or ghost The intention of the offering
can then be more precisely formulated But if the crisis is acute,
sacrifice would, whatever opinion, if any, might be held about its
cause, be made at once to God. Mgr. Mlakic was clearly recording
what he witnessed or heard at the time it happened from a witness
when he described how when lightning set fire to a byre its owner
entered its flaming interior to save his family and cattle. His first
act, however, was to spear a beast of the herd, saying 'God, what
do you do to us?' Then he gave his attention to saving people and
beasts.[1]

If there is no urgency a sacrifice may be put off till a time convenient for the sacrificer. The collective sacrifices and sacrifices in
honour of spirits of one kind or another are normally held in the
villages during the rains, and even in cases of sickness, if it is not
acute, in dry-season camps Nuer prefer to put off animal sacrifice
till they return to their villages. They may consider that though a
sickness is due to neglect of some spirit there is no pressing need
for immediate sacrifice. To keep the spirit content in the meantime they may sacrifice a cucumber, if they have one, or offer it
some tobacco or a libation; or they may make an animal sacrifice
in intention by devoting to the spirit then and there an animal by
rubbing ashes on its back and then wait till they are back in their
permanent homes to sacrifice it. Consequently one rarely sees
animal sacrifices in dry-season camps.

A sacrifice is also a feast, and a feast is more suitably held in the
surroundings of huts and byres. Nuer, especially the older people,
think of the *cieng*, the homestead and village, rather than of the
wec, the cattle camp, as their home. This is all the more weighty
a reason in the case of collective sacrifices, because the kin who
should attend them and have rights in the sacrificial flesh may be

[1] Op. cit

scattered in the drought. There is also plenty of beer and porridge in the rains to add to the meat of the sacrifices for feasting, and little or none in the dry-season camps, for even if their millet is not exhausted people are often too far from their granaries to transport it. Moreover, the social activities which are the occasion of collective sacrifices take place, largely because there is plenty of food, in the rains. I think also it is possible that there is more, and more serious, sickness in the rains and hence the greater need for sacrifices then.

It does not seem usually to matter at what time of day a sacrifice takes place, though the early morning is preferred on big occasions when oxen are sacrificed; but I have witnessed sacrifices when the sun was high and also in the evening. Early morning and evening are the most convenient times because then the men are at leisure and it is cool, but the early morning has the additional advantage that it gives time for what are sometimes lengthy ceremonies to be performed with slow dignity. I suppose that if there were need Nuer would sacrifice at night, but I have never known this happen, and it would cause certain inconveniences.

There is no particular spot at which the rites must be performed. The ceremony may be held in the space in front of the dwelling-huts if it is on a domestic scale. This is a suitable place for sacrifice, for a man often erects there a *riek*, post-shrine, and there also is the wife's *buor*, mud wind-screen (Plate V), which also has a certain sacred significance, being the woman's counterpart to the *riek*, as well as serving its practical purpose. But in major sacrifices of the collective type, when there may be many persons present, the sacrifices are likely to be held in the kraal, where there may also be a *riek* (Plate VI), or at its edge, on account of the cattle, or even if they are absent, to avoid the tethering-pegs incommoding those making the invocations It is not, however, a matter of importance and anywhere convenient will do—properly speaking Nuer have no fanes.[1] It is the same for place as for time. They do not worry about such details God is at all times and everywhere, there are no specially sacred times and places for sacrifice Likewise, there are no specially sacred persons who must make sacrifice: any man

---

[1] God, spirits, and ghosts are associated with the *riek*, which may be in the courtyard, in the kraal, or at the side of the *gol*, the central hearth in the byre, which is the symbol of the family conceived of as a group of agnates and hence of the lineage; and for women, with the *buor*, the symbol of the elementary family, the domestic group

can offer sacrifice on behalf of himself or others, intermediaries
are not required.

Before giving an account of the succession of acts which constitute a sacrifice it is advisable to say further that though the acts
are almost always the same and performed in the same order they
are much more elaborate on some occasions than on others. A
mortuary ceremony must begin between dawn and sunrise and is
carried out by long, slow, solemn stages. The rites of sacrifice at
marriage ceremonies are, on the contrary, often carried out in a
perfunctory manner, giving the impression that they are regarded
as little more than a formality. Likewise there is much variation
in the attention paid to the rites by those present but not taking
an active part in them. In some sacrifices they pay little attention
to them, or even ignore them altogether, continuing their dancing
or talking among themselves about their own affairs. Thus, in my
experience, at sacrifices in marriage ceremonies only close kin of
the persons immediately concerned take much, or even any, interest in the ritual. Even sacrifices in honour of a spirit may be
performed in a perfunctory manner, it being thought that all that
is required is that a beast be offered so that the spirit may know
that it has not been forgotten. But on occasions of serious sickness,
of grave danger, and of death the spectators sit quietly in a line or
semicircle and give silent attention to what is being said and done
The amount of attention paid and its intensity depend on the
nature of the occasion and the degree to which spectators are
personally involved.

Therefore the many attempts that have been made to explain
primitive religions in terms of supposed psychological states—awe,
religious thrill, and so forth—are, as far as the Nuer are concerned,
inept because the feelings of officiants and spectators are, in so far
as they are discernible, clearly different on different occasions and
in different parts of the same ceremony. This is obvious to anyone
who sees a few Nuer sacrifices. Some people are paying attention
and others not. Some are solemn, others gay. Wedding and funeral
sacrifices do not evoke the same response, nor do initiation and
incest sacrifices, nor even the opening and closing sacrifices of a
mortuary ceremony. The feelings of close kin are not the same as
those of distant kin. There is no need to labour the point. What is
important in sacrifice is not how people feel, or even how they
behave—a serious mien when the occasion is a solemn one is a

matter of sentiment and good manners, not of religion. What is important is that the essential acts of sacrifice be carried out and, especially in personal sacrifices, with a right intention, which is a matter of disposition, not of emotion.

III

Almost all sacrifices, whether personal or collective, have the same general features. A description of one is therefore, apart from details, a description of almost all. The victim is brought to the place of sacrifice and there are performed in succession the four acts which compose the sacrificial drama· presentation, consecration, invocation, and immolation. Other features may be added, such as libations and aspersions and, mostly in sacrifices to spirits, hymn-singing, but these are supernumerary acts. The essential rites of the sacrifice proper are the four I have mentioned. They form what might be called the canon of sacrifice.

The first act is the *pwot*, the driving into the ground of a tethering-peg and the tethering of the animal to it. The officiant presents the victim to God The man who stakes the victim is called *pwot yang*, the tetherer of the cow, and as in collective sacrifices this is generally done by the master of ceremonies of the family concerned he is commonly referred to in a sacrificial context by this title. Sometimes, after the victim has been staked, a libation, of milk, beer, or water, is poured over, or at the foot of, the peg.

Then takes place the *buk*, the rubbing (with ashes), the act of consecration (Plate VIII). The man who is about to speak the first invocation rubs ashes of cattle-dung lightly on the victim's back with his right hand. Each speaker does this in turn, and in some sacrifices all present place ash on the victim's back whether they make invocations or not. I discuss later (pp. 261–2 and 279–81) the meaning of rubbing ashes, when I shall try to show that it is not only a consecration of the beast to God but also an identification of man with ox.

Then takes place the *lam*, the invocation (Plate IX) The officiant, holding his spear in his right hand, speaks to God over the consecrated victim. The invocation states the intention of the sacrifice and matters relevant to it. Occasionally, when a sacrifice is a very perfunctory affair, no words are spoken. When asked about the omission Nuer say that the sacrifice is the *lam*, by which they

PLATE IX

Invocation

mean that the intention is implied in the sacrifice itself in the circumstances in which it is made. However, even in the most perfunctory rites, it is more usual for a few formal phrases to be spoken by the officiant as he consecrates the victim, either in a scarcely audible patter or even silently. He is addressing God and not the people present. This is what Nuer call a *lam me tot*, a short invocation. They say *'ca be lam e bec'*, 'they will not invoke (God) much'. Normally, however, and always in a serious situation which also permits leisurely action, there is a *lam me dit*, a long invocation. The officiant walks up and down past the tethered beast, brandishing his spear, and uttering his words loud and clear —he is then addressing the audience as well as God, and they may interrupt him with promptings, advice, and even argument. In a long address of this kind certain petitionary formulae recur again and again but it has no set form or prescribed words. Each speaker may say what he likes so long as what he says is true and also in some way relevant to the intention of the sacrifice. These long rambling addresses, sometimes taking over an hour to deliver, contain, besides a statement of intention and petitions, all sorts of affirmations, exhortations, reflections about life, anecdotes, and opinions; and also complaints, for on very formal occasions the speaker must reveal any grievance he may have in his heart As there may be several such invocations by different persons before the victim is slain, a sacrifice may be a very lengthy affair, and for a European rather tedious to assist at. He has to sit in the sun for several hours listening to addresses which are difficult for him to follow. Some of the sentences may be inaudible, the speaker speaking too low or having his back turned to the audience, who may also be talking among themselves; and the invocations are apt to require a more detailed knowledge of past events and relationships than a stranger is likely to have. These difficulties are added to by a marked tendency in the invocations towards periphrasis and aposiopesis.

The word *lam*, which has much the same range of meaning in other Nilotic languages, expresses a number of interconnected ideas, one or other of which is stressed according to the direction of interest. In reference to God it has to be translated 'to invoke'. In reference to a sacrificial victim it can be translated 'to sacrifice'. With reference to a man the ordinary meaning is 'to curse', more rarely 'to bless'. It may also refer to a formal pronouncement in ordeals, and in animal stories to the ordeal itself. 'Invocation' would seem best to cover all these special senses. For the verbal form I shall generally use the phrase 'to make an invocation'. Nuer usually employ it in what we call a passive or intransitive mood when speaking of sacrifices, saying *'ba lam'*, 'an invocation is made', or *'be lam ke lam'*, 'he will invoke with an invocation'; but since it is understood that it is God (though it may be in some refraction and sometimes coupled with ghosts) who is invoked it is legitimate also to use the phrase 'to invoke God' even when this is not a word-for-word translation of what is said in Nuer.[1] Even in curses and blessings it is God who is implicitly, if not explicitly, invoked, since the desired action can come only from him. A curse is therefore an imprecatory, and a blessing a benedictory, address to God

The full significance of the *lam* will emerge later when the symbolism of the spear and the role of the ox have been discussed. Here I define only its outward character as a ritual form of speech. The word indicates a distinctive form of address rather than its content, which varies according to circumstances. We can perhaps best grasp its distinctive character by contrasting invocation (*lam*) with prayer (*pal*) *Pal* is to make a simple and direct petition to God for some favour, usually of a general nature, such as the petitions I recorded in Chapter I, and the supplication is so often spoken with a pleading of the hands that the word implies this gesture—*be tet pal*, praying with the hands, being understood. The word may also be used to refer to congregational hymn-singing to spirits, though since this is frequently done to the accompaniment of hand-clapping the word *pat*, to clap, is often used instead. The form and character of the *lam* are different Its characteristic accompanying gesture is brandishing a spear, and although it contains petitions (*lang kwoth*) which are the same as those uttered in praying these are not its main or typical feature. The invocation has an incisiveness prayer lacks. What is said in it is more definite and particular; and its clauses are mostly affirmations, formal statements, rather than petitions, and these affirmations, declarations of what is, have a sort of virtue in themselves.

---

[1] The difficulty is that the verb 'invoke', unlike the now rarely used 'invocate', cannot be used intransitively in English as the verb *lam* can be used in Nuer However, the grammatical distinctions we make between transitive and intransitive and between passive and active do not entirely suit the Nuer language.

I do no mean by this that an invocation is a spell—far from it—
but there is a difference between an assertion and a supplication.
Thus in a sacrifice for sickness what is said is not so much may the
sick man be healed as that his sickness is ot no account and that
he will be healed in the moment of sacrifice. Intention and what is
intended are brought together. The sickness is finished, it is blown
away, it is no more And here we have again to emphasize the
significance of the identification of sickness with sin. If the sacrifice wipes out the sin it wipes out also the material form in which
it is manifested and known. That this emphasis is required is confirmed by a letter I have received from Dr. Mary Smith in which
she tells me that the Nuer at her mission do not use the word *lam*
if they are speaking of praising or giving thanks but only, and
always, where sin is involved. But the validity of the assertion that
the evil is no more depends on the general validity of all else that
is said. Nuer say that a man must make invocation in truth
(*thuogh*). Even in recounting the most trivial details in a history
of events which have led up to a situation in which sacrifice is
necessary every statement made in the presence of God must be
true; and I think this, rather than just a desire to interrupt or dispute, accounts for the emendations, additions, and contradictions
of the assistants. The victim offered to God has placed on its back
by the *lam* what is said in the *lam*, and if the sacrifice is to be
efficacious what is said must be true

Now takes place the immolation, what Nuer generally call the
kam yang, the giving, or offering, of the victim when speaking of
personal sacrifices, and the *nak*, the killing, when speaking of collective sacrifices By the use of one or the other word they indicate
whether a sacrifice is for them more a religious or a festal event,
whether its purpose is mainly piacular or social. Nuer do not, in so
far as I have observed or heard, wait for the animal to urinate
before killing it, as do some of the other Nilotic peoples An ox is
speared on the right side, and so expert are the Nuer that I have
never known a second thrust to be necessary or the beast to move
for more than a few seconds after the thrust has been made Sheep
and goats have their throats cut (Plate X) A bovine victim should
fall well to make a perfect sacrifice. Falling well means falling
cleanly on its side, preferably on its right side, and with its head
in the desired direction, which in most sacrifices is towards the
huts and the people who sit outside them I have been told that

should an ox fall badly, and there is another handy, they repeat the sacrifice I have not, however, seen this done, and in my experience those present say that the animal has fallen well whichever way it falls. I have also been told that a lion will not eat an animal it has killed if it falls on its left side, but most Nuer ridiculed this statement.

We may, indeed, note here that Nuer are not a highly ritualistic people. We have already noted that they are not particular about the time and place of sacrifice or who performs the rite, that neither sacrificer nor officiant has to submit to any ceremonial interdictions, and that there is no prescribed content of their invocations, neglect of which would invalidate the rite. There is a certain air of casualness and lack of ceremony about the whole sacrificial procedure. So, although it is better if the ox falls well, it does not much matter if it does not. Nuer are more interested in purpose than in details of procedure. An oblation must be made to validate a social status or relationship or so that people may be free from evil and danger—small details of ceremony do not matter

Sacrifice proper finishes with the *kam yang* or *nak*, the offering or killing of the victim, and since these expressions describe the culminating movement of the drama they can stand for the whole sacrifice and have the general sense of 'to sacrifice'. In this final moment, at which the invocation may be intensified (Plate XI), the consecrated life has gone to God.

Nuer say that God takes the *yiegh*, the life, and I have heard them say also that he takes the *tie*, the soul. This raises a problem touched on earlier (p. 157). They also say that what in sacrifice belongs to God are the *riem*, blood, which soaks into the ground, and the *wau*, chyme or perhaps a mixture of chyme and chyle. In what sense do Nuer speak of the blood and the chyme being what God receives? No doubt we have here to take into consideration the different levels at which Nuer conceive of Spirit. I have heard them say that after sacrifice to a spirit you can see the flesh of the speared beast twitching as the spirit pulls at it, and we have earlier noted in the hymn to the river-spirit *buk* the emphasis on red blood and also how the fetishes are said to 'eat' the 'soul' of offerings. But, as I have said before, the word *cam*, to eat, even in reference to fetishes is a metaphorical usage. I think that it may be accepted that there is no question of Nuer believing that in animal sacrifice Spirit, even as most materially conceived of, eats the blood and the chyme, not even in the sense of consuming their essence. Clearly, they are not materially consumed. Nuer do not say that Spirit feeds on (*mieth*) or eats (*cam*) or drinks (*madh, ruidh*) them. They do not use these words, but say that God, or a spirit, *kan*, takes, them. It is not a question of eating anything—what eating there is is done by the people—but of taking something, the life. This would seem to be a matter of great importance in an estimation of Nuer religious thought.

When, therefore, Nuer say that the blood and the chyme belong to God we are to understand, I would suggest, that this is a way of saying that the life belongs to him. It is true that we cannot say for the Nuer, as for the Hebrews, that the blood is the life. The word for life, *yiegh*, is also the word for breath, so that if we were to say that anything 'is' the life we would have to say it of the breath; though even here the word 'is' must not be taken to imply identity but a symbolic relationship. We must rather suppose that the blood and the chyme, and especially the blood, are also symbols of the life.

Human blood has for the Nuer a peculiar psychical value. When kinsmen and neighbours fight they use clubs instead of spears. No doubt this convention is most easily explained as making homicide a less likely outcome than if spears were permitted and, should it happen that a man be killed, of making a settlement easier to bring about on the grounds of absence of intent, but there may be a different, or at any rate an additional, reason for it. It may be that behind it is the notion that not the same responsibility is felt if the life-blood does not flow as it would from a fatal spear wound —that in a sense the man has not taken the life, that the death happened of itself, as Nuer would put it. That Nuer have some such idea is shown by the fact that a ghoul may be killed with impunity, but only if he is beaten to death with clubs and his blood is not shed. The blood of a man slain with the spear is moreover thought to enter in some way into the slayer, and he must therefore at once have his arm cut by a leopard-skin priest to let it out. This must mean that blood is thought to have some vitality of its own. The rite of initiation must be held in a homestead because the blood of the initiates must not be shed outside the home, and care is taken to bury it in the holes into which it flows lest dogs eat it. These examples, and others could be cited, show that human blood has mysterious properties but they do not justify our saying that Nuer regard the life as something contained in the blood Moreover, in the case of cattle, which is the case at issue, we have to bear in mind that Nuer have no objection to shedding their blood They do so when they cut their horns, when they castrate them, and when they pierce veins in the necks of cows (*bar*) in the dry season for veterinary purposes or, more usually, to obtain blood for boiling or roasting for their own consumption. But if the blood is not thought of literally as containing the life, the life of a sacrificed ox ebbs with its flow so that Nuer say either that God takes the life (or breath) or that he takes the blood—the blood and the breath being symbols of the life, as also appears to be, in a lesser degree, the chyme.

The chyme (*wau*) is what makes the flesh and maintains the life of the beast. Dr. Lienhardt tells me that *wei*, the word for it in Dinka, means in that language also 'life' and 'breath'. It does not appear to have so important a place in Nuer ritual as it has in the ritual of some other Nilotic peoples. The only reference in my notes to its sacramental use in connexion with sacrifice is to its being smeared on a Dinka at his adoption into a Nuer lineage, but Father Crazzolara says that sometimes after sacrifice the head of the family takes some of the chyme and after adding some of the beast's blood and his own spittle he rubs this mixture on his own breast, back of neck, and maybe also forehead, and perhaps also on the same parts of members of his family.[1]

God takes the *yiegh*, the life. Man takes the *ring*, the flesh, what is left over after the sacrifice. The carcass is cut up and skinned as soon as the animal falls In most sacrifices the meat is consumed by members of the family and kin of the person on whose behalf it was made. In marriage and most other collective sacrifices it is divided among relatives, both paternal and maternal, in traditional portions, and the age-mates of the owner of the beast and representatives of lineages collateral to his may also have rights to shares If the principal officiant is not a member of the family or of the close kin but a master of ceremonies of the family or a priest or a prophet, he also receives his share. This part of the proceed-

---

[1] Op cit , p 80. Among the Shilluk, at any rate in their sacrifices to end feuds, the chyme of the victim is put on the youths to indicate unity A beast eats a bit here and a bit there in the stomach it becomes one (D S Oyler, 'The Shilluk Peace Ceremony', *Sudan Notes and Records*, 1920, p 299)

ings is of general interest and not merely for those directly concerned in the rites. If it is at all a public occasion people, whether
they are concerned in the matter or not, gather round to watch
the meat being cut up and handed to those to whom it is due, and
there is often much shouting and argument as the distribution is
goodhumouredly disputed and men tug at the carcass and snatch
or beg pieces of meat Even outsiders who get in the way and beg
persistently enough are likely to receive pieces of it. According to
the circumstances those who on such an occasion receive meat
take it to their homes, maybe in different villages, for cooking and
eating, or it is cooked by women of the homestead in which the
sacrifice took place and eaten there by groups, according to sex,
age, and kinship. The meat is cooked, served, and eaten as would
be that of a wild beast slaughtered in hunting. It is boiled, though
tit-bits may be roasted in the embers of a fire. I want to make it
clear indeed that the cutting up of the victim, the preparation of
its flesh, and the eating of it are not parts of the sacrifice. To
regard the eating of the animal as part of the sacrificial rite would
be like regarding a wedding feast as part of the marriage service
in our own country But if it does not form part of the rite and
has no sacramental significance it forms part of the whole ceremony in the broader sense and has a social significance. We have
always to remember that a sacrifice, even piacular sacrifice, fur-
nishes a feast and that in the circumstances in which Nuer live
and by convention this means that neighbours are likely in one
way or another to share in it.

IV

The ordinary Nuer sacrifice is carried out in the manner I have
described—*pwot, buk, lam, nak (kam yang)*, presentation, consecration, invocation, immolation. In some sacrifices, however, there
are differences of order and procedure.

Mortuary ceremonies open with the slaughter of one or more
beasts before sunrise, and as the invocations do not take place till
later in the day they are not spoken over the victims as in other
sacrifices. I do not think that this reversal of phases has in itself
any special significance Since the cattle have to be killed before
the sun rises it is convenient to postpone the invocations, which are
very lengthy on this occasion. Moreover, though in the mortuary

ceremony which I witnessed the speakers of the invocations did not as they spoke walk up and down past tethered victims, as in normal sacrifices, they walked up and down past the dead man's possessions to which had been added the heads and hides of the slaughtered beasts; and I believe this to be the usual practice. As these heads and hides represented the victims it may be said that the invocations were said over them *post mortem* What is of significance is rather the fact that the cattle must be slaughtered before the sun rises. The sacrifices concern death and the ghost of a dead man, so that the killing before sunrise is in accord with the association of east and light with life and of west and darkness with death. This part of the ceremony is for the dead man. The sacrifices are for him. Another sacrifice, which concludes the ceremonies, is for the release of the living. This explains also another difference, one of procedure.

It is understandable that on this occasion there is no formal presentation, for the beasts are killed at their habitual tethering-pegs in the kraal; but that there is also no consecration with ashes calls for comment. The explanation I would put forward, and which I discuss further in later chapters, is that the rubbing with ashes is, besides a consecration, an identification, at any rate in sacrifice which has a piacular meaning, of life of man with life of ox. Here sacrifice is for the dead. His soul, as we have seen earlier, goes to the abode of the ghosts with the souls of the cattle slaughtered at his mortuary ceremony. It is not for the living, so the living do not identify themselves with the victim in the usual manner.

There are some peculiar features in other sacrifices, apart from the supernumerary acts, such as libations, I have mentioned as sometimes accompanying the main rites, but they are only variations in the mode of slaughter or special acts performed after the sacrifice has been made.

In sacrifices in which the idea of separation is strong, as in cases of incest, to sever kinship, and in one of the mortuary rites, instead of the ox being speared and then skinned it is thrown on the ground and cut longitudinally in half, an operation known as *bak*. They begin the cutting by making an incision in the throat, so that the animal is soon dead, and they then cut towards the tail, slitting even that in two. Finally, they split the head in two with an axe. In other sacrifices in which the same idea is present the animal is speared, or its throat is slit, but instead of being skinned it is cut in two laterally across the belly (*ngok*). This is done at ceremonies in honour of a *colwic* spirit, and also in rites performed to avoid misfortune coming to a man whose wife has been unfaithful or who takes a widow in leviratic marriage.

In sacrifices to spirits associated with rivers and streams and with creatures which live in them (generally the crocodile), and also sometimes in a sacrifice to God for rain, the victim—a sheep or goat, not an ox—may be bound and pushed under the water among the reeds and weeds. When sacrifice is made to the python-spirit the victim is suffocated. The openings of its body are stuffed with grass and it is jumped on and pummelled to death. In practice it is assumed to be dead at an early stage and the point of a spear is inserted in its throat to begin the skinning. Nuer regard this as a Dinka mode of sacrifice, as indeed it is, contrasting suffocation with *yiedh*, stabbing with the spear, their own normal mode of sacrificing oxen.

I have not seen a sacrifice to the python-spirit, but I have seen an ox suffocated in a different and rare ceremony. I think that perhaps what I witnessed should not be regarded as a sacrifice at all, at any rate in the usual sense, for the beast does not seem to have been consecrated and there was no invocation. It has more the appearance of what we might better describe as a magical rite, almost certainly of Dinka origin. I feel nevertheless that, as it was the only occasion I saw a killing by suffocation, I should give a brief description of it When a girl is espoused early in life, probably before the commencement of the menses, the premature payment of bridewealth may cause her to be barren unless a special ceremony is performed. In western Nuerland, where I saw it, it is called *gorot*.[1] I believe that in eastern Nuerland a rather different ceremony is performed. On the occasion when I was present it took place in the girl's home after her marriage had been consummated. An ox was thrown and its forelegs and back legs tied in pairs It'was then slowly suffocated, grass being first pushed up its anus with a stick, and then into its mouth and nostrils (Plate III). During its sufferings the husband and a youth of his age-set, the wife and a maiden of about her age, and a small boy and a small

[1] J Kiggen (op cit , pp. 108 and 117) gives this word as the name of a different ceremony, for a woman without children who has smallpox He says that a small gourd is opened, beer is poured into it, it is rubbed over the woman, and a goat is killed The rite I describe is probably his *guur*, the meaning of which he gives as 'animal sacrifice to the Dinka god'.

girl sat on its flank. After a while they rose and the ox's throat was cut. Dr. Lienhardt tells me that this mode of slaughter by cutting the throat, otherwise unknown among the Nuer in the killing of oxen, is the usual manner of sacrificing oxen among the Dinka. The ox was then cut up and from each joint and major organ a bit of meat was sliced off. The bits were cooked and then minced. The conductor of the rite, a female diviner, threw some of the mincemeat towards the hut where the husband and wife were cohabiting and placed some of it in the mouths of the spouses. Both spat it out. The husband told me afterwards that the putting of the meat into his mouth was the most humiliating part of the rite because he had never before allowed food to touch his lips in the presence of his wife. The small boy was then seated on the husband's lap and the small girl on the wife's lap. A gourdful of the mincemeat was emptied into the husband's cupped hands and he transferred it to the cupped hands of the boy. The action was repeated by the wife and the small girl. A pot of boiled blood was then taken into the hut and the diviner scraped some of it with a mussel shell across the mouths of husband and wife and the companions of their own age. The door of the hut was then closed and the butter was placed on the fire While it was melting, a boy, the wife's brother, circled the hut outside with the boiled hump of the ox on the point of a fishing-spear. When he stuck the hump through the first window of the hut the diviner asked 'what will you give me?' and someone in the hut answered that she would give a brown calf. The action was repeated at the other windows of the hut, the answer referring to either a brown or a black calf. Then the door was opened and the diviner hung round the wife's neck the stomach lining of the ox and the skin of its umbilicus to which brass rings and part of its tail had been attached. She then anointed husband and wife and their companions and others present with the butter. On their departure the husband's people took the meat of the ox home with them, except the head, which remained with the wife's people who had provided the ox. I was told that the purpose of the ceremony was to ensure that in spite of the unusual circumstances of betrothal a child would speedily be born to the union.

I cannot explain the symbolism, if it has any, of this particular rite, but in cases of sacrifice proper in which a victim is slain in an unusual manner the symbolism is manifest The beast is cut in

PLATE X

Immolation

twain to sever a relationship. The beast is drowned because the sacrifice is associated in one way or another with water. The beast is suffocated because that is how the python kills its prey. All this is mimicry, symbolic action by which some peculiar feature or some particular purpose of the sacrifice is expressed. The different modes of slaughter do not constitute different kinds of sacrifice but merely variations of the rite.

There are also variations in the manner of disposal of the carcass. In sacrifices in settlements of feuds the sacrificial ox is not skinned and its flesh then distributed in fixed traditional portions, but as soon as it falls all the men fall upon it and hack it to pieces with their spears, each taking what he can slice off and get away with. This is called *koak*. A scene of great confusion results and those taking part in the scrimmage are lucky if they are not injured by the spears used to cut off pieces of the flesh. An animal found dead in the bush is treated in the same way; and according to Father Crazzolara also cattle burnt in a byre struck by lightning.[1] Dr. Howell says that when an elephant is killed by hunters it is hacked to pieces in the same manner: 'the chaos which follows has to be seen to be believed'[2] Occasionally sacrifices are holocausts, as when sacrifice is made to God to stay a plague or murrain, or to the durra-bird-spirit for the birds to leave the millet and return to the bush. The victim is left lying where it falls and its flesh is not eaten. I believe that it is the same with an ox sacrificed before an advancing enemy. In these instances the victims are slain in the bush and not, as in ordinary sacrifices, in the homestead.

These variations in the disposal of the carcass would seem to be connected with special circumstances in which sacrifice is some-times made. We have a clue to the general scramble for meat at sacrifice to conclude a feud in the other occasions when a scramble is customary. Then the animal does not belong to anyone. An elephant's tusks belong to the first and second spearer but its flesh is the right of all who participate in the hunt. There are no indivi-dual rights in it. Likewise a beast found dead in the bush was a wild creature that belonged to no one and it did not die as a result of anyone's efforts. Similarly cattle burnt to death in a byre, although they belonged to the owner of the byre, were not slaugh-

[1] Op cit , pp. 96–97
[2] P. P. Howell, 'A Note on Elephants and Elephant Hunting among the Nuer', *Sudan Notes and Records*, 1945, p. 100

tered by him but by God, and when God took them they ceased to be his. It would seem likely therefore that some such idea of the beast belonging to no one is present in the sacrifice to end a feud. The holocaust appears to be, at any rate usually, a manner of disposal, like the burnt offering of the Hebrews, when sacrifice is made on behalf of the whole community against a common danger, plagues and murrains and an enemy. Here sacrifice is not made to serve any individual interest nor the exclusive interests of particular lineages or clans but the interests of all the people alike. The reason for abandoning the carcasses, however, seems to be the idea that the evil has entered them through the sacrificial act.

It remains only to mention briefly some other peculiar features of ritual attached to some sacrifices. A small piece of the hide of a victim may after any sacrifice be tied to the *riek* shrine as a memento, but after sacrifice to a spirit a more elaborate memorial, a *yik*, may be constructed. This is a small mound of ash and mud with a *riek* set in the middle of it. The bones, or some of them, of the victim may be buried in the mound. In sacrifices for incest and in settlement of feuds the gall of the victim is drunk in infusion. This has nothing to do with the sacrifice itself but is a post-sacrificial act to cleanse the bodies of those who have been contaminated or to protect those who run a risk of contamination. It is a sort of medicine to counteract physically the consequences of the breach, or the possible breach, of an interdiction. It is something extra added to the sacramental action of the sacrifice proper. Some sacrifices are accompanied by the rite of aspersion. I discuss this later.

V

I have given some account of the structure of the Nuer sacrificial rite which, allowing for the variations and peculiar features I have mentioned, is the same for all sacrifices, those of the collective type as well as those of the personal type. Most sacrifices, as we have already noted, have a markedly piacular purpose. They are made in times of trouble and their general object is always the same, to get rid of the evil or threatening evil by offering to God a victim whose death will take it away. Nuer express this in various ways. They say that the evil 'will be finished with a thing (*duor*)'—that is, with an oblation. They say that it 'goes into the earth with the blood of the cow'. They say that 'the cow shields (*gang*)' the persons threatened by it. They say that God 'turns away'—as we have seen that in a sense the evil is he, in a certain aspect of the relation of Spirit to man, so, in this sense, it is he who is 'finished with a thing', he who 'goes into the earth' with the blood, he against whom the ox 'shields' man.

But though sacrifices made in times of trouble have this basic piacular meaning in common, certain tones in it are emphasized more in some sacrifices than in others, and this is sometimes indicated by some special word being used in reference to the intention. These words lie within the circuit of the general term denoting a piacular offering, *kam*, to give. An examination of them will shed further light on the character of the whole class of piacular sacrifices, and hence on the meaning of sacrifice in general. I speak now only of personal sacrifices, those which have a piacular intention.

When the notion of redemption is strongly marked the word *kuk*, with the verbal form *kok*, seems generally to be used when speaking of the sacrifice and in the invocation made at it. A *kuk kwoth*, sacrifice to God (or to some spirit), appears to be regarded as a ransom which redeems the person who pays it from a misfortune that would, or might, otherwise fall on him. By accepting the gift God enters into a covenant to protect the giver of it or help him in some other way. Through the sacrifice man makes a kind of bargain with his God.

In violent storms Nuer, fearful of the lightning, throw small pieces of tobacco into the air, asking God to take them, and saying that they have paid him ransom with this offering When a man in sudden illness or danger takes off a bead or bracelet and throws it away he says 'grandfather [God], take thy cow [bead or bracelet], I have paid thee ransom (*kok*), let my sickness depart'. When an ox is sacrificed there is the idea that the evil goes into the ox and then into the earth with its blood, and there seems to be here the idea of its going into the bead and residing there, for I was once about to pick up a bead I saw lying on the ground in the bush when a Nuer stopped me, saying that it had probably been given to God as an offering by a sick man and if I took it the sickness might enter into me. Likewise, when Nuer sacrifice before crossing a river or wading into a lake to fish, and ask for the protection of the female spirit *buk* against the dangers of the water, they say 'take thy cow, we are ransomed (*kok*)'. In a story of how a girl, Nyanding, was sacrificed to the river which bears her name she is said to have been paid in ransom to the river. The river was bought, as it were, by her sacrifice, just as the hippopotamus had to buy the river in one of the Nuer just-so stories Fox had found hippopotamus on land, where he had been created, and exacted from him, in payment for taking him to a river, the flesh around his mouth—which accounts for his funny face today. When they arrived at the river hippopotamus had to pay it (*kok*) the marrow of his leg bones before it would receive him—which accounts for their having no marrow, so Nuer say, in them today. 'Bought' and 'buy' are renderings I discuss below.

When in serious sickness an animal is sacrificed Nuer may say '*ca kwoth kok ke yang*', 'God is paid a cow [in ransom]'. I was present when a Nuer was defending himself against silent disapproval on the part of his family and kinsmen of his frequent sacrifices. He had been given to understand that it was felt that he was destroying the herd from inordinate love of meat. He said that this was not true. The oxen he had killed—and he had killed his own favourite ox among them—had been sacrificed to his mother-in-law's and wife's spirit *deng*, which came from Dinka-land and was frequently troubling his children and his wife and her brother with sickness. It was all very well for his family to say that he had destroyed the herd, but he had killed the cattle for their sakes. It was '*kokene yiekien ke yang*', 'the ransom of their lives with cattle'. He repeated this phrase many times as one by one he recounted cases of serious sickness in his family and described the ox he had sacrificed on each occasion to placate the spirit *deng*. If his sons saw fit to complain let them regard their sisters. Would they not get the cattle of their sisters' bridewealth? And were not the cattle killed to save their sisters' lives?

The word *kuk* would seem therefore to suggest that God, or a spirit, is placed by the sacrifice under an obligation A woman says 'God, take thy cow and give me a child', and Nuer say of the river-spirit that 'it is given a gift and then it gives life to the people'. The child and the life are given to suppliants in return for the gifts they make. The action of the rite is not effective in itself. God, or a spirit, is not constrained by the sacrifice to grant the favour asked for. An animal sacrificed to God is his animal anyhow, and what he gives the suppliant in return is a *muc*, a free gift Nevertheless, my impression was, at any rate where spirits of the air and of the earth are concerned, that Nuer feel that the recipient of a sacrifice is at fault if it does not fulfil its part of the bargain. A costly sacrifice having been made, *cuong*, right or justice, is on the human side in the matter. Thus the man of whom I was speaking above said during his harangue that after all the sacrifices he had made to the spirit *deng* on account of sickness in his family, his little daughter had been bitten by a snake and died. He had given all these oxen to *deng* and look what had happened! He felt aggrieved and had consulted a prophet of *deng* who had told him that if the spirit had taken his daughter it would compensate him for his loss; and it had indeed done so by giving him twins: '*ca col e kwoth ke cuek*', 'it [the death of the daughter] was compensated by the spirit with twins'. The use of the word *col*, as will be seen later, here implies that the spirit was in debt to the man. This Nuer Job complained that the spirit had only compensated him because he told it that he had had enough of it and that it could take all his children if it pleased, for then he would have finished with it because it would have nothing more to take from him.

The word *kok* occurs in the other Nilotic languages with much the same range of meaning, outside its sacrificial usage, as it has today in Nuer, for one most frequently hears it used today to describe the purchasing of goods from an Arab merchant. That a word which had chiefly, and perhaps primarily, a sacrificial meaning should come to be employed for the recent practice of buying something from a shop, a commercial sense it has also in other Nilotic tongues, sheds some light not only on Nuer ideas about trading but also on their ideas about sacrifice. Since the present range of meaning of the word includes buying and selling one might say that God or a spirit is 'bought' by sacrifice. The dangers of translation that beset one at every step in an attempt to understand and make intelligible Nuer religious ideas are here very apparent, for once we use the word 'bought' the associations it has among ourselves rush in to colour the Nuer conception. But Nuer do not regard purchase from an Arab merchant in the way in which we regard purchase from a shop. It is not to them an impersonal transaction, and they have no idea of price and currency in our sense. Their idea of a purchase is that you give something to a merchant who is thereby put under an obligation to help you. At the same time you ask him for something you need from his shop and he ought to give it to you because, by taking your gift, he has entered into a reciprocal relationship with you. Hence *kok* has the sense of either 'to buy' or 'to sell'. The two acts are an expression of a single relationship of reciprocity. As an Arab merchant regards the transaction rather differently mis-understandings arise. In the Nuer way of looking at the matter what is involved in an exchange of this kind is a relation between persons rather than between things. It is the merchant who is 'bought' rather than the goods, just as it is God or a spirit who is bounden by sacrifice; or it can be better put by saying that the partners, Nuer and merchant, man and God, *kok* each other. The general notion conveyed by the word is therefore that of exchange. This sense covers, as do our own words 'ransom' and 'redemption', both religious and commercial usages. In both there is the idea of a relationship expressed in gift and counter-gift. The mere fact that the word has been made use of to denote what we regard as plain and simple commerce shows that some idea of a bargain is implied in its sacrificial use. Whatever else it may also be, sacrifice can be regarded, as Socrates says in the *Euthyphro*, as being in a sense a 'commercial technique', a way of doing business between gods and men. A bargain is struck. There is an exchange This is further shown by the use of the verb *luel*, not in reference to any particular kind or situation of sacrifice but in invocations at per-sonal sacrifices. A consideration of its use shows us better what sort of exchange Nuer sacrifice is.

One of Professor Westermann's texts records a sacrificial in-vocation made on behalf of a sick man. I would translate it as follows· 'God, what is this? Leave him with us; let him recover. Turn about, take thy cow. It has been decreed for the life. It is thou who hast spoken thus. Take the cow that it may be in ex-change for the life (*bi je luele yei*). It is thou who hast created us; it is the cow which is exchanged for life (*e bi yang a luel ne yei*). Take the goat and the cucumber; and let him recover! In what have we erred? Give us the life Thou ait our father. Why must we always suffer? Give us the life, we pray thee, our father.'[1]

In other contexts the word *luel* means 'to exchange' or 'to change'. Something takes the place of another thing equal to it —a simple exchange of two things considered to be of more or less

---

[1] Op. cit , pp 116–17 The sentence 'Take the goat and the cucumber' would not occur in any actual invocation, for the two things would not be sacrificed at the same time Whoever spoke the text has inserted a gloss in the sense of 'Take the cow [ox], that is to say, the goat or the cucumber' [as the case may be].

equal value by the persons concerned in the exchange, as when a man who is leaving his neighbourhood exchanges his old byre for a bull calf or when a man exchanges an ox with certain markings desired by his partner to the exchange for one with his own favourite markings. The difference between *kok* and *luel* is that between the reciprocal relation between persons in an exchange and equivalence of objects exchanged. In either case the action is immediate, unlike that implied by use of the words *ngual*, to borrow, and *gwal*, to lend In loans a man makes a gift and the recipient later returns it or something of greater value. There are two distinct and separate movements between which there is a long passage of time. In its piacular context, therefore, the word *luel* means that the life of the victim is exchanged in the moment of its immolation for the life of a man. In the sacrificial situation the two things are of equal value, so that the one can be substituted for the other. This puts men and cattle in a very peculiar relationship to each other, a matter I discuss in Chapter X.

In personal and piacular sacrifices the animals are substitutions for men To this extent sacrifice is an exchange, but it is also something very much more than just a simple exchange. It is not a simple idea at all but a very complex one in which many other elements are present. I discuss the problem in more general terms later, but we may here note how other terms are used to describe personal sacrifices which emphasize rather the related ideas of propitiation, expiation, atonement, and purification.

Sometimes the word *lor* is used to describe a sacrifice The word means 'to go to meet', perhaps its most common usage being to describe the formal greeting that Nuer, especially women, make to a visitor of importance when they go from their homes to receive him outside their homestead or village. The word has therefore the further sense of 'to honour', as would appear to be the case also in Dinka and other Nilotic tongues But in the religious sense of the word people go out of their villages to meet a plague or other danger not with the purpose of bringing it to their homes to give it hospitality there but with the opposite purpose of preventing it from entering their homes. They go out to meet and stay a plague or murrain with sacrifice. They say '*bane je luor*', 'let us go out to meet it'. The well-known prophet Ngundeng of the Lou tribe did this in times of epidemics, sometimes, I was told, sacrificing dozens of oxen and leaving their carcasses in a line in the bush He also used to sacrifice before his followers as they advanced to battle. His son Gwek appears to have met his death while making such a sacrifice before a military patrol sent against him Mr. Coriat, one of the officers on this patrol, has described how the Nuer attack was launched 'Two long lines of men rushed out to either flank in an attempt to surround the troops while the main body of Nuer in the centre advanced more slowly but singing lustily and driving ahead of them a solitary white bull The order to fire was given The leading men and the bull reached to within 120 yards of the square before they fell and within a few minutes the whole mass of Nuer were fleeing in all directions. A long pursuit over rough and broken ground followed. Gwek, arrayed in a leather skirt with an iron skewer clutched tight in his hand and a brass pipe, the pipe of Dengkur [Ngundeng], lying beside him, was picked up dead beside the white bull.'[1]

Other prophets acted in the same manner in epidemics and war. It has also been described to me how a whole section of the eastern Jikany Nuer went out to meet smallpox which was advancing into their territory. They went out to meet it with goats and sheep and pots of beer, and they slaughtered the animals and left their carcasses and the pots of beer in a line over which the smallpox should not cross. It was described to me as being like a *kegh*, a boundary line—more closely in meaning a line a leopard-skin priest makes on the ground before advancing warriors halt them so that a fight may be prevented.

When I was living in a small village on the Sobat river swarms of locusts descended on it and on its gardens, and the people went out to meet (*lor*) them in a body, leading a fawn-coloured goat (roughly the colour of the locusts) and beating their ox-hides, where the gardens adjoined the bush, and there sacrificed the goat. It fell with its head towards the bush. This was regarded as a favourable sign as it was in that direction that the people wanted the locusts to go They soon departed. The carcass was left where it fell. I have earlier described how people go out to meet durra-birds which are eating their crops and how they make a similar sacrifice and leave the carcass in the bush. Nuer use the same word when speaking of the sacrifices made by kinsmen of twins at their birth. They say '*ba cuek luor*', 'the twins are met [with sacrifice]'.

---

[1] P Coriat, 'Gwek, the Witch-Doctor and the Pyramid of Dengkur', *Sudan Notes and Records*, 1939, p 237

On those occasions on which Nuer use the word *lor* in a religious context the danger is definite and immediately before them, and it has to be met with sacrifice to propitiate God so that of his kindness he may stay its approach It is true that they speak of going out to meet the smallpox, the locusts, the durra-birds, or whatever the threatening thing may be, but when they say that they 'meet it with a cow', that is, by sacrifice, we are to understand that the 'it' is not the thing itself but Spirit manifested in the thing. It is a vehicle of Spirit and only God can stay it. We have then in the concept of *luor* another element in sacrificial intention, homage to God by a whole community, or on its behalf, at a time of common crisis.

The word *kier*, with the verbal form *kir*, is more difficult to translate than the other words used for sacrifice because it has no meaning outside its sacrificial usage I have translated it by 'expiation' because that idea together with the idea of purification seem to me to be strongly represented in the situations of its use, the appeasement of God or spirits when an event which places people in a state of danger, usually grave, has taken place. The danger, which is Spirit itself, is not merely possible, nor is it seen to be approaching. It is already present and people must rid themselves of it before it injures them or causes them further injury.

Nuer say of a spirit which has made a man seriously ill '*ba kwoth kier ke del*', 'expiation is made to the spirit with one of the flock'. They say of the sacrifice made after the burial of a man that '*ba kier piny ke del*', '[the dead man] is expiated in the earth with one of the flock'. They say of a byre which has been struck by lightning that '*ca kir ke ghok*', 'it has been expiated with cattle', and of a man killed by lightning that '*ca je kir ke det kene ruath*', 'he was expiated with some of the flock and with oxen'. When a speckled vulture settled on a man's head (pp. 88–89) expiation was made (*ca kir*) by sacrifice. I have also heard it said of sacrifices made on account of the birth of twins '*ca ke kir*' 'they [the twins] have been expiated'. One does not visit the home of a kinsman who has begotten twins without something to sacrifice in one's hands. Further examples of the use of the word *kier* for sacrifices are given by Father Kiggen, on account of a man being lost and on account of a bad dream.[1]

It may seem a peculiar expression to speak of a man, twins, and

[1] Op cit, p 145

a byre being expiated and it is true that it is not they who are expiated but the death of the man, the birth of the twins, and the striking of the byre by lightning, or rather, since these events are all signs of God's presence it is Spirit itself which is expiated. This is what is said, literally, in the first example of the use of *kier* I have given, '*kwoth* (Spirit) is expiated with one of the flock'. A payment is made to get rid of it and the state of danger its presence means. It is expiation in that sense, not in the sense of paying penalty for fault, for in the examples I have given the idea of fault, or at any rate of some definite fault, is negligible, if not altogether lacking. What we observe is a feeling of something dangerous being in the village, a sort of miasma, which must be dispelled if the people are to be at peace, and a defilement from which the people must be cleansed. In some of the examples the ideas of defilement and purification are apparent Where this sense is strong the sacrifice is often accompanied by the rite of aspersion, and it may be noted that the word *kir* has in some of the other Nilotic languages the sense of 'to asperse', 'to sprinkle', and similar meanings.

We have seen that the *lor* concept adds the idea of honouring to that of an exchange or bargain in the general meaning of sacrifice. The *kier* concept adds something more. Sacrifice in the situations for which this word is used is made to prevent misfortune, or further misfortune, by an oblation. The danger is not disposed of till there has been an act of human will, a turning to God in sacrifice. Only when expiation has been made will it be wiped out. And the expiation is not just a payment, it is also the recognition of a debt. This aspect of sacrifice is most clearly brought out in the concept of *cuol*.

The ideas of expiation and purification are also markedly present in those sacrifices for which Nuer use the verb *col*, but there is a further and different emphasis as well. *Col* in its most general sense means, as in the other Nilotic languages, to pay compensation for an injury, and it is perhaps best translated 'to indemnify'. Indemnification for homicide or bodily injury, or indeed reparation made for any injury, may be spoken of as *col*. The word is also used in a religious sense when speaking of sacrifices to wipe out (*woc*) by indemnification the wrong done to God or a spirit by sin, such as, for example, having harmed a totem; when sacrificing for sickness if the sickness is thought to be due to some particular

PLATE XI

Death of victim and end of invocation

fault; and, most specifically, to describe mortuary rites. The implication is that just as, let us say, a woman who has been wronged by her daughter's husband exposing his nakedness to her must be indemnified by a gift, so if God or a spirit is wronged by some act or neglect he or it must be indemnified by sacrifice In the religious sense of the word it can perhaps best be translated 'to atone' and 'atonement'.

As the use of the word *col* implies in all other contexts that reparation for some wrong or fault is due we may suppose that it has something of the same sense when it is used with reference to mortuary ceremonies A mortuary ceremony is known as *col woc*, an expression which might be translated by some such phrase as 'the wiping out of debt' As it is not necessarily felt that any definite wrong has been done for which reparation must be made we may ask why this expression is used. I would answer that not only do Nuer seem to regard death itself as a kind of payment of debt, but they also seem to regard the dead man's kin as being involved in the debt, just as they would be had he incurred a debt to someone in his lifetime. The death still clings to them till they have made atonement by sacrifice and have been purified from its contamination by a purificatory rite which, while being particularly noticeable in the mortuary ceremonies, may accompany any sacrifice, such as those referred to by the terms *kier* and *cuol*, in which the idea of pollution is accentuated. The rite is known as *kith*, a word which means 'to sprinkle' and may be translated in its religious use as 'to asperse'. The aspergillum is a handful of wild rice, a plant which has other religious associations It is dipped in water or milk or blood and water mixed and shaken over the persons involved in whatever the calamity may be, and in rites concerning death over the dead man's possessions as well The word *kith* is also used for the sprinkling of beer at a ceremony in honour of a spirit over the ox dedicated to it, the beer being thrown over the animal's back by hand or blown over it from the mouth, a rite also called 'the bathing (of the ox)'; but here different ideas are expressed (pp. 42–43).

We may suppose that Nuer would not use so many different words when speaking of sacrifice unless the rite meant for them sometimes more one thing than another thing; and in our examination of these words we have found that they do indeed express rather different conceptions. No doubt these conceptions are only

variations of a single general meaning, are logically interconnected, and shade into one another, but they indicate nevertheless
distinct differences of emphasis. What all of them express, however, is the central piacular idea of substitution of lives of cattle
for lives of men That is on the surface. We have to inquire further
if we are to understand its interior meaning.

CHAPTER IX

SPEAR SYMBOLISM

WHEN I think of the sacrifices I have witnessed in Nuerland there are two objects I see most vividly and which sum up for me the sacrificial rite: the spear brandished in the right hand of the officiant as he walks up and down past the victim delivering his invocation, and the beast awaiting its death. It is not the figure of the officiant or what he says which evokes the most vivid impression, but the brandished spear in his right hand.

We have noted that the *lam* or invocation states the intention of the sacrifice. Its words are a projection of the will and desire of the person as he turns towards Spirit; and an essential part of the action is the brandishing of the spear. As the officiant walks up and down delivering his oration the movements of the spear in his right hand emphasize his words· opening and closing his fingers on it, poising it in his hand, raising it as though to strike, making little jabs with it into the air, pointing it towards the victim, and so on. These movements are an integral part of the expression of intention, and there is more in the action than meets the eye.

In Nuer ritual the meaning of symbolism is generally at once evident to ourselves, at any rate in its main import, for there is an intrinsic relation between the symbol and what it stands for. When an animal is cut in half in cases of incest. to allow inter-marriage between distant kin, before a man takes his dead brother's wife in leviratic union, at the closing of an age-set, in mortuary ceremonies, and on other occasions, we can at once perceive how the purpose of the rite is expressed in the severing of the carcass. A relationship of one kind or another between persons is being severed. Likewise the symbolism of the rite, common among primitive peoples, of putting out fires and relighting them at a man's mortuary ceremony, and in the case of the rehabilitation of a homicide the relighting of them with fire-sticks, is at once evident for us. The past is finished with; one begins anew.

The shaving of the head of a bride at her marriage, of a boy at his initiation, of a kinsman at a mortuary ceremony, and of a homicide at the settlement of a feud expresses, and brings about, the passing from one state to another as obviously for us as for Nuer Again, we can see immediately also the appropriateness of the action to the situation and purpose in the ritual making of a line or boundary (*kegh*). A leopard-skin priest cuts a line between opposing factions to forbid combat. The dominant lineages of the Gaagwong and Leek tribes may not, for a mythical reason, tether their cattle in a common kraal, but if they cannot conveniently avoid doing so a line of earth is thrown up between the sections of the kraal occupied by each. On the other hand, whilst there is generally a ridge of raised earth dividing adjacent gardens of neighbours this is absent when the owners of them are members of the same *ric* or age-set. When in certain ceremonies Nuer throw ashes into the air or asperse their bodies we do not have difficulty in perceiving that they are expressing the idea of evil being blown or washed away Another, and final, example is that of a man who leaves the tribal territory where he was born and brought up to reside in the territory of a different tribe He may then—it may not be a regular practice, though I was told that a man might die of *nueer* were he not to take the precaution—take a pot of earth from his natal territory and mix it in an infusion with earth from the territory of his adoption, and drink the infusion, on each occasion adding more of the new earth and less of the old, thereby slowly making the transference from his old to his new home. We have no difficulty at all in understanding and entering into this symbolism Likewise we readily understand the imagery of various rites I have described in this book, such as the bending of a bracelet to close the jaws of crocodiles, the placing of the corpses of infant twins on branches of trees, and many other rites.

Since we at once perceive the meaning of the symbolism of the ritual action we may suppose that Nuer also perceive its logical fitness to its purpose; and, indeed, it is often certain that they do so, for if asked to explain what they are doing they interpret the symbolism of a rite in terms of its purpose. The symbolism is manifest to them, as it is to us. But there is a deeper symbolism which is so embedded in ritual action that its meaning is neither obvious nor explicit. The performer may be only partly aware or even unaware that it has one. Interpretation may then be difficult for a person of alien culture, and the door is open for every kind of extravagant guesswork to enter. Nevertheless. if it be rash in such circumstances to put forward symbolic interpretations of ritual acts, or features of them, we are sometimes compelled to make the attempt, as in this excursus on the spear, by the very emphasis given to them by the culture we are trying to understand.

Since we have no spears ourselves and nothing which takes their place in our lives it is difficult for us to appreciate their importance for Nuer Nuer have no knives, other than that (*ngom*) used for cutting the marks of manhood at initiation, so that their fighting-spears, besides their use as weapons, have to serve where other peoples use knives.[1] A man's fighting-spear (*mut*) is constantly in his hand, forming almost part of him—when he is fighting, hunting, travelling, herding, dancing, displaying himself with his oxen, playing with his comrades, and so on—and when he lays it down it is within his reach; and he is never tired of sharpening and polishing it, for a Nuer is very proud of his spear. In writing a preliminary account of Nuer age-sets many years ago and without reference to the symbolic significance of the spear I wrote that 'one is surprised at the real feeling a Nuer expresses for his spear, almost as though it were animate and not a mere weapon'. Later I came to realize better that in a sense it is animate, for it is an extension and external symbol of the right hand, which stands for the strength, vitality, and virtue of the person. It is a projection of the self, so when a man hurls his spear he cries out either 'my right hand' or the name of the ox with which he is identified.

The spear, being an extension of the right hand, stands for all that the right hand stands for, for what is strong, virile, and vital, and consequently for masculinity and hence for the paternal kin and the lineage Therefore during the discussions about bridewealth in the byre of the bride's home on her wedding day the bridegroom's people sit on the right side of the byre and the bride's people on the left side Therefore, also, when the carcasses of oxen sacrificed at marriage ceremonies are divided among the kin, the right fore and hind legs are the portions of the father's brothers and sisters and the left fore and hind legs are the portions of the mother's brothers and sisters. The left side symbolizes evil

---

[1] Being the only thing they have which cuts and is therefore suitable for shaving—their other spears only pierce—the verbal form of the word for fighting-spear, *mut*, besides its meaning of 'to spear' means 'to cut' or 'to shave hair'. When used in the last sense it often refers to ritual shaving of the head, and it may then be used for the whole ceremony of which shaving of the head forms part, as the final marriage ceremony of consummation and ceremonies in connexion with death.

as well as femininity, and there is here a double association, for the female principle is also associated with evil directly, as it were, and not merely through the convergence of femininity and evil in the concept of the left side. Thus we have two opposites, the one comprising the left side, weakness, femininity, and evil, and the other comprising the right side, strength, masculinity, and goodness.[1]

That the right side is the good side and the left side the evil side may have been noted in various places in this book. When a fruit or animal is cut in two at sacrifices the left half may be either thrown or given away and only the right half be consumed by the people of the home. It is propitious for a sacrificial ox stabbed with the spear to fall on its right side and unpropitious for it to fall on its left side A dead man is buried to the left of his hut or windscreen, the side of misfortune. A woman is said to warn her son that when he visits his bride to cohabit with her she may crouch to the right side of the entrance to the hut so that he has to enter by the left side. If she does this he must order her to the other side lest some ill come to him.[2]

When I was in Nuerland I was only half aware of the significance of left and right for Nuer. When writing this book I found therefore that in several respects my observations, or at any rate what I had recorded, were insufficient to answer certain questions that arose from a further consideration of the left–right polarity. It occurred to me that if the representations were as I supposed them to be then, for example, when Nuer deform the horns of their favourite oxen with which they identify themselves, it should always be the left, and never the right, horn which is trained downwards (Plate XIII). Or again, when Nuer erect the sacred pole, associated with God, the spirits of their lineage, and also with its ghosts, at the entrance to their windscreens, which is their practice, it should always be to the right of the windscreen (taking, in this case, bearings from within it). My recollection,

---

[1] Among many primitive peoples the slight organic asymmetry between the left hand and the right is made the symbol of absolute moral polarity. Robert Hertz has treated the subject systematically in a brilliant essay, 'La prééminence de la main droite', *Revue philosophique*, xxxiv, 1909 (reprinted in *Mélanges de sociologie religieuse et de folklore*, 1928)

[2] Left and right are of course relative to the orientation of the person. Thus when a man takes his bearings from the entrance to hut or windscreen what is left from the inside will be right from the outside. I do not think, however, that the point of orientation affects the argument, for it is conventional that in reference to any particular matter the one side is left and the other right

PLATE X

Youth wearing *thiau* (arm-rings)

confirmed to some extent by the evidence of my photogiaphs,[1] supported these conclusions, but I asked Dr. Lienhardt and Dr. Howell to verify them, which they have been able to do. It should follow also that a husband sleeps on the right side of the hut and his wife on the left side, and here again Dr. Lienhardt has been good enough to confirm that this is the invariable practice. He has made a further and important observation. I was aware that the west is associated with death and the east with life, but I did not know, till he told me, that east is identified with right and west with left, thus bringing into the left–right polarity the polar representations not only of life and death but also of the cardinal points east and west. I am indebted to Dr. Mary Smith for the further observation that Nuer speak of 'right-handed peace' ('*mal me cuec*'). They would never speak of left-handed peace

It is in accord with what we have learnt of the associations with left and right in Nuer thought that Nuer youths should emphasize the contrast between the two hands by putting the left arm out of action altogether for months or even a year or two. This they do by pressing a series of metal rings (*thiau*) into the flesh of the left arm from the wrist upwards so tightly that sores and great pain result and the arm is rendered useless for any purpose other than the display of fortitude and as a passive instrument for the right hand to play upon (Plate XII). A ring on a finger of the right hand is rubbed up and down the discs on the imprisoned left arm to accompany the compliments and endearments of courtship. Such a mutilation is only fully intelligible in terms of symbolic associations. Here the fact that it is only the left horn of favourite oxen which is debased (if the right is trained at all it is trained upwards) is of great significance, for, as will be seen, a man and his favourite ox are identified What he does to his left hand he does to his ox's left horn: what he does to the ox he does to himself.

It is perhaps important to add that Nuer do not think of the left hand as being in a material sense evil. Left-handed persons suffer no disabilities at all and are not considered in other respects as different from other people Nuer do not, in my experience, attach any importance to the matter, but simply say of a left-

[1] All deformed horns in the photographs are left horns. Some branches in them, however, are to the left of the windscreens, but Nuer erect branches for practical purposes as well as for religious reasons, and I do not think it is possible to distinguish between them by sight

handed man that his left hand is his right hand. It is the quality of leftness, not the thing that is left, the hand itself, which is significant for them. Similarly, the left half of the severed carcass of a sacrificial animal is not intrinsically evil. It is always eaten by someone. It is bad symbolically, not in itself, and symbolically only in certain contexts or for certain people.

It is suggested that the spear as a projection of the right hand symbolizes the vitality of man, the manhood of man with the associations of lineage values that go with it. It is within the logic of the representation that we speak only of men. The spear stands for masculinity. Women do not bear fighting-spears. The spear does not go with femininity. Hence also boys do not bear fighting-spears till at their initiation to manhood they are given them by their fathers. Before this event they are something in between men and women, and this is shown by the fact that they milk the cows, a feminine task that men may not undertake. That neither women nor boys bear spears means that they do not go to war and also that they do not sacrifice. It is not just that a woman may not slaughter the sacrificial victim —it is not, in any case, important who slaughters it—but that, not being able to bear the spear, she cannot make the sacrificial invocation, which is made by the spear in the right hand as well as by the mouth. She can indeed address Spirit at sacrifices, but if she does so she prays (*pal*); she does not invocate (*lam*). This is understandable when we think of the spear as an extension of the right hand and hence as representing strength, masculinity, and goodness. Sacrifice, like war, belongs to that side of life, what we ourselves call the spear-side.[1]

0 5 10 CENTIMETRES

---

[1] I was told that a wife may act as master of ceremonies in her husband's place and shout out the spear-name of his clan at a wedding. This is the *twoc ghok* mentioned later.

FIG. 4

Instrument used in wedding invocations

It is important here, and before we proceed further with the argument, to note that the spear we are concerned with is the *mut*, the metal fighting-spear (or, in a more restricted sense, spear-head), the only spear used in sacrifice. It is not a *bidh*, a metal fishing-spear, and it is not a *giit*, a fighting-spear fashioned out of substances other than metal. We have further to bear in mind that though spears are now easily obtained by purchase from Arab traders this is a very recent development. There is no iron in Nuerland, and what metal spears the Nuer used to possess were procured in one way or another from neighbouring peoples, and it is certain that till recently there were very few of them. Nuer made up for the deficiency by fashioning spears from horn and bone and hard wood. Spears fashioned from these materials were still plentiful when I was living in Nuerland, though they were taking on more and more a purely sentimental and ceremonial value, being often used in dances but seldom for fighting and hunting. Since, however, the spears of the ancestors, the names of which are cried out in invocations, were iron fighting-spears, and since Nuer could not have done without some of these cutting blades, there must always have been a certain number of them, and also a certain number of iron fishing-spears (for which horn, bone, and wood substitutes are unsuitable), but, as Dr. Howell has pointed out, they were few in number, this accounting, in his opinion, for the high value—several head of cattle—placed upon them.[1] I agree with him that it must have been very rare for a man to have had more than one *mut*, the *giit* spears being regarded as supplementary to it. This must consequently have been a very valuable possession and, if lost, most difficult to replace; and it was not just a private possession but a family heirloom passed from father to son down the generations This does not mean that it was a relic. It was for practical use and therefore when worn was presumably replaced; otherwise one would see these ancestral spears today. However, the age of a spear has no great significance for Nuer For them,

It is not a sacrificial invocation It must be a very rare occurrence for a woman to play this role. Probably she can only take the part if she is acting on behalf of the bridegroom's family and hence holds in her hand, not a spear, but the instrument called *dang* (Fig 4). and also if she is an old woman, of whom Nuer say 'she has become a man'. There is one occasion when women bear spears Twins go through a fictional wedding before they can go through a real one In this ceremony men array themselves as women, and women as men

[1] P P. Howell, 'On the Value of Iron among the Nuer', *Man*, 1947, No 144.

even if the spear a man's father gives him at his initiation has been bought from an Arab merchant, and is not in fact the spear the father received from his father and the father's father from his father, it is ideally so regarded and thus serves as a symbol of filiation The spear is thus a point at which two complex social representations meet, that of the person and that of the lineage. Consequently I do not think that the high assessment of spears in cattle can be assigned to scarcity alone or even that scarcity was at any time the primary consideration. Spears, both fighting- and fishing-spears, were something more, and fighting-spears something much more, than weapons of war or of the chase. They were almost parts of the person. I have seen Nuer enraged when neighbours have borrowed their spears without permission, especially if they have lost them, their anger being out of all proportion to the offence if we think of the matter solely in terms of economic value, for the economic value of spears is negligible at the present day. It is the audacity and the insult which outrage the owner, as though someone had taken, and perhaps lost, part of his person, and all the more so in the case of the fighting-spear, with which are bound up his manhood and his participation in his lineage, as we see from the manner of his receiving it at his initiation.

I have discussed elsewhere[1] the ritual of initiation and I do so again in connexion with the role of cattle in Nuer religion. All that need be said here is that when a boy is initiated into manhood and takes on the full responsibilities of that status he is presented by his father with a *mut*, a metal fighting-spear, and an ox —the two objects in which, as I have said, the whole drama of sacrifice is centred I discuss here only the spear. A boy may before initiation possess a fishing-spear, but even today he is most unlikely to own a fighting-spear. Even should he do so, he would still be presented with a spear by his father at his initiation, for it is a ceremonial gift expressing formal recognition of his manhood and all that that means in the social life of the Nuer, and also the handing over by one generation to another. It is not just a spear, but a new status also that he is being given. The boy is now boy no longer but man and warrior and soon to be husband and father. He takes part in feuds and wars and raids. He also for the first time engages in dances and displays with oxen, both of which among the Nuer are martial exercises as well as play intimately

[1] 'The Nuer Age-Sets', *Sudan Notes and Records*, 1936

associated with courtship; and also in the pursuits of herding and hunting. All these activities require the use of the spear, but it is important that we recognize that it is not the acquisition of a weapon, whatever its economic value might have been in the past, nor even its utility, great though that may be, that gives a crucial significance to the gift of a spear at initiation. Its significance is moral, not merely utilitarian. It is not the spear itself, nor its possession, which is stressed but the activities associated with it: war and raiding, dancing and display, and herding. The uses of the spear itself and the evaluations of its uses as an index of social personality are blended, so that the spear is not just a weapon but also something which stands for a very complex set of social relations.

But the investment of a youth with a spear at his initiation would seem to be something more, for, as we will see in discussing the sacrificial role of cattle, initiation is not only into the social life of adults but also into a new relationship with the cattle which has an important religious side to it There is now established an identification, deriving from the sacrificial situation, between the initiates and cattle and, looked at from this point of view, the rites of initiation may be said to have a sacramental character. The boy enters into communion with the spirits and ghosts of his lineage through the cattle. 'The spear of the cutting (initiation)' is thus a symbol of a sacramental change as well as of a change in social status. In both symbolic aspects it is an extension of, and stands for, the right arm and represents strength, strength of the soul as well as strength of the body of the person; and, as I shall attempt to show, in both the symbolism is also a representation of the collective strength of the lineage to which the person belongs.

I have suggested that the fighting-spear has a symbolic meaning for Nuer besides what it means for them as a weapon and tool—that it is a projection of the self and stands for the self. This is most important for an understanding of Nuer sacrifice Its manipulation in the most common, and for a study of religion the most significant, sacrifices, the personal and piacular ones, expresses, if our interpretation is right, the throwing of the whole person into the intention of the sacrifice. It is not only said but also thought, desired, and felt. Not only the lips make it but also the mind, the will, and the heart. This interpretation makes the miming with the spear intelligible for, as an extension of the right arm, it stands for the whole person [1] It is for this reason that a spear must be carried during the invocation and not in order to slay the animal at the end of it. Other invocations by other men may follow before that is done, and the quick dramatic thrust into its heart which concludes the rite may be made by anyone, and not necessarily by a man who has made an invocation or by a spear used in the invocation.

But we have also to note that on many sacrificial occasions— those of a collective kind held in structural situations—when a man makes an invocation he does so as the representative of his clan (where 'clan' is used in this context 'clan or lineage' is to be understood—a man may be speaking in reference to his maximal lineage). He identifies himself with the clan by identifying his spear with that of the ancestor of the clan It is his own spear which he brandishes but the name of the spear he shouts out as he does so is that of the spear of the ancestor of the clan, the clan spear-name. This is characteristic of sacrifices of the collective type, and it is towards them that the discussion is now directed

Each of the Nuer clans has a spear-name and sometimes a large lineage of a clan has a secondary name which is different from that of another lineage of the same clan. This spear-name is shouted out by a representative of the clan while he brandishes a spear in his right hand, in war, at weddings, and on other public occasions when the clan as a whole is concerned—ideally, that is, and never actively and corporately. It is especially shouted out as an exordium to sacrificial invocations on occasions of collective significance (pp 288–9) It is '*mut gwara*', 'the spear of our fathers' On such of these occasions as require the services of a leopard-skin priest he calls out the spear-name '*mut Geaka*', 'spear of Gee', a spear-name which combines the representation of the priestly office with that of the Nuer as a whole.

It is essential to note that, with two exceptions, no actual spears of the ancestors of the clans exist, and it is not held by Nuer that they ever did exist, except in the sense that the ancestors had their own spears. The virtue is in the idea of 'the spear of our fathers', not in any material clan relic. Consequently, in invocations any spear will serve the purpose of the rite and represent that of the

---

[1] Among the Shilluk the officiant rubs his spear on the back of the victim, as the Nuer places his right hand on its back (D S Ovler, *Sudan Notes and Records*, 1920, p 298)

ancestor of the clan and hence symbolize the clan as a whole. Any spear will do, but, for the reason I have stated, there must be a spear; and when Nuer sitting in my tent recounted to me what is said in invocations they gestured with their right hands as though they held spears in them, for they found it difficult to speak the words without making the gestures, just as in recounting what is said in prayers (*pal*) they found it difficult to do so without moving outstretched hands up and down.

Published literature on the Nuer records information about only two actual spears of clans. The one about which we are told most is the spear, called *wiu*, of the Gaatgankir clan, who are regarded by all, including themselves, as being of Dinka origin, and the spear is a Dinka, and not a Nuer, type of spear. A mysterious origin and power are attributed to it It is believed to have been held by Kir, the ancestor of the clan, when he was cut out of the gourd in which he was found, and it is also associated with the air-spirit *wiu*, which is regarded as being in some sense immanent in it. When I was in Nuerland it was in the charge of a family of leopard-skin priests of the Tar lineage of the eastern Gaajak tribe. I did not myself see it, but it has been described by Mr H. C Jackson, who saw it in 1922 near the Pibor river.[1] He records that it was decorated with cowrie shells and beads and was housed in a special grass hut where visitors treated it with great deference. He says that it was prayed and sacrificed to, especially before raids on the Dinka and Burun peoples;[2] that if two sections of the Nuer wished to engage in fighting among themselves it would be placed between them to prevent an engagement; and that oaths were taken on it I was told that only old people would look upon it. The importance of this spear to our discussion of clan spear-names is that, as I will explain later, all such spear-names have an

---

[1] H C Jackson, op cit , pp. 168 and 179–81

[2] We are probably to understand, in view of Nuer religious conceptions in general, that Nuer respect (*thek*) the spear and pray and sacrifice to the spirit *wiu*, which is in the sky as well as in the spear. Mr R T Johnston reached the same conclusion with regard to a similar spear among the Bor Dinka. He observes that 'the spear by itself, except by association and as a symbol, is not sacred' (op. cit , p 127) Dr Lienhardt tells me that when the Government, with remarkable lack of imagination, confiscated and removed this spear lest it should become a focus of opposition to the administration the Dinkas' faith was in no way lessened. The only result was that the spirit associated with the spear, no longer having a recognized material symbol in a single place, manifested itself all over the tribal territory, defying any further intervention

association with the spirit *wiu* through the further association of this spirit with lightning and hence with the idea of striking, so that the spear *wiu*, perhaps also because it has a material existence, has become the prototype of clan 'spears'. Of the other spear, that of the Thiang clan and tribe, who occupy a territory I have not myself visited, we are told by Mr. B. A. Lewis only in whose possession it is and that it is called *mut bah thiang*.[1] Dr P. P Howell, who gives its name as *mut bar thiang*, tells me that he has not seen it but Nuer have described it to him as being nearly worn through with much polishing. It is unknown whether any cultic practices like those I have mentioned above are connected with it.

Apart from the Gaatgankir and the Thiang spears the spear-symbols of the Nuer clans and lineages are only names. Through the association of a tribal community with the clan dominant in it the spear-name of this clan is shouted out in invocations when the whole tribe goes to war but, except in this context, which I discuss below, in which a political group is merged conceptually with a clan or lineage, it is only called out in reference to a descent group as an exclusive group Thus, when I asked a Wot tribesman whether his tribe had a tribal spear he replied: 'We have many spears. One lineage (*gol*) has one spear, another lineage has another spear, a third lineage has a different spear, and so on.' By 'spear' he meant a spear-name, not an actual spear. Consequently, if two persons have the same spear-name there is likelihood of agnatic relationship, and spear-names are therefore often spoken of in connexion with proposed marriages. One hears Nuer saying in discussions about the permissibility of a proposed marriage 'what about their spears?', 'they have the same spear, they cannot marry', or 'their spear is different to ours, we can marry their daughter'.[2] At a wedding the masters of ceremonies on the bride's side and on the bridegroom's side, each acting as representative of his clan, begin their formal announcements that the marriage negotiations have reached a successful conclusion (*twoc ghok*) by shouting out their clan spear-names. The spear-name is also shouted out by the master of ceremonies as the opening words of the sacrificial invocation he makes when a Dinka boy is adopted

---

[1] B. A Lewis, op cit, p 82.
[2] Should the two clans have the same spear-name this is not always a bar to the union, for secondary spear-names may indicate that they belong to different clans, or other circumstances may be taken into consideration

into the lineage of the man who has given him domicile, the expression for adopting being either *lath buthni*, to be given shares (in sacrificial meats) and hence to be given agnation, or *lath muot*, to be given a spear (-name), and hence to be made a member of the clan. He also shouts it out in sacrificial invocations at mortuary ceremonies, at settlement of blood-feuds, at initiations, and on other occasions which concern the whole clan (p 288). When, as mentioned above, clan and tribe are identified politically in war and raiding a representative of the dominant clan of the tribe brandishes a spear and calls out the spear-name of his clan on behalf of the whole tribe. This man, called *ngul*,[1] is usually, perhaps always, a leading man of the senior lineage of the dominant clan, that descended from the eldest son of the ancestor of the clan Thus in the Lou tribe this rite is performed by a man of the Gaaliek lineage of the Jinaca clan. Likewise the Tar lineage who have charge of the *wiu* spear are descendants of Thiang, the eldest son of the founder of the clan; and the Thiang clan who own the *thiang* spear are descended from Thiang, the eldest son of Gee.

I cannot always explain the meaning of these spear-names or even translate them, and Nuer themselves cannot always say for certain what they mean, for they arose in ancient days It is clear, however, that they are charged with symbols expressing the unity and continuity of clans and lineages. I give a few examples, choosing those in which the meaning is more or less evident The Jiruet lineage have *mut tora*, spear of the monorchid This lineage respects monorchids, whether they be man or beast The Gaatiek clan have *mut yier*, spear of the stream, because their ancestor came out of a stream. The Gaatnaca clan have *mut ghama*, spear of the thigh. This seems to refer to the loins of the ancestor from whom they sprang. The Gaaliek lineage of this clan have the secondary spear-name *mut tang*, spear of the spear-shaft, because the *ngul*, whom I have referred to above, of the Lou tribe is of this lineage. He uses a spear-shaft in war ritual The Gaatleak clan have *mut leak*, the word *leak* being simply, it would seem, taken from the clan name itself. Many leopard-skin priests are members

[1] He is also called *ngul ghok*, *ngul* of cattle, an expression which probably refers to the taking of enemy cattle on raids, and *gwan muot*, possessor of the spear As he may break a spear-shaft in two and throw the pieces in the direction of the enemy he is further known as *gwan tang*, possessor of the spear-shaft. I was told that he may also invoke God for success in hunting in time of famine

of this clan and, as I have explained, they use *mut Geaka*, spear of Gee, as an alternative expression. The Thiang lineage have a secondary spear-name *mut Thiang*, spear of Thiang, which is the name of their ancestor.

When a man calls out his clan spear-name he often does so with embellishments, which are further symbolical representations of the clan. They refer to its ancestor, its spirits, its totems, its ghosts, its cattle, or its origin and traditions. Thus a Gaatgankir clansman in making invocations adds to *mut wiu* such expressions as *mut kwe, mut jangemo me coali Kir*, and *mut gwara. Kwe* is the fish-eagle and also a colour distribution of cattle. The shining of the spear is likened to the white face of the fish-eagle against its black body and to the white splash on the head of a dark coloured cow or ox. *Jaangemo me coali Kir* means 'that Dinka who is called Kir' and refers to the Dinka origin of the clan. *Mut gwara* means 'spear of our fathers'. The spear in the hand of the speaker, the spear *wiu*, the spear used to cut open the gourd in which the ancestor was found, and the spirit *wiu* all seem to be fused in the representation. In a similar manner the Gaawar clan may add to their spear-name *mut wang*, spear of the eye (I think), such expressions as *mut nhial, mut puara*, and *mut kwoth nyota*. I do not know why the spear is called 'spear of the eye' (if that is the right translation). *Nhial* is the firmament and *puar* is a cloud. Their ancestor fell from the sky and the clan is therefore associated with sky, clouds, and rain. When he fell he had in his hand a sprig of the *nyuot* tree, a tree associated with rain. Hence the *kwoth nyota*, the spirit of the *nyuot* tree.

Thus the spear-name is either that of the ancestor of the lineage or clan or in some way signifies him, and the elaborations of it, such as by reference to a spirit or a totem, are also just different ways of denoting the lineage or clan as a whole, for the name of the ancestor stands for the whole clan, both here and elsewhere. We have noted earlier (p 169) how in myths a lineage is personified for the purpose of the action of the story, the name of the lineage or of its tribal territory being used to indicate its ancestor. Nuer sometimes even insert the name of a lineage into a genealogy as its founder, though the form of the word shows that it is the name of a group and not of a person; or they give the founder a composite name, appending the name of the lineage to the personal name, for example, Nyang Gaaliek, Nyang being the name of the person and Gaaliek the name of the lineage of his descendants.

I have attempted to show that the spear brandished in sacrificial invocations stands for the person and that when this person speaks as a representative and on behalf of the clan, as he does in collective sacrifices, it stands for the clan. In the one case it is the right hand (vitality) of the individual and in the other the right hand (vitality) of the ancestor (the clan) which is emphasized. In the second case the spear is closely associated with the idea of the clan as a battle host

When we ask why clans should be symbolized by a spear, or rather by the idea of a spear contained in a spear-name, and not by something else, we cannot give an acceptable answer in terms of the scarcity, and therefore high value, of iron nor in terms of simple utility. The symbol is not *yieth* or *you*, iron.[1] Nor is it the *bidh*, the fishing-spear, which is perhaps even more essential for Nuer than the fighting-spear, for they have no substitute for it and could not survive without a good supply of fish. It is the *mut*, the iron fighting-spear. The fact that the wood, horn, and bone pointed spears do not figure as symbols might suggest that it is because it is made of iron, which lasts longer and makes a more efficient weapon, that the *mut* is the symbol of clans, but it appears to me to be a more satisfactory explanation that it is because the *mut* not only stands for the right hand and hence vitality but is also the symbol of going to war and of making sacrifice.

The word *mut*, besides meaning a fighting-spear, has a general sense of taking part in war and raiding: '*ce Nath wa mut*', 'the Nuer went raiding'; '*ca mut nang Jaang*', 'war was taken (by the Nuer) to the Dinka' The idea expressed by the word *mut* in these examples is not so much the general idea of war and raiding as the idea of a collectivity, the clan or lineage in its political or tribal embodiment, going to war or going on a raid Hence Father Kiggen correctly translates '*te ke mud mediid*' (his spelling) as 'they have a big army'.[2] By synecdoche 'spear' stands for 'battle host'.

---

[1] It is true that Nuer lick any metal in taking an oath (p. 297), but I regard this as being a derivation from licking a spear, for which any metal stands as a substitute, in the same way as the honorific titles of the Gaatgankir clan, son, and daughter, of iron, derive from the *wiu* spear The words *yieth*, metal, and *yiedh*, to spear or to stab, are surely connected.

[2] J. Kiggen, op cit, p 206 One may ask, in the light of this discussion about

It is, I believe, in some such sense of the clan militant that we should interpret the spear symbolism of the clans Nuer always speak of 'spear' where I have used the expression 'spear-name'. However, not only are there in almost all cases no actual spears, but it is not even the idea of any particular spear that they have in mind. What they have in mind is the clan as a whole for which the spear stands as a symbol not just as a spear but as representing the collective strength of the clan in its most conspicuous corporate activity, for clans and lineages are most easily and distinctly thought of as collectivities—through their identification with tribes and tribal segments—in relation to war. That the representation is of the clan as a battle host is shown by the Nuer statement about their clan spears that they only exist in the sense that 'they are in the mouths of men when they go to battle'. Two remarks made by Nuer give further support to an interpretation along these lines. One man said of all clan spears that *'tuokdien e wiu'*, 'their origin is *wiu*', and that *wiu* is the *kwoth*, spirit, of all clan spears. There was some discussion about this remark among Nuer present, and I gathered from it that all clan spears in this wide and symbolic sense of the word *mut* as the battle host signify the clan as a social group in relation to God in the conception of him as Lord of Hosts. The man could not have meant that other clan spears were derived or copied from the spear *wiu*. That would have made no sense, both because there are no actual spears and also because the Gaatgankir clan who own the spear *wiu* are regarded by everybody as a Dinka clan of later origin than the true Nuer clans. That a spiritual conception of *wiu* was meant is further evident from a remark made to me by another Nuer, a man of exceptional ability, that when the Gaatgankir clan reach ten generations from their ancestor Kir—when they have grown up, so to speak—they will doubtless cease to respect (*thek*) the

the *mut*, why it is that the title of spiritual leaders in Dinkaland is taken from the fishing-spear (*buth*) instead of from the fighting-spear An explanation might be put forward in terms of the analysis I have presented Whereas among the Nuer the fighting-spear is the symbol of the clan because what is being symbolized is exclusiveness and opposition, among the Dinka the fishing-spear is the symbol of spiritual leadership because what is being symbolized is inclusiveness and unity. This is a guess but it receives some support from the fact that among the Nuer, at any rate in western Nuerland, when a leopard-skin priest goes to settle a feud he is accompanied by a kinsman called the *gwan biedh*, the master of the fishing-spear, which is the title of the Dinka spiritual leaders However, this may be a loan from the Dinka spear *wiu*, as they do at present, and will respect (the word is here used to balance the statement and not literally) only its name As we should put it, they will not then feel the need for a material symbol of the spiritual relationship, and a verbal or ideational symbol will suffice. The association of clan spears with the spirit *wiu* is clear to us when we recall that the spirit is also associated with lightning with which, in this hypostasis, God strikes as man strikes with the spear.[1]

In invocations in which clans are involved as such God is appealed to, as I have explained earlier, in some refraction by which he is figured as their patron. This is the '*kwoth gwara*', 'the God of our fathers' It is on such occasions also that the spear-name of the clan is shouted out as an exordium to the invocation. This is the '*mut gwara*', 'the spear of our fathers'. I would suggest that we have here in the spear-name a symbolic representation of the clan in its relation to God. God is invoked in relation to the clan through the spear of the ancestor held in imagination in the hand of one of his descendants.

If this interpretation is right, then in those sacrifices in which the clan as a whole is concerned the calling out of the clan spear-name by the officiant identifies the whole clan with the intention of the sacrifice as spoken in the invocation. The sacrificial spear in his hand becomes through the exordium the clan sacrificial spear through which in symbol the whole clan offers up the victim to God. The officiant in such sacrifices must therefore be a representative of the clan, what the Nuer call a *gwan buthni*; whereas in personal and piacular sacrifices, in which appeal is made on behalf of an individual or a number of individuals, anyone can officiate and the officiant is usually a senior member of the family or kin of the sacrificer. The intention, and therefore character, of the sacrificial act is different in the two cases. In the first it is of the nature of a validation, in the second of the nature of a *piaculum*, though in some situations there may be a broad overlap. Religion has always these two sides, the one concerned chiefly with the social life and the other with the relation of the individual soul to its God.

---

[1] Nuer, however, use for God striking a man with lightning the verbs *mar*, to strike, and *pim*, to strike in the sense of 'to hit' or 'to punch', and not *yiedh*, to strike in the sense of to thrust or to stab.

CHAPTER X

THE SACRIFICIAL ROLE OF CATTLE

I

NUER are very largely dependent on the milk of their herds, and in their harsh environment they probably could not live without them, any more than the cattle could live without the care and protection of their owners. Their carcasses also furnish Nuer with meat, tools, ornaments, sleeping-hides, and various other objects of domestic use, and their sun-dried dung provides fuel for the great smouldering smudges that give protection from mosquitoes to man and beast alike. Women are more interested in the cows, and this is natural for they have charge of milking and dairy work. Men's interest in the cow is, apart from their value for breeding, rather for their use in obtaining wives, and they are interested in the oxen for the same reason, and also because they provide them with a means of display and, which is the matter I am about to discuss, a means of sacrifice. But for all Nuer—men, women, and children—cattle are their great treasure, a constant source of pride and joy, the occasion also of much foresight, anxiety, and quarrelling; and they are their intimate companions from birth to death. It is not difficult to understand, therefore, that Nuer give their cattle devoted attention, and it is not surprising that they talk more of cattle than of anything else and have a vast vocabulary relating to them and their needs.

Though I restrict myself here to a consideration of the religious significance of their cattle for Nuer we must not for a moment forget that this is bound up with their secular uses Otherwise it will not be appreciated what it is that Nuer surrender in sacrifice, the most precious thing they possess Nevertheless, if cattle were only used for food and obtaining wives writers about the Nuer, and also about other Nilotic peoples, might have been content just to draw attention to the great interest these peoples have in them. But cattle figure so prominently in their lives in ways not directly concerned with their maintenance or their use for practical pur-

poses that European observers have perceived that in the relationship between men and cattle there is something more than can be
stated in simple terms of husbandry and exploitation. I mention
only those whose observations refer specifically to the Nuer. Ernst
Marno says that we may speak of their veneration (Verehrung) of
cattle, that the largest and finest ox of a herd is regarded as a
guardian genius (schützende Genius), and that they refer to this
beast by the same name, '*nyeledit*', as they assign to the conception of a Supreme Being and to thunder.[1] Likewise, Mr. H. C.
Jackson tells us that the bull which a youth receives from his
father at initiation 'is a kind of guardian spirit of its owner who
calls upon it in times of stress and difficulty', and in another place
he speaks of this bull as the 'tutelary spirit' of its owner.[2] Captain
H. H Wilson says of the Nuer that, like the other Nilotic peoples
of the White Nile, 'what religion they possess is centred in the
cow';[3] and Professor D. Westermann writes that 'the attachment
of a man to his cows and of a boy to the bull with which his father
presents him may almost be called religious'.[4] There is, however,
no evidence at all that cattle are venerated or in themselves are in
any way regarded as guardian spirits, and in so far as it may be
true to say that Nuer religion 'is centred in the cow' or that their
attachment to cattle 'may almost be called religious', in so far, that
is, that we may legitimately speak, as Marianne Schmidl did in
her interesting paper on the subject,[5] of '*die sakrale Stellung des
Rindes*', it is for a different reason

Another writer about the Nilotic peoples and a very experienced
anthropologist, my teacher Professor C. G. Seligman, said about
Nilotic cattle that 'it is difficult to describe their importance to
their masters or the love and care the latter have for their beasts,
but it is certainly no exaggeration to say that it amounts to what
psychologists would term "identification".'[6] What seems chiefly to
have persuaded Professor Seligman to use this word is the Nilotic

[1] Ernst Marno, op cit , pp 343 and 349–50. What he says about '*nyeledit*' is
unintelligible.

[2] H C Jackson, op cit , pp 94 and 96

[3] *The Anglo-Egyptian Sudan*, edited by Lieut.-Col Count Gleichen, vol. 1,
1905, p 140

[4] Ray Huffman, *Nuer Customs and Folk-Lore*, 1931, p vii

[5] Marianne Schmidl, 'Die Grundlagen der Nilotenkultur', *Mitteilungen der
Anthropologischen Gesellschaft in Wien*, LXV. Band, Wien, 1935 See also
Johannes Weissenborn, *Tierkult in Afrika*, 1904, p 16

[6] C G and B. Z. Seligman, op cit , p 169.

custom of taking personal names from their cattle in addition to the personal names they are given soon after birth. I have discussed elsewhere[1] the general social significance of names and other modes of address among the Nuer and here I speak only of their cattle-names and principally of their ox-names, these being of chief importance.

These names are often spoken of in writings about the Nuer as bull-names, but ox-names, in the use of the word 'ox' to denote a castrated bull, is a more correct designation [2] Nuer speak always of such a name as *cot thak*, the name of an ox, and *thak* is a castrated animal in contrast to a *tut*, an entire animal. It is true that when a youth takes his name from a beast it may be entire, but it will be castrated later. Nuer may not castrate a male calf till it is nearly two years old, but they do so before it is likely to gender with the cows. It is not for pedantry that I make the distinction: it has a logical, and perhaps psychological, appositeness to the equation of man and ox in sacrifice.

Ox-names are essentially the names of men, males who have passed through the rite of initiation to manhood. Boys may take ox-names in play but only in imitation of their elders. Likewise, maidens may take ox-names, from bull calves of the cows they milk, but they are mainly used only between girls themselves and in the nature of a game, copying their brothers; and the names are short-lived. Married women use cow-names among themselves, but, here again, this is similitude, and it has none of the significance of the ox-names of men. Perhaps also here again the distinction between the copy-names of boys, girls, and women and those taken by men may be important because of its logical relation, which concerns our present discussion, to the fact that men, and not boys or women, are the sacrificial agents. The two sides of the standard equation are the human male and the bovine male, man and ox

When a boy is initiated his father gives him in sign of his manhood an ox or, as I have explained, a bull calf which will later be castrated; and this ox, which he describes as '*thak gareda*', 'the ox of my cutting (initiation)', becomes his *dil thak*, what I have spoken about as his favourite ox (Marno's '*Lieblingsstier*'), though

---

[1] 'Nuer Modes of Address', *Uganda Journal*, 1948.
[2] Throughout the literature on the Nuer, 'ox' or 'steer' or 'bullock' should in most cases be substituted for 'bull'.

the word *dil* has generally the sense of 'pure', 'true', 'perfect', or 'aristocratic'. It is the ox of perfection. It is the young man's friend and companion. He plays with it and fondles it. He composes poems about it and sings them to it, and he gets a small boy to lead it round the camp in the morning or evening as he leaps behind it chanting poems. He walks among the cattle at night ringing a cattle-bell and singing of his kin, his loves, and his cattle, and he praises this ox among all other oxen. He makes tassels to hang from one of its horns, and he loves to see it toss the tassel in the air with a sweep of the neck. He acquires an iron bell to hang round its neck, and no music, unless it be the ox's lowing, is sweeter to his ears than its tinkling in the pastures. He goes to the edge of the camp to meet it when it returns from grazing in the evening. He is never tired of describing its points, and as he does so, and also in dancing, he may hold up his arms in imitation of its horns. Should the ox die he is downcast; and should he die it must be sacrificed at his mortuary ceremony.

The youth now also enters through this ox into a new kind of relationship with God, the guardian spirits of his family and lineage, and the ghosts of his ancestors. When he has tethered it in the kraal for the night he may pet it, removing ticks from its belly and scrotum and picking out adherent dung from its anus; and he may at the same time rub ashes on its back. Ordinarily I think he does this simply because the ox, which has suffered from parasites throughout the day, gets relief from its back being rubbed, but I was told that he may occasionally as he does so speak a few words to God or to the ghosts. While it is not until a man marries and has children and an independent household that he sacrifices

Fig. 5
Hollowed-out ambatch log, used as stool, &c.

animals, dedicates them to spirits, and in other ways makes formal use of them for religious purposes, nevertheless, the ox a father gives his son at initiation provides him with a direct means of communication with the spiritual world It is more than a possession, more even than part of his social personality—it is a point of meeting between soul and spirit and has therefore a sacramental character also.

From the colours, their distribution, the shape of the horns, and other peculiarities of the ox of his initiation a youth takes, or is given by his companions, his *cot thak*, his ox-name. It may be the same word as that by which the ox's markings are indicated, but generally it combines the name for the markings with a prefix descriptive of something connected with the ox. For example, a man whose favourite ox is black and white (*rial*) may call himself *Luthrial* or *Luerial*, *luth* being a large cattle-bell and *lue* a long tassel attached to one of the horns. At first only his age-mates may know his new name, but the older people soon get to know it too, for they hear his mates greet him by it and they also hear him shout it out as he displays himself with the ox in the cattle camps which are formed soon after initiation. Also, young men of about the same age call out their ox-names, with many embellishments, to one another at dances, often after a bout of duelling with clubs, and when in a dance two lines of youths stand opposite each other and shower ox-names on one another preparatory to a spectacular jump into the air in unison.

The calling of a youth by a name the same as, or derived from, that by which his favourite ox is referred to is perhaps the most striking example of, and evidence for, what Professor Seligman speaks of as 'identification'. Indeed, in listening to Nuer poems one is often in doubt whether it is the ox or the man that is being spoken about. The representations are never entirely distinct. Somewhat different, though related and also very striking, is the custom called *thak moc*, the calling out of the (name of the) ox. A man shouts out the name of his favourite ox—the ox's name, not his ox-name, which may be an elaboration of the ox's name —when he hurls his spear at an enemy or at his quarry when hunting or fishing, for example, '*ma rial*', 'black-and-white (ox)', or '*thakda ma rial*', 'my black-and-white ox'. In some of my earlier writings I have translated *moc* by 'invocation' and 'to invoke', following Driberg's translation of the Lango *gwongo*,[1] but I avoid doing so in an account of Nuer religion partly because I have in it used these words to translate another word, *lam*, but also because nothing is in fact invoked, and it is precisely the use of the words in connexion with oxen that has led to the erroneous conclusion that a favourite ox is a sort of 'tutelary spirit' The ox is not called on, but called out. It is not an invocation but a cry of excitement and triumph as the striker strikes his foe or prey. That the ox is not being called on for aid is conclusively shown by the fact that in the same circumstances a Nuer may shout out instead '*tet cueda*' followed by a kinship term, usually that referring to the mother's sister: '*tet cueda malene*', 'my right hand, my mother's sisters'. Nuer are not calling on their mother's sisters for aid but using an emotive ejaculation, in which the ideas of strength (the right hand) and good-will (the mothers' sister) are combined. When they cry out the names of their oxen the ejaculation is a triumphant assertion of the self, for which the ox stands as a symbol. Also a man may cry out the name of his ox on occasions when there is no question of success or failure: as he brandishes his spear as though to strike in dancing, when making spectacular leaps into the air (*rau*), and sometimes in making a sacrificial invocation It is both self-expression and a drawing of attention to the self.

It should be borne in mind that a man normally retains his ox-name and continues to be called by it and also to shout out the name of the ox from which it is derived long after the ox is no more in his possession. A man may part, though always with regret, with a favourite ox for marriage or sacrifice, or the ox may die. It is then replaced by another favourite, though when a man is older and has a herd of his own he may not identify himself in quite the same way or to the same extent as when he was young with any one particular ox. If another ox takes the place of the first favourite, the ox of initiation, its owner may take, or be given, a new ox-name derived from this second ox, the new name then either taking the place of the old or both being used, but most men keep for life the ox-names they acquire at the time of their initiation. It is the name of this ox that a man shouts out in war, hunting, dancing and leaping, and in sacrificial invocations, and

---

[1] J H Driberg, *The Lango*, 1923, pp 109–10: 'One who takes a hostile spear on his shield invokes by name a favourite bull belonging to his father or maternal uncle (*guongo twon*).'

by which, in one or other form he is addressed by his peers; though it has long ago departed. Fundamentally, therefore, it is not the ox of initiation itself with which there is 'identification' but ox, the idea of oxen. The ox of initiation is the prototype of the ox–man relationship, and it is a kind of focal point at which the feelings a Nuer has towards cattle converge and run over into demonstration by word and gesture. When the ox is long ago dead the relationship continues, because ultimately it is not one between a man and a particular beast but a general relationship of a human being to cattle, an essential feature of which, I am about to suggest, is the sacramental equation of man and beast in sacrifice. Any ox will therefore serve the purpose, or, indeed, no ox at all—only the memory, or rather the idea, of an ox.

We may ask why the identification is with oxen and not with bulls. It might be expected that a man, who is himself a *tut*, a bull, not only in the general sense of 'male', but also in a common metaphor of speech derived expressly from cattle, would take his name from a bull rather than from an ox. The commonsense answer is that Nuer castrate all but a very few of their bulls, so that there would not be enough entire animals to go round, and this may be the right explanation. Even if it is not, or is not a sufficient explanation, we must here take it as given that the equation is between man and ox. We may, however, note further the fact, on which emphasis is later to be laid, that since an ox or a surrogate for an ox is almost always the sacrificial victim, the sacrificial equivalence is between men (the sacrificers) and oxen (the victims). If a beast is entire it is castrated before sacrifice. It is perhaps also necessary to remark that Nuer evaluation of bulls and oxen is not ours. Our representation of an ox, in contrast to a bull, is a docile, inferior, and slightly contemptible beast destined for the slaughter-house In the Nuer representation a fat ox is a thing of grandeur and beauty It is oxen which arouse their admiration. Bulls evoke utilitarian interest rather than emotional and aesthetic attention.

The facts I have related make it understandable that Professor Seligman should have spoken of 'identification' of men with their favourite oxen. Had he had either a first-hand or a wider knowledge of the Nuer he would no doubt have elaborated his theme, and especially by drawing on their ceremonies of initiation for illustrations

A youth takes his cry and his personal name from the markings
and other traits of the ox his father gives him at initiation. By the
rites of initiation boys are made men,[1] and this means, among
other things, a conspicuous change in their relation to the cattle
They now cease to look after the calves and sheep and goats and
to perform the more menial services of kraal and byre. Instead
they tend the adult cattle The most marked change is that
whereas before initiation they helped the women milk the cows
they now altogether cease to milk. But these external and evident
changes are accompanied by a deeper, and hidden, transforma-
tion, men and oxen being brought into an intimacy of relationship
on a different plane to that of mere proximity and association,
however close, so that in some way an equation is brought about
between man and ox. Such would seem to be the interpretation of
certain very peculiar, though outstanding, features of the initiation rites. I have described these rites and discussed their social
significance elsewhere,[2] and in this place I shall only draw attention to those features which have special relevance to our immediate subject.

The rites direct our attention throughout to the relationship
between men and cattle It is the *wut ghok*, the man of the cattle,
to which he stands in a special ritual relationship, who opens and
closes the periods of initiation. During initiation the initiates may
not have any contact with the cattle, which are a danger to them
till their wounds are completely healed and they formally pass
out of seclusion. The prohibition extends even to rubbing ashes
of cattle-dung over their bodies, a daily practice common to all
men and boys; and Dr. Mary Smith tells me that Nuer say that it
may harm the lads if the smoke of the smudges reaches them,
though the fact that they drink milk suggests that the interdiction
really concerns their relation to the oxen rather than to cattle in
general, just as the interdiction on women drinking milk during
their periods concerns their relation to cows and not to cattle in
general. In the terminal rite of initiation, when the initiates are

[1] Or, perhaps, one should rather say 'Nuer men', for Nuer do not regard other
people as 'men', whatever their age They think of *wut*, manhood, as something
specifically Nuer. Consequently Dinka who have already been initiated in their
own country have their foreheads cut in the Nuer fashion across the scars of
their Dinka initiation if they become members of Nuer communities

[2] 'The Nuer Age-Sets', *Sudan Notes and Records*, 1936. Since this article was
written I have obtained further information which has not been published

'loosened' (*lony rar*, the verb *lony* being that used for loosening cattle from their tethering-pegs) they re-establish their contact with the cattle. They are pelted (smeared) by their seniors with cattle-dung (*buk ke war*) Then they wash in a stream On their return to the homestead they beat the cattle with wild rice, and afterwards rub themselves with ashes of cattle-dung They spend the rest of the day leaping and chanting behind the oxen given them by their fathers and possibly, if they are lucky, by their paternal and maternal uncles also, which are the first oxen they can call their own. The fact that after initiation there is an interdiction on men milking also seems to point to an opposition between women and cows on the one side and men and oxen on the other side and further to emphasize the equation of man and ox.

One might perhaps feel that one was attributing to the facts a symbolical significance which the evidence does not sustain were it not that further, and very striking, observations push one to the interpretation put forward. Thus, the name of the dances held at the initiation ceremonies is *ruath*, the word for a bull calf from the time it is weaned, that is to say a bull, normally destined to be an ox, which has broken with its dam in the same way as a youth at initiation cuts, as we would put it, the apron strings which before have tied him to his mother, especially in the matter of food, as some of the symbolism of the rites indicates. Further, between the cutting of the marks of manhood on a boy's forehead and his ceremonial emergence from seclusion (or exclusion from the normal life) he is known as *cot*, which appears to be the same word as that used for a hornless cow or ox. It is remarkable also that Nuer compare to the initiation of youths the cutting (*ngat*) of the horns of favourite oxen (they are entire animals at the time) so that they will grow against the cut at fancy angles, generally in a curve across the muzzle (*ma gut*) They say that the operation, which is performed before castration, is the *gar*, the cutting of the marks of manhood, on the young bulls If the operation has not already been carried out before a father presents a young bull to his son at initiation it is likely to be one of the young man's first acts in the period immediately following his own initiation. I have noted earlier how soon after their initiation youths, if they can procure the metal, fasten bracelets up their left arms so tightly as to render them, for the time of

PLATE XIII

Ox with trained horn

their wearing, incapable of use, and that they also render useless the left horns of their favourite oxen by deforming them.

Human thought and expression are inevitably constructed out of man's experience of the world around him. There is nothing that should surprise us in Nuer speaking metaphorically of boys by the same word (*ruath*) as they use for young bulls and for the male young of other animals, and, by contrast, of men by the same word (*tut*) as they use for adult bulls and adult males of other animal species It is natural—it would be remarkable were it not so—that Nuer use cattle metaphors in speech and gesture Nevertheless, the evidence, some of which I have presented, suggests that there is more in it than that Whether Professor Seligman's psychological use of the word 'identification' is correct is a question that lies outside my own competence and the scope of this book, but it cannot be denied that there is a moral identification, a participation imposed on the individual by his culture and inextricably bound up with religious values. When henceforward I speak of identification it is to be understood in this sense

II

We have noted that there is a personal side and a collective side to Nuer religion and that we may speak of personal and collective types of sacrifice We have noted also that in the collective type the officiant represents the whole clan, that the spear he holds in his hands is that of the ancestor of the clan, and that he invokes God as the God who created his ancestor and the God of his fathers. We have further noted that the sacrificial victim, although in fact it is an ox or a surrogate for an ox, is not spoken of as *thak*, ox, but as *yang*, cow, a general term referring to any bovine beast, with a plural form *ghok*, meaning 'cattle'. This suggests that the victim embodies the general idea of the equivalence of cattle and men in the sacrificial act, and there is certainly what we may speak of as a collective identification of clans and lineages with their herds. This is expressed in the honorific titles of clans and lineages We have been discussing hitherto the equation of man with ox These titles introduce us to the idea of an enduring relationship between a social group and its ancestral herd.

On the day when, by the cutting of lines on his forehead, a boy becomes a man there is much rejoicing of his kinsfolk, and especially of his father and paternal kin. In talking to Nuer about this day they have impressed on me that what is uppermost in the minds of the older men, particularly at the initiation of an eldest son, is that the continuity of the family and lineage is now assured. Initiation is the threshold to marriage and the birth of sons who will remember their forebears; for as soon as the period of healing and seclusion is over the initiates embark on a full sex life leading to courtship, marriage, and begetting. An initiate is part of a lineage and clan and his initiation is seen in terms of its collective life. His new relationship with the cattle is then not only a personal one, important though that is, but the personal relationship is incorporated in a more general lineage one.

Nuer conceive of the ancestor of a clan, and likewise the ancestors of its component lineages, as having possessed a herd, the descendants of which have had, and continue to have, though distributed among different families, a constant relationship with the descendants of their original owners and are still thought of as one herd This ancestral herd is a fiction, for the cattle are being constantly dispersed and replaced by others at marriages, but conceptually it is an enduring collectivity. There is ideally a constant attachment, the clan and its herd forming a joint community down the generations, so much so that a common, perhaps the commonest, explanation of a division in the clan is the fighting of bulls of the ancestors of the divided parts. The social cleavage is represented in tradition as a cleavage in the herd

The unity of clans and lineages is symbolized in the names of the ancestral spears, which we have already discussed, and in honorific titles, chiefly derived from the names of cows. In both cases we are dealing with ideas and not actual things, with the idea of a clan spear handed down as an heirloom and with the idea of the present herds of the members of a clan being descended from the ancestral herd Nuer say that '*mut kene paak jalke kel*', 'the spear and the honorific title go together'. If a man has a certain clan spear he must have one or more honorific titles which go with it. Both have come down together from *tuok nath*, the beginnings of the Nuer. The *paak*, a word found with the same meaning in some of the other Nilotic languages, may be described as an honorific title used as a mode of salutation or address. It is commonly used on ceremonial occasions, as on formal visits, at dances, and at marriage and initiation ceremonies. Otherwise it is mostly a complimentary usage which expresses a formal relationship of reserve, as between a husband's mother and her son's wife, and then it is chiefly a woman's mode of address.

The title consists of *gat*, son (of), or *nya*, daughter (of), followed by a word which usually refers to a cow said to be that on whose milk the ancestor of the clan or lineage was nurtured in infancy, though it may refer to the place where the clan or lineage is said to have originated, or to some object connected with its ancestor, or to its totem. Nuer say that clans either '*ba paak ka kwi yang-dien*', 'are saluted by reference to their cow' or '*ba paak ka kwi ciengdien*', 'are saluted by reference to their (original) village site', but since the salutation generally refers to a cow the expressions '*paak*', 'honorific salutation', and '*paakene yang*', 'honorific salutation of cow', are synonyms. The words are often exceedingly difficult to translate, or even to discover the meaning of, especially when they relate to cows, for here the Nuer language proliferates symbolism in luxuriant elaborations of fancy, and representations of ancestral cow, ancestral home, totem, and totemic spirit, are sometimes fused in the titles, which are built out of a number of residues all of which derive from and express lineage values. I have listed and discussed some of these honorific titles elsewhere,[1] and there is no need here for a detailed consideration of them. We have only to note the central place the idea of a cow has in them, the cow standing for the herd and hence also for the lineage of its masters.

It need not surprise us that it is a cow that is referred to and not an ox or bull. It would be inappropriate to refer to an ox since, as I understand the matter, the whole point of using a symbol from the herds is to express in a single representation the idea of the unity of a lineage and its cattle, the cattle which sustain the lineage by their milk (the cow suckles the ancestor) and by constant calving provide them with bridewealth for marriages whereby sons are born and the lineage continued, and with a means of maintaining communication with Spirit and ghosts. Male animals do not answer the requirements of the symbolism. The great majority of the bulls are castrated, and, if not later disposed of in marriage, those which survive murrains are sacrificed, and the animals which are left entire are not thought of as being, like the

[1] 'The Nuer Tribe and Clan', *Sudan Notes and Records*, 1934, pp 25-29.

male members of a human lineage, a line of descent. In tracing back the lineage of a beast, which Nuer can sometimes do to several generations, they do so by the points of the dams and not the points of the sires an ox of certain markings was born of a cow of certain markings and it of a cow of other markings. Descent in the herd is, so to speak, traced matrilineally; and it is the cows which are seen as the stable element, which calve cow-calves, which calve cow-calves in their turn, and so provide the constant and continuous nexus between herd and lineage. Consequently, if at marriage most of a herd is dispersed and only a core is retained, it is some cows which are kept so that the herd may be built up anew through them. Therefore, it is to the cows of the ancestors, and not to their bulls, that the honorific titles of clans and lineages refer.

The lineage-herd equation can thus be considered as a collective expression of the man–ox equation. The one does not derive from the other but they are parts of a single complex representation, which finds its most logical expression in the rites of sacrifice. The name of the ox of the speaker may be shouted out in sacrificial invocations because its name stands for his own, but when the sacrifice is on behalf of a whole clan the exordial words are the spear-name of the clan, which goes together with the cow-title of the clan, representing the relation of the clan to its ancestral herd. The two symbols, ox-name and spear-name, represent two aspects of the sacrificial relationship between men and cattle, the personal and the collective. The one or other aspect is emphasized according to the nature of the sacrifice

III

The facts we have examined, taken severally or together, point to the conclusion that there is the idea of equivalence between men and cattle, and the only plane on which there is anything that can be called equivalence is that on which men and cattle are things of the same order, so that one can be substituted for the other, namely in sacrifice, or in other words in relation to God We have seen that in those sacrifices which have the most significance for the study of Nuer religion, the personal ones, the lives of oxen are substituted for the lives of men This is not only evident in what

Nuer say but is indicated also in the rites themselves, and especially in the rite of consecration In discussing this rite I speak for the present only of personal sacrifice.

When ashes are rubbed on the back of an animal in giving it to a spirit I speak of the act as one of dedication When they are rubbed on its back in sacrifice I speak of it as consecration. It is useful to make this distinction for several reasons. Animals are not dedicated to God except on rare occasions when sacrifice is to take place shortly afterwards, but they are consecrated to him in sacrifice. Cows are the animals usually dedicated to spirits, whereas it is oxen which are sacrificed. Though even a cow dedicated to a spirit may ultimately be sacrificed and at least one of its male calves is destined for sacrifice, sacrifice does not follow dedication, if at all, for months or even years after the dedication What is devoted by dedication to a spirit is the animal and its milk, but when ashes are rubbed on the back of a beast at sacrifice what is devoted is its life. That there is a difference of meaning between the two acts is shown by the fact that an animal which has been dedicated to a spirit by ashes being rubbed on its back has ashes again rubbed on it when it is sacrificed to that spirit. It is—if we care to use these terms—dedicated to the spirit in the first act and consecrated for sacrifice to it in the second. The difference is that the rubbing of ashes in dedicating an animal to a spirit is the sign and the manner of its passing out of man s possession (though in fact he does not part with it) into a spirit's possession, whereas the rubbing of ashes in consecrating an animal for sacrifice is a substitution of life of man for life of beast and hence also an identification of man with beast, sacrificer with victim.

It will be remembered that in sacrifice the animal is consecrated with ashes, has an invocation spoken over it, and is speared. I have already discussed the *lam* or invocation What concerns us now is the *buk*, the consecration. This word, which in other Nilotic languages has the sense of 'to smear' and sometimes of 'to sacrifice', means in Nuer 'to rub' or 'to smear' and generally 'to rub with ashes'. In a sacrificial context it describes the placing, and usually lightly rubbing, of ashes on the victim's back It is clear that it is a rite of consecration, the animal's life being thereby devoted to God, but also in the personal and piacular sacrifices it is, as we have seen, sanctified for sacrifice in substitution for the life of a man It would seem, therefore, that the laying of the right hand on the animal's back identifies the man who lays it, or the person on whose behalf he is acting, with the beast, the right hand standing, as we have earlier noted, for the whole person If this is so, then it is himself, or the person for whom he is proxy, that the officiant offers up; or, to put it in another way, in the act of consecration the representations of man and ox, of sacrificer and victim, are fused.

This interpretation is supported by the fact that when ashes are ritually rubbed on persons the meaning which fits the action best is unity, solidarity, or identification, the expression of the idea of 'I am with you', as when, for example, before initiation a boy's father, maternal uncle, and family's master of ceremonies rub (buk) his forehead with ashes, uttering an invocation, or when a man returns from a long journey and his father rubs ashes on his forehead. It is confirmed by two other observations. As we have noted, there is no laying of hands on cattle sacrificed at mortuary ceremonies, nor is there, Dr. Smith tells me, in sacrifices at colwic ceremonies. They are given to God, but the person on whose behalf they are sacrificed is dead. Also, cattle slain for reasons other than for sacrifice may have an invocation said over them but there is no laying on of hands.

I discuss this question again later in relation to the whole rite of sacrifice and the various theoretical interpretations of it which students have put forward. We may here note further, however, that the fact that it is ash which is placed on the back of the victim and not something else and that this ash must be that of cattle-dung (pou) and not wood-ash (ngeth) may be significant, for the ash is taken from the gol, the household smudge which symbolizes for Nuer the home in various senses Gol means primarily the home in a domestic sense It is identified with the father of a family, gol so-and-so being the 'home' of that man and hence his 'family' also But it can also be used for the lineage, 'the family' in that wider sense. The ash comes from the gol which represents the family or the lineage, and the officiant who places it on the animal's back represents, according to the type of sacrifice, either the members of the family or the members of the lineage.

IV

It may be asked how the fact that in piacular sacrifice an ox is substituted for a man affects the general relationship of men to cattle. The answer is that all cattle are reserved for sacrifice. It is not just that in a particular ceremony a particular ox stands for a particular man. The equivalence is a general one between men and cattle. Some caution is necessary here. Nuer are very fond of meat, and whether an animal is killed in sacrifice or dies a natural death its flesh is eaten All cattle, sheep, and goats, except those sacrificed in holocausts, eventually go into the pot. Also, it is very noticeable that on ceremonial occasions which are not also occasions of calamity, most people show more interest in the festal than in other aspects of the ceremonies. People show their desire for meat without reserve and it is the festal character of sacrifices which gives them much of their significance in the life of the Nuer. This is perhaps most noticeable at weddings, when, moreover, those who get the flesh are not those who sacrifice the animal; and also on those occasions when men scramble for meat Further, Nuer themselves recognize that some men are too eager to sacrifice an ox, sheep, or goat on the slightest excuse, a craving for meat rather than a pressing need for spiritual aid being the incentive for sacrifice. It is undoubtedly true that it is sometimes craving for meat which reminds a man that sacrifice to some spirit is long overdue, religious obligations providing a ready excuse for a feast. However, the fact that Nuer accuse men of making unnecessary sacrifices to have feasts of meat in itself shows that animals should not be slaughtered except in sacrifice; and there is indeed a very strong feeling, amounting to a moral injunction, that domestic animals—sheep and goats as well as cattle—must not be slaughtered except in sacrifice and, save in very special circumstances, they are never slaughtered for food, a fact noted by Ernst Marno nearly a century ago.[1] This injunction explains why Nuer are not expected to, and do not, provide meat for guests, and also why I was unable to buy beasts from them for food for my own household.

[1] Op. cit., p. 348. The Dinka likewise do not slaughter cattle for food (see that curious book *The Ethiopia Valley*, n.d , pp 10 and 39, by Hatashil Masha Kathish, a Dinka convert to Christianity). This is the case among many African pastoral peoples.

The very special circumstances in which cattle are killed for food are times of severe famine and in what are called *nak*, or in some parts of Nuerland *kanar* or *cuel*, camps. Within my own short experience, in 1931, a year of great hunger, the Lou Nuer killed many oxen for food, and during a famine in western Nuerland in 1935 a great number of beasts were slaughtered to keep the people alive. Dr. Howell says that in the Zeraf valley in 1943, likewise a year of famine, animals were being killed for food.[1] The Lou Nuer even have a reputation, of which they are ashamed, for killing oxen when hungry, for not waiting, that is, till faced with starvation. How often this situation used to occur is not, and cannot, be known If it is not altogether a modern phenomenon, we may suppose that it was much less likely to have arisen before rinderpest depleted the herds and imposed peace prevented their rehabilitation through raiding, the milk supply thus being lessened.[2] *Nak* camps are presumably so called because they are formed for the express purpose of killing (*nak*) oxen. They are formed in some years only, in the rains or at the commencement of the dry season, by youths, each of whom takes an ox to the camp where one by one they are slaughtered and the young men gorge themselves on their flesh. Now that cattle have become scarcer two youths may share a single animal, though it is still thought that there ought to be an ox to a man. There is some doubt about the precise significance of this custom. When I published an account of the Nuer age-set system[3] I considered that it did not form an integral part of the rites of initiation but was only incidentally connected with them. I may have been wrong in this conclusion, and my own later researches revealed features which incline me to accept Dr. Howell's contention that they are connected with the age-set system.[4] Certainly there is more in the *nak* than merely killing oxen for feasting. That it has a ritual significance is clear from the fact that the youths who take part in it are segregated. Girls are not allowed to enter, or at any rate to sleep in, the camps. Abstinence is imposed at a time when the company of girls and their favours are a Nuer's chief interest. Nor may the

---

[1] P P Howell, 'The Age-Set System and the Institution of "*Nak*" among the Nuer' (with a Note by E. E. Evans-Pritchard), *Sudan Notes and Records*, 1948, p 180 I was told that on raids on the Dinka pillaged oxen were slaughtered for food.   [2] E E Evans-Pritchard, *The Nuer*, 1940, pp 19–20.
[3] 'The Nuer: Age-Sets', *Sudan Notes and Records*, 1936.
[4] P P. Howell, ibid.

young men attend dances, which therefore do not take place at this time Also, they may have no contact of any kind with the herds other than with the oxen with which they are segregated. It is to be noted further that the borrowing from kin and neighbours of oxen for slaughter by youths whose families are unable to provide them with suitable animals is no ordinary loan but is of a peculiar and ritual character. The owner of a beast who is asked for it by a youth may not refuse the request, and not only for social reasons but also, says Dr Howell, because 'he would run the risk of spiritual contamination resulting in sickness or even death among the members of his family'.[1] Nor may he demand repayment for some years. These facts considered in the light of the great reluctance, to say the least of it, of Nuer to kill an ox other than for sacrifice suggest strongly that a slaughter on this scale has some religious significance. I asked Dr Lienhardt and Dr. Smith to inquire about this matter. The former informs me that an old man makes an invocation over one of the oxen, which stands for all of them, and the latter that the older men who have contributed the beasts make invocations over them, though they do not consecrate them with ashes. It would seem, therefore, that if their slaughter is not a proper sacrifice it has to some extent a sacrificial character. It is significant also that not only is the killing obligatory but also that each youth ought to provide an ox for slaughter, an ox for a man, for we seem to have here again the equivalence of a man with an ox, which is the basis of piacular sacrifice; and it can easily be seen that the death of an ox at the termination of the rites of initiation would be a sacramental act appropriate to the whole setting of initiation.

Except on those rare occasions when dire necessity or custom compels them to do so, Nuer do not kill cattle except in sacrifice, and it is regarded as a fault to kill them '*bang lora*', 'just for nothing', the Nuer way of saying that they ought not to be killed for meat This is clearly shown apart from the facts I have already instanced, by the statement that an ox slain simply from desire for meat may *cien*, take ghostly vengeance on, its slayer, for it has *cuong*, right, in the matter. Maybe Nuer do not take this very seriously, but that they say it at all is an indication of how they regard the matter, for, as we have seen, they fear ghostly vengeance and hold that it operates only because God is permissive,

[1] Ibid, p 176

seeing that an injustice has been done. The man had no right to take the life of the ox and by doing so he committed a fault. In sacrificial invocations Nuer explain to God why the life of the ox is being taken, and they may also address the ox and tell it why it is being killed—not that they think it understands They are justifying themselves in taking its life.

Consequently I was not surprised to learn from Dr. Mary Smith, whom I asked to inquire into the question, that when cattle are killed in time of famine Nuer, though they do not consecrate the beasts, may make an invocation over them asking God that 'the meat may be soft in their stomachs and not bring them sickness'. This does not constitute sacrifice, there being no sacrificial intention, but it shows that there is a feeling of guilt about killing animals for food even when hunger compels it, and we can say that all cattle, and also sheep and goats, are reserved, or set apart, for sacrifice and their lives should not be taken, except in the special circumstances I have mentioned, for any other purpose. In that sense we may speak of cattle as being 'sacred'. If we do so, however, we must note that they are not sacrificed because they are regarded as sacred intrinsically, or for reasons extraneous to the sacrificial situation, but, on the contrary, they are regarded as sacred only because they are reserved for sacrifice and in the sense defined by that purpose. I have discussed beasts of the herd only and not those of the flock because, as we have noted earlier, in sacrifices they are 'cattle', surrogates for oxen. It is pre-eminently their role to play the victim's part in sacrifice and they are consequently also reserved for sacrifice, but the sacrificial equivalence is always between *ran* and *yang*, man and 'cow', never between man and sheep or goat, for even when it is a sheep or goat which is being killed the ideal equivalence is preserved in speech.

In order that the sacrificial killing of beasts of the flocks and herds may be seen in a wider setting both of the taking of lives of creatures and of the eating of flesh, it should be realized that, except for fish, Nuer seldom kill wild creatures but rely almost entirely on the flesh of their domesticated animals for meat. For religious reasons they are averse to killing birds, except occasionally the ostrich, to which the same symbolism does not attach, for its feathers; and also reptiles, except the turtle and the crocodile (perhaps occasionally the monitor lizard). But even where there is no objection to killing animals, as in the case of mammals, Nuer seldom go out of their way to kill them. They do not go out to hunt lions, leopards, and hyenas, unless they molest the flocks and herds, and usually they only pursue those graminivorous animals which come to drink near their camps and seem to offer themselves for slaughter. It is not that it is thought to be wrong to kill them, but that except in time of famine, Nuer are little interested in hunting. They speak of it as a Shilluk and Dinka practice beneath the serious attention of a Nuer who can boast of a herd—as a pursuit, that is, of foreigners or of men without cattle. Even those who deliberately set out to hunt elephants and giraffe do so less to obtain meat than to acquire ivory and hair which can be exchanged for cattle, sheep, and goats This lack of interest in hunting may be due to the fact that their flocks and herds supply them, through sacrifice, with meat and to the nature of their country which renders hunting difficult, but, whatever the reason, they are not interested, so that any killing of animals outside sacrifice is rare; and we may here say again, as has been said before in a rather different context, that the Nuer mind is turned inwards towards his own society of men and cattle. He is not unobservant of nature but he sees it with a contemplative and not with a predatory eye that seeks to destroy and exploit. He sees wild creatures as something in their own right, and his disposition is to live and let live. His folk-stories reflect this attitude and the feeling that killing, like death, is something which has come about almost by accident and is not in the original nature of things

A large part of Nuer folk-lore consists of stories about animals.[1] There are stories about ogres, a cycle of adventure stories about how cunning fox tricked hyena; many just-so stories which tell why hyenas limp, why plovers have thin legs, why guinea-fowl crouch, why millepedes are blind, why cows have no upper incisors, and so forth; and stories of yet other sorts. God sometimes figures in these stories as a judge in a way which appeals to the Nuer sense of humour as well as to our own. For example, fish, finding that they were visible to man in the water and hence easily speared, appealed to God who let them be invisible. God sometimes figures

---

[1] I have not published the folk-stories I collected among the Nuer. Some of those given by Miss Huffman (*Nuer Customs and Folk-Lore*, 1931, pp. 88–104) show Anuak influence Those recorded by Capt V H. Fergusson ('Nuer Beast Tales', *Sudan Notes and Records*, 1924) have Nuer themes but may be Atwot, or even Mandari, versions of them, for *nill*, the jackal, and *tjong*, the hawk, are two main figures in them, and these are not Nuer words.

in them because the animals are made to act like men after the manner of fables. They are given human speech and feelings. live in villages and camps, and have kinship relations on the pattern of human relations; and as men stand in a certain relationship to God in real life, so the animals are placed in a similar relationship in the make-believe of the stories. Miss Huffman says of these stories that the Nuer 'implicitly believe' in them.[1] This was not my impression. It appeared to me that they realize that their folk-tales are just tales which are true only in the sense that they are, as we say, true to life, a dramatization of real situations and an accurate characterization of human and animal, and indeed also of spiritual, qualities. It does not, therefore, worry them that their folk-stories may not accord with, and may contradict, both evidences of the senses and those of tradition and myth, and also each other.

These stories reflect an attitude of mind about man's relation to other creatures, and I mention them in this place, without, however, laying great stress on their significance, because they tell of an original age of innocence in which all creatures lived in amity in a common camp. Various stories, though separate tales and not related as parts of a coherent structure or dramatic plan, nevertheless taken together give us a picture of man at that time, or rather in that state, for the setting of myth and folk-lore lies outside time. He is entirely simple He does not suffer from hunger, because what later became his stomach lives a life of its own in the bush where it feeds on small insects. He does not have to labour to live because, according to another story, which contradicts the last one, a single grain of millet soaked in water makes a sufficient meal. In this Nuer Eden there is no desire and mating, for the male and female organs are also not yet part of man and woman but live apart from them and separate from each other As other, and once again contradictory, stories have it, man does not know how to beget or woman to bear Man has no knowledge of fire and he does not know the spear. Then all changed The new order is sometimes presented as arising from a quarrel in the camp started, it would seem, by fox persuading mongoose to throw a club into elephant's face. The animals separated and each went its own way and began to live as they now live and to kill each other. Stomach entered into man and he is now always hungry. Elephant taught

[1] Ibid, p 88

him how to pound millet so that he now satisfies his hunger only by ceaseless labour. The sexual organs attached themselves to man and woman so that they are now constantly desirous of each other. Mouse taught man how to beget and woman how to bear. Dog brought fire to man And we are told that while fox was plotting to sow dissension among the beasts he gave man the spear and taught him how to use it. It was then that man began to kill, and his first killing seems to have been that of the mother of cow and buffalo, or rather the mother of cattle, for at that time cows and buffaloes were the same. This led to a feud between men and cattle, buffaloes avenging their mother by attacking men in the bush and cows by causing men to quarrel and slay one another

It may perhaps sharpen our focus on sacrifice to know not only that Nuer seldom kill wild animals but also that they can imagine a state in which man did not kill, that there might have been a beginning to killing as to coitus, to pounding grain, and to other things men do now Viewed in relation to the dialectic of the stories, the killing of cattle is then seen not to be, as it were, derived from a state of nature in which men kill animals for food, as just one sort of killing among others, but as a product of a new dispensation in which cattle are allotted a sacrificial role and are set apart for this purpose. Other animals may, as a matter more or less of chance, and now and again, be killed, but it is the role and destiny of cattle to be slaughtered in sacrifice. Sacrificial slaughter thus stands at the very centre of the idea of killing, and sacrificial flesh at the very centre of the idea of feasting.

We may conclude, therefore, that the observations we have made earlier concerning the relationship of a man with his favourite ox, the ritual of initiation, &c., must be viewed in the light of the identification of men with cattle in sacrifices A Nuer does not look upon his cattle as a stockbreeder or dairy farmer does, for in his case his relationship to his beasts is complicated, apart from their use in marriage, by their reservation for sacrifice. And it is not just that he must not kill cattle except in sacrifice because if he were to slaughter them for meat he would lower his resources for food, marriage, and religious purposes. It is not merely a negative injunction It is not 'thou must not kill' but 'thou must sacrifice'. It is not that they must only kill for sacrifice but that they must sacrifice to kill.

We must not be led astray by this conclusion to suppose that in the everyday life of the Nuer they think of and treat their animals in a 'religious' manner. They do not even treat those dedicated to spirits in any special way Ordinarily Nuer think of their beasts from the practical point of view of herdsmen who are largely dependent on them for food and are dependent on them entirely for marriage. But if it would be a mistake to leave out of considera-tion the practical uses of cattle it would be no less a mistake were we to ignore the religious significance they have for Nuer. This is easier to do for two reasons. Firstly, because Nuer are themselves reticent in speaking of their cattle in this connexion. They tend to be reserved in discussing religious matters, and it may even be said that a certain secrecy adheres to them; and those whom a Euro-pean tends to know best, the younger men, have less awareness of the sacramental role of cattle than the older people. Secondly, because we have no direct experience of our own which associates animals with anything similar in our culture. We are, therefore, inclined to reason that cattle have ritual significance because they have great practical value. If this were really so the cow, and not the ox, would be the object of identification, but, apart from that consideration, an attempt to interpret the religious importance of cattle on this one-way track of reasoning changes the whole character of the relationship between men and cattle. It makes the animals themselves to be in some way the object of religious atten-tion, and nothing could be farther from the truth

The religious significance of cattle is of a very different kind. Cattle are necessary to Nuer not only for food and marriage but also for salvation, for the sanctification of their social undertakings and for overcoming evil in its twofold character of sickness and sin As Professor Westermann's text has it, 'she (the cow) was ordered (by God) for the deliverance of souls'.[1] This soteriological function pertains to cattle as much as their economic, bridewealth, and other functions. It is not just that in Nuer sacrifices something that for other reasons is valuable obtains through its consecration and sacramental death a religious significance, which would con-sequently be secondary and momentarily derived from the imme-diate sacrificial act. The sacrificial role is always dormant in cattle, which in sacrifice are being used for an ordained purpose for which they are set apart. This is why the rubbing of ashes on an ox's

---

[1] Or, as I have translated the passage (p 224): 'It [the cow] has been decreed for the life [of man] '

back while uttering some short prayer or invocation is a rite which can at any time be performed. The animal, even when not dedicated to a spirit, is already destined for sacrifice. The sacrificial situation is present, as it were, in the act, though no actual sacrifice is made.

When, therefore, we seek to estimate what their cattle are to Nuer and how they see them, we have to recognize that they are the means by which men can enter into communication with God, that they are, as Father Crazzolara puts it, 'the link between the perceptible and the transcendental'.[1] In fulfilling this role, his cattle shield a man and his family from disaster, and he conceives of them also collectively as a herd which from the beginning of time has helped his fathers in distress, performing in each generation the same sacrificial service. In the time of the ancestor of his clan the 'cow' gave her life for his salvation and so it is today. Whence springs the identification of man with ox, of lineage with herd, and of men with cattle.

[1] J. P. Crazzolara, 'Die Bedeutung des Rindes bei den Nuer', *Africa*, 1934, p 320

CHAPTER XI

THE MEANING OF SACRIFICE

I

THE points I have tried to establish with regard to Nuer sacrifice are as follows (1) There are two broad types of sacrifice, that which is chiefly concerned with social relations—changes of social status and the interaction of social groups—and that which is concerned rather with the moral and physical welfare of the individual Our attention has been mostly directed to the second, the personal and piacular type, because of its greater importance for an understanding of Nuer religion, but it was not possible to draw a firm line of demarcation between the two classes. (2) The piacular sacrifices are performed in situations of danger arising from the intervention of Spirit in human affairs, often thought of as being brought about by some fault. In such sacrifices ideas of propitiation and expiation are prominent. They centre, however, in the general idea of substitution of life of ox for life of man. (3) Almost all sacrifices consist of four movements—formal presentation, consecration, invocation, and immolation. It is particularly in the invocation and consecration that we must look for the meaning of the whole drama. The invocation states the intention of the sacrifice, and it is made with the spear in the right hand. The spear represents the virtue and vitality of man and through it, as well as by speech, he throws his whole self into the intention In symbol the spear is the man. When a whole lineage or clan is concerned in the sacrifice the spear is that of the ancestor of the lineage or clan and represents the whole group which, through its representative, offers up the victim. (4) The consecration by placing ashes on the back of the victim with the right hand is also, at any rate in the piacular sacrifices, a gesture of identification of man with victim; and this is a special and emphatic expression within the sacrificial situation of an identification which has a more general denotation, perhaps arising from that situation, for in sacrifice man and ox can be said to be really equivalent So if in symbol the sacrificial spear is the man, so also is the sacrificial victim. We may now ask ourselves what light is shed by what we have discovered about Nuer sacrifice on theories of sacrifice put forward by anthropologists and others and attempt, with the aid of these theories, and in terms of them, to reach a deeper understanding of it.

Much has been written about the nature of sacrifice, and this is not surprising in view of the central position it has had in the Hebrew and Christian religions and in the religions of pagan Greece and Rome. As is well known, there have been two main theories of sacrifice, the communion theory and the gift theory. The communion theory was given wide currency by Robertson Smith in his *Lectures on the Religion of the Semites* (1889). Briefly, his theory was that primitive sacrifice, and particularly early Semitic sacrifice, was a feast in which the god and his worshippers ate together. It was a communion or act of social fellowship—not a gift, not a tribute, not a covenant, not an expiation, not a propitiation. All these ideas were either much later or, if present in the earliest forms of sacrifice, were secondary or even merely germinal. Moreover, the sacrificial victim was a sacred beast, not in virtue of being set apart or consecrated for sacrifice, but intrinsically. It was the totem of the clan and hence of the same blood as the people who slew it and ate it. But in a sense it was also the god himself, for the god was the ancestor of the clan and therefore kin to both his worshippers and their totemic victim. By sacramentally eating their god, the theanthropic and theriomorphic victim, the worshippers acquired spiritual strength.

The totemic part of this theory is unacceptable, since there is almost no evidence that can be adduced in support of it, either from the literature concerning the early Hebrews, with whom Robertson Smith was chiefly concerned, or from accounts of primitive peoples, to which he made appeal. Moreover, I think that every competent Old Testament scholar would today admit the accuracy of Buchanan Gray's conclusions that the idea of gift rather than that of communion was predominant in even the earliest Hebrew sacrifices known to us, that the ideas of expiation and propitiation were present in these earliest sacrifices, and that it is clear that by the time of Deuteronomy a eucharistic intention was present.[1] Even, therefore, in its more reasonable form, minus the totemic character of the victim, Robertson Smith's attempt to

[1] Buchanan Gray, *Sacrifice in the Old Testament Its Theory and Practice*, 1925, pp 1–82

show that festal communion between worshippers and their gods was the original form of Semitic sacrifice could only be a highly speculative hypothesis for times for which records, and hence evidences, are totally lacking Nor do ethnographic accounts support it with regard to predominantly theistic religions, such as that of the Nuer. They only show, if their conclusions are correct, that among some peoples, such as some of the Bantu[1] who have a cult of the ancestors, sacrifices are sometimes communion feasts at which the ghosts and their living kinsmen are thought to feed together on the victim.

The communion theory as held by Robertson Smith and those who have accepted his interpretations gives us little aid towards understanding the nature of Nuer sacrifices to God, and they do not lend it support. The idea is excluded by definition in the case of their holocausts The flesh of other victims can only be said to be in any sense sacred in such sacrifices as those in which parts of it may not be eaten by the sacrificers. In their common sacrifices of wild cucumbers the victims are in any case inedible. In none of their sacrifices is there any suggestion that God partakes of the essence of the flesh. What goes to him is the life, and it would be to extend the communion theory beyond legitimate bounds to say that his taking—not consuming—the life and man's eating of the flesh constitute a communion in the sense given to the idea by its upholders. Moreover, though men eat the carcass, and any man may partake of the flesh, their eating of it, however important socially this festal side to sacrifice may be, is not a sacramental meal but an ordinary commensual act of family or kin which, moreover, falls outside the sacrificial rites Those who eat the flesh are not thought to gain spiritual strength by doing so. It might be held that the juices of the cucumber, and occasionally the chyme of a beast, have a sacramental use in the sacrificial situation, but the same could not be maintained of the flesh of animal victims. In the etymological sense of the word 'sacrifice' it is the life which is made *sacer* by the consecration, not the flesh which the sacrificers and others eat.

It is only in a mystical, and not in a material, sense that Nuer sacrifice might be called a communion, in the sense that through sacrifice man communicates with God, who is invoked to be present (*in-vocare*) to receive the life of the consecrated victim and

[1] W. C. Willoughby, *The Soul of the Bantu*, 1928, pp 396 seq

to hear what it is that those who make the sacrifice desire of him. It is communion in this sense of union, of a *communio* established through the victim, that H. Hubert and M. Mauss were speaking of in their 'Essai sur la nature et la fonction du sacrifice'[1] when they said that in sacrifice a communication is established between the sacred and the profane by the intermediation of a victim. We may readily accept that the victim is an intermediary between God and man, in that they are brought together in the offering of its life. And if we ask why communion should be through a life, we are given an answer by the fourth-century neo-Platonist Sallustius,[2] that two living objects which are distant from one another can only be brought into union ($\sigma\nu\nu\alpha\phi\eta$) by means of an intermediary ($\mu\epsilon\sigma\acute{o}\tau\eta s$) of the same order, a third life.

We have, nevertheless, to bear in mind that the purpose of Nuer piacular sacrifices is to establish communication with God rather in order to keep him away or get rid of him than to establish a union or fellowship with him What Georges Gusdorf[3] says of religious sacrifice in general, that it is made not only to the gods but against the gods, is very true for the Nuer, in whose piacular sacrifices prophylactic and apotropaic features are very evident They are made in times of trouble, present or feared, and the trouble comes from God and in a sense is God. Sacrifice is made to persuade him to turn away from men and not to trouble them any more. It is made to separate God and man, not to unite them. They are already in contact in the sickness or other trouble The sacrifice is intended to rid the sufferer of the spiritual influence whose activity is apparent in the sickness. There is here a paradox. God is separated from man by an act which brings them together. The solution of the paradox would seem to lie in a distinction between two kinds of union, union on a material plane which is to be dissolved in the moment of sacrifice by bringing about union on a moral plane. This solution is consistent with the Nuer representation of sickness in which the sickness itself, the moral or spiritual state of the sufferer, and the action of Spirit form a complex whole; and also with the essential ambiguity of their conception of God as the source of good and ill.

[1] Op cit, p 133
[2] Sallustius, *Concerning the Gods and the Universe*, edit with Prolegomena and Translation by Arthur Darby Nock, 1926, pp. 29–30 (sect. xvi of text)
[3] *L'Expérience humaine du sacrifice*, 1948, p 78

II

Much older than the communion theory of sacrifice is the gift theory, supported among anthropological writers by Sir Edward Tylor and Herbert Spencer. For Tylor[1] sacrifices are gifts made to a deity as if he were a chief. This would not be a happy explanation for Nuer sacrifice, as they have no chiefs. For Spencer[2] sacrifice has developed from the placing of offerings on the graves of the dead to please their ghosts. This would also not be a happy explanation in the case of the Nuer, who do not make offerings in this manner to the dead. Other writers who regard sacrifice as being essentially a gift to gods stress a variety of motives· to nourish the gods, to obtain favours from them, to propitiate their wrath, to draw nearer to them, to create harmony between God and man, to expiate sins; or they emphasize their eucharistic, commemorative, or other intentions

Now Nuer sacrifice is clearly a gift of some sort. They say that they are giving God a thing, a gift. But it is a gift which is immolated, it is that which makes the offering a sacrifice And the gift must be a life or something which stands for a life. Moreover, a gift is a far from simple idea. It is a symbol which may have many different meanings and shades of meaning. We have to determine what sense or senses it has in Nuer sacrifices.

In their piacular sacrifices to God, which I am now discussing, they give something to get rid of some danger or misfortune, usually sickness. We found that the general idea underlying such sacrifices was that of substitution, the life of a beast being given in exchange for the life of a man. The ideas of purchase, redemption, indemnification, ransom, exchange, bargain, and payment are very evident in Nuer sacrifices, as the words by which they refer to them indicate; and they are not peculiar in this. for, as Hubert and Mauss rightly emphasize, there is probably no sacrifice in which there is not some idea of redemption and something of the nature of a contract.[3] As in the reciprocity of all giving and receiving, as Mauss points out also in his 'Essai sur le Don',[4] sacrifice establishes a contractual relationship between persons, those who give and those who receive. We can say definitely that a relation-

---

[1] *Primitive Culture*, 1913 ed , chap xviii
[2] *The Principles of Sociology*, vol ii, 1883, p. 102.   [3] Op cit , p 134
[4] *L'Annee sociologique*, 1925, pp 53–60 (Eng trans by Ian Cunnison *The Gift*, 1954, pp 12–16)

ship of this kind, based on a sort of exchange, is involved in Nuer sacrifices; but if they include, they go beyond, the dialectic of exchange and contract, even when thought of in terms of persons and not of things, for we can hardly speak of simple exchange or contract when one side in reality gets nothing and the other side may get nothing too.

This is an old problem. Since in most Nuer sacrifices men eat the carcass of the victim, what is God supposed to receive? Nuer say that he gets the life, but they also sense that, as this is his already, he gets nothing. It is his already not only in that it is no longer man's because man has consecrated it to him, so that in the sacrificial invocation the officiant tells God to take 'thy cow' and not 'my cow' or 'our cow', sometimes putting his hand on the beast or pointing at it with his spear as he does so to direct attention to the devoted animal, and uses the expressions *kam yang*, to give a beast in the sense of delivering what is due, and *kan yang*, to take a beast in the sense of taking what is the right of the taker. Nor is it his only in the wider sense that all beasts of the flocks and herds are in a general way of speaking devoted to him, being reserved for sacrifice to him, so that they ought not to be killed for any other purpose. The victim is always his in a yet more general religious sense which extends beyond, and is not derived from, the sacrificial situation, in the sense, that is, that everything belongs to him. In giving a beast to God man without doubt loses something but God, to whom it belongs anyhow, gains nothing But though this sense of God's ownership may be general it is not unprecise. Thus, Nuer do not complain when a beast is killed by lightning or sickness, for God has a right to take his own, and here also they speak to God about it as '*yangdu*', 'thy cow', so the expression is not determined by formal consecration, which merely gives greater emphasis to it All life belongs to God. It comes from him and to him it returns, and when he wants it he takes it. Indeed, his taking a beast by lightning or sickness has a certain similarity to sacrifice in that Nuer say that God takes the life of the beast in the place of the life of its master, the beast, as they say, in this manner shielding the man; but it differs otherwise from true sacrifice where man makes an offering of his own accord, and what he offers is a consecrated life.

If God gains nothing have we then to interpret Nuer sacrifice in terms of what man loses, in the sense of abnegation the word

(277)

'sacrifice' has come to have in our own language? Is it that man deprives himself of something that should take the emphasis? This also is an old problem. It cannot be denied that, although there is no sacrificial tariff, Nuer feel that the greater the crisis the greater should be the offering. At least some cattle should be slaughtered to stay a plague, and their carcasses are abandoned. In mortuary ceremonies oxen, and even cows, must be sacrificed In cases of serious sin or grave sickness it is desirable to sacrifice an ox if one can be spared. In lesser crises a goat or a sheep suffices, or even a cucumber. All this suggests that the greater the danger the higher should be the payment, the more valuable the gift or substitute and the more complete the surrender of it But though it may be so, the matter is more complex. It is of course true that cattle are by far the most valuable possessions of the Nuer, but, though doubtless their high value is an important consideration, we have to remember that it is not merely a question of relative value but also one of religious tradition and convention Men and oxen have a symbolic equivalence in the logic of sacrifice, so that whatever is sacrificed is an 'ox'. If there were enough oxen one might always sacrifice an ox, and in symbol and by surrogate one does so; but as there are not enough, other offerings have to take their place and oxen be kept for the greater crises and those important ceremonial occasions when quantity of meat is a primary consideration. When an ox is sacrificed it is not just a matter of making the highest bid for divine favour when it is most needed, on the principle that the greater the gift the greater will be the return. This is evident from the fact that the victims in marriage ceremonies must be oxen, for here the ideas of substitution and exchange are least in evidence and the purpose of sacrifice is social rather than religious Nor, in piacular sacrifices, should the holocaust be taken as evidence that it is simply a matter of the greater the need the greater must be the surrender, for when the carcasses of victims are abandoned to stave off plagues and murrains there is the idea of the evils entering into their bodies, and since the sacrifices are made on behalf of everybody no one can eat them They are holy for all and not, as in some sacrifices where one half of the victim is abandoned, only for certain persons.

But valuable though his beasts are to Nuer and great the loss of them—even though he may feast on their carcasses he still loses them—they themselves freely explain that it is not so much what is sacrificed that is important as the intentions of those who sacrifice. If a man is poor he will sacrifice a goat, or even a cucumber, in the place of an ox, and God will accept it. A man should give according to his circumstances, and the sacrifice is not less efficacious because it is a small thing The emphasis is not on the receiving but on the giving, on the sincerity of intention. It is a question, Nuer say, of the heart or, as we would say, of disposition. It is clear, indeed, that if God is prepared to accept a cucumber instead of an ox it is not merely the thing itself which is significant, for a cucumber can have no use or value for him. We should fix our attention on the suppliant as well as on what he offers, for what he offers is not only whatever it may happen to be but also the expression of an interior state. If a cucumber costs man nothing and benefits God not at all, we have surely to seek deeper into the ideas of payment, substitution, or exchange for the meaning of sacrificial gifts.

All gifts are symbols of inner states, and in this sense one can only give oneself, there is no other kind of giving. This has often been said and in the sense in which it is said it is true. But the idea is a very complex one. When Nuer give their cattle in sacrifice they are very much, and in a very intimate way, giving part of themselves. What they surrender are living creatures, gifts more expressive of the self and with a closer resemblance to it than inanimate things, and these living creatures are the most precious of their possessions, so much so that they can be said to participate in them to the point of identification.

But it is not only in this rather general sense of identification of men with cattle that Nuer can be said to offer up themselves in offering up their cattle in sacrifice. We have seen that one of the chief features of their sacrifices is the rubbing of ashes along the backs of the victims. It is true that this may be regarded as an act of consecration but it is also, to a greater or lesser degree, an act of identification. Identification of sacrificer with victim is a common interpretation by ancient and modern writers on the subject. Indeed, it is quite explicit in some religions, in particular in certain Vedic, Hebrew, and Muslim rites, that what one consecrates and sacrifices is always oneself, and this is sometimes symbolically represented by laying of hands on the victim. It is an interpretation which makes good sense for Nuer piacular sacrifices. I have not, it is true, heard Nuer say that this is what the laying on of hands means to them—it is our interpretation, what it means to us—but I have already given reasons for my conclusion that this meaning is implicit in their sacrifices also, and I do not think that their piacular sacrifices, where the life of an animal is substituted for the life of a man, are intelligible unless this is granted.[1]

But if a man gives himself in sacrifice he does so in the symbolism of substitution, in what Loisy calls a 'figuration' (*Essai historique sur le sacrifice*, 1920). He is acting a part in a drama. It is the ox which dies, not he Once again, this is an old problem. In trying to solve it we must recall that the purpose of Nuer piacular sacrifices is either to get rid of some present evil or to ward off some threatening evil, and also that the evil is very often connected with ideas of sin, fault, and error, and hence with feelings of guilt. The notions of elimination, expulsion, protection, purification, and propitiation and expiation cannot easily be separated out in these sacrifices, though in any particular sacrifice it may be possible to say that one or other notion is most in evidence The sense of fault is, as we have noted, clearly expressed in the sacrificial rites, in the confession of grievances and resentments, which is a feature of some sacrifices, and also in the sacrificial invocations, which must state a true account of everything which has led up to the crisis But it is most clearly and dramatically expressed by the common practice of all present placing ashes on the back of a beast and then either washing them off or slaughtering it. Nuer say that what they are doing is to place all evil in their hearts on to the back of the beast and that it then flows into the earth with the water or the blood. This is not done in most piacular sacrifices, but in almost all such sacrifices someone places ashes on the victim's back on behalf of those for whom the sacrifice is being made; and Nuer say of the sacrifice that whatever evil has occasioned it is placed on the back of the victim and flows away with its blood

[1] It is quite explicit among the neighbouring Shilluk people. The Rev D S Oyler ('The Shilluk Peace Ceremony', *Sudan Notes and Records*, 1920, p 298) describes how in a sacrifice by their king he says in his invocation over the victim 'the flesh of this animal is as my flesh, and its blood is the same as my blood'. I asked Dr. Mary Smith to discuss with Nuer the rubbing of ashes on sacrificial victims in the light of what has been said about it in this chapter Nuer told her that it was done to show God his animal and also so that the bad or evil would go out of them into the ox—they said it was '*lueh ni tek*', 'exchanging life' (life of man for life of beast) She concludes 'it certainly seems to me that you are right when you draw this conclusion from these actions and what they say'.

into the earth. We have also seen how in some animal sacrifices, and always when a cucumber is sacrificed, the evil is said to go into the left half of the victim, which is therefore abandoned, and how in the case of other offerings they are entirely abandoned for the same reason. They are asking God to take away the evil and that the evil may be ransomed or expiated or wiped out with the victim It is clear, therefore, that the laying on of hands is not only a consecration and an identification but also a transference on to the victim of the evil which troubles the sacrificer, and which, as we have noted earlier, is in a sense Spirit itself. It is put on to the victim and departs with its life. The victim thus has the role of scapegoat. This does not mean that the victim is made responsible for the evil. There is no suggestion of *poena vicaria*. The ox is not punished in the place of the man but is a substitute for him in the sense of representing him. In the laying on of hands the ideas of consecration, identification, and transference seem to be blended in the representation of a substitute. If this is so, it would follow that what the sacrificer is doing is to identify himself with the victim within the meaning of the transference. In other words, he identifies that part of himself which is evil with the victim so that in its death that part may be eliminated and flow away in its blood. As Gusdorf,[1] quoting Nietzsche, aptly remarks, 'en morale, l'homme ne se traite pas comme un *individuum*, mais comme un *dividuum*'. The same idea is expressed when in danger Nuer throw away as an offering to God something representing themselves and in substitution for themselves—a bead, a tassel, or some other small object of personal adornment or a lump of tobacco—that the evil may depart with it and they be spared.[2]

In sacrifice, then, some part of a man dies with the victim It can be regarded both as an absolution and a rebirth; and also as a self-immolation (the psycho-analysts use the word 'suicide').[3] Funda-mentally, however, if we have to sum up the meaning of Nuer sacrifice in a single word or idea, I would say that it is a substitu-

[1] Op cit , p 178
[2] Dr. P. P. Howell (*A Manual of Nuer Law*, 1954, p 218) has recorded a most interesting, and as far as I know unique, act of self-mutilation for the same purpose An elder of some social standing committed an act of bestiality with a cow and was so overcome by shame and remorse that, in addition to sacrificing a beast, 'as an act of expiation he cut off one of his own fingers with a spear' Dr Mary Smith was told by Nuer that a man who committed such an act would take his own life
[3] R. Money-Kyrle, *The Meaning of Sacrifice*, 1930, pp 248, 252, *et passim*

tion, *vita pro vita*. If it were not so it would be difficult to understand at all why offerings to God should be immolated. The life can only be given by its liberation through death, as Professor E. O. James emphasizes in his *Origins of Sacrifice*.[1] Substitution, a common enough interpretation of sacrifice,[2] is the central meaning of the rites—they are a giving or exchange or an expiation in that sense—whatever other ideas are mixed up in it or become attached to it.

But to sum up the meaning of Nuer piacular sacrifices in a single word scarcely does justice to the very complex set of ideas they express We have found it necessary to use a variety of words in speaking of them. communion, gift, apotropaic rite, bargain, exchange, ransom, elimination, expulsion, purification, expiation, propitiation, substitution, abnegation, homage, and others. According to situation and particular purpose one element in this complex of meaning may be stressed in one rite and another element in another rite, or there are shifts in emphasis from one part of the sacrificial rite to another. The matter becomes yet more complicated and resistant to precise definition when we take into consideration the scale on which Spirit is figured to Nuer on different levels, and also their collective sacrifices, for in this chapter I have so far been discussing only sacrifices to God and only those made to him which belong to the piacular class.

III

In piacular sacrifices to God the *do ut des* notion, some sort of exchange or bargain, may never be entirely absent but it appears in a refined and sublimated form. The favour requested does not follow automatically the sacrifice, *ex opere operato*. God is not compelled by the sacrifice to grant it It is indeed obvious, to Nuer as well as to us, that, apart from there being no means by which bargaining with God can be conducted, it is no use trying to haggle with him, because he is master of everything and can want nothing Nor is there any idea that God is at fault if he does not give what is asked for in sacrifice; in his dealings with man he always has the *cuong*, is in the right. But when we examine sacri-

---

[1] 1933, *passim* His interpretation, as I understand it, of primitive sacrifice in terms of the *do ut possis dare* motif does not, however, accord with Nuer ideas.

[2] Given, among anthropologists, some emphasis by Edward Westermarck (*The Origin and Development of the Moral Ideas*, 1908, vol. ii, pp 616 seq)

fices to spirits of the air and of the earth the relations between Spirit and man are somewhat different and colour the meaning of the sacrifices accordingly. The lesser spirits are in competition, and if one of them has a cow dedicated to it its prestige is thereby increased. They do not, as God does, own all the beasts anyhow, but only those men give to them. This is why one dedicates beasts to the spirits but only rarely and in very special circumstances to God, for there is little point in giving him what is his already. Likewise, a sacrificed life, which is God's anyhow, is something spirits are thought to gain. Further, since God needs nothing he does not ask for anything. He does not demand sacrifices of men and cause them ill if they are not made The spirits do. They demand attention, and they are not to be satisfied with cucumbers. They require bloody offerings. And if they are not given animal sacrifices they seize their devotees and make them sick Nuer, therefore, do not hesitate to bargain with these spirits, speaking through their mediums, in a downright way which astonished me. The sense of the bargain is always the same: if we give you an ox or a sheep or a goat will you leave the sick man alone that he may recover, or what do you require of us this year in sacrifice that we may not be troubled by you? The lower in the scale is the conception of Spirit the more it is thought of as taking delight in what is offered

Thus even though sacrifices to God and to the spirits may both have a piacular purpose and though the apotropaic element in both is very evident they cannot have precisely the same meaning Even in piacular sacrifices to God there may be much variation of meaning, as, for example, between those in which the idea of expiation is most in evidence, such as those made to wipe out some definite sin like incest, and those made so that people may recover from wounds and ailments not attributed to specific offences and which, therefore, do not have the same moral connotation. But in either case the general attitude is the same. Man approaches God through sacrifice and asks for aid. It is man and not God who benefits by the sacrifice. Man's attitude in these sacrifices contrasts with his attitude in the case of sacrifices to spirits who have seized people to exact gifts from them or may do so if they are not satisfied. It is true that men generally have a feeling that the spirits would not have troubled them if they had been given their due and that their devotees have only themselves to blame if they have neglected them, and also that men give to the spirits for the same reason that they often give to God, that they may be left alone. But the psychology of gifts to spirits is different. Here the substitution is blended with the idea of propitiation and satisfaction rather than of expiation or solicitation for aid, and the experience is on a different level of thought Man does not wrestle with God, but here man and a spirit are pitted against one another, and the huckstering is conducted through a human agency—is, in fact, between humans, between the sacrificer and the representative of a spirit, a prophet and generally a very minor one. God has no such representatives The leopard-skin priests are men's representatives to him, not his representatives to men. We are here faced again with the problem of the one and the many; and we see in these differences of attitude in sacrifices to God and in those made to lesser spirits a facet of the ambiguity of the idea of Spirit, the source of good and ill, as represented in the paradox of unity and plurality.

Thus we see that in Nuer sacrifice there are different shades of meaning. The pattern varies. There are shifts of emphasis. Any attempt to present a general interpretation, to put forward a simple formula to cover all Nuer sacrifices, meets with further difficulty when we turn to the collective and confirmatory sacrifices. Here the intention is clearly different. God, or whichever of his refractions may be involved, is not angry and therefore does not have to be propitiated. No sin has been committed which must be expiated, and there is no situation requiring expiation in the broader sense of payment to be rid of a state of danger due to the presence of Spirit. Life is not usually endangered so there is no need for substitution. Initiations and weddings are occasions of mirth, and even mortuary ceremonies, though they are solemn occasions, mark the end of mourning and therefore have a joyous side to them. There may always be some element of anxiety in these *rites de passage*, and perhaps also—it is difficult to say—of a feeling of the possibility of fault. In some confirmatory sacrifices, those concerned with death, these elements are manifest, but in others, such as marriage ceremonies, they are not evident and the stress is rather on ensuring the success of a social activity and validating it. As I have said earlier, we cannot make a rigid distinction between the one type of sacrifice and the other. Mortuary sacrifices might be placed in either class, according to the point of view.

But in initiation and marriage ceremonies the sacrifices are only incidents in a succession of ceremonial acts, and they have a maximum of festal, and a minimum of religious, significance. The sacrifice adds strength to what is being accomplished by other means and it provides a meal for those attending what is primarily a social gathering, so much so that those who have a right to the carcass of the victim in marriage sacrifices may demand that a bigger ox be slaughtered than that provided. In these ceremonies we have to distinguish between the religious rite of sacrifice and the secular rites and ceremonial acts which it accompanies and sacralizes, and both from the feasting on porridge and beer and the flesh of the sacrificial victims and other acts of simple sociability. A boy is initiated into manhood by the making of six incisions across his forehead and by various other acts of a ritual and ceremonial character. The sacrifice is something extra added to these acts which protects the lad from harm, makes God and the ghosts witnesses of his change of status, and provides a feast for the living witnesses, his ever-hungry kinsmen and neighbours. Likewise in marriage, though sacrifices must be made to mark and secure the completion of the stages leading to the full union of man and wife as well as to give the visiting relatives-in-law a meal, the union itself is brought about mainly by other than religious acts: payment of bridewealth, wedding ceremonial and festivities, and so forth. The sacrifices form only a part of the whole series of ritual and other activities, and a part in which the religious content is reduced to a minimum, the movements of the sacrifice being conducted in a perfunctory manner. To indicate the place of the religious element in the total event, one might perhaps compare it among ourselves to grace before a festal meal on some important ceremonial occasion. There is, therefore, a difference of attitude and hence of meaning between the collective and the personal sacrifices. We must suppose that in the laying on of hands in the former by representatives of the lineages which offer up the victims the ideas of identification and of transference of evil are not so prominent as in the piacular sacrifices.

Yet we cannot exclude these killings from the general category of sacrifice. We can, nevertheless, say that the most typical collective and confirmatory sacrifices, those sacrifices which lack, at any rate to any marked degree, piacular significance, are least important to an understanding of the character of Nuer religion. The role of this religion in the regulation of the social life, its structural role, is subsidiary to its role in the regulation of the individual's relations with God, its personal role. The two roles are of different orders and have different functions, and it is the second which has the greater interest for us, for though Nuer religious activity is part of their social life and takes place within it they conceive it as expressing essentially a relationship between man and something which lies right outside his society; and it is, therefore, within the framework of that conception that our study of their religion has to be made and its central act of sacrifice has to be understood.

CHAPTER XII

PRIESTS AND PROPHETS

I

It has been noted that women do not make sacrifice and that though any man can make it only senior men who are fathers of families, 'bulls' as the Nuer call them, do so. Personal sacrifices are usually, as in most cases of sickness, performed by the head of the family or some senior kinsman and neighbour, but sacrifices which have more than domestic import and are thought of as involving a whole lineage or clan—collective sacrifices—have to be performed by a person called *gwan buthni*, whom I have spoken of as the master of ceremonies.

The verb *buth* means 'to share', and since collateral lineages of a clan and also clans with common ancestry may claim portions of the flesh of sacrificial victims at each other's collective sacrifices, there is said to be *buth* between them. They are to one another *jibuthni*, people who share. The word is also used when speaking of the adoption of a captured Dinka into his captor's lineage. He is said to be *lath buthni*, given shares A sacrifice is made and in the invocation at it the guardian spirit of the lineage is asked to receive the Dinka into its care and the ghosts of the ancestors are informed of what is being done. The Dinka is smeared with the victim's chyme. He now counts as a member of his captor's lineage and has a right to partake of the meats of its sacrifices and also to claim a portion of the meat at sacrifices by any other lineage to which this lineage stands in a *buth* relationship. *Buth* has consequently the further meaning of agnation. *Jibuthni* are agnates. *Lath buthni* is to be given agnation. Agnates are people who share in the flesh of sacrifices.

Buth relationship is stated also in terms of the division of elephant tusks or of cattle exchanged for them. When hunters kill an elephant the right tusk goes to the *koc*, the man who first speared it, and the left tusk to the *gam*, the man who speared it next. The tusks are cut into portions to be used as armlets—one of the most precious of Nuer possessions—or are exchanged for cattle, and the portions of ivory or the cattle are divided among those relatives of the spearsmen who receive cattle of bridewealth and bloodwealth and the flesh of sacrifices. Those standing in a *buth* relationship to the spearsmen also have rights in the tusks. This means in practice that a section of the tusk, or its equivalent in cattle, goes to the particular *thok mac*, minimal lineage, of the spearsman's clan to which the *gwan buthni*, master of ceremonies, of his family belongs, and it is this man who gets it.[1]

Each family has its master of ceremonies, who is a member of a lineage collateral to that of its head and therefore one of his distant agnatic kinsmen. A son takes his father's place in this service. The same man may act on behalf of the heads of several families of the same minimal lineage, and one of his close agnatic kin may act in his stead, since he carries out his functions not as an individual but as representative of a group. The office is not necessarily reciprocal, for a man may act as master of ceremonies to a family of one collateral lineage and have as master of ceremonies to his own family a man of a different collateral lineage. Also, a family may have more than one master of ceremonies, the second belonging to a different collateral lineage from the first. Moreover, it would seem that if one of the persons who usually acts in this capacity is not available his place may be taken by any distant kinsman who can be held to represent him. Nuer are very latitudinarian in such matters; but the point we have to note is that on certain occasions a whole clan or large lineage offers up the sacrifice, and the officiant ought then to be someone outside the family and close kin most immediately concerned who represents the interest of the wider group, which participates in the sacrifice through him.

A master of ceremonies functions at weddings, mortuary and *colwic* ceremonies, settlements of blood-feuds, adoptions, initiations, severings of kinship to allow intermarriage or cohabitation, the building of new byres, and the division of elephant tusks. On these occasions he calls out the clan or lineage spear-name and then makes an invocation, usually prior to animal sacrifice. By calling out the spear-name he identifies the whole clan or lineage with the offering. When the victim has been killed he cuts through the scrotum (*juak tem*), this being the commencement of the skin-

[1] See also P P Howell, 'A Note on Elephants and Elephant Hunting among the Nuer', *Sudan Notes and Records*, 1945

(288)

ning in ordinary sacrifices at which he officiates, and Nuer often refer to him in his sacrificial role as 'the cutter of the scrotum' Does this usage symbolize the principle of agnation? Possibly, for after the sacrifice by which a Dinka is adopted into his captor's lineage it is said *'ca juak tem'*, 'the scrotum has been cut', to signify that the Dinka is now a member of the lineage. If we are right in thinking that it may have this meaning, then the cutting of the scrotum is a most appropriate symbolic act, for the *gwan buthni* represents, as a member of a collateral lineage, the unity of the clan as a corporation of segments, the principle of fission which is in the very nature of a lineage structure. The master of ceremonies receives some of the sacrificial meat at sacrifices at which he officiates and he generally has a right also to the hide or half of it. He has also a right, as I have explained, to a section of any elephant tusk that comes into possession of the family he serves, and the first turtles and the skins of the first leopards and serval cats killed by its sons are given to him. He receives a calf or sheep from the husband's people when one of its daughters is married

The role of the *gwan buthni* in sacrifice is seen to be a social role rather than one of a specifically religious kind. He does not function in virtue of any qualities in himself. He is a *dwek*, a layman, not a *kuaar*, a priest. He is called upon to make the first invocation when the sacrifice concerns the interest of a whole clan or lineage His clan or lineage alone is involved or if, as in marriage, another clan is also involved he acts on behalf of his own group alone; and consequently he addresses Spirit in the refraction by which it is represented to the clan—maybe in a totemic refraction or just as *'kwoth gwara'*, 'God of our fathers' His role in the proceedings is, therefore, determined primarily by the nature of the social activities in connexion with which he is asked to make sacrifice and not by any specifically religious considerations.

II

When sacrifice is made in consequence of some sin or to end certain states of interdiction, of sin-potential—in circumstances, that is, which involve the notion of *nueer* or of notions akin to it— it is desirable, and sometimes necessary, for the rite to be performed by a *kuaar twac* or *kuaar muon*, a priest of the leopard-skin or of the earth. It might seem that it is in no way here the nature of the social group involved which requires an officiant from outside the family and close kin, but the nature of the circumstances which occasion the sacrifice, circumstances which call for consecration and invocation to be made by someone with special religious qualities. Nevertheless, as will shortly be evident, although the exclusive sacrificial functions by which priestly office is defined have a special sacramental character, they arise, like those ideas of sin with which they are particularly concerned, from situations which require for full understanding a knowledge of the social structure.

When the Government of the Anglo-Egyptian Sudan first began to take an interest in the Nuer the attention of its officers was at once drawn to what became known as 'leopard-skin chiefs', for these men were distinguished from the rest of the Nuer by the leopard-skins they wore over their shoulders (Plate XIV). It was thought that they were some kind of 'chiefs' or, in the language of those days, 'shaikhs' or 'sultans' through whom the Government might conduct its administration. It soon became apparent, however, that they lacked any real authority; and it is clear that, although the exercise of their religious functions has an important political role, they have no political, administrative, or judicial office. I have discussed the political significance of their religious functions in *The Nuer*,[1] and I limit further discussion of them here to what is necessary for an understanding of the topics treated in the present book.

The word which Europeans have translated 'chief' and which I translate 'priest' is *kuaar* (pl *kuar*).[2] This person is often referred to as *kuaar twac*, priest of the (leopard-) skin, or as *gwan twac*, possessor of the (leopard-) skin, on account of the leopard-skin he wears over his shoulders. In its original sense the word *kuaar* conveys to Nuer a category of persons with traditional ritual functions Its opposite is *dwek* (pl. *dueghni*), an ordinary person who has no such functions, a layman. Used by itself the word *kuaar* would normally, perhaps invariably, mean for a Nuer a leopard-skin priest, but combined with other words it may be used

[1] Chap IV.
[2] He is referred to in all government files as 'leopard-skin chief', and rather than make for local confusion I used this designation in my reports and later, with a caveat, in my earlier books In a book on Nuer religion I feel that a title should be used which indicates better his religious character

PLATE XI

Leopard-skin priest

to refer to other persons with traditional ritual functions, such as the *wut ghok* or man of the cattle, though this usage is loose and should perhaps be regarded as derived by analogy from its primary use to denote a leopard-skin priest. When the Government chose certain leading persons in the various Nuer communities and appointed them 'Government Chiefs' with administrative and judicial duties and privileges these chiefs became known as *kuar biei*, chiefs of the cloth (the robes of office presented to them by the Government), either because Europeans referred to them as *kuar* or because Nuer saw a resemblance between the robes and the leopard-skins worn by priests. Both are worn over the right shoulder. *Kuaar* became as well the title by which Europeans are addressed by Nuer, perhaps for one or other of the same reasons. The word has thus gained a wider range of meaning.

A more usual title than *kuaar twac* or *gwan twac* is *kuaar muon*, priest of the earth, the word *mun* (gen *muon*) meaning 'earth' in the sense of 'soil', and if it were not that in the literature on the Nuer the priest of whom we speak is always designated by reference to his leopard-skin I should be inclined to write of him as the priest of the earth, because the leopard-skin title is taken only from his badge whereas the earth title is derived from a symbolic association with the earth of deeper significance It is said that a leopard-skin priest (henceforward generally referred to simply as 'priest') will not approach people when they are making pots lest the pots crack; and in this sense he may be said to respect (*thek*) the earth. If anything goes wrong with the standing crops he may be asked to anoint (*yir*) the earth with butter. He may also be asked to anoint seed and digging-sticks with butter before sowing. When a priest is buried, his corpse, so that it will not be in contact with the earth, is placed between hides on a light platform erected in the grave, which is dug in his hut if he dies while the people are in their villages. These and other observances express a mystical relationship of priests with the earth in virtue of which their curses are thought to have special potency, for, as was noted earlier (p 167), they can affect not only a man's crops but his welfare generally, since human activities all take place on the earth. However, in spite of the power attributed to their curses, I have never known Nuer stand in awe of them nor have I known the power to be used outside a situation of feud; and then a priest's threat to curse is regarded as a routine convention It gives the injured party an excuse to accept compensation without loss of honour.

It is a matter of surprise that the Nuer priesthood should have this association with the earth and take its most common title from it. There is no cult of the earth such as we find in West Africa. Priests are not traditionally linked to a particular territory as are the 'fathers of the land', ritual agents who are such in virtue of being descendants of first settlers, among some other Nilotic peoples. Nor can a satisfactory explanation be advanced in terms of agricultural activities. Nuer do not highly esteem cultivation of crops and may be presumed to have engaged in it even less in the past when cattle were more numerous Cattle husbandry receives more of their attention and is their absorbing interest, but it and fishing, which is also most important for them, so far as they are the object of ritual attention, are the concern of other, and less important, ritual specialists than the priest of the earth. Moreover, Nuer do not attach much importance to such ritual as he performs in connexion with the crops, and it is entirely secondary to his other functions. On the other hand, it can be seen that the association of priesthood with the earth is a representation which accords with the general idea of man being identified with the earth and God with the sky, the priest being essentially a person who sacrifices on behalf of man below to God above.

Lineages of leopard-skin priests are found in all tribal sections, and in most parts of Nuerland they are in the category of *rul*, strangers, and not of *diel*, members of the clans which own the tribal territories. It is necessary that they should be widely spread, because their services are essential to Nuer everywhere, and it is significant that they are generally not members of lineages identified with political groups, because they have to act as peacemakers between such groups. The two best-known priestly clans, the Gaatleak and the Jimem, have no tribal territories of their own but live, as families and small lineages, in most or all territories owned by other clans They are like Levi, divided in Jacob and scattered in Israel Their priestly filiation goes back to Gee, the first man and the first priest, from certain of whose sons the priestly virtue (*ring*) has passed down the generations However, although their powers are hereditary, and although all members of a priestly lineage can, therefore, act in a priestly capacity, in practice only certain families do so, and these families can function as priests wherever they happen to reside. Moreover, persons who do not belong to a priestly family can become priests, transmitting their powers to their children, by what the Nuer call *tetde*, by hand. This means that such a man is given a leopard-skin by a priest and told to carry out priestly services. In some myths of origin of the Jikany tribes the leopard-skin was given by the ancestors of the dominant lineages to their maternal uncles that they might serve as tribal priests. The structurally opposed lineages of the clan were then in the common relationship of sisters' sons to the line of priests, which thus had a mediatory position between them.[1] A layman is still today sometimes invested with the leopard-skin and the priestly powers that go with it, and I have known a Dinka chosen for the purpose This in itself teaches us much about the way Nuer regard their priests. Priestly duties are tiresome and ill-rewarded, but somebody has to perform them. Nuer society is very far from being a hierocracy.

The chief services a priest performs are in connexion with homicide and the importance of his office derives from this essential function. Only he can perform these services,[2] which are to release the slayer from the state of extreme danger his act has placed him in and, where circumstances are such that an active blood-feud is likely to develop if a settlement is not reached, to give the slayer sanctuary, to negotiate a settlement, to perform sacrifice to enable normal social relations to be resumed, and to rehabilitate the slayer. All these functions, in addition to having a political significance, are also essentially religious acts or derive from the priest's sacred character

As soon as a man kills another he hastens to the nearest priest, who draws the point of a fishing-spear down his right arm from where it joins the shoulder and sacrifices a beast, called *yang riem*, the cow of blood. Were the slayer to eat or drink before this has been done it would be serious *nueer* and cause certain death, for the blood which is drawn is thought to be in some way that of the slain man which has passed into him. If there is likelihood of blood-vengeance the slayer then takes sanctuary in the home of

---

[1] I recorded this fact in *Sudan Notes and Records* (1935, pp. 46–48), but I have only recently realized, in the light of Dr Lienhardt's research among the Dinka, the significance of it

[2] Except perhaps on such rare occasions as when a priest himself or one of his family is killed. I was told that then an elder of the aristocratic clan of the tribe might act in the priest's place.

the priest, his family and cattle being dispersed to homes of kinsmen, leaving his homestead deserted. He will not be molested
there because of the sacred character of the priesthood For the
same reason the priest and any who accompany him can move
between the parties without fear and so conduct negotiations for
settlement It is essential that a blood-feud be settled if the parties
to it live in the same neighbourhood, not only for reasons of
security, but also on account of the serious danger both the dead
man's kin and the slayer's kin are placed in by the homicide, a
danger in which the whole community is involved. Settlement by
payment of compensation (*cut*) to the family and kin of the dead
man prevents them from taking vengeance and thus causing a
further disturbance of social life. It also pacifies the ghost, who
may trouble his family and kin if a wife is not soon married to his
name with *ghok thunga*, cattle of blood-guilt. Consequently, even
when a man is slain by a close paternal kinsman cattle, though
fewer, have to be paid to provide him with heirs, and if vengeance
is taken and a man on each side is killed compensation has to be
paid for both so that their names may not be blotted out. The payment is rather for this purpose than to satisfy honour. Only vengeance can do that. This is why the kin, even when they are ready
to accept compensation, at first refuse it, and why, even after
acceptance, a feud is always liable to break out again. But neither
consideration seems to weigh with Nuer so much as the need to
rid themselves of the condition of *nueer*. This threatens chiefly
the kin of the slain. but the kin of the slayer, the wives of both lots
of kin, and all their neighbours are also subject to interdiction If
either side eats or drinks with the other or from vessels which the
other has used the penalty is death, and it may be brought on
kinsmen on either side by a person who belongs to neither party
eating or drinking in the homes of both. This intolerable state of
interdiction can only be ended by sacrifice by a priest when compensation has been paid, since it requires the consent of both
parties. We have, therefore, to distinguish between the cattle paid
to compensate the kin of the dead for their loss and to provide the
ghost with a wife from those paid for sacrifice, just as we had to
distinguish between the cattle paid in indemnity for adultery and
the beast paid for sacrifice. This is shown by the fact that should
a man kill his wife, though no compensation can be exacted and
the question of providing heirs does not arise, he will hand over

to her kin the beasts required for sacrifice to get rid of the state of uncleanness resulting from the homicide. We have here to distinguish also the priest's role in making these sacrifices, which only he can perform and the performance of which is the essentially priestly role in blood-feuds, from the sanctuary he provides and the mediation he offers. The first is a sacramental act only a priest can perform, the others are acts he can perform because people, as we would say, have respect for the cloth. It is a distinction between priestly office and priestly status. In certain cases, as in those of accidental homicide, neither sanctuary nor mediation would be required of him; but it is always necessary that he makes the customary sacrifices if the state of *nueer* is to be ended, and it must be ended if the parties have to come into contact with each other in the course of their ordinary social life. Although today the Government exacts compensation for homicide and takes charge of the slayer, priestly sacrifice is still required before a blood-feud can be settled.

I am not certain about all the details of procedure in settlement of a blood-feud, and they probably vary from one part of Nuerland to another and even from one case to another, but the main, and usual, actions are as follows.[1]

When, usually after some months (the mortuary ceremony for the dead man having first been held), negotiations have been completed and the cattle brought together from the homes of the various kinsmen who have contributed to the payment the priest, accompanied by some of his kinsmen, and when relations are not too strained by a representative of the slayer's party, drives them to a place near the home of the dead man, where his kinsmen have gathered. When, after inspection, all are accepted they are tethered in a neighbouring homestead as they may not enter the kraal of the dead man's family till sacrifices have been made. One of the oxen, called *yang ketha*, the cow of the gall-bladder, is consecrated by the priest, who then makes an invocation over it to God that the feud may be closed. In the course of it he addresses also the ghost of the dead man and tells him that his death has been paid for and that his kinsmen will marry a wife to his name to bear him a son. The priest then slays the victim and as soon as

---

[1] For a fuller account see H. C. Jackson, op. cit, pp 102–4. my book *The Nuer*, pp. 152 seq; J. P Crazzolara, op cit, pp 106 seq; and P P Howell, *A Manual of Nuer Law*, chap ii

it has fallen the dead man's kin hack it to pieces in a wild scramble. The gall-bladder is extracted and placed on one side This is later squeezed into a gourd containing water and a little milk and is drunk by members of the dead man's family and paternal and maternal kin and, if one is present, by the representative of the slayer's party. The priest gives them also cleansing medicines, *wal nueera*, to drink After this ceremony the parties can eat and drink together without risk, though if feelings have run high they are unlikely, for reasons of sentiment, to do so. Were at any time before it is performed a man inadvertently to break the interdiction a priest would be summoned to save his life by sacrifice and medicines.

Next day before sunrise the dead man's kin go to where the cattle of compensation have spent the night in a neighbouring homestead and sacrifice the one entire bull among them and cook and eat its flesh The cattle may now be brought into the dead man's homestead and their milk drunk. Some of them are later distributed among the dead man's paternal and maternal kin while the rest are entrusted to relatives to look after, or are temporarily tethered in his kraal, until they are used to marry him a wife, the bride cohabiting with his brother. It is unlikely that all the cattle will have been handed over at the ceremony for closing the feud. The last ones to be paid, maybe years later, are the *ghok pale loc*, the cattle of relieving the heart, and a beast known as *yang tul coka*, the cow of the breaking of the bone, because after it is sacrificed one of its bones is held at either end by representatives of the two parties while the priest severs it in two. The left half of the bone is thrown away The two parties then consume the flesh together The earlier ceremony ended the state of *nueer*, and the purpose of this later ceremony seems to be to bring the parties into amity again These final cattle may not be paid, and the final ceremony therefore not be held, if the parties to the feud do not strongly feel the need for a lasting settlement

The state of feud, which is a state not only of social conflict but also of spiritual danger, was ended by the sacrifice of the *yang ketha*. But the priest still has a duty to perform, to bring the man who incurred the blood-guilt back into the life of the community. The cutting of his arm put him out of immediate and acute danger, but the death he has caused still clings to him till these final rites, which are like those which end a period of mourning.

The priest and one or two of his kinsmen escort the slayer to his neglected home where huts and byre are in disrepair and grass has grown up in courtyard and kraal He consecrates an ox, preferably a black one or one with black markings, utters an invocation to God, saying that compensation has been paid and sacrifice made to remove the state of feud and asking that the slayer may now rest in peace in his own home. He sacrifices the ox, known as *yang miem*, the cow of the hair, because afterwards he cuts the slayer's hair or a token lock of it. It has not been cut or tended since the homicide. The priest then starts to hoe up the weeds in the kraal, and he and his kinsmen to clean up the homestead. He also kindles fire with fire-sticks (*piec mac*), lights three fires, sacrifices a goat, removes its intestinal fat, and places a piece of it on each fire where the flames consume it. The slayer is now rid of the *thung*, the blood-guilt, and can repair his byre and huts and settle down to normal life.

The leopard-skin priest also conducts the taking of oaths A Nuer may at any time lick a spear or metal bracelet as a sign that he is speaking the truth, and I was told that a man would not do so if he were lying, though he might pretend to lick it But formal rites of purgation are conducted by a priest If a man denies that he has killed another he undergoes an ordeal by drinking milk from the herd of the dead man handed to him by the priest in the presence of the dead man's kin Should he be lying he would die of *nueer*. To kill a man and not to confess to the killing is a heinous offence in Nuer eyes because it puts the kin on both sides in jeopardy. In questions other than homicide, which would usually, I think, concern rights in cattle, the priest digs a hole, representing a grave, and accuser and accused either step over it or take hold of the shaft of the priest's spear placed above it as they make their declarations Or the declarations are made by them as they sit on the priest's leopard-skin The priest then utters an invocation over a tethered victim that whoever is lying will die. The late Mr. Hamer, who witnessed this rite, told me that the priest caught the blood of the beast, a goat, in a gourd and mixed it with earth scraped from the ground in front of the skin. He placed a lump of this mixture in the mouths of the two men, who chewed and swallowed it. They then stood up and, facing one another, stepped across the skin. In a text written by a Nuer at the American mission, and sent to me by Dr. Mary Smith, the priest first addresses the victim, a sheep: 'now, sheep, thy blood is shed to death on account of the man who is at fault'. He then calls on God: 'O God of heaven, God of our fathers, God who created all things, God of the universe, God of the flesh (*ring*), I call on thee to look upon these persons, that the man who is at fault may die Now, I know that thou, O God, listenest to my speech (*rietda*).' If a guilty man who has taken an oath that he is innocent falls sick he gets the priest to sacrifice for him and give him medicines, promising reparation for the wrong he has done.

A leopard-skin priest is also, at any rate usually, called in to sacrifice an ox if close relations commit incest. In cases of slighter incest, between, that is, persons more distantly related, some lesser specialist, a diviner, or just the head of the family, performs the sacrifice, or the man who has committed incest himself sacrifices a cucumber or cuts in two the fruit of a sausage-tree. The priest consecrates the ox, makes an invocation over it to God that he may spare the partners to the sin and that the offence may depart with the blood of the victim. The beast is then held down on the ground and the priest inserts the point of his spear in its throat and cuts towards the breast. He severs the beast in twain, hacking its head in two with an axe. As he makes the final cuts the parties to the offence tug at the carcass on either side and pull it apart. One half is eaten by the priest and his friends and the other by the relatives of the principals, the principals themselves abstaining The priest squeezes out the gall from the victim's gall-bladder into water in a gourd, adds *wal ruali*, incest-medicine, and the principals and their relatives drink this mixture.

Sacrifices in connexion with homicide, ordeals, and, at least usually, serious incest are the exclusive domain of the leopard-skin priest. If he is called on to make sacrifice on other occasions it is because it is felt that his doing so adds weight to the intention; but it is not necessary that he should act and unless he happens to be a neighbour it is unlikely that he would be summoned.

Since a good deal has been written about the importance of 'rain-makers' in this part of Africa it is perhaps wise to note also that the leopard-skin priest is never spoken about in relation to rain When questioned, Nuer say that he might be asked to sacrifice for rain and to perform some other and minor ritual acts, such as putting a hyena's skull in water, to the same purpose; but they make it clear that they attach no great importance to these procedures. Any Nuer can pray to God to send rain, and his prayers may be supported by placing a sprig of the *nyuot* tree in water, though this is best done, together with sacrifice of one of the flock to *kwoth nyota*, spirit of the *nyuot* tree, by a member of the widely scattered Gaawar clan on account of their association with both rain and the tree (p 72). Some Nuer said that a prophet's prayers and sacrifices for rain might be effective, and they seem to have had some faith in those of the prophet Gwek; but I found that in general Nuer showed little interest in the subject They certainly do not think that anyone can 'make' rain. Whoever it may be, priest, prophet, member of the Gaawar clan, or just an ordinary person, he can only pray to God to send the rain. They say, 'There is nothing we can do if it does not rain. God has given us nothing [to make it]. We are merely ignorant folk.' When I urged that surely there was something they could do, a Nuer replied, 'Oh well, the leopard-skin priest may sacrifice a cow [probably a goat was meant] and pray to God for rain, and that is all, perhaps God will give it and perhaps he won't.' When I asked about Car, a well-known prophet, whether he could bring rain, I was told, 'Oh well, he will pray to his spirit [an air-spirit] and ask for rain, but that is all.'

In whatever circumstances a priest acts as intermediary between men and God the virtue which gives efficacy to his mediation resides in his office rather than in himself. Consequently, it does not matter what sort of person he is, socially, psychologically, or morally. The virtue derives from the office having been established by God at the beginning of things as part of the social order. Consequently the priest is a traditional public functionary thought of as having always existed and as representative of man, rather than of any particular men, to God in certain critical situations Therefore when he invokes God at sacrifice he does so in phrases which recall the universal and enduring character of his role: '*Kwoth muonda*', 'Spirit of our earth', '*Kwoth Jagei*', 'Spirit of all the Nuer' (*Jagei* has here this sense), and '*Kwoth rieng gwani*', 'Spirit of the virtue of our fathers'.

When we examine the critical situations in which the priest is called upon to exercise his functions we see that the priesthood can be regarded either as a political institution functioning within a set of religious ideas and values or as a religious institution functioning within a set of political ideas and values. His essential and distinctive role is that which he plays in homicide, that is to say, when two social groups, groups of kin and local and political groups, are in a state of violent opposition to each other and the whole community is involved in consequence, directly or indirectly, in a state of interdiction. He functions as administrator of oaths in a similar setting. The oaths either arise out of homicide or concern matters which may result in homicide. There are strong feelings of hostility between the parties; otherwise oaths, with their terrible consequences, would not be taken. Serious incest may provoke similar feelings, because, Nuer ideas about incest being what they are, the persons concerned in it may belong to different descent groups and, indeed, are for various reasons likely to do so. In situations of *nueer* in which hostile feelings are not aroused, as when twins are born or a person is killed by lightning, the head of the family or its master of ceremonies officiates. These are family and lineage affairs. So, whereas the *gwan buthni* acts in sacrifice on behalf of an exclusive social group, the leopard-skin priest for the most part performs sacrifices in situations in which two groups are opposed to one another and which therefore require a person unidentified by lineage attachment to either to act on behalf of the whole community. The priest thus has a central position in the social structure rather than in religious thought, for his priestly functions are exclusive not because, on account of the sanctity of his office, only he can perform sacrifices, but because representatives of neither party to a dispute can effectively act in the circumstances obtaining. As he entirely lacks any real political authority or powers it is understandable that he could not carry out his functions unless during their performance his person was sacrosanct. The presence of a priesthood adds nothing to the dominant ideas of Nuer religion. It is rather these ideas which give to a political role· its necessary attributes. Put in another way, the Nuer have priests who perform certain politico-religious functions but their religion is not intrinsically a priestly religion.

Another hereditary and traditional functionary is the *wut ghok*, the man of the cattle, sometimes also spoken of as *kuaar ghok*, the 'priest' of the cattle, or *ring ghok*, the 'virtue' (literally, 'flesh') of the cattle. There are men of the cattle in every tribe and tribal section, and they belong to lineages of a number of different clans, all those I have come across being of true Nuer descent. As in the case of the leopard-skin priestly lineages, any member of a lineage of men of the cattle can perform the services attached to that office, but in practice only some, and senior, persons would normally be called upon to do so. These services have less religious and social importance than those of the *kuaar muon*, and a man of the cattle is not by virtue of his office a person of social importance One hears of him chiefly in connexion with his ability to perform rites to cure sick beasts and to make barren cows fertile, usually by spitting on grass and beating the animal's back with it while asking God to make the beasts well or fertile In times of murrain he may sacrifice an ox to God. I was told that after consecrating it he would speak in this vein: 'What, God? Take this ox, it is thine. Thou art master of the world, the world is thine and it is thine affair alone. What, God? Do not kill all the cattle. What will our children eat? No one will live. Oh God, take thy cow and spare a portion of the herds. God, I am a man of the cattle and I have come to sacrifice this beast; take it, it is thine.' Nuer say that he addresses '*kwothde*', 'his spirit', that is Spirit as figured in relation to his office, the God of his fathers. He may also on raids lash a tethering-cord in the direction of enemy herds to ensure booty. He may be consulted about the time of moving to dry-season camps He is said to sprinkle people with milk in time of sickness, and at his own mortuary ceremony his kinsmen and possessions are aspersed with milk. He is buried in fresh cattle manure. He cannot accept cattle in compensation for adultery with his wife. His curse can cause cattle to die and a man to have diarrhoea if he drinks milk. All these customs and notions give him that mystical association with cattle which is indicated by his title and also by his badge of office, a circle or two of tethering-cord round his neck

As I have explained earlier (pp 255–6), initiation of boys to manhood is intimately bound up with their relation to the cattle. It is therefore appropriate that it should be a man of the cattle who in each tribe determines when a new age-set should commence and when it should close, performs sacrifices to open and close the periods of initiation, and names the sets, and this is the most important public function of any man of the cattle. We see here again how, as in the cases of the masters of ceremonies and the leopard-skin priests, the chief religious function of men of the cattle, their formal sacrificial and ceremonial role, is concerned with group activities In their case the activities are relations

(301)

between successive age-groups within the age-set system and not between kin-groups or local and political communities.

It is remarkable that, considering what cattle mean to Nuer, the man of the cattle is not socially or ritually so important a figure as the priest of the earth. Doubtless this is because his functions in the organization of the age-sets are not so often brought into play, nor so striking and important, spiritually and socially, as the priest's functions in homicides and the feuds that arise from them. There is an opposition in thought between the two. It cannot often happen that a man of the cattle quarrels with a priest of the earth; yet Nuer volunteer the information that if they quarrel and curse one another the man of the cattle asks the leopard-skin priest on what he expects to live if all his cattle die, and the priest counters by asking the man of the cattle whether he intends to take his cattle up to the skies as he can no longer pasture them on earth Nuer say that since both are placed in an impossible situation they exchange gifts to dissolve the curses Mr. P. Coriat in a Government Report of 27 February 1931 remarks that some of the Karlual tribe were feeling the need for a man of the cattle (for some reason they did not, I suppose, have one at the time), and he adds that the reason for this is a belief that if a man quarrels with a leopard-skin priest his cattle will not be acceptable as sacrifices as the earth cannot absorb their bones and blood. Therefore the services of a man of the cattle are necessary, so that the sacrifices will go direct to heaven. Mr. Coriat's observation suggests that Nuer tend to think of the man of the cattle in relation to the above and of the leopard-skin priest in relation to the below. This may be so, but I have no clear evidence that the former is classed as a *ran nhial*, a person of the above.[1]

As I have said earlier, the word *kuar* may be used in a general sense to describe persons with ritual powers in contrast to *dueghni*, laymen. I do no more than mention the titles and functions of some others than those we have been discussing, because they are not prominent figures in Nuer society and play only occasional and minor roles in their religious life. The *kuaar yika* or *kuaar ytini*, priest of the mat or mats, acts as arbitrator between the

---

[1] To P W. Schmidt (op cit , pp. 2–4, *et passim*) the problem is solved in terms of culture-complexes With agriculture go mother-right, evidences of which he finds among the Nuer, and an earth-religion. With cattle husbandry go father-right and a Sky-God religion Nuer culture is a mixture of the two

husband's people and the wife's people should the wife die in her first child-birth, and it is possible that he performs sacrifice in the course of the negotiations.[1] The word *kuaar* is also occasionally used instead of the more usual word *gwan*, possessor, in the titles of the *gwan muot* (or *ngul* or *ngul ghok*), possessor of the spear, who performs rites for success in war and hunting (p. 243); the *gwan biedh*, possessor of the fishing-spear, a kinsman of the leopard-skin priest who acts in homicide cases as his assistant in western Nuerland (p. 246); the *gwan nyanga* or *gwan thoi*, possessor of crocodile or of grass, who performs rites to protect people during fishing (p. 67); the *gwan biedh*, possessor of the fishing-spear, or *kuaar juaini*, priest of grass, who performs rites for the same purpose (p. 74); the *gwan pini*, possessor of water, who performs ritual against floods in western Nuerland, and the *gwan keca*, possessor of durra-bird (p 71). When asked about these specialists, Nuer say that when God created men he designated people to carry out certain functions, and their descendants have continued to perform them. I have, however, never heard *kuaar* used in speaking of the *tiet*, diviner or leech (p. 95) Nor is it ever used of persons possessed by spirits of the air or owners of nature sprites or fetishes, none of whom have traditional offices.

III

Gwan kwoth, possessor of a spirit, is an expression which may refer to what I have called a prophet or to someone who has a sprite or fetish or a totemic or totemistic familiar. All these persons may make sacrifice to their particular spirits on their own behalf or on behalf of others when they or others have been seized by the spirits or desire protection against dangers the spirits are associated with. I have already discussed them in earlier chapters, and here I speak further, though briefly, only of the prophets A prophet, as we saw in Chapter II, is a person who is possessed by a spirit of the air or occasionally a *colwic* spirit, the possession giving him spiritual powers lacking in other persons, including the leopard-skin priests. The possessed is thus also the possessor.

[1] I have no detailed account of his functions. Mr. Jackson (op. cit , p 151) gives a different account of them, and Dr Howell's account (*A Manual of Nuer Law*, p 54) differs from mine in one important particular I imagine that the *kuaar yika* was not often called upon to act

Some of the chief characteristics of a prophet can be seen by comparing him to the priest. The priest is a traditional functionary of Nuer society, the prophet is a recent development. The priest has an appointed sacrificial role in certain situations of the social life, particularly in homicide and blood-feud; the prophet's functions are indeterminate The priest's powers are transmitted by descent from the first priest—a social heritage; the prophet's powers are charismatic—an individual inspiration. The virtue of the priest resides in his office, that of the prophet in himself. The priest has no cult; the prophet has certain cultic features. But the most outstanding conceptual difference is that whereas in the priest man speaks to God, in the prophet God, in one or other of his hypostases, speaks to man The priest stands on the earth and looks to the sky. Heavenly beings descend from the sky and fill the prophets. The prophet is the mouthpiece of a spirit, its interpreter; it is he who speaks but he speaks under its control. We can only understand Nuer faith in their prophets, and also their fear of them, when we know that when they speak as prophets it is Spirit which speaks by their lips, theopneustic speech The prophet in making his declarations says, 'I am such-and-such', naming the spirit, and '*kwoth a lar*', 'Spirit says', just as the Old Testament prophets say, 'saith Yahweh', or the Prophet Muhammad says, 'saith Allah'. What the prophet says and what Spirit says are all mixed up together, the two being interspersed in such a manner that they cannot be separated. When we reflect on the dangerous quality in Spirit we do not have to wonder at the reverence Nuer show the vehicles of this manifestation of it in their midst. Another important difference is that while the priest has, when acting as priest, dealings only with Spirit in its most comprehensive sense of God the prophets deal with particular spirits, 'spirits of the air' or 'children of God'. God does not enter into men and inspire them. It will readily be seen that there is a fundamental difference, and one that will be still more apparent when a short account of prophets has been given, between the representative of man to the divine and the representative of the divine to man.

But though Nuer regard priests and prophets as very different sorts of persons they do not think of them as being opposed to one another Government officials, who were very hostile to the prophets and described them, confusing prophets with diviners and leeches, most inappropriately as 'magicians', 'necromancers', and

'witchdoctors' and as 'reactionary upstarts' and 'anti-tribal', speak
of them, indeed, as having undermined the traditional privileges
of the priests But this is not a Nuer way of looking at the matter
They do not think of their leopard-skin priests as being privileged
persons. Also, I have never heard a Nuer contrast priest with prophet or suggest that there could be rivalry between them as such.
Moreover, some of the best-known prophets were, like Jeremiah
and Ezekiel of the Old Testament, both priests and prophets.

Owing to the action taken against them by the Government I
had no opportunity to get to know any Nuer prophets well enough
to reach an understanding of the *forma mentis* of a prophet [1]
According to Nuer tales about them their behaviour was most
abnormal. The first prophet, or at any rate the first to achieve
fame, was Ngundeng son of Bung, of the Lou tribe, a prophet of
the spirit *deng*, who died in 1906. He acquired his powers by pro-
longed fasts. It is said that he lived for weeks by himself in the
bush, eating animal and human excrement, that he used to sit on
a cattle-peg in his kraal and let it penetrate his anus, that he used
to wander about the bush for days mumbling to himself or sit in
his cattle byre doing the same, and that when in such a mood he
would refuse all food except ashes, which he had cooked for him.
Mr Coriat says that he was in the habit of falling into trances on
the top of the roof of his cattle byre.[2] After he had established
himself as a prophet he seems to have given up his solitary wanderings, though he still used to shut himself up in his hut from time
to time to undergo long fasts Nuer say that when the spirit *deng*
seized him he could climb into the air without support and could
also run up and down from the ground to the top of his byre. His
son Gwek, described by Mr. Coriat as of squat body, misshapen
arms and legs, and a short toad-like head, also had a reputation
for daemonic exhibitions. Mr. Coriat records that he would spend,
and spent during Mr. Coriat's visit to his home, all day shouting
from the top of what has been described as a pyramid, a remarkable feat both of agility, for the pyramid was most difficult of
ascent, and of endurance.[3] Perhaps we would be right in seeing in
the habit of mounting to tops of byre and pyramid a symbolic

---

[1] When I began my studies Gwek, the leading prophet, had already been
shot; Dwal, the next most prominent, was in prison; so also was the well-known
prophet Car (I declined the administration's offer that I might visit them in
prison); and the influential prophet Buom was banished in the course of them

[2] Op. cit , p 224   [3] Ibid , pp 226-9.

expression of the prophet's relation to Spirit, the spirit in him lifting him up, as it were, to its own realm.

The construction of this so-called pyramid (*bie*), a conspicuous landmark in Lou tribal territory, was begun by Ngundeng and completed by Gwek. It was a huge mound of earth and debris some fifty to sixty feet high with a base diameter of about a hundred feet It was surmounted by elephant tusks and a spear decorated with an ostrich egg and feathers and encircled at the base with dozens of elephant tusks, numbers of which were also buried in the mound.[1] The purpose of the mound seems to have been to honour *deng* and increase the prestige of his prophet, though it may have expressed also the feeling of the above quality of Spirit. It became a cult centre, people from the whole of eastern Nuerland, and even from the west of the Nile, bringing cattle there for sacrifice, and Ngundeng and Gwek kept in a kraal near by a herd of cattle with black and white markings (*rial*) dedicated to *bungdit*, the mother of *deng*, with whom these markings are associated All this is more in accordance with Dinka than Nuer thought and custom, and there is some reason to suppose that the idea of the mound was, like the *deng* conception itself, borrowed from the Dinka There is said to be a similar, though smaller, mound at Thoc, in eastern Gaajak country, built by a prophet called Deng, son of Dul. Ngundeng's mound was blown up with high explosive by the British administration during a punitive expedition in 1928 against his son's followers However, much of it still remains, and Dr. Lienhardt tells me that it is said at the present time that sometimes at night a strange light is seen shining from it; and when a recent eclipse of the sun occurred people said that Ngundeng was returning. Another prophet, Deng Leaka, a prophet of the spirit *diu*, a Dinka of the Gaawar tribe, also acquired his spirit by fasting and solitude He left his home and wandered in the bush where for many days he sat under a tree without eating. When found he was engaged in collecting hundreds of shells of the giant land snail and arranging them in rows. This abnormal side to the prophets is to be seen in their unkempt hair and their beards, both of which are objectionable to ordinary

[1] Captain H H Wilson in *The Anglo-Egyptian Sudan*, edited by Count Gleichen, 1905, vol 1, p 140, information from Major C. H Stigand, *Sudan Notes and Records*, 1918, p 210, II. C. Jackson, op cit , p 158, P Coriat, op cit , p 224

PLATE XV

Prophet

Nuer The photograph of a prophet in Plate XV was taken by
Major-General Sir Charles Gwynn early in the present century.
We see from it how different is the appearance as well as the
representation of a prophet from that of a priest!

The ascetic and abnormal element in the prophetic personality
would seem to have been mixed up with personal ambition, a
striving after renown, power, and riches, a combination which
made the prophets outstanding figures in Nuerland. Reports by
administrative officials constantly denounced them for their greed
and ambition and for being 'plausible and unscrupulous' and
'charlatans'. Though these reports do not show great sensitivity
in distinguishing between the ideas of holiness and morality, there
is an element of truth in what they say. We have noted that it was
not just by chance that a man acquired an air-spirit. There is
nothing an ordinary Nuer desires less than to be in contact with
Spirit. He seeks by sacrifice to rid himself of it or to keep it at a
distance, for it is dangerous to him But a prophet sought inspiration, entry of Spirit into himself and its filling him; and in seeking
it he could not but have been aware of the influence it would bring
him. Gwek seems to have been what we should call avaricious,
though I never heard Nuer say so, and the only prophet of distinction I met, Buom of Dok country, whose spirit was *teny*, was, I
would say, a man of cunning whom Nuer themselves regarded as
selfish and greedy to acquire large herds. The hostility I sensed
among his neighbours may have been due in his case to the support given him by the Government, which had appointed him a
'chief', but I think it is true to say in general that though Nuer
feared their leading prophets, their fear, shown in the great outward deference, and in the case of women one might say veneration, they paid them, was tinged with resentment and hostility.
They were glad to have people with such powers among them, but
it always goes against the grain with Nuer to have to put themselves in an inferior position towards anyone; and in the main we
may agree with Capt V H. Fergusson when he wrote. 'None
of my Nuer [the western Nuer] will tolerate injustice in his everyday life even from a witchdoctor [prophet].'[1] Their attitude to
their prophets displayed the same ambivalence that they showed
towards the spirits of the air themselves and indeed to Spirit in
any form. They wanted it and at the same time did not want it

[1] *Sudan Notes and Records* 1923, p 107

A very complex representation would seem to be involved here, in which ideas about persons and ideas about Spirit are mixed together with regard to a man who in one way of thinking about him is man and in another way of thinking about him is Spirit and who is also conceived of as both man and Spirit.

As explained in Chapter II, the chief function of such prophets as gained any considerable following and became political figures was their hermeneutic role in warfare. They spoke the directions of the spirits of the air for raids on the Dinka[1] and for resistance to the slavers and the administration and made sacrifices to them. Their other functions were subsidiary and were exercised by lesser prophets also healing, particularly curing barrenness of women, staying of epidemics lethal to men or cattle, and exorcism of troublesome spirits. They were also credited with power to foretell events and with a more than usual insight (*gwic*). A prophet heals people by rubbing his spittle on them or by sprinkling them with water, milk, or butter, and his inspiration gives him foreknowledge, but he, like anyone else, relies on sacrifice in times of trouble; and he may be asked to sacrifice for any purpose except on those occasions reserved to the priesthood. People ask him to sacrifice on their behalf, not because they cannot make sacrifice themselves, but because sacrifice by him is felt to have special efficacy in that he has a special and intimate association with Spirit. Nevertheless, though prophets, like priests, may sacrifice on behalf of other people, the distinctive character of the prophet is not, as it is of the priest, his sacrificial role, but his revelational role deriving from spiritual inspiration. Hence, so I have been told, women, as well as men, may become minor prophets, though I believe only an old, and possibly barren, woman, of whom Nuer say '*coa wut*', 'she has become a man', would do so. A female prophet would not sacrifice.

I mentioned briefly, because I have treated the matter elsewhere, the political significance of the Nuer priests, their office being a politico-religious institution of the traditional social order. The prophets can also be regarded from the same point of view, as a politico-religious institution which has recently emerged in answer to changes in the social order. It may be hard to believe that people with prophetic powers have not always existed among the Nuer, but there is no evidence that they have; and all Nuer with whom

[1] They acquired substantial herds from their share of the booty

(308)

I have discussed the question stated that in old days, before *deng*,
the first of the air-spirits to fall to earth, entered into men towards
the end of last century there were no prophets at all, only the *kuar*,
the priests. I have suggested in an earlier book that their appearance might be explained by historical events—the expansion of
the Nuer and, more particularly, the threat to their independence
by northern Arab slavers, the Mahdists, and Anglo-Egyptian rule,
which required, if it were to be met, greater political unity and
the development of political authority. This view accords also
with what has been said in general about the relation of Nuer
religious conceptions to their social structure It is possible that
some of the prophets might have established political authority
and leadership overriding local loyalties and sectional interests
had they been allowed to, for prophetic powers tend to become
hereditary, passing to whichever son is susceptible Thus the
mantle of Ngundeng fell upon his son Gwek, who was more a
political, and less a religious, figure than his father had been, and
the mantle of Deng Leaka fell upon his son Dwal The Government effectively stopped development in this direction Direct
British administration was instituted, and no more influential
prophets emerged. On the other hand, far from the idea of spirits
—air-spirits, totemic and totemistic spirits, nature sprites, and
fetish spirits—dwelling among men having been eclipsed it has
spread more widely and in ever-increasing variety This was
already beginning to happen when I was in Nuerland (in the years
1930, 1931, 1935, and 1936), but the Nuer of the areas in which I
carried out most of my research, the Lou and eastern Jikany tribes,
had heard of only a few of the many spirits already familiar to
those to the west of the Nile. So strongly have they now invaded
these territories that, Dr Lienhardt tells me, they have established
themselves among the Anuak, who live yet farther to the east and
had no knowledge of them as late as 1940 If my interpretation of
the emergence and proliferation of new religious conceptions in
terms of structure and structural developments is correct it would
follow that we have here a counterpart in religious thought to an
increasing fragmentation and individualization amounting by
this time to a breakdown of the traditional social order.

Historical circumstances have brought the Nuer into closer
communication at all points with foreign ideas; and the breakdown of their traditional way of life and the taking over of some

of these ideas are part of the same process of change. As we have noted, they say of their air-spirits which inspire their prophets, and also in general of spirits which have fallen from above to earth, that they took them over from foreign peoples, mostly from the Dinka; and it is also possible that, as Mr. H. C. Jackson suggests,[1] there is a relation between the appearance of prophets among the Nuer and the spread of Dervish influence, for it was about the time of the Mahdist upheaval that their first prophets arose, and I was expressly told by one Nuer that the first spirit they heard of entering men was *madi* (?al-Mahdi) in the lands of the north and that afterwards they heard of *deng* and then of other spirits.

Although the emergence of prophets can be interpreted in terms of historical events and structural changes just as the priesthood can be interpreted in terms of the functioning of the traditional tribal system, the prophet's significance for an understanding of Nuer religious thought calls for comment not required in the case of the priest. The rise of prophets and the increase of every other kind of 'owners' of spirits may indeed be a response, first to a challenge and then to disintegration, but it is a response made within a set of religious conceptions and has, therefore, a significance for the study of those conceptions without regard to whatever it may have been which occasioned the response. That the response should have taken a religious form does not surprise us, for that has been a common enough reaction to European rule in Africa and elsewhere, and the Nuer are, in any case, conspicuously religious. What claims our attention is rather the kind of religious form it took, a form which is at the same time both a development of potentialities in their traditional religion and a change in its character. We have seen in an earlier chapter how the Nuer notion of Spirit lends itself to refraction without limits. If this had not been so all the new spiritual conceptions which have arisen in the course of the last two generations could not have come into existence without entirely changing the character of Nuer religious thought As it is, they have partly changed it.

[1] Op. cit , p 91

CHAPTER XIII

SOME REFLECTIONS ON NUER RELIGION

THE theories of writers about primitive religion have not been sustained by research. During the last century what was presented as theory was generally the supposition that some particular form of religion was the most primitive and that from it developed other forms, the development being sometimes presented as a succession of inevitable and well-defined stages. The form of religion presented by a writer as the most primitive was that which he considered to be the most simple, crude, and irrational; to exhibit most conspicuously 'crass materialism', 'primeval stupidity', 'naive eudaemonism', 'crude anthropomorphism', or 'daemonic dread'. Many such origins have been propounded: magic, fetishism, manism, animism, pre-animism, mana, totemism, monotheism, &c. All this was for the most part pure conjecture. The determination of the *primordium*, in the absence of historical evidences, was, as Schleiter, among others, has shown, quite arbitrary.[1]

Nuer religion, like any other, has, of course, a history, but we can only trace it in so far as it survives in the memories of the Nuer themselves, for reports by travellers, which start barely a century ago, are on this matter slight and unreliable. Ethnological research can supply us only with indirect evidences; archaeological research, were it to be undertaken, probably with none at all. However, Nuer statements, supported by ethnological evidences, enable us to say with a fair degree of probability what have been the main lines of development during the last hundred years Now, if we take the Nuer as we find them today and as we have good reason to think them to have been in the recent past, an account of their religion at least shows the inadequacy of most of these so-called evolutionary theories and exposes the conceit of the assumptions on which they were based. The Nuer are undoubtedly a primitive people by the usual standards of reckoning, but their religious thought is remarkably sensitive, refined, and intelligent. It is also highly complex.

[1] Frederick Schleiter, *Religion and Culture*, 1919, p 39

Explanations of primitive religions were often couched at the same time both in terms of historical origins and of psychological origins, which made for great confusion, especially as the logical and chronological senses of 'primitive' and 'origin' were also seldom kept distinct. The psychological explanations were very varied, changing with changes in psychological theory. Intellectualist interpretations were succeeded by emotionalist interpretations and they by psycho-analytical intepretations. Religion was discussed and explained in terms of association of ideas, of personification of natural phenomena, of awe, of thrill, of fear, anxiety and frustration, of projection, and so forth. Most of these theories have long ago been discredited as naive introspective guesses

Certainly one cannot speak of any specifically religious emotion for the Nuer. One can only judge by overt behaviour on occasions of religious activity and, as I have noted, on such occasions Nuer may be afraid, anxious, joyful, indifferent, or in other states, according to the situation and the degree to which they are involved in it. Miss Ray Huffman says that their religion is one of fear,[1] and I feel I ought to say, and I do so with her permission, that this is the one point with which Dr. Mary Smith finds serious fault in my account of it. She, like Miss Huffman, holds that it is a religion of fear, even of terror. For me this is an over-simplification and a misunderstanding. It is true that Nuer, like everyone else, fear death, bereavement, sickness, and other troubles, and that it is precisely in such situations that they so often pray and sacrifice. It can be admitted also that, in that these troubles are manifestations of Spirit, they fear Spirit and wish to be rid of it. But we cannot say that on that account their religion is simply one of fear, which is, moreover, a very complex state of mind, and one not easy to define or assess. On the contrary, it is because Nuer are afraid of these misfortunes that one might speak of their religion as one of hope and comfort. But I think what fits the facts best is to say that it is a religion of both fear and trust, which may be opposites but are not contraries, or that the Nuer attitude towards Spirit might be described as ambiguous, and perhaps as ambivalent. The question is much complicated by the different ways Nuer represent Spirit to themselves and their different attitudes to it at different levels of representation. We have further to recognize

[1] Op. cit, p. 56.

(312)

that the sense of guilt which is often so evident in misfortunes is not just fear but a complex psychological state, and also that it varies in intensity from one situation to another Nuer thought in these matters is involved, for a serious danger may not be just an adventitious intrusion of Spirit into human affairs. It often has a moral significance It is then not so much regarded as a natural crisis which can be overcome by spiritual aid as a moral crisis brought about by human action, and of which the outcome, it is thought, may depend on so delicate and indiscernible a factor as intention. Faced with so complex and variable a problem, to speak of Nuer religion simply as one of fear or awe, or as a projection or as cathartic, and so forth, must be a distortion, and one that does not greatly help us to understand it. All emotions enter into it; they blend; and there is nothing constant that we can say is characteristic of the religious life, which is rather to be defined in terms of disposition than of emotion.

Sociological theories of religion have frowned on evolutionary and psychological explanations alike. They have rather sought to understand primitive religions, or certain aspects of them, as products of social life |Fustel de Coulanges, Robertson Smith, Durkheim, Mauss, Hertz, and others have shown successfully that many features of these religions can be understood only by sociological analysis, by relating them to the social structure. This is true of Nuer religion I do not think, for example, that the configuration of Spirit, the faults which are regarded as sins, and the roles of master of ceremonies, priest, and prophet in sacrifice can be fully understood without a knowledge of the social order. But Durkheim and his colleagues and pupils were not content to say that religion, being part of the social life, is strongly influenced by the social structure. They claimed that the religious conceptions of primitive peoples are nothing more than a symbolic representation of the social order. It is his society that primitive man worships in the symbol of a god It is to his society that he prays and makes sacrifice. This postulate of sociologistic metaphysic seems to me to be an assertion for which evidence is totally lacking It was Durkheim and not the savage who made society into a god.|

All these theories about primitive religions, evolutionary, psychological, and sociological, suffered from a common weakness. The facts on which they were based were both inadequate and unreliable. Indeed, such wide generalizations could only have been put forward at a time when systematic studies of the religions of primitive peoples were lacking, and by persons with no direct, however slight, experience of them. That they were in reality *a priori* assumptions posited on the facts rather than scientific conclusions derived from them became increasingly apparent as new knowledge of these religions came to light and their variety and complexity were better appreciated. It is indeed surprising that these writers, whose speculations were for the most part attempts to explain religion as a general phenomenon, should have turned their attention exclusively to the religions of present-day primitive peoples or to the earliest forms of the higher religions—to those religions, that is, about which information was the most lacking and the most uncertain—rather than to the contemporaneous world religions with their vast literatures and known histories, to Christianity, Islam, Hinduism, Buddhism, and others. Had they done so, however, and, even more, had they conducted research into what these religions mean to ordinary people rather than into how philosophers, theologians, lawyers, mystics, and others have presented them, they would have seen how inadequate their theories were. Also. the religions of primitive peoples could not then have been treated, as they so often were, as something so unlike the religions of civilization that they appeared to require a special kind of interpretation and a special vocabulary.

The insufficiencies of the theories of primitive religions I have mentioned are apparent to all students today, but little has been put in their place. Certainly one reason for this is that though during the last thirty or so years many and intensive investigations of primitive peoples have been made there have been few systematic studies of what we may call, in order to include a wider range of phenomena than are usually placed under the rubric of religion, primitive philosophies. The word 'philosophy' is used here, for want of a better, in the general sense of the German 'Weltanschauung'. That more studies of the kind have not been made can be attributed to some extent to a lack of interest among anthropologists, and this is perhaps in part to be accounted for by the fact that the theories they inherited from earlier students could not be broken down into problems permitting investigation in the field. No one can put to the test of observation a theory that magic preceded religion or that when a people worship a spiritual being

it is nature or their own society that they worship. We have, therefore, in the study of primitive philosophies to begin anew to build
up a body of theory and to formulate problems in the light of it.
There is only one way in which this can be done A number of
systematic studies of primitive philosophies has to be made. When
that has been done a classification can be made on the basis of
which comparative studies can be undertaken which possibly may
lead to some general conclusions. This book is intended as a contribution which it is hoped may be useful in the building up of
a classification of African philosophies

Such a classification of African philosophies must naturally be
by reference to their chief and characteristic features. Among all
African peoples we find in one form or another theistic beliefs,
manistic cult, witchcraft notions, interdictions with supernatural
sanctions, magical practices, &c., but the philosophy of each has
its own special character in virtue of the way in which among that
people these ideas are related to one another It will be found that
one or other belief, or set of beliefs, dominates the others and gives
form, pattern, and colour to the whole. Thus, among some peoples,
notably a large proportion of the Bantu, the dominant motif is
provided by the cult of ancestors; among others, some of the
Sudanic peoples for example, it is found in the notion of witchcraft, with which are bound up magical and oracular techniques;
among others, such as the Nuer, Spirit is in the centre of the picture
and manistic and witchcraft ideas are peripheral; and among
other peoples yet other notions predominate. The test of what is
the dominant motif is usually, perhaps always, to what a people
attribute dangers and sickness and other misfortunes and what
steps they take to avoid or eliminate them.

Nuer philosophy is, as we have seen, essentially of a religious
kind, and is dominated by the idea of *kwoth*, Spirit As Spirit
cannot be directly experienced by the senses, what we are considering is a conception *Kwoth* would, indeed, be entirely indeterminate and could not be thought of by Nuer at all were it not
that it is contrasted with the idea of *cak*, creation, in terms of
which it can be defined by reference to effects and relations and
by the use of symbols and metaphors. But these definitions are
only schemata, as Otto puts it, and if we seek for elucidation beyond these terms, a statement of what Spirit is thought to be like
in itself, we seek of course in vain. Nuer do not claim to know

They say that they are merely *doar*, simple people, and how can simple people know about such matters? What happens in the world is determined by Spirit and Spirit can be influenced by prayer and sacrifice. This much they know, but no more; and they say, very sensibly, that since the European is so clever perhaps he can tell them the answer to the question he asks.　　　　*!*

Nevertheless, we can reach certain conclusions about the basic features of the conception. We have seen that Nuer religion is pneumatic and theistic Whether it can rightly be described as monotheistic is largely a matter of definition. I would say, for the reasons I have given, that it can be so described in the sense already discussed, for at no level of thought and experience is Spirit thought of as something altogether different from God. It follows from the conception of God as Spirit that though he is figured in many diverse figures he can be thought of both as each and as all alike and one But if we say that in spite of the many different spirits Spirit is one and that Nuer religion is in this sense monotheistic we have to add that it is also modalistic. Spirit, though one, is differently thought of with regard to different effects and relations.

We have, indeed, in this matter to be particularly careful not to be led into false conclusions. A theistic religion need not be either monotheistic or polytheistic. It may be both It is a question of the level, or situation, of thought rather than of exclusive types of thought On one level Nuer religion may be regarded as mono-theistic, at another level as polytheistic; and it can also be regarded at other levels as totemistic or fetishistic. These conceptions of spiritual activity are not incompatible. They are rather different ways of thinking of the numinous at different levels of experience. We found these different ways of thinking reflected in the complex notions involved in sacrifice, and also in the variety of Nuer attitudes towards Spirit, ranging from love to fear, from trust to apprehension, from dependence to hostility.

Since the basic feature of Nuer religion is the idea of Spirit it is not surprising that certain features of other African religions are unimportant among them or even entirely lacking. The conception of ancestral ghosts is altogether subordinate. Animistic ideas are almost entirely absent Witchcraft ideas play a very minor role, and magic a negligible one Both are incompatible with a theo-centric philosophy, for when both fortune and misfortune come from God they cannot also come from human powers, whether innate or learnt. Likewise, it is easily understandable that there is no idea of an impersonal force, a dynamism or vital force, which we are told is characteristic of some African religions It is true that when Nuer speak of *kwoth* without specifying any particular representation of it the impression may be conveyed that it has an impersonal character; but it is always understood that what is being referred to is Spirit conceived of either as God or as some particular hypostasis or refraction of him, though it may not be known which of them is concerned in the situation they have in mind. Moreover, it is certain that, for the most part at any rate, the many representations of Spirit we find in Nuerland today are a fairly recent introduction and development, and Nuer are aware of this. Another negative feature of Nuer religion is the complete absence of ritual, in the sense of ceremonial, interdictions, so prominent among other African peoples No interdictions on food, drink, or sexual intercourse condition the efficacy of religious rites (nor, for the matter of that the success of any undertaking), and, there being no ritual interdictions, there can be no ideas of ritual purity and impurity. Nuer interdictions are not of a ritual order at all, but of a moral one, so that breaches of them result in a state of moral impurity or sin, of which the resultant situation and manifestation may be sickness or other misfortune. And what counts in sacrifice is not the outward, physical, state of the sacrificer, but his moral state, the sincerity of his intention.

We can say that these characteristics, both negative and positive, of Nuer religion indicate a distinctive kind of piety which is dominated by a strong sense of dependence on God and confidence in him rather than in any human powers or endeavours. God is great and man foolish and feeble, a tiny ant. And this sense of dependence is remarkably individualistic. It is an intimate, personal, relationship between man and God This is apparent in Nuer ideas of sin, in their expressions of guilt, in their confessions, and in the dominant piacular theme of their sacrifices. It is evident also in their habit of making short supplications at any time This is a very noticeable trait of Nuer piety, and my conclusions are here borne out by Dr. Lienhardt's observations. He tells me that when he was in western Dinkaland he had in his household a Nuer youth whose habit of praying to God for aid on every occasion of difficulty greatly astonished the Dinka In prayer and sacrifice alike, in what is said and in what is done, the emphasis is on complete surrender to God's will. Man plays a passive role. He cannot get to God but God can get to him. Given this sort of piety, we are not surprised to find that the prophet is more influential than the priest.

In this sense of the totality of Nuer religious beliefs and practices forming a pattern which excludes conflicting elements and subordinates each part to the harmony of the whole, we may speak of their religious system. This does not mean, however, that it is an entirely consistent set of ideas. On the contrary, like other religions, it contains unresolved ambiguities and paradoxes, as that God is remote from men, a *deus absconditus* in the sky, and also very near to them, a *deus revelatus* in human enterprises and affairs; and that he is both friend and foe, whom one summons for aid and asks to turn away, seeking at the same time union with him and separation from him. It might, indeed, be argued that the breaking up of the conception of Spirit into a number of different representations, evoked in different situations, could be regarded as a means of resolving both ambiguities; but there would be certain difficulties in this view. Both must always have been there, whereas the spirits are a new phenomenon. Also, they are not regarded as something different and apart from God, so that the ambiguities are not really resolved Moreover, although some of the spirits have a capricious side to them and Nuer may be said to have in a way an aversion to some of them, they are, nevertheless, a coming down of Spirit to earth into a homely relationship to men, so that while they may trouble them they also put themselves at their service. In them man and Spirit meet A prophet, indeed, seeks so complete a union with a spirit that he is no longer himself but the spirit. That these spirits have come into Nuer thought during the last few decades might, therefore, be rather interpreted, at this level of interpretation, in terms of the sufferings Nuer have endured in them.

It is in the nature of the subject that there should be ambiguity and paradox. I am aware that in consequence I have not been able to avoid what must appear to the reader to be obscurities, and even contradictions, in my account When one looks at Nuer religion from one angle it seems to be like this and when one looks at it from another angle it seems to be like that, and this and that do not always correspond. The difficulties of investigation and presen-

tation have been further added to by the great increase in the
number and types of spiritual forms.

The taking over from neighbouring peoples of new spiritual
conceptions has, if not produced, greatly accentuated the paradox
of the one and the many, one of the chief problems of Nuer religion
today, and one to which I have had to devote particular attention
And it has made yet more apparent a further problem, to which
I have also given special attention—that of the relation of symbol
to what it symbolizes—for every new representation requires, if it
is to acquire more than nominal distinctness, a visible, material
symbol. Indeed, our difficulties are everywhere greatly increased
by historical changes in Nuer religion. I have attempted to interpret these changes by relating them to other social changes going
on at the same time. I think that to some extent they are elucidated by this sort of interpretation, but one has to admit that it is
not susceptible of proof, and also that Nuer have borrowed much
from their neighbours at various times—for example, not only
spirits but also such ideas as *ther*, *kor*, and *thiang*—without our
being able to give sure reasons for the loan or the time of it. We
can only suppose that since such ideas as I have mentioned are
intimately connected with women, they have entered Nuerland
through the intermarriage of Nuer with Dinka and Anuak But
if one has to admit that religious conceptions have some autonomy
and pass from one people to another without our being able to say
why they do so, we can show that they are much altered in the
process, being made to conform to the already existing set of ideas
into which they are taken. The ideas of *deng*, *colwic*, and *kor* are
very different among the Dinka and the Nuer, that of *ther* has a
very different place in Nuer thought to that which it has in Anuak
thought, and *nyikang* is a very different figure in Nuer religion
from what it is in Shilluk religion.

The new conceptions of Spirit Nuer have borrowed from neighbours or have developed within their own culture are thought
of as having appeared at points of time in events in relation to
persons. But though they are always so presented in myths and
traditions there is a difference between such personal experiences
in stories which account for a relationship of a social group to a
spiritual form and the personal experience each man has in the
critical events of his own life and of the lives of those near to him.
I have throughout my account emphasized, especially in my

discussion of sacrifice, the difference between the personal and collective aspects of Nuer religion and that the first is more important for an understanding of its fundamental character. We learn from the collective expression of religion more about the social order than about what is specifically religious thought and practice Its personal expression tells us more of what religion is in itself. If we recognize that the collective expression is only one form of religious activity we shall not make the mistake of trying to explain Nuer religion in terms of their social structure alone.

Sociological writers, as I have already observed, have often treated religious conceptions, because they refer to what cannot be experienced by the senses, as a projection of the social order. This is inadmissible. That Nuer religious thought and practices are influenced by their whole social life is evident from our study of them. God is conceived of not only as the father of all men but also under a variety of forms in relation to various groups and persons. Consequently we may say that the conception is co-ordinated to the social order. Also, he is conceived of not only as creator but also as guardian of the social order who punishes transgressions, which are breaches of interdictions which serve to maintain the social order. But the Nuer conception of God cannot be reduced to, or explained by, the social order.

In my first book on the Nuer I gave an account of their ecology, their modes of livelihood, and their political structure. I tried to show that some features of their modes of livelihood can be understood only if we take their environment into account, and also that some features of their political structure can be understood only if we take their modes of livelihood into account. I did not, however, try to explain their modes of livelihood as a function of their environment or their political structure as a function of their economy In my second book I tried to show how some features of their family and kinship systems were more intelligible when seen in relation to tribal and lineage systems; but it is not suggested that they could be explained in terms of them./In this final volume I have tried to show how some features of their religion can be presented more intelligibly in relation to the social order described in the earlier volumes but I have tried also to describe and interpret it as a system of ideas and practices in its own right.

When the purely social and cultural features of Nuer religion have been abstracted, what is left which may be said to be that which is expressed in the social and cultural forms we have been considering? It is difficult to give a more adequate answer to this question than to say that it is a relationship between man and God which transcends all forms. It is not surprising therefore that we cannot give any clear account of what for Nuer is the nature of this spiritual relationship. We feel like spectators at a shadow show watching insubstantial shadows on the screen. There is nothing Nuer can say of the nature of God other than that he is like wind or air. They can speak of their experience of Spirit but can tell us nothing of Spirit itself. The spirits of the air are little more than names to them. Were a possessed man, when asked what possessed him, to utter a new name there would be a new spirit. It is much the same with the totemic representations of Spirit. They are not in themselves of a spiritual nature but only material symbols which serve to differentiate Spirit in its relation to some people from its relation to other people A study of the symbols tells us nothing of the nature of what is symbolized. Spirit in itself is for Nuer a mystery which lies behind the names and the totemic and other appearances in which it is represented.

We can, therefore, say no more than that Spirit is an intuitive apprehension, something experienced in response to certain situations but known directly only to the imagination and not to the senses. Nuer religious conceptions are properly speaking not concepts but imaginative constructions. Hence the response to them is imaginative too, a kind of miming Words and gestures transport us to a realm of experience where what the eye sees and the ear hears is not the same as what the mind perceives. Hands are raised to the sky in supplication, but it is not the sky which is supplicated but what it represents to the imagination Formal respect is paid to an animal not on account of what the animal is in itself but on account of what for some people it stands for in thought as a symbol. The spear he bought from an Arab merchant in the hands of an officiant representing a clan is in the mind's eye the spear of the ancestor in the drama of sacrifice. The ancestor's spear does not exist, and a man may make sacrificial gestures with this non-existent spear merely by moving his hand as though he held a spear in it, the ancestral spear being represented by nothing but a thought. A piacular ox is the sacrificer himself and in the ox he dies in symbol. But the sacrificer is not present. The hand of the officiant on the back of the ox represents his hand And when we look for the ox about to be slaughtered we see a cucumber. To the mind sickness caused by sin is the sin and in the mind it is wiped out by the sacrificial act. We seem indeed to be watching a play or to be listening to someone's account of what he has dreamt. Perhaps when we have this illusion we are beginning to understand, for the significance of the objects, actions, and events lies not in themselves but in what they mean to those who experience them as participants or assistants If we regard only what happens in sacrifice before the eyes it may seem to be a succession of senseless, and even cruel and repulsive, acts, but when we reflect on their meaning we perceive that they are a dramatic representation of a spiritual experience. What this experience is the anthropologist cannot for certain say. Experiences of this kind are not easily communicated even when people are ready to communicate them and have a sophisticated vocabulary in which to do so. Though prayer and sacrifice are exterior actions, Nuer religion is ultimately an interior state. This state is externalized in rites which we can observe, but their meaning depends finally on an awareness of God and that men are dependent on him and must be resigned to his will. At this point the theologian takes over from the anthropologist

INDEX

buth, to share, 287.

butter, use of, in mortuary ceremony, 151

'buy', 222 sqq

Bwoogh Kerpel, Nuer leader, 172

byre, burning of, expiated, 54–55, 227–8

cak (*chak*). creation. various uses of the word, 4–5; means to create not to beget, 8; creation, 124, created, 12, 156

cak ghaua, creator of the universe, 4

cak kwoth, a freak, 5

cak nath, creator of men, 5.

Calotropis procera, 66

cam, to eat, 101, 158, 212.

cany, to despise, 58, 182

Cany major lineage of the eastern Gaajak, 66–67.

Car, prophet, 299, 305 n 1.

Catholic Mission at Yoahnyang, 49.

cattle: ancestral herd, 258, blood-wealth, 288, bridewealth, 64, 259, 288, castration, 250, 254, 256, compensation for incest, 184, for adultery, 185–7, dedicated, 38, 43; -egret, as totem, 70–71, of ghosts, 163–4; given by God, 6; hides, respect of Jikul clan for, 75–76, husbandry, 292, 'identification' of cattle and owner, 249, 252–5, 257, and initiation, 238–9, laying of hands on, 262; lions and, 79; -markings some Nuer lineages respect cattle with certain markings, 74–75, -names, 142, 250, peg-sprite, *biel loi*, 98; personal names taken from, 250; -raids on Dinka by Nuer, 45, religious significance, 248–9, respect towards cow and milk, 180 n 1, 'sacred', 266, sacrificial role of, 248–71, animals should not be slaughtered except in sacrifice, 263–71; secular uses, 248; soul attributed to, 157.

child, small, 156

children remarks about, 15; of God (*gaat kwoth*), 3, 8.

Christianity, 48–49, 314

chyle, 212.

chyme (*wau*), 56, 212, 214.

cieh joka, ghost's wife, 164.

cien, to haunt, 157, 161, 165, 173–6, 265

cieng (community), 89, homestead, 205

cieng Gangni, lineage (Lak tribe) respect the monitor lizard, 65–66

ciengbalangni (or *nyier*), 'river people', 89

clan identification of clans and lineages with their herds, 257–8, leader, 243; spear-names, 31, 148, 240–1, see also under *mut* (spear-name of lineages)

clans honorific titles, 259, see also under honorific titles.

cobra· *fajook*, name of spirit of tree-cobra, 79, respect for, 68–69, 82; -spirit, 68–69, -sprite, *biel rir*, 98.

cok, black ants, 12

col, dark, 53, 57

col, to indemnify, 66, 223, 228

col, spirit of the air, 30, 33, 57

col woc, mortuary ceremony, 190, 229.

collective aspect of Nuer religion, 320

colwic of the Rek Dinka, 60 n 1, ceremonies, sacrifices at, 54 sqq, 262, etymology, 53; *gwan colwec*, owner of a *colwic*, 60, mortuary ceremony not held for a *colwic*, 54–55, Nuer, special features of, 60–62, Nuer term *coa kwoth* ('he has become Spirit') applied to, 61, patron spirit, 53; shrine, 57 n 1, spirits, 3, 28–30, 52, 54, 93, 113, 116, 118, 319

communion theory of sacrifice, 273–5

community (*cieng*), 89

confession, 193

consecration. act of, 261; of sacrifice, 272, *buk*, 2nd sacrificial act, 208

Cordia rothii, 72

Coriat, P , 226, 302, 305–6.

cot, applied to youths during initiation, 256

cot thak, ox-name, 250, 252

Coulanges, Fustel de, 313.

cow. milk, 40; bathing of, in beer, 42–43; -names, 250, reference to in honorific titles, 259; cattle lineage traced through, 260.

cows· dedicated, 51, 53; not dedicated to God, 41 n 1; fertility of, 99

Crataeva religiosa, 66

crazy (*yong*), 18

Crazzolara, Father J P , 4, 8, 10, 13, 20, 32, 53, 99 n 2, 100, 102, 161, 219, 271, 295 n 1

creation (*cak*) (*chak*), various uses of the word, 4–5

creation myth, 6.

creator of men (*cak nath*), 5, of the universe (*cak ghaua*), 4

creature-Spirit expression, 133

crocodile control of, 95, eggs, 130, symbolic use of, 134, -spirit, 66–67, 78, 93, 126–8, 135–7, 141, 266

crocodiles, 19, 78–79, 136, respect for, 92

Crowfoot, Mrs G M , 203

Cuaagh lineage, 168.

PRINTED IN GREAT BRITAIN
AT THE UNIVERSITY PRESS, OXFORD
BY CHARLES BATEY, PRINTER TO THE UNIVERSITY

CPSIA information can be obtained
at www.ICGtesting.com
Printed in the USA
BVHW060038100920
588456BV00003B/86

9 781376 189025